◆ ◆ ◆

AN ENCYCLOPEDIA
OF RELIGIONS
IN THE UNITED STATES

· AN ·
ENCYCLOPEDIA
OF RELIGIONS
IN THE UNITED STATES

*One Hundred Religious Groups
Speak for Themselves*

◆ ◆ ◆

Edited by
WILLIAM B. WILLIAMSON

Crossroad · New York

1992
The Crossroad Publishing Company
370 Lexington Avenue, New York, NY 10017

Printed in the United States of America

Library of Congress Cataloging-in-Publication Data

An Encyclopedia of religions in the United States: one hundred religious groups speak for themselves / edited by William B. Williamson.
   p.   cm.
  Includes index.
  ISBN 0-8245-1094-1
  1. United States—Religion—Dictionaries. 2. Christian sects—United States—Dictionaries. I. Williamson, William Bedford, 1918–.
BL2520.E53 1991
291'.0973—dc20   91-14252
                                    CIP

CONTENTS

◆ ◆ ◆
PREFACE

This book is a firsthand and comprehensive survey of the current religious scene in the United States. It developed from a student-participation college course entitled "Religion in the United States," for which twenty-four self-descriptions were selected from major religious groups such as Baptists, Roman Catholics, and Episcopalians. In order to make this volume more useful, the concept of the course was expanded to include all religious groups of 100,000 adherents or more as well as other interesting groups such as the Fellowship of Religious Humanists, Unity, and some American groups of world religious heritage such as Zen Buddhism and the Sufi Order.

Following the course's original format and pluralist-ecumenical tone, all Judeo-Christian bodies and others identified as religious groups were invited to respond by furnishing a self-description of their group in full outline form, including:

1. A general self-description of their group or branch and the reasons for their existence;
2. The founder and/or major leaders;
3. Their unique doctrines, forms of worship, organization, and function;
4. Their contribution to and estimated influence in the United States;
5. Significant terms and names (with definitions);
6. Bibliography (giving four or five helpful books).

The earlier list of twenty-four self-descriptions has been expanded by approximately seventy-five more groups or branches. A significant value of this book will derive from these self-descriptions, which reveal who the group believes it is and what it says it practices. Statistics may occur as part of the self-description, simply as an item of specific information. The self-revelatory feature of this book will make it of interest to general readers as well as to scholars and clerics.

Another special feature of the book is the introductory chapter, "Religion in the United States," which gives a historical sketch of the development of the religious phenomenon in America generally and also of specific religious groups that the development records. It will help to orient the reader both historically and ecclesiastically for the study at hand. The table of contents is arranged in alphabetical order.

The book is intended to be used in a number of settings as a general handbook of religious groups, a resource book for general and church libraries, a textbook for courses in religion in the United States, and a resource book for adult discussion groups. Its many-faceted contents can be approached in different ways for either individual or group use. It can be studied chronologically as in the typical history introduction. Or one can study a particular religious family or heritage, emphasizing sectarian developments in the free religious environment of the United States.

I am grateful to those who prepared the self-descriptions of the various religious groups, whose names appear at the end of the invidiual descriptions. I am grateful also to the following colleagues: Elaine D. Schultz, for helpful criticisms, and the critical reading of everything I wrote; Keith J. Hardman, for his critical reading of the introductory chapter; George G. Storey, for his editorial assistance in shortening overlong self-descriptions and his critical reading of everything I wrote; Michael Renninger, my former honors student, for his contribution of several pages in the introductory chapter on the Roman Catholic Church and for his critical reading of the entire manuscript; Ms. Judith Fryer and David Mill, reference librarians at Ursinus College; Mrs. Sally Rapp, secretary extraordinary from Ursinus College; Miss Suzanne Kern, a devoted and friendly typist who helped to prepare the final manuscript for publication; and Dr. Linda Jessup, whose steady skill and spirit pulled it all together to make possible a "hard copy." The author is also grateful to his grand-daughter Jennifer Lynn Baran for the conception and preparation of Appendix C. Worthy of thanks also are the author's family for doing things to help, but mostly for accepting the fanaticism and devotion necessary to prepare a book such as this one.

RELIGION IN THE UNITED STATES
Introduction and Historical Survey

Religion in the United States, as everywhere, has been shaped by the history, geography, economics, and politics of the country. Because of the United States' relatively short history, however, this shaping is more obvious and easily recognized.

The earliest Americans—the American Indians—were animists, a religion called primitive in many textbooks. Animism is based on the belief that all beings, natural objects, and nature itself possess spirits and thus life. Animists also believe they must deal with these spirits religiously in the affairs of their daily lives.

The native Americans believed in a Great Spirit and developed elaborate rituals and magical rites. These were led by shamans, who wore headdresses, masks, body paint, and amulets appropriate to each rite, from healing the sick to securing the favor of a particular spirit. Even contemporary native Americans, although most participate in "the white man's religion," maintain loyalty to the beliefs and practices of their ancestors. In sickness and death, in the face of vital tribal decisions, they practice the ceremonies, dances, and rituals of their heritages, as these have been colored by the experiences of living and surviving in a hostile world.

The first European religion to come to the United States was Roman Catholicism. Following the landing of Christopher Columbus in the Bahamas in 1492, Spain, Portugal, and France sent Roman Catholic missionaries into the colonies they established. Protestant missionaries from Holland, England, Germany, and Sweden soon followed, but Spanish missionaries had already won the West Coast from Mexico to the state of Washington, and French missionaries had won Louisiana and the southeastern portions of Canada.

Protestantism in the United States owes it origins to immigration from England, first of the Anglicans, Pilgrims, and Puritans, and then of others. According to George Tavard: "Presbyterians and Congregationalists . . . settled in New England, the Quakers founded Pennsylvania on principles that opened up [the colony] to all religions; Anglicans were established in Virginia. . . . Baptists evangelized the southern states and . . . Methodists settled in Georgia. Methodism spread widely through the Great Revival of 1742. . . . Later with the emigrations from Germany, Lutheranism established itself . . . throughout the continent."[1]

Three pairs of terms characterize religion in the United States: pragmatic and experimental, humanistic and concerned with the humanist way of life, and evangelistic and Pentecostal. It is pragmatic and experimental in its concern for being flexible and open toward social changes and for adapting both concept and practice to meet society's needs. It is humanistic in its belief in the primary importance of humans and a way of life that guarantees their rights and the quality of human life today. It is evangelistic and Pentecostal in preserving and extending the missionary zeal that first brought religion to America and the emphasis on the dynamic use of Pentecostalism (the "gifts of the Spirit") to convert and "save" the unbeliever.

The unique pragmatic and experimental religious expression in the United States is known as American (or civil) religion, a highly pragmatic "religion" that has no theological or institutional structure and no form of worship. It is a way of life based on belief in God and in a set of values (often undefined but quite real) that inspires a common religious sense and forms a kind of national religion.

Will Herberg has noted that this American phenomenon "influences and is influenced by the 'official' religions of American society. . . . It is the characteristic American religion, undergirding American life . . . despite all indubitable differences of region, section, culture and class."[2] Other scholars have been harshly critical. Joseph Fletcher called it "the American Shinto"; *Newsweek* carried a full account of what it called "the Protesting Protestants" in which it noted the need for "a radical transformation of Protestant Christianity"; and a *Philadelphia Bulletin* article called American religion "a false religion" confusing politics and religion.

Another unique religious expression in the United States is humanism, or the humanist way of looking at life and human experience. Humanism also has no theological or institutional structure or form of worship, yet its concern for the dignity of humans and their rights and for the quality of human life here and now might be called religious. Indeed some humanists do call themselves religious yet put their emphasis on human beings and human activity (under "Ethical Culture Movement" below, see "Fellowship of Religious Humanists"). Some humanists, however, reject all supernaturalism and have been condemned by fundamentalists as "secular humanists" bent on destroying "true" religion and even the United States itself. Nevertheless, humanism has been an influence in religion in the United States mainly by helping religious institutions rethink their beliefs and by paying more attention to human experience in belief and practice. It has also helped soften the expression by mainline religions of the relations between God and people and between people themselves.

A third characteristic, more specifically identified with Protestantism, yet of such an influential nature that it must be considered a key part of religion in the United States, is its evangelism and Pentecostalism. Evangelism describes the spirit and attitude of American religion for most of its history.

Pentecostalism is a Protestant emphasis that many religious groups adopted that is characterized by biblical literalism in dynamic preaching about humanism and its dangers, about God's judgment and eternal damnation, and about salvation, usually achieved in revival services designed to provoke emotional fervor to be "saved" from Satan and "the world."

A contemporary and somewhat more sophisticated offspring of the Pentecostal movement is the charismatic movement. Charismatics emphasize a Pentecostal "baptism in the Spirit," which confers the "gifts of the Spirit" identified by Paul in 1 Corinthians 12:8–10, 28, including speaking in tongues, the gift of prophecy, the interpretation of tongues, faith, wisdom, knowledge of divine things, the power of healing, the recognition of spirits, and the performing of miracles. One significant difference between Pentecostalists and charismatics is that the latter come from all Christian bodies, not just Protestant denominations. Charismatic services in the late twentieth century may have adopted "the old-time religion" spirit of the Protestant evangelical Pentecostal movement, but the charismatic movement is now ecumenical in nature as Protestants and Roman Catholics pray, worship, and share in the ecstasy of "the gifts of the Spirit."

U.S. Religion at the Gate of the Twentieth Century

As early as 1880 and continuing until 1925, when immigration was drastically curtailed, America was flooded with millions of newcomers, who radically altered the composition of the population. So marked was this change that the U.S. Immigration Commission designated it the new immigration, as contrasted with the old immigration. The "old" referred to people who had come from the British Isles, Belgium, Denmark, France, Germany, the Netherlands, Norway, Sweden, and Switzerland. The so-called new immigration referred to the flow of people then coming from Austria-Hungary, Bulgaria, Greece, Italy, Montenegro, Poland, Portugal, Romania, Russia, Serbia, Spain, Syria, and Turkey.

The two lists of countries suggests the vast cultural differences between the two immigrations. The first group was predominantly Protestant; the second was Roman Catholic, Orthodox, or Jewish. Other differences in the countries of origin included (1) movements toward representative and popular government versus absolute monarchies; (2) the presence of what we might call a progressive peasantry versus peasants who were just one generation removed from serfdom; and (3) peoples who were mainly Teutonic versus those who were mainly of Latin, Slavic, Semitic, and Mediterranean strains. These radical differences were greatly accentuated by a dramatic increase in the volume of immigration around the turn of the century, as these figures indicate.

Years	*No. of Immigrants (millions)*
1850–1879	2½ per decade

1880–1889	5¼
1890–1899	3¾
1900–1909	8¾
1910–1919	6½

While the causes of the increased immigration were mostly economic, the new immigration constituted a major problem for religion in the United States. Millions of new immigrants had been uprooted from their inherited faiths and transplanted to a new land. Many tended to form tight ethnic colonies that maintained the language, dress, and manners of the old country. But the second generation, more especially the young, tended to drop items of their old culture and adopt that of their new country. The question that the religions of the United States faced was, Would the immigrants abandon, along with the other customs peculiar to their ancestral heritage, the faith of their fathers and mothers? They had come from countries where religion had been a normal accompaniment of citizenship, whereas in the new land there was no state church, with the institutions of government and religion separated by constitutional definition.

For Protestants in general the adjustment was easy. In the United States, denominations related to those the immigrants had known in the old country were available. Roman Catholics had a more difficult time. Very few areas were predominantly Catholic; indeed the atmosphere was overwhelmingly Protestant. The early days had known no Eastern churches and very few Jews. But increased immigration had changed the overall religious makeup, which now included an increase in non-Christian nationals. The Jews were more numerous, and so were Orientals.

The earliest tendency of national groups was to live together in a colony and to use their newly formed churches as a social center. This was of great benefit to Catholicism. The Roman Catholic Church, unlike the Protestants, who had concentrated on secondary and higher education, emphasized the primary school of parochial education. Roman Catholics, always believers that the Christian religion should be an integral part of education, built not only churches but schools and thus assumed more responsibility for indoctrinating the faithful's children and youth. Much of the success of the Roman Catholic Church in the United States is due both to the comprehensive nature and organization of the church itself and to the zeal and fervor of its people. The Roman Catholic population grew from 12 million members at the turn of the century to over 16 million in 1910.

At the gate of the twentieth century, Christianity in general was approaching what some have called its golden age. The liberal giving of great industrialists who were also churchmen made growth possible far beyond the remotest dreams of nineteenth-century religious leaders; the names read like an early *Who's Who:* Cook, Gould, McCormick, Morgan, Rockefeller, Vanderbilt, and even the practical atheist Carnegie. Other factors explaining growth were the increasing tendency to develop lay leadership in local and national churches and the adoption of "big business" efficiency, order, and organization in running churches and church boards.

Another symptom of change accompanied the golden era. The Baptist and Methodist churches, once "the poor man's churches," overnight became wealthy. The less-educated masses, once successfully reached by these two religious bodies, now turned to the new Pentecostal groups. Such groups were especially strong in the southern and the central and western states, where the appeal traditionally had been more emotional. The fundamentalist movement of 1910 was a similar phenomenon. An early pamphlet entitled *The Fundamentals: A Testimony to the Truth* set forth five fundamentalist doctrines, alleging, "No Christian can deny any one." Those who did not conform to the statement were called modernists, and a battle began between the two camps of Protestants that raged on for years. An outgrowth of the fundamentalist movement was the nationwide evangelistic campaign, such as that of the colorful Billy Sunday, whose antics and down-to-earth preaching reached many. Another outgrowth was the trial of John T. Scopes, who was charged with teaching evolution. One of the more serious consequences of the fundamentalist movement was witch-hunts conducted by the most zealous for nonbelievers. One notable example was the trial of Harry Emerson Fosdick, which brought about his resignation from the First Presbyterian Church in New York City. Several denominations were split wide open by such doctrinal radicalism.

In spite of the fundamentalists, or perhaps because of them, there were strong evidences of efforts toward unity among Christian churches. Several attempts at unity within the religious families separated by the Civil War or by physical-legal reasons were noted among the Lutherans, Methodists, and Reformed, all with the purpose of repairing earlier rifts. And after World War I several organizations that cut across denominational bounds were formed: the Young Men's and Young Women's Christian Associations, the Student Volunteer Movement, Christian social action groups, and the Peace Movement. Furthermore, led by John R. Mott and others, several Protestant groups began to work together in many fields, such as in foreign and home missions councils and in the Federal (later called National) Council of Churches. And the Protestant Episcopal Church opened to all like-minded groups a concrete offer for union—a forerunner of later unity movements.

Conclusion

No conclusion to the survey of religion in the United States can be accurately drawn without a review of the five most active religious phenomena of the late twentieth century:

1. Civil religion
2. TV religion

3. Decline of mainline Protestantism
4. Changes in Roman Catholicism
5. Pluralism

The last half of the century has witnessed the use (or perhaps overuse) of the concept of civil religion from our Judeo-Christian heritage to support a parochial interpretation of the political institutions of the United States, along with an emphasis on the concepts of God, of the God-given rights of humans, and of the God-willed destiny of the nation. These concepts may be vague, ambiguous, and perhaps empty, but they are considered good, even "holy" by many, and they have been proven vote-getters in elections.

Witness the appeals to civil religion in the inaugural address of John F. Kennedy in January 1961. He declared, "I have sworn before you and Almighty God the same solemn oath our forebearers prescribed nearly a century and three quarters ago." Kennedy also subscribed to "the belief that the rights of man came not from the generosity of the state but from the hand of God." And he concluded by saying, "Let us go forth . . . asking His blessing and His help, but knowing that here on earth God's work must truly be our own."[3] Twenty years later Ronald Reagan attained the highest office literally by preaching the slogans of civil religion while wrapping himself in the American flag with an appeal to stand tall as an American.

Another reason for Ronald Reagan's success was the support of right-wing, conservative (some scholars say reactionary) Protestants, more particularly the TV preacher-evangelists. As a matter of fact, the phenomenon of so-called TV religion was a very potent force in the 1980s. Many of the leading figures were connected only distantly to established religious groups, and many of them used their television pulpit to build a church or to amass their own wealth. All of these preachers were Protestants, all conservative evangelicals, and some of them identified themselves as right-wing Republicans.

An indication of the overwhelming coverage of TV religion is a survey from the early 1980s that showed that Jerry Falwell, Jimmy Swaggert, and Rex Humbard appeared on Philadelphia channels at least four times a week; Jim Bakker, James Robison, and Oral Roberts at least three times a week; and "Pat" Robertson and the "Hour of Power" twice a week. Several of these men (e.g., Bakker and Robertson) owned their own TV stations or even networks. Amazingly, even the moral difficulties of some of the popular TV preachers seemed only a minor hindrance to the lucrative "ministries" of TV religion generally. It is quite obvious that religious broadcasting is big business in the United States. In 1980 more than 1,300 radio and 36 television stations devoted all or most of their time to religion.

Oral Roberts, a veteran of electronics, raised enough to launch a multimillion-dollar "City of Faith" at Tulsa, Oklahoma, complete with a university, a multistoried university clinic, a research center, and a 777-bed hospital. Jerry Falwell, in addition to his large and influential Baptist Church in Lynchburg, Virginia, and the "Old Time Gospel Hour" on television, established and built the Christian Liberty College and founded a denomination—the Liberty Baptist Fellowship. Pat Robertson, founder of the Christian Broadcasting Network, Virginia Beach, Virginia, and of his "700 Club," also built a multimillion-dollar international headquarters for his operation. Jim Bakker founded and did well with his "PTL Club," which was modeled on the Johnny Carson show and was entertainment deluxe for many American Christians. Bakker later had personal problems following an alleged moral lapse and, after an FCC investigation, was convicted of misusing donated funds and with income tax evasion.

Another interest of several of the TV evangelists, especially "Pat" Robertson and Jerry Falwell, is politics. Robertson organized a 1980 rally in Washington, D.C., for a day of "humiliation, prayer, and fasting," followed by a lobbying of members of Congress, asking them to be "of God's mind" as they considered legislation. Robertson later made a run for the 1988 Republican nomination for president of the United States. Falwell founded the Moral Majority with Paul Weyrich in 1979, which announced objectives of distributing sermon materials on political issues to ministers and organizing them to get their parishioners registered to vote. Actually the Moral Majority also worked for the defeat of liberal politicians.

"Mainline Protestantism" is a friendly name for what we could call the founding denominations—namely, the Episcopalians of Jamestown; the Congregationalists, Presbyterians, and Baptists of Plymouth; and the latecomers: the Methodists and a few other WASP (or white, Anglo-Saxon, Protestant) groups. This informal alignment of Protestant groups "defined the spiritual and moral ethos of the U.S.," according to a *Time* article on May 22, 1989. Yet *Time* author Richard N. Ostling reports that "America's 'old guard' Protestant churches confront an unprecedented decline." He notes that "the United Church of Christ (which included most Congregationalists) has shrunk 20% since 1965, the Presbyterian Church 25%, the Episcopal Church 28%, the United Methodist Church 18% and the Christian Church (Disciples of Christ) 43% [after a de facto schism]. Together, these five groups suffered a net loss of 5.2 million souls during years when the U.S. population rose 47 million." Ostling also points out that black Protestant groups have gained, and Roman Catholic membership has grown a solid 16 percent. "The boom in the conservative evangelical churches (including Fundamentalists, Pentecostals and Charismatics) has caused some to envision a religious revival."[4]

Ostling's explanations are varied. He acknowledges "cultural and demographic changes, organizational reshuffles," a general lack of "marketing and communications that the Evangelicals employ to win new members," "a preoccupation with political and social issues at the expense of good old fashioned faith," and the fact that "the traditional denominations . . . are increasingly unsure what [their] message is."[5] Ostling does note that of a list of 500 fastest-growing Protestant congregations, 445 were outside the mainline groups. He also comments that many of the losses of the mainline churches are "backdoor" losses, that is, dropouts into irreligion or antiauthority movements. Ostling's conclusions are also varied. He believes the possibility of mainline Protestantism regaining its former status and clout is small. Another analyst, however, seems to think that the mainliners' present struggles could one day give them special strength "in a humbling," because of their "dethronement" and the need to adapt their churches to the twenty-first century.

The Roman Catholic Church, despite *Time*'s reported growth in membership, has had its share of problems and changes, or, as a *Newsweek* article called it in 1985, crisis. Such phenomena of unrest began with Vatican II (1962–65) and have continued to concern Catholics ever since. Indeed, Pope John Paul II convened a Synod of Bishops in 1985 in order to assess the many troubling issues created by Vatican II.

When Pope John XXIII convened the Second Vatican Council, he prayed that the Roman Catholic Church would "open its windows" and allow some "fresh air" to permeate its entire structure.[6] Without doubt, the council was the most significant event in the life of the Catholic Church in the twentieth century, and Catholics throughout the world are still struggling to give concrete expression to the radically revised self-understanding of Roman Catholicism that is contained in the documents of the council. This struggle touches almost every aspect of church life, but for the sake of clarity we may discuss it under the rubrics of model, method, magisterium, ministry, and minorities.

The council modified the self-confident, hierarchical, and clericalized ecclesiology that had been prevalent since the Council of Trent and adopted instead a model of the church as "the People of God."[7] The foundational role of the laity and the relative autonomy of the local church were keystones of this new ecclesiological model. Collegiality tempered the monarchical power that the papacy had acquired over the centuries. In addition, the council rejected the notion that the church of Christ is strictly identical with the Roman Catholic Church,[8] thus providing a strong impetus for ecumenical dialogue. This new ecclesiological model was accepted with great enthusiasm, especially in the United States, where much of the American democratic tradition of governance was adapted for use in church administration. These developments, however, have led to certain tensions between the central ecclesiastical authorities in Rome and the various local churches.

This shift in ecclesiology was a direct result of a change in Catholic theological method. Most of the council documents reflect a renewal in Catholic biblical, patristic, and liturgical studies. Whereas historical-critical theological methods had met with Roman condemnation in the first half of this century, the council employed the results of these same methods in its deliberations and documents. The result has been a general emancipation of theological method from the traditionalist and scholastic schools that had dominated the church for four centuries. This newfound freedom has led to a tension between theologians and Roman authorities over the nature of orthodoxy and the teaching of truly "Catholic" doctrine.

The struggle over orthodoxy highlights a growing debate in the Catholic Church concerning the proper function of the magisterium. When Pope Paul VI rejected the majority opinion of his own theological commission and restated the church's ban on artificial birth control in 1968, many European and American Catholics voiced public dissent. Since that time, more and more American Catholics have questioned the normativity of magisterial teachings, especially in the field of medical and reproductive ethics. There is also a growing debate between Roman authorities and Catholics in developing countries over the proper role of the church in regard to peace and economic justice. These tensions continue to grow, and some theologians fear that there will be, in the words of Bernard Haring, "an exodus of the most alert and intelligent people" from the Roman Catholic Church.[9]

Many of these developments presuppose an active participation by the laity in the life, governance, and mission of the church. This renewal in ministry was symbolized by the changes in the Catholic liturgy that were mandated by the council. In an attempt to ensure the "full, conscious, and active participation" of all those who gathered for worship,[10] the council urged that the vernacular language be adopted in the celebration of the liturgy. The rites of the church also underwent a complete restructuring. As a result, the role of the ordained priest has undergone a redefinition, and there has been a dramatic rise in the exercise of various ministries by members of the laity. This increase in lay ministry has been coupled with a marked decline in the number of candidates for the priesthood. This decline in ordained ministry will pose a significant challenge for Roman Catholics in the near future, and there are already many dioceses in the United States that have parishes that are staffed by someone other than a priest.[11] This situation has led many Catholics to call for a change in the church discipline concerning those who may be ordained.

Finally, it must be noted that the face of the Catholic Church is changing throughout the world. The role of so-called minorities in the church presents both a challenge and an opportunity to the church. Women (and men) are addressing themselves to what they perceive as an inherent sexism in Catholic theology and ministry, and they are raising important questions about the equality of the baptized and the nature of ordained ministry. Afro-American and Hispanic Catholics will constitute fully one-third of the American Catholic Church by the year 2000.[12] By that same year, two-thirds of all Catholics will live south of the equator.[13] These trends will force the church to shift its theological and administrative models away from the western European systems that have been prevalent for so long. As the minorities become the majority in the church, Catholic theology and praxis will have to change if the church is to remain responsive to the "signs of the times" and the needs of the modern world.[14]

Historically, every major church council has been followed by a period of difficulty and adjustment. The years since the Second Vatican Council have certainly been no exception. The move toward theological and pastoral models that are infused with the fresh air of the council has met with some hesitation and resistance. It is clear, however, that Catholics throughout the world have been committed to the vision of Roman Catholicism as articulated by the council, and they are struggling to respond appropriately in the life and ministry of the churches in communion with Rome.

The finest summary statement on the contemporary health and viability of Judaism in the United States is in the conclusion of Gilbert S. Rosenthal's book *The Many Faces of Judaism*. Rosenthal writes:

> American Judaism has come a long way in a short three hundred years. In America today there are about six million Jews; more than three thousand rabbis and almost four thousand synagogues; seminaries and parochial schools; native-born scholars; four hundred thousand children in religious schools, including more than eighty thousand students attending the hundreds of all-day schools for intensive Jewish education. Thousands study Hebrew language in high school and colleges; thousands take adult study courses in congregation and Jewish colleges; thousands are enrolled in youth groups and in Jewish or Hebrew-speaking camps; and thousands visit or study in Israel each year.
>
> Today it is easier than ever to keep kosher and observe the Sabbath and holidays—at least in the major centers of Jewish life—and many Jews do so. It was unheard of to find a yarmulke on a college student in a secular university twenty years ago, and an observant college professor was a great rarity. Today these are commonplace. Despite the many problems of American Jewry—the high rate of mixed marriage, widespread Jewish illiteracy, a low birth rate, and rapidly decaying Jewish neighborhoods in the inner cities—we have made great progress since the first generation of immigrants came here a little more than three centuries ago.
>
> And a greater variety of Jewish beliefs and experiences is found in this country than in any other land or at any other time in Jewish history. We have discussed and compared the four main religious movements and two minor schools of thought. There are others. Jews are finding Jewish identity in small religious fellowships or havurot, in informal synagogues and home worship, and in a variety of religious, secular, cultural, social, and Zionist organizations. This American Jewish community is rich with choices and blessed with alternatives. Even within the four major religious movements there are many smaller schools of thought. Surely each Jew can find a philosophy to satisfy a personal quest for Judaism and Jewish life.[15]

The fifth unique contemporary religious phenomenon in the United States is pluralism. The dictionary defines "pluralism" as "the quality or condition of existing in more than one part or form," or "the theory that reality is composed of a multiplicity of beings, principles, or substances." Religious pluralism in the United States is a result of the history, geography, economy, and cultural facts of the country itself, since to this new land immigrants from many countries brought many different kinds of religious expressions and institutions, which made us a pluralistic society and guaranteed pluralism in religion. Roman Catholicism, Protestantism, and Judaism were aware quite early that many religious groups practiced a diversity of expressions in the new land and that many more groups would most likely multiply in this environment. Contemporary religion in the United States bears this out. For example, in 1977 an investigation of the diversity of religion in the United States revealed that there were over eight hundred separate groups or denominations of Christians and two hundred different non-Christian groups.

Surveys in the late 1980s continue to support the view that the United States has been transformed from an informal religious culture dominated by the mainline Protestant churches to a pluralistic one. In the days after the Revolutionary War, the United States was as Protestant as a modern Middle East nation is Muslim. Roman Catholicism was still only 2.5 percent of the population, and less than one out of one thousand was Jewish. Yet by the middle of the twentieth century, the Roman Catholic population had reached 25 million, and the Jewish population was over 5 million. In addition, both Roman Catholics and Jews had achieved a social status almost equal to that of the "landed" mainline Protestants, expressed in the attainment of higher economic and educational levels.

The urbanization of society in the United States contributed not only to the social equality of Roman Catholics and Jews with Protestants but also to the expansion of pluralism to include religious groups from the Far East and Near East and a continued fracture of Christian and Jewish religious groups in the United States. Indeed, even the right to disbelief has accounted for a number of "religious" groups in the United States, in fulfillment of De Toqueville's observation that the strength and vitality of American religious life lay in the respect of free choice. He concluded that it was the voluntary character of American religion that had given it a dynamism often lacking in countries where people are religious by coercion or national habit.

Two interesting phenomena of the contemporary religious scene in the United States are the "Jesus People" and the reverse missionary efforts of Hare Krishna and the Unification Church. The Jesus People movement is a religious phenomenon born to match the social and political upheaval of the 1960s. Several groups are representative. The Berkeley Christian Coalition developed from the youth flower-child culture in the late sixties under the leadership of Jack Sparks as an offshoot of the Campus Crusade for Christ.

Called at first the Christian World Liberation Front, it was reorganized in 1975 as the Berkeley Christian Coalition to function primarily as a religious body with beliefs and ministry similar to Protestant Christianity, with the addition of a life-style seeking beauty and creativity.

A second group is the Children of God, which developed from the movement Teens for Christ and offered both a religious revival and a colonial system to the California youth culture of the late 1960s. It was led by David Brandt Berg (called Moses David by the media). Sixty colonies were established in the United States and some overseas, each colony headed by a shepherd. Each colony member vowed to forsake all to follow Jesus, to study the Bible and the writing of Moses David, and to preach the gospel to all people. The colonies practiced communal sharing of property and income and avoided all "worldly" entanglements.

A third group is the Jesus People, or International Christian Ministries, founded by Duane Pederson via a free "underground" type of Christian newspaper, the *Hollywood Free Paper.* They offered Bible study groups, Christian "rock" festivals, coffeehouses, and help for drug abusers, and their influence spread across the nation. They established the Jesus People Practicollege for members to train for group leadership. Their beliefs were those of evangelical Protestant Christianity—strongly Bible oriented, with Pederson's books as an important supplement.

Two interesting phenomena are the reverse of the usual, as they involve missionary efforts from abroad. The first was from India, a modified Hinduism in the form of the International Society for Krishna Consciousness, which was brought to the United States by Bhaktivedanta Swami Prabhupada in 1965. The second was from Korea, a modified Christianity called the Holy Spirit Association for the Unification of World Christianity (also known as the Unification Church, the "Family," and the "Moonies"), brought to the United States by Sun Myung Moon and his followers in 1971.

From an overall point of view, religion is still a major force in the United States. Although the statistics may not show the continued strength and influence of mainline religion, the strength of nontraditional Christianity in the United States is obvious from the same statistics. Discounting TV religion, many Protestant religious groups are growing—often in reverse proportion to formerly stiff membership demands and in direct proportion to the informality and friendly fellowship these groups provide. This comment on the late 1980s could lead us to conclude that general religion thrives in the United States, mainly because, in the words of de Tocqueville, "every man is allowed freely to take that road he thinks will lead him to heaven."[16]

Notes

1. George Tavard, *Understanding Protestantism* (Glen Rock, N.J.: Paulist Press, 1959), p. 96.

2. Will Herberg, *Protestant, Catholic, and Jew* (Garden City, N.Y.: Doubleday, 1955), p. 77.

3. *New York Times,* January 21, 1961, p. 8.

4. Richard N. Ostling, "Those Mainline Blues," *Time,* May 22, 1989, p. 94.

5. Ibid., pp. 94, 96.

6. Pope John XXIII, "Address on Pentecost Sunday," *The Pope Speaks* 6, no. 3 (1960).

7. Vatican Council II, "Dogmatic Constitution on the Church (Lumen Gentium)," translated from the Latin and reprinted in *Vatican Council II: The Conciliar and Post Conciliar Documents,* ed. Austin Flannery (Collegeville, Minn.: Liturgical Press, 1975), pp. 359–69.

8. Ibid., p. 357.

9. Bernard Haring, as quoted in the *National Catholic Reporter* 25, no. 27 (April 28, 1989): 5.

10. Vatican Council II, "Constitution on the Sacred Liturgy (Sacrosanctum Concilium)," in Flannery, *Vatican Council II,* p. 7.

11. Archdiocese of New York, *Clergy Report,* June 1989, p. 2.

12. Ana Maria Pineda, "The Hispanic Presence: Hope and Challenge for Catholicity," *New Theology Review* 2, no. 3 (August 1989): 30–33.

13. William McConville, "Catholicity and Belonging," *New Theology Review* 2, no. 3 (August 1989): 8.

14. Vatican Council II, "Pastoral Constitution on the Church in the Modern World (Gaudium et Spes)," in Flannery, *Vatican Council II,* p. 905.

15. G. S. Rosenthal, *The Many Faces of Judaism* (New York: Behrman House, 1989), pp. 156–57.

16. Alexis de Tocqueville, *Democracy in America,* 2 vols. (New York: Vintage Books, 1954), 1:436.

♦ ♦ ♦

ADVENTISTS

ADVENT CHRISTIAN GENERAL CONFERENCE

General Description

Organized in 1860, the Advent Christian (General) Church has approximately 20,000 members in 340 congregations in the United States and Canada. The church maintains mission work in Nigeria, Mexico, the Philippines, Japan, Malaysia, and India. Another 15,000 people attend Advent Christian congregations in these countries.

The denomination grew out of the Advent Awakening of the 1840s, fueled by the prophetic preaching of William Miller, a farmer and U.S. Army captain who through his study of Scripture became convinced of the imminent return of Jesus Christ. One of five denominations that grew out of this awakening, the Advent Christian Church practices Sunday worship, emphasizes justification by faith alone in Jesus Christ, and holds as its distinctive doctrines the following: conditional immortality, soul sleep during the intermediate state between death and the return of Christ, and a historic interpretation of Bible prophecy.

The Advent Christian Church's contribution to religious life in the United State occurred primarily in the mid-1800s, when emphasis on the imminent return of Jesus Christ was minimized by prevailing postmillennial interpretations of Bible prophecy. The Advent Awakening was the first of several movements within evangelical Christianity that focused upon the crucial nature of Christ's second coming. Mission work among freed slaves and overseas was a key part of the Advent Christian Church in the last half of the nineteenth century.

Today denomination headquarters are in Charlotte, North Carolina. It holds membership in the National Association of Evangelicals.

Significant Terms

Conditional immortality. The belief that man's soul is not created immortal but gains immortality only through the grace of God as a gift bestowed at the resurrection. The gift is given to the faithful but not to the wicked. Hence, it is conditioned upon one's acceptance of Christ as Savior (John 3:16). Those without Christ will not be eternally tortured in a burning hell but will be consumed and cease to exist.

Historicist interpretation of Bible prophecy. In opposition to dispensationalism and other interpretations, this school of prophecy stresses that the prophetic passages of Scripture have been fulfilled throughout human history and not during the time immediately before the return of Christ.

Millerism. This term describes both the teaching of William Miller that Christ would return "in or about 1843–44" and the movement that evolved from his proclamation. It was originally coined by the opponents of that teaching. His followers slowly came to accept and use the term, as they did the term "Millerite" in reference to themselves.

Sleep of the dead (or soul sleep). A belief that upon death man becomes unconscious and remains so until the resurrection and judgment—in opposition to the view that the soul either ascends to heaven or descends to hell immediately upon death. Rather, man enters a state of unconsciousness best described in human terms, as it so often is in the Bible, as a "sleep." The condition of the soul between death and the resurrection is sometimes referred to as the intermediate state.

Bibliography

Dean, David A. *Resurrection: His and Ours*. Charlotte, N.C.: Venture Books, 1976. Dean, a graduate of Westminster Theological Seminary, provides a theological and historical perspective on the beliefs of the Advent Christian Church. The most concise book on Advent beliefs available.

Hewitt, Clyde E. *Midnight and Morning*. Charlotte, N.C.: Venture Books, 1984. Hewitt, a historian with a doctorate from the University of Chicago, focuses on the life of William Miller, on his theological understanding and ministry, and on the founding of the Advent Christian Church in 1860. The first of a projected seven-volume work on the history of the Advent Christian Church.

Prepared by Rev. Robert Mayer, director of publications.

SEVENTH-DAY ADVENTIST CHURCH

General Description

"Seventh-Day Adventist" is the name adopted as a denominational title in 1860 by one branch of Adventists—those who keep the seventh day as the Sabbath. The people who first took the name in 1860 were already Adventists, not only in the broad sense of believing in the nearness of the Second Advent (in various parts of the world in the 1840s and earlier, many had believed that), but also in the restricted sense of having developed from the Millerite movement, which Miller had called Adventist. By adopting the name, the Sabbath-keeping Adventists distinguished themselves from the other descendants of the Millerite movement.

The full title "Seventh-Day Adventist" is the official name of a specific Christian denomination with a specific body of doctrines, of which the Sabbath and the Second Advent form only a part. It does not apply to those (mostly small groups) who observe the seventh day and hold to the nearness of the Advent but who differ in other doctrines and hence are not part of the denomination. The name is not denied, however, to those of like faith who are separated by circumstances from organizational connection with the whole body.

History

Seventh-Day Adventists are doctrinally heirs of the Adventist, or Millerite, movement of the 1840s. Also they are heirs of an earlier widespread awakening, in many countries, of interest in the Second Advent, of which the Millerite movement was a part, along with premillennialism.

The denominational name and basic organization were adopted between 1860 and 1863. Since at least 1844, however, the group had been organized as a distinctive and well-defined body of individuals, groups, and local churches who were developing and holding common doctrines that distinguished them clearly from others.

By about 1850 the fusion of scattered groups of Sabbath-keeping Adventists in New England and New York was assured by a series of conferences under the leadership of James and Ellen White and Joseph Bates. During the period from 1848 through 1850, differences were resolved, and the main outline of doctrines held in common was laid down. Thus was formed the nucleus of the church years before the name or the church organization existed.

In 1848 James White, at the urging of his wife, began to publish *Present Truth,* in Middletown, Connecticut; the next year, *Advent Review,* in Auburn, New York; and later in 1850, *Review and Herald,* at Paris, Maine, later at Rochester, New York, where a small publishing house was established. The *Review and Herald* became the official denominational organ. In all of this Ellen G. White's counsels furnished the inspiration, and James White provided the leadership and much of the preaching, writing, and promotion. The publishing house, operated at first in Rochester, New York, was moved to Battle Creek, Michigan, in 1855, where it soon became the headquarters for the denomination.

During the 1850s doctrines were developed, mostly in articles on various biblical subjects, often called forth as answers to opponents. J. N. Andrews, a young man in his twenties with a scholarly bent, wrote numerous expositions on the Sabbath, the sanctuary, the beasts of Revelation 13, and other prophetic topics. His articles, closely reasoned and forcefully expressed, formed a basis for other pamphlets and books on these subjects. Uriah Smith, later known for his exposition on the Books of Daniel and Revelation, began to write on the prophecies.

In a general meeting at Battle Creek in 1860, the denominational name was adopted, and a committee was formed to incorporate the publishing house. The Seventh-Day Adventist Publishing Association was incorporated in 1861. In 1861 also the churches of Michigan were organized into a "conference" (in the Methodist sense of the word); later, other conferences were formed. In 1863 a General Conference met, and a constitution was framed.

Numerous institutions were established at the Battle Creek headquarters, including, in 1866, the Western Health Reform Institute, which in 1877 became the Medical and Surgical Sanitarium and later the Battle Creek Sanitarium. In 1874 Battle Creek College was founded, and in 1985 the American Medical Missionary College.

In 1868 evangelists launched a thriving work on the Pacific Coast. In New England, lay evangelism was fostered through tract and missionary societies, begun in the late 1860s and organized on a denomination-wide basis in 1874. Publications in different languages were printed for use among foreign-speaking people in the United States, and the influence of this evangelism spread. In the late 1860s the Adventist teachings were carried to Europe (to Italy and Switzerland) by an independent missionary named Czechowski, who did not represent the denomination, and groups of adherents to the doctrines were formed who had no contact with the original groups.

In 1874 the General Conference sent J. N. Andrews to Europe. This was the beginning of a worldwide expansion. As Seventh-Day Adventists entered other lands, they found people who were already looking for Christ's return and some who were observing the Sabbath, who joined the movement in Germany, Russia, Argentina, Brazil, and elsewhere.

In the later 1870s house-to-house selling began of Seventh-Day Adventist publications, which led in the early eighties to the printing of subscription books on Seventh-Day Adventist doctrines for sale to the general public. This innovation was so successful that it became one of the standard methods of evangelism.

In the early years of the twentieth century, the church rounded out its worldwide expansion, yet it also turned its attention to administration in order to facilitate the work in the areas where it had already become established. Local conferences were brought together in areawide or nationwide union conferences during the period from 1894 to 1901; in 1913 divisions were formed on a continental basis.

In 1901 planning and control over the various phases of work of the church became more centralized with the formation of the first General Conference departments, in place of several independent organizations. An enlarged and more widely representative General Conference Executive Committee assumed the guiding role.

In later years, as all parts of the globe were assigned to the various divisions, new territories were entered and in turn became bases for further expansion as indigenous leadership was developed. The church became truly worldwide, though it has continually been challenged by the existence of further unentered regions. The worldwide membership is distributed approximately as follows: 35 percent in Latin America; 30 percent in Africa; 16 percent in Asia; 12 percent in North America; 4 percent in Australia, New Zealand, and Oceania; and 3 percent in Europe.

Beliefs and Doctrines

The Seventh-Day Adventist Church is a conservative Christian body, worldwide in extent, evangelical in doctrine, and professing no creed but the Bible. It places strong emphasis on the Second Advent, which it believes is near, and observes the Sabbath of the Bible, the seventh day of the week. These two distinguishing points are incorporated into the name Seventh-Day Adventist. The church is administered by a democratic organization ranging from the local churches, through the conferences (or missions, or sections; the terminology varies in different countries) and unions, to the General Conference, with its several geographic divisions and other administrative units in various parts of the world.

The Seventh-Day Adventist Church has consistently refused to adopt a creed or confession, preferring to base all beliefs on the Bible. However, several statements of general beliefs have been published.

Church membership, granted by vote of the local congregation, is based on conversion and baptism by immersion, following instruction in and acceptance of the doctrines of the church and its standards of behavior, which include total abstinence from liquor and tobacco.

The distinctive Seventh-Day Adventist message may be summarized as "the everlasting gospel"—the basic Christian message of salvation through faith in Christ—in the special setting of the threefold message of Revelation 14:6–12. The call there is to worship the Creator, "for the hour of his judgment is come," and to take a stand for God in the crisis. This message is epitomized in the phrase "the commandments of God and the faith of Jesus."

Organization and Practices

The local church administration is partly based on a presbyterian pattern, although ministers are not chosen by the congregation but are assigned by the conferences (or missions, or sections), composed of a number of churches. Departmental activities are supervised by representatives of the conference. Groups of conferences form union conferences, and these are the constituents of the General Conference, the worldwide administrative body. The General Conference Executive Committee functions not only through geographic administrative divisions but also through advisory departments, committees, and commissions.

The church organization is representative of its international composition. The General Conference Executive Committee includes members from all the divisions. Each division has its president (who is a vice-president of the General Conference), officers, executive committee, and representatives who belong to the General Conference Executive Committee, serving somewhat as a subcommittee, operating in its own section of the globe. The Seventh-Day Adventist Church operates in 184 countries and areas of the world, using 671 languages.

Two distinctive activities and practices of the Seventh-Day Adventists are their devotion to the principle and practice of tithing and their zeal in carrying forward an extensive program and chain of institutions in the field of health care. An Adventist pamphlet entitled *Seventh-Day Adventists: Their Work and Teaching* points out that "every member, every convert, every church-school pupil . . . the native convert . . . as well as the new follower from the ranks of the highly cultured, all alike are instructed in the elemental rudiments of stewardship, the result of which is the practice of tithing" (p. 67). Seventh-Day Adventists believe that one-tenth of their income belongs to God for the advancement of his kingdom. Such a belief runs through the entire organization and its work and is the basis for the financial structure and strength of the Seventh-Day Adventist Church.

Seventh-Day Adventists also believe that good health and good religion are closely allied, and therefore they support and carry the "gospel" of good health by establishing medical institutions and programs at home in the United States and in all the countries where they have missions. Adventists in fact own and operate more hospitals and treatment centers in the United States than any other religious group. In their institutions not only are the sick treated and nurses and other staff persons trained, but instruction in healthful and godly living is given, which results in better men and women. The Adventists also own and operate a medical college in California where the Bible's teachings on health care are coordinated with a general medical education. No doubt these two distinctives are somewhat responsible for the growth and the popularity of the Seventh-Day Adventist Church.

Significant Terms

The blessed hope. The hope of the Christian: the second advent of Christ.

Effort. An evangelistic campaign or series of meetings to proclaim the doctrines of the church to the public.

Finishing the work. Fulfilling the gospel commission of Christ.

Investigative judgment. A pre-Advent judgment conducted in heaven and relating to the destiny of the human family.

The message. A shortened from of "the three angels' messages" of Revelation 14, which Seventh-Day Adventists believe are being proclaimed now. Also, the entire body of Seventh-Day Adventist teachings.

Present truth. An aspect of biblical truth especially applicable now.

Regional conferences. Church administrative units managed for and by blacks in the United States.

Right arm of the message. The church's teaching regarding health. See "the message" above.

Sundown worship. A special family hour at sundown Friday and Saturday evenings marking the beginning and ending of the seventh-day Sabbath (Exod. 20:8-11).

Week of prayer. A week of devotion set aside each year during which members gather for several prayer meetings in the churches or in homes.

Bibliography

Froom, Le Roy Edwin. *The Prophetic Faith of Our Fathers.* Washington, D.C.: Review & Herald Publishing Association, 1950–54.

Nichol, Francis D. *The Midnight Cry.* Washington, D.C.: Review & Herald Publishing Association, 1944.

Schwartz, R. W. *Light Bearers to the Remnant.* Mountain View, Calif.: Pacific Press Publishing Association, 1979.

Seventh-Day Adventist Encyclopedia. Rev. ed. Washington, D.C.: Review & Herald Publishing Association, 1976.

Spalding, Arthur W. *Origin and History of Seventh-Day Adventists.* 4 vols. Washington, D.C.: Review & Herald Publishing Association, 1961–62.

Prepared by M. Carol Hetzell and revised by F. Donald Yost, director, archives and statistics.

• • •

ASSEMBLIES OF GOD

General Description

The Assemblies of God (AOG) is an outgrowth of the late nineteenth-century world revival and Pentecostal awakening. The denomination was organized in Hot Springs, Arkansas, April 2–12, 1914. Since 1918 its international headquarters have been in Springfield, Missouri. The AOG was founded to (1) achieve better understanding and unity of Pentecostals, (2) combine efforts of missionary endeavors, and (3) combine printing interests.

It is currently the largest Pentecostal denomination in the world, with over 16 million members and adherents worldwide at the end of 1986. The AOG is the largest member denomination of the National Association of Evangelicals. The denomination also belongs to the Pentecostal Fellowship of North America and the Pentecostal World Conference.

Beliefs and Doctrines

The Bible is the all-sufficient rule of faith and practice.

Salvation is through the blood of Jesus Christ and results in a life of holiness (1 John 1:7–9).

Baptism is in the Holy Spirit, with evidence of speaking with other tongues as the Spirit gives utterance (Acts 2).

Divine healing is through the atoning blood of Jesus Christ (James 5:14–15).

The return of Jesus Christ is premillennial (1 Thess. 4:16–18).

Church ordinances are Holy Communion and water baptism by immersion.

Organization

AOG government is a mixture of presbyterian and congregational elements, with local church sovereignty in the choice of pastor and management of local affairs. Presbyteries function at district and national levels. There are fifty-seven district councils (following state lines for the most part). The local district council credentials ministers, not the national body.

At the national level, the *General Council* is a legislative body composed of ministers and one lay delegate from each affiliate church; it meets biennially.

The *General Presbytery* is a lesser legislative body meeting annually, having three representatives from each district council and three from each of the four foreign mission areas. The *Executive Presbytery* is a policy board that meets six times a year and is composed of five elected officers and eight regional representatives.

Contributions and Influence

In 1986 there were 10,886 churches, 2,135,104 members, 30,204 ministers, 1,404,974 Sunday school enrollees, 18 U.S. colleges and Bible institutes, 85 military chaplains, and 398 home missionaries. Special areas of ministry are benevolence, education, home missions, men's and women's groups, publications, radio, Sunday school, and youth.

AOG missionary work is evangelistic rather than institutional. There are 1,464 foreign missionaries, 188 countries served, 102,343 national workers, 110,538 foreign churches and preaching points, 14,241,714 foreign membership, and 283 foreign Bible schools.

Significant Terms

Christian. An individual who has accepted Christ as Savior.

Salvation. The redemption of man from the consequences of sin through Christ's atonement.

Holy Spirit baptism. The impartation of the Holy Spirit of God to an individual distinct from and subsequent to the salvation experience. It is evidenced by speaking in a language one has not learned—that is, by speaking in tongues (also called glossolalia).

Premillennialism. The belief in the millennial (i.e., thousand-year) reign of Christ on earth, which will come at the beginning of the millennium rather than at its end.

The church. The universal body of Christians everywhere and of every era.

Bibliography

(All items are published by Gospel Publishing House, Springfield, Mo.)

HISTORY AND DOCTRINE

Bicket, Zenas J. *We Hold These Truths*. 1978.

Blumhofer, Edith L. *The Assemblies of God: A Popular History*. 1985.

Brumback, Carl. *Like a River: The Early Years of the Assemblies of God*. 1961, 1977. Formerly published as part 2 of *Suddenly . . . From Heaven*.

Carlson, G. Raymond. *Our Faith and Fellowship*. 1977.

McGee, Gary B. *This Gospel . . . Shall Be Preached: A History and Theology of Assemblies of God Foreign Missions*. 1959, 1986.

Menzies, William W. *Anointed to Serve*. 1971.
Riggs, Ralph M. *We Believe*. Rev. ed. 1960.
Womack, David. *Wellsprings of the Pentecostal Movement*. 1968.

HOLY SPIRIT
Bicket, Zenas J. *Walking in the Spirit*. 1977.
Brumback, Carl. *What Meaneth This?* 1947.
Harris, L. Thomas. *The Holy Spirit: A Pentecostal Interpretation*. 1980.
Horton, Stanley M. *What the Bible Says about the Holy Spirit*. Rev. ed. 1986.

Prepared by the Office of Information and revised by Juleen Turnage, secretary of information.

♦   ♦   ♦

BAHA'I FAITH

General Description
The Baha'i Faith is an independent world religion based on the belief that the Promised One of all revealed religions appeared in the person of Baha'u'llah ("glory of God"). His cause is the establishment of God's kingdom on earth and marks the coming of age of the human race.

Central Figures
Baha'u'llah (1817–92), prophet-founder of the Baha'i Faith and the manifestation of God for this day.

The Bab ("the gate"; 1819–50), herald of the Baha'i Faith, regarded also as the manifestation of God.

Abdu'l-Baha (1844–1921), the son of Baha'u'llah and his successor.

Principles, Teachings, and Laws
The fundamental principle of Baha'i is that religious truth is not absolute, but relative. Religion is one, coming from one God and unfolding his purpose for humankind through continuous and progressive revelations. Missions of manifestations, including those of Abraham, Moses, Buddha, Jesus, Muhammad, the Bab, and Baha'u'llah, represent successive stages in the spiritual evolution of humanity.

God is unknowable essence. We know him only through his manifestations. The purpose of man is to know and love God and to carry forward an ever-advancing civilization.

The covenant of Baha'u'llah protects the unity of faith and safeguards the integrity of teachings.

Prayer and fasting are spiritually obligatory.

Baha'i accepts donations and contributions from members only.

The oneness of humankind is a pivotal social principle. The organic unity of inner and outer realities of man includes the elimination of all forms of prejudice, the equality of men and women, the harmony of science and religion, elimination of extremes of wealth and poverty, universal compulsory education, development of each individual's unique talents and abilities, independent investigation of truth, establishment of a universal auxiliary language, seeking a spiritual solution to economic problems, using consultation as the basis of resolving all major problems, establishing world peace, and developing divine civilization.

According to its social laws, Baha'i prescribes monogamy, upholds chastity, makes marriage conditional on the consent of both parties and sets of parents, forbids the unprescribed use of alcoholic drinks and narcotics, prohibits involvement in partisan politics, requires obedience to the laws and authority of one's country, and applies some laws at the determination of the House of Justice.

Forms of Worship

Baha'i houses of worship present services that include the recitation of Baha'i writings and the scriptures of other divinely revealed religions; a cappella music is allowed.

Individuals are to pray daily in private. Congregational prayer is prohibited except in prayer for the dead. The introduction of rituals is prohibited.

There are nine holy days on which work is suspended. Every nineteen days, Baha'is gather for a spiritual feast. (The Baha'i calendar consists of nineteen months of nineteen days each, with intercalary days between the penultimate and last Baha'i months.)

One's work is performed in the spirit of service, which is regarded as worship.

World Order of Baha'u'llah

The World Order is dependent upon the Covenant of Baha'u'llah, which is established in his Most Holy Book and in the Book of his Covenant. Baha'u'llah appointed Abdu'l-Baha as his successor and as the center of his covenant and the interpreter of his word. He ordained the institution and principles of his world order and established the spiritual and administrative center of the Baha'i world sect in Haifa, Palestine (now Israel).

The will and testament of Abdu'l-Baha delineated the functions of divine institutions and elaborated the administrative and spiritual principles by which they operate. The order was crowned by the twin institutions of *guardianship* and the *Universal House of Justice*. Shoghi Effendi (1896–1957) was appointed by Abdu'l-Baha as his successor and interpreter of Baha'i scripture and the sole guardian of the faith. The Universal House of Justice (first elected in 1963) was named protector of the faith and was empowered to legislate on matters not written in Baha'i writings.

The Baha'i administrative order comprises two branches: the *rulers* and the *learned*. Rulers are elected by governing councils at local, national, and international levels (in local and national spiritual assemblies and in the Universal House of Justice). Nominations, campaigning, and electioneering are forbidden. The learned, or Hands of the Cause of God, are appointed only by Baha'u'llah, Abu'l-Baha, or Shoghi Effendi. Other appointed advisers are the Continental Boards of Counselors, the Auxiliary Board members, and officers of the International Teaching Center. The primary functions of the learned are the propagation and protection of faith. There is no priesthood or clergy in Baha'i.

The Mashriqu'l-Adhkar ("dawning place of the mention of God") is the institutional complex for the integration of the spiritual, humanitarian, educational, and scientific pursuits of Baha'i Faith. It includes the House of Worship—a nine-sided building with a sanctuary providing a serene atmosphere for prayer and meditation, which is open to people of all faiths—and the buildings and organizations that support the House of Worship, including homes for the aged, an orphanage, educational institutions, scientific institutes, service agencies, and institutes for human development.

Contributions and Influence

The American Baha'i community, vitalized by America's spiritual destiny as indicated by the leaders of the faith, is the major contributor toward the development of the Baha'i administrative order throughout the world. The Baha'i Faith was first publicly represented in the United States in 1893 at the World Parliament of Religions in Chicago. There are now more than 1,600 local spiritual assemblies, and the national Baha'i community forms a significant part of the worldwide Baha'i community, which is the most widespread religion in the world outside of Christianity.

The Baha'i Publishing Trust of the United States publishes materials on the faith for the American public and for the worldwide Baha'i community. Baha'i has permanent schools or institutes in Arizona, California, Maine, Michigan, and South Carolina. It has an educational FM radio station in South Carolina.

Activities of the Baha'i community include promotion of human rights, advocacy of world unity and peace, encouragement to eliminate prejudice, and support of the equality of women and men.

Significant Terms

Manifestation of God. A messenger or prophet of God, as revealer of the divine will and founder of the religion.

Baha'i. A follower of Baha'u'llah.

Babi. A follower of the Bab.

Bibliography

(Except as noted, all items are published by the Baha'i Publishing Trust, Wilmette, Ill.)

Abdu'l-Baha. *Secret of Divine Civilization.* 1957. 3d ed., 1975.

Baha'u'llah. *Gleanings from the Writings of Baha'u'llah.* Translated by Shoghi Effendi. 1939. 2d ed., 1976.

Hatcher, W. S., and J. D. Martin. *The Baha'i Faith: The Emerging Global Religion.* New York: Harper & Row, 1984.

Shoghi Effendi. *God Passes By.* 1944. 3d ed., 1974.

——. *World Order of Baha'u'llah.* Compilation of letters of Shogi Effendi. 1938. 2d ed., 1974.

The Universal House of Justice. *The Baha'i World: An International Record.* Vol. 18, *A Compilation.* Wilmette, Ill: Baha'i World Center, 1986.

——. *The Promise of World Peace.* Wilmette, Ill: Baha'i World Center, 1985.

Prepared by the U.S. Baha'i Office of Public Information.

◆ ◆ ◆

BAPTISTS

General Description

Baptists include a family of Christian denominations with over 25 million baptized believers in 115 countries. Their 23,070,102 members in this country represent the largest Protestant denomination family in the United States. Three of the four largest groups belong to the National Council of Churches as well as the World Council of Churches.

Baptists originated in an effort to recover the simplicity and truth of New Testament life and thought. The two basic principles of the original Baptists were believer's baptism and religious liberty.

Founder

Baptists can name no single leader or founder. They trace their history as a denomination to a refugee congregation of English Separatists in Amsterdam, Holland, where they became Baptist in 1609, under the leadership of John Smyth, an Anglican clergyman who became a Puritan, then an Independent, then a Baptist.

Famous Baptists of the past include John Smyth, Thomas Helwys, Roger Williams, John Clarke, John Bunyan, John Milton, John LeLand, Isaac Bakkus, William Carey, Adoniram Judson, Luther Rice, John Clifford, Walter Rauschenbusch, Augustus H. Strong, William Newton Clarke, Samuel F. Smith, E. Y. Mullins, A. T. Robertson, Alexander Maclaren, George W. Truett, Edgar J. Goodspeed, Helen Barrett Montgomery, Shailer Matthews, Albert W. Beaven, and Charles Evans Hughes.

Prominent living Baptists include Ralph D. Abernathy, Marian Anderson, Gene Bartlett, Robert Byrd, Jimmy Carter, C. Emmanuel Carlson, Van Cliburn, W. A. Criswell, R. H. Edwin Epsy, Coretta Scott King, James Forbes, Herbert Gezork, Billy Graham, Charles Grassley, Samuel H. Miller, Carl Radmacher, and Gardener Taylor.

Beliefs and Doctrines

The New Testament is regarded as a divinely inspired, trustworthy, authoritative—an all-sufficient rule of faith and practice. Baptists hold to a regenerate church membership, believer's baptism, symbolic significance of the ordinances (or sacraments), separation of church and state, freedom as an inherent right, the priesthood of all believers, and the church as a gathered company of believers baptized on personal confession of faith in Jesus Christ as Lord and Savior. Distinguishing marks include "a regenerate church membership safeguarded by believer's baptism, congregational in polity coupled with an associational principle, and the necessity of freeing the church from interference by civil government" (N.H. Maring and W.S. Hudson, *A Baptist Manual of Policy and Practice,* Valley Forge: Judson Press, 1976, pp. 207–8).

There are two ordinances: baptism of believers by immersion, a symbol of burial and resurrection, the acted parable of spiritual birth; and the Lord's Supper, symbol of the body and blood of Christ, the occasion of memorial, communion, fellowship, renewal, and consecration—the acted parable of spiritual nurture from the Living Bread and the Water of Life.

A pamphlet, *The People Called American Baptists,* notes that

> American Baptists affirm that God is sovereign over all and that this sovereignty is expressed and realized through Jesus Christ. Therefore, we affirm the Lordship of Christ over the world and the Church. We joyously confess that Jesus Christ is Saviour and Lord. We are called in loyalty to Jesus Christ to proclaim in the power of the Holy Spirit the Good News of God's reconciling grace, and to declare the saving power of the gospel to every human being and to every human institution. We celebrate Christ's charge to make disciples of all nations and to bear witness to God's redeeming reign in human affairs. (p. 21)

Forms of Worship

Simple forms of worship include congregational singing, choral selections, Scripture reading, prayer, with a special emphasis on preaching of the Word, the heart of which is the good news of God's redemptive grace in Jesus Christ.

Organization

The basic unit is the local congregation, conducting its own affairs under the leadership of Christ. Local autonomy, however, is combined with the associational principle in the interest of avoiding the tendency to an isolated self-sufficiency.

Contributions and Influence

Baptists have maintained a strong emphasis on the free church tradition, including the supremacy of the spirit over form and ceremony, the necessity of the church to be free from civil coercion, the freedom of local congregations to order their own church life, and the evangelical expression of the gospel over against the sacramental.

Baptists are largely responsible for the achievement of religious liberty in the United States. Baptists in colonial New England and Virginia led a heroic struggle for freedom "which culminated victoriously in the omission of any religious tests or restrictions when the Constitution of the United States was being framed" (Robert C. Torbet, *Baptist Leadership* [leaflet], p. 3). During the past 150 years, Baptists have grown from a ratio of 1 out of 45 to approximately 1 out of 9 in the total U.S. population.

Significant Terms

Associational principle. Congregational polity is balanced by devotion to the associational principle, in which individual churches work together in association with other churches for the purpose of carrying out mission and cooperative ministries.

Autonomy. Every Baptist congregation—even those that are a part of the conventions, such as the Southern Baptist Convention, the National Baptist Convention, or the American Baptist Churches, U.S.A.—is autonomous and independent from any other structure.

Born again. Baptists do not use the phrase "born again" exclusively, but decades of tent evangelism and crusades have made more people think of it as a Baptist term. On the basis of Jesus' statement to Nicodemus (John 3:3), most Baptists use the term to call attention to God's promise that sinners will be forgiven if they believe Jesus died to save us from our sins.

Ordinance. Baptists do not observe sacraments, but they do observe two ordinances: baptism by immersion, and the celebration of the Lord's Supper (or Holy Communion).

Priesthood of all believers. Although Baptists do ordain professional clergy, they believe that every Christian has a special ministry to serve Christ.

Religious freedom. Baptists are not alone in their devotion to religious freedom, but the concept plays a special part in their history and consciousness. Roger Williams was a Baptist when he founded the Rhode Island colony for religious freedom. The Baptist minister John Leland was particularly influential in encouraging the passage of the First Amendment to the U.S. Constitution. Today, Baptists strongly resist the interference of government in religious matters, and this stand often leads Baptists to resist periods of prayer in schools.

Saved. This term, used by Baptists and many other groups, means "born again."

Soul liberty. According to this concept, each individual has the competency to determine his or her own theology and tenets of faith, on the basis of study of the Bible (especially the New Testament) and the guidance of the Holy Spirit.

Bibliography

Brackney, William, ed. *Baptist Life and Thought*. Valley Forge, Pa.: Judson Press, 1983.

Childers, James Saxon. *A Way Home*. New York: Holt, Rinehart & Winston, 1964.

Maring, Norman H., and Winthrop S. Hudson. *A Baptist Manual of Polity and Practice*. Valley Forge, Pa.: Judson Press, 1963.

Payne, Ernest A. *The Fellowship of Believers: Baptist Thought and Practice Yesterday and Today*. London: Kinsgate Press, 1945.

Robinson, H. Wheeler. *The Life and Faith of the Baptists*. London: Kingsgate Press, 1946.

Woolley, Davis C., ed. *Baptist Advance*. Nashville: Broadman Press, 1964.

Prepared by Willis Hubert Porter and revised by Philip E. Jenks, American Baptist Churches, U.S.A.

AMERICAN BAPTIST ASSOCIATION

General Description

The American Baptist Association was organized in 1924 in Texarkana, Arkansas/Texas, by merging the Old General Association of Baptist Churches with representative churches from additional states. The General Association was originally organized in 1905. A definition of the body is, "A national group of independent Baptist churches voluntarily associating in the effort to fulfill that New Testament commission to the churches, maintaining a minimum of organization so designed as to guarantee the complete sovereignty and equal representation of the churches" (I.K. Cross, *What Is the American Baptist Association?* [leaflet], p. 1).

They are sometimes called the Landmark Baptists, Missionary Baptists, or both names combined.

> The churches of the American Baptist Association are a progressive group with a mind to maintain the purity and simplicity of the churches of the New Testament, and to enlist as many people to these principles as they can through the preaching of the Gospel and the teaching of church truth. They claim to be the descendants of the ancient Donatists, Waldeneses, and Anabaptists. Like their predecessors, they are constantly called dissenters and non-conformists because they are determined to use the Bible as a complete rule of faith and practice. (Cross leaflet, pp. 12, 13)

American Baptist Association members to not accept the sixteenth-century Reformation origin of Baptists. Nor do they accept the concept of a universal, invisible church.

Beliefs and Practices

American Baptist Association members believe that they are the successors of the church of Jesus called out during his personal ministry on earth; that this church has been perpetuated through all centuries; that there is no other kind of church in the New Testament except the local congregation, which is its highest governing body; and that all ordinances are under the complete control of the local congregations. They believe that baptism, to be valid, must be administered by a scriptural Baptist church.

American Baptist Association churches have no affiliation with any organizations other than their own fellowships. They strongly disapprove of the activities of both the National and the World Council of Churches.

Activities

American Baptist Association mission work in the United States and around the world consists of social work as a mission activity. They have Bible institutes, colleges, and seminaries throughout America and a number of foreign countries. The association publishes Sunday school and youth literature and a number of books for their own churches and any others who choose to use them. Headquarters are in Texarkana, Texas. They also operate local and national youth camps.

Significant Terms

Clergyman. A term sometimes used to refer to ministers of the gospel in general.

Deacon. A man who has been ordained by a local congregation to assist in the ministries of that church.

Pastor. A minister, always a man, who has been ordained and called by a church as its leading minister.

Reverend. A term accepted by some of the preachers, but not preferred by most, to identify their office.

Bibliography

(All items are published by Bogard Press, Texarkana, Tex.)

Christian, John T. *A History of the Baptists.* 2 vols. Originally published by Broadman Press, 1922.

Cross, I. K. *The Church: Local or Universal?* 1982.

——. *Landmarkism: An Update.* 1984.

Glover, C. N., and A. T. Powers. *A History of American Baptist Association.* 1979.

Prepared by I. K. Cross, public relations, American Baptist Association.

AMERICAN BAPTIST CHURCHES, U.S.A.

See main entry under "Baptists."

BAPTIST BIBLE FELLOWSHIP MISSION

The Baptist Bible Fellowship is "a group of Independent pastors and churches majoring in global evangelism. [We] are convinced that [we] can do more collectively than individually in committing [ourselves] to carrying out the Great Commission. All that is required to be part is believing in and fellowshipping with like-minded pastors and churches for the purpose of world evangelism."

Excerpts from a letter of July 21, 1989, from Dr. Bob Baird, mission director, the Baptist Bible Fellowship Missions, Springfield, Missouri.

BAPTIST GENERAL CONFERENCE

General Description
The Baptist General Conference (BCG) is a fellowship of 137,000 members in 800 churches, located from Maine to California and Hawaii, from Florida to Alaska, but mostly in the northern tier of the United States. National headquarters are in Arlington Heights, Illinois.

Article 3 (Identity Statement) of the BCG articles of incorporation and constitution states that the denomination is "a fellowship of Baptist churches whose theology is biblically evangelical; whose character is multi-ethnic; whose spirit is positive and affirmative; whose purpose is to fulfill the Great Commission through evangelism, discipleship and church planting and whose people celebrate openness and freedom in the context of Christ's Lordship."

The BCG is affiliated with the Baptist World Alliance and National Association of Evangelicals.

History
Gustaf Palmquist, a Swedish immigrant converted in an English-speaking Baptist church in Galesburg, Illinois, baptized three fellow immigrants in the Mississippi River near Rock Island, Illinois, in early August 1852. On August 13 the four organized the first Swedish Baptist Church in America. (Sweden had only one Baptist church at this time.) For the next several decades the mission of Swedish Baptists was focused on evangelizing Swedish-speaking people in America and Canada. In 1879 delegates representing

3,000 members in 65 Swedish Baptist churches organized into the Swedish Baptist General Conference of America. In 1945 the name was changed to the Baptist General Conference.

In 1894 the first Swedish Baptist Church was organized in Winnipeg, Manitoba. In 1984 the Canadian BCG churches amicably separated from the U.S. BCG. The 70 Canadian churches, located in five provinces, are known as the Baptist General Conference of Canada.

Schools

In 1871 John Alexis Edgren, a former sea captain and a brilliant student of the Bible and languages, founded a seminary in the Chicago's First Swedish Baptist Church, where Edgren was pastor. The purpose of the school, which began with only one student, was to train ministers for the 30 Swedish Baptist churches, which had about 1,500 members in seven states. For several years, the seminary was the Swedish Department of the Baptist Union Theological Seminary in Chicago.

In 1914 the school was moved to St. Paul. In 1965 the seminary moved to a new 240-acre campus in Arden Hills in suburban St. Paul and now has almost 600 students, including more than 100 in a satellite campus in San Diego. In 1972 Bethel College moved to its new campus adjacent to the seminary; in 1989 it had 1,800 students.

Leaders

F. O. Nilsson (1809–81). A Swedish sailor who was converted in New York City in 1834. He was the first Baptist preacher in Sweden and founder of the first Swedish Baptist Church in Minnesota.

John Alexis Edgren (1839–1908). A Swedish sailor and Union Navy captain during the U.S. Civil War; founder and dean of Bethel Seminary, 1871–87.

Carl Gustaf Lagergren (1846–1941). Dean of Bethel Seminary, 1889–1922.

Gustave Avrid Hagstrom (1867–1953). Missions leader and pastor; president of Bethel, 1914–41.

Henry C. Wingblade (1883–1977). President of Bethel, 1941–54.

Carl H. Lindquist (1916–). President of Bethel, 1954–82.

Ola Hanson (1864–1929). Missionary for thirty-nine years among the Kachin tribe in Burma; translated the entire Bible into Kachin.

O. L. Swanson (1867–1949). Missionary for forty-three years in Assam, India.

Walfred Danielson (1888–1959). Bethel Junior College dean; secretary of the first BCG world mission board, 1944–54.

Lloyd W. Dahlquist (1906–). BCG general secretary, 1959–69.

Warren R. Magnuson (1921–). BCG general secretary, 1969–87.

Beliefs and Doctrines

The BCG has always been in the mainstream of American evangelism. While there is a diversity of belief in eschatology, on the role of women in church leadership, and on the five points of Calvinism, there is unity on the inerrancy of the Scriptures and the crucial doctrines of Christology, including the Virgin Birth, full deity and humanity, impeccability, substitutionary death, bodily resurrection, physical ascension, and visible and literal return. In 1951 the BCG adopted a twelve-point Affirmation of Faith that covers the following: the Word of God, the Trinity, God the Father, Jesus Christ, the Holy Spirit, Regeneration, the Church, Christian Conduct, the Ordinances, Religious Liberty, Church Cooperation, and the Last Things.

Organization

The local church is the basic unit of BCG life and ministry. Each church is autonomous and under the lordship of Jesus Christ, free to call her pastor, organize for ministry, disburse mission funds, and evangelize her community. The eight hundred BCG churches are organized into fourteen geographic districts of uneven numerical strength, each under the leadership of an executive minister, elected by delegates from the churches to the district annual meeting. The districts serve to organize church planting, provide Christian education and camping, and provide opportunities for associational fellowship and spiritual encouragement.

The BCG is a voluntary fellowship of eight hundred regularly organized Baptist churches in the United States and the islands of the Caribbean (six churches) that subscribe without reservation to the Affirmation of Faith. The cooperative ministry of BCG churches is accomplished through the work of two ministry boards (for world missions and home missions) and the board of regents of Bethel College and Seminary. Supervising the ministry of the three boards is a twenty-three-member board of overseers. The president of the BCG is the administrative officer of the board of overseers and chief executive officer of the BCG. The executive directors of the two ministry boards—each elected to five-year terms—report directly to the president of the BCG. Robert Ricker was elected in 1987 to a five-year term as first BCG president.

The Standard is the official news magazine of the BCG. Founded in 1911, this sixty-four-page monthly has a circulation of 20,500.

World Missions

Johanna Anderson sailed to Burma in 1888. She was the first overseas missionary sent by U.S. Swedish Baptists. Between 1888 and 1944, when the BCG organized its own world missions board, BCG churches sent out and supported hundreds of missionaries, most of them serving with the American Baptist Foreign Mission Society. In 1944 the BCG elected its first world missions board, and currently about 144 missionaries serve in twelve fields: Argentina, Brazil, Cameroon, Ethiopia, Ivory Coast, France, Japan, Mexico, Philippines, Thailand, Eastern Europe, and the Middle East. The BCG world mission board is in the midst of a Decade of Vision program (1985–95) with goals of 1,225 churches and 95,000 baptized believers in the BCG overseas field.

Distinctives

While the BCG has much in common with other Baptist denominations, the sum of several characteristics marks the BCG as significant in today's spectrum of evangelism: (1) it takes a strong stand on an inerrant Bible; (2) it is irenic in relationship with other fellowships, rather than judgmental; (3) churches are governed by different forms of government, some with multiple boards, some with one board; (4) it has an ethnic diversity—eighty-nine churches represent twelve different multicultural groups; (5) the denomination's college and seminary seek academic excellence by balancing keen minds with warm hearts; and (6) in the States and overseas, both home and world mission boards are involved in aggressive church-planting programs.

Significant Terms

Board of overseers. This group directs the affairs of the conference, develops policies, and is responsible for the administration of mission activity and for business affairs. It is also responsible to ensure that the spiritual and charitable objectives of the conference are fulfilled. Twenty in number, overseers are elected to serve five years and represent the fourteen districts and the three boards of the conference.

Board of regents. Fifteen persons are elected by delegates of the BCG at the annual meeting for five-year terms. They are responsible to the conference for maintaining the integrity of both the instruction and the atmosphere within Bethel College and Seminary.

District. Fourteen associations of the BCG churches, uneven in geographic area and in number of churches, cover the eight hundred conference churches in the United States. District churches meet annually to receive reports and set strategy for starting mission churches. Each district is headed by a district executive minister, elected for a five-year term.

Executive director. BCG boards of home missions and world missions are each headed by an executive director. They are elected for a five-year term by the conference and are accountable to the BCG president.

President. The president is the chief executive officer of the board of overseers and the Baptist General Conference and is responsible to the board of overseers for his duties and activities. The president is elected to a five-year term at the annual meeting of the conference by nomination of the board of overseers.

Bibliography

Anderson, Donald E., ed. *The 1970s in the Ministry of the Baptist General Conference.* Arlington Heights, Ill.: Board of Trustees, BCG, 1981.

———. *The 1960s in the Ministry of the Baptist General Conference.* Evanston, Ill.: Harvest Publications, 1971.

Guston, David, and Martin Erikson, eds. *Fifteen Eventful Years: A Survey of the BCG, 1945–60.* Chicago: Harvest Publications, 1961.

Olson, Adolf. *A Centenary History, As Related to the BCG of America.* Chicago: Baptist General Conference Press, 1952.

Olson, Adolf, and Virgil A. Olson. *Seventy-Five Years: A History of Bethel Theological Seminary, 1871–1946.* Chicago: Conference Press, [1946].

Prepared by Donald E. Anderson, editor, The Standard.

BAPTIST MISSIONARY ASSOCIATION OF AMERICA

General Description

The Baptist Missionary Association of America (BMAA) is a cooperative group of about 1,500 missionary Baptist churches, mostly in the southern states. They exchange letters of membership, members, and pastors with other Baptist groups that are missionary in practice. It was organized as a distinct group in 1950 in order to uphold church sovereignty more positively, which includes equal representation of churches in the cooperative meetings and the sending forth of missionaries by voice vote of messengers of the churches rather than by boards of the denomination.

It traces its roots back through the American Baptist Association, organized in 1925; the General Association of Baptists in the United States of America, organized in 1905; the Philadelphia Baptist Association, organized in 1707; church associations among the Welsh Baptists in the 1600s; various groups of Baptists under different names during the Middle Ages; and associations among the Macedonian churches during the time of the apostle Paul.

Founder and Leaders

Baptists do not look back for their founder to any one human but rather look to the Lord Jesus Christ as their founder and head. They were first called Christians at Antioch of Syria (Acts 11:26). Through the centuries after that and based on doctrines believed and practiced that are identical to what today's Baptists believe and practice, they were known by different names, some denoting leaders or geographic locations or practices, such as Montanists, Paulicans, Cathari, Donatists, Novations, Albigenses, Waldensians, Anabaptist, and others.

Although some Baptists claim to trace their roots in America to Roger Williams and the church that he founded at Providence, Rhode Island, the BMAA churches trace their roots to John Clarke and the church that he established at Newport, Rhode Island. Both churches were begun in 1638, but Williams's church shortly ceased to exist. According to John T. Christian, "Not one Baptist Church or minister came out of the Providence church of this period or was anywise affected by the baptism of Williams" (*A History of Baptists,* [Texarkana: Bogard Press, 1922] 2:40). W. A. Criswell, pastor of First Baptist Church in Dallas, states his agreement with Christian. Earlier outstanding leaders of BMAA sentiments were J. R. Graves and J. M. Pendleton. More recent leaders have been D. N. Jackson, W. J. Burgess, J. E. Cobb, C. C. Winters, W. J. Doorman, and G. E. Jones.

Beliefs and Doctrines

Besides what Baptists of most groups believe in general, the BMAA believes that baptism can be administered only by authority of a local church and that the pastor or administrator must himself have been previously baptized (immersed). This was not the case with Roger Williams and Ezekiel Holliman, who immersed one another, then proceeded to establish the church at Providence. The BMAA believes that the Lord's Supper should be administered only in a local church capacity and that all participants should be members of that local church. This is commonly called closed communion.

Of the two scriptural offices recognized in Baptist churches—pastors and deacons—it is believed that only men qualify to hold these offices. Also, absolute equality of church members, pastors, and churches is upheld locally and in associated assemblies, with every member privileged to vote in the local church, with all ministers on the same level, and with all churches represented by an equal number of messengers in the cooperative association of churches. The BMAA believes in the premillennial, bodily, and visible return of Christ, followed by his thousand-year reign of peace on earth.

Forms of Worship

Worship forms are ordinary and simple, with singing, prayer, giving of offerings, choral selections, reading of the Scriptures, and preaching the usual worship in BMAA churches.

Organization

The national cooperative body of churches is a fellowship or association of churches by means of messengers, which are on an equal basis of representation. The association is merely a servant or instrument of the churches for their united efforts and to reach common goals, and it has no authority over any of the sovereign local churches in its fellowship.

Contributions and Influence

The conservative attitude of BMAA churches and their uncompromising position on Bible doctrines and moral teachings, especially their opposition to drugs, alcohol, abortion on demand, and other social evils and political liberalism, has had a wholesome impact upon American society, religion, and politics.

Baptists made a contribution to religious freedom in America when John Clarke, not Roger Williams, was instrumental in getting a grant for the colony of Rhode Island, with full religious liberty included. The system of democratic government practiced by local Baptist churches and known to Washington, Jefferson, and other Founding Fathers of this country gave them a pattern for the American republic and democratic government guaranteed by the Constitution.

Significant Terms

Many BMAA ministers prefer to be called "elder" or "pastor," rather than "reverend." The cooperative work is done under the term "association," which signifies fellowship, rather than "convention," which means a gathering of representatives.

Bibliography

(Other material is published by Baptist News Service, P.O. Box 97, Jacksonville, Tex. 75766-0002.)

Burgess, W. J. *Baptist Faith and Martyrs' Fires*. Texarkana, Tex.: Baptist Publishing House, 1964.

Duggar, John W. *The Baptist Missionary Association of America, 1950–1986*. Texarkana, Tex.: Baptist Publishing House, 1988.

Prepared by John W. Duggar, Th.D., past president of the BMAA of America and president emeritus of BMAA Theological Seminary.

BLACK BAPTIST CHURCHES

The settlement of blacks in America, both as slaves and as freemen, brought them into new and strange conditions of life to which they had to adapt themselves or perish. Because slaves were denied the full status of human beings and thus the full protection of the law, blacks were exploited and dominated, even spiritually, in ways that were to condition and limit them for centuries. Yet the hostile environment gave rise and impetus to the many organizations, groups, and churches that sprang up wherever blacks lived in large numbers.

As early as 1700, slaveholders in the South were providing religious teaching and places of worship for their slaves. However, blacks were limited to seats in the gallery, while whites sat on the ground floor. Often such worship places were buildings on a plantation where white ministers (occasionally with black assistants) would somewhat regularly hold services and teach the children and youth. Eventually, black ministers were liberated to perform a full-time ministry among the slaves. Such ministers soon developed a most influential status among blacks, as well as in the eyes of white clergy and other white leaders.

The first black Baptist church in the United States was organized at Silver Bluff, near Augusta, Georgia, in 1773—to be followed by churches in Petersburg, Virginia (1776), Richmond (1780), Williamsburg, Virginia (1785), Savannah, Georgia (1785), and Lexington, Kentucky (1790). The first black pastor, Rev. Andrew Bryan, was a former slave who was called to the church at Savannah.

The so-called black religion of the United States is not a racial religion but is the expression of a religious experience that is the product of the conditions under which blacks struggled and developed. Black religion has the spiritual, emotional, and sociological factors found in other national and cultural religions, yet its distinctive flavor developed from the special background and habits of a transplanted and abused people. Thus, any discussion about the black Baptist churches must include an understanding of the situation out of which they grew and were forced to endure.

In his book *The American Dilemma,* Gunnar Myrdal notes that

The American Negro problem is a problem in the heart of the American. It is there that the interracial tension has its focus . . . . "The American Dilemma," . . . is the ever-raging conflict between, on the one hand, the valuations preserved on the general plane which we shall call the "American Creed," where the American thinks, talks and acts under the influence of high national and Christian precepts, and, on the other hand, the valuations on specific planes of individual and group living, where personal and local interests . . . jealousies . . . consideration of community prestige and conformity . . . group prejudice . . . and all sorts of miscellaneous wants, impulses, and habits dominate his outlook.[1]

In other words, the white churches of America really reflect the mores of the community rather than the Christian creed of equality. The problem of black religion in the United States is thus really the problem of American race relations and a failure in brotherhood. E. Franklin Frazier, in his work *Negro Youth at the Crossways,* marks the beginning of black religion in America as the "coming of the Methodists and the Baptists to influence the masses of . . . slaves into a form of Christianity that they could make their own."[2]

Indeed, the overwhelming majority of the blacks in pre–Civil War America were either Baptists or Methodists. It is estimated that at the beginning of the Civil War, there were approximately 200,000 black Methodists and

150,000 black Baptists. That difference was soon reversed, however, perhaps because of the lack of formality of the Baptists and the more formal episcopal structure of the Methodists. This reversal continued to the end of the Civil War, when, aided by a revival movement among newly freed blacks, the black Baptist churches numbered over 1 million members.

The formal organization of black Baptists began prior to the Civil War with a weak association in 1836. The first truly national organization was effected in 1880 with the formation of the Foreign Mission Baptist Convention. It was followed in 1886 with the American National Baptist Convention and in 1893 with the Baptist National Educational Convention. Finally the Baptist Convention of America was established in 1895 by a merger of the three organizations. This convention remained intact until 1915, when a disagreement arose over the incorporation of the convention and ownership of the publishing house. The group opposing the incorporation continued to function under the name National Baptist Convention in America, and the incorporating body chose the name National Baptist Convention of the U.S.A. The latter group is now the largest body, claiming 6.5 million members, while the former group claims a membership of 3.5 million. Another dispute arose in 1961 over election and tenure procedures for convention officers, resulting in organization of a new body, the Progressive Baptist Convention.

Black Baptist doctrine is very much the same as that of white Baptist churches, although some say it is somewhat more Calvinistic. Black Baptist worship is much more "popular" and emotional than that of white Baptist churches, especially that of the American Baptist Convention or the Southern Baptist Convention. It is largely evangelistic in spirit, and preaching is primarily emphasized.

The black Baptist patterns of organization are similar to those of the white Baptist churches. Each local church is autonomous, although local churches do unite in associations, usually along state lines for fellowship, consultation, and mutual help. There are comparable state (and national) conventions offering the extension of the mission of the church to foreign lands and in the important areas of education, social work, and similar interests. It is claimed that the old animosity between the conventions has been replaced by a spirit of cooperation, although no movement toward reunion is discernible. Talks concerning union with the American Baptist Convention by the National Baptist Convention of the U.S.A. have been held.

In the late 1960s a student gave me a copy of "The Predicament of the Negro Baptist Church,"[3] a volume of three lectures delivered by Homer J. Tucker at the National Baptist's Deacon Convention in 1962. This self-criticism of the black Baptist churches is an enlightening account that describes the "predicament" as "unpleasant, trying and dangerous"; Tucker uses it to explain the situation in which black Baptists find themselves by virtue of the race problem in the United States. Indeed, Tucker insists that the black church is the product of a slave culture and is made what it is by the customs and socioeconomic practices of the white-dominated environment. Tucker quotes H. A. Richardson, who wrote that "the emotionalism of the . . . Negro Church, together with the evangelical awakening and the substitute of tones, voices, and ecstatic expression for the lack of ability to read or to interpret the Scripture properly, did much to set the pattern for the church's standard of worship and practice."[4]

Tucker concludes his work with the following reflections.

> The Negro Church, as it now stands, with its ministers poorly trained, its church organization ill-planned, few accredited seminaries, a weak denominational structure, undemocratic and un-Christian practices in the local church where the domineering practice of most ministers, with little help . . . from qualified lay leaders, is not effective in recruiting its best qualified youth for Christian service . . . .[5]

Tucker then gives a number of recommendations for strengthening the black Baptist churches that he declares will develop "a church which reflects the image and work of Christ . . . [with] Christian service to all people, as the Gospels spell out plainly, without respect of persons."[6]

A more recent work by Peggy L. Shriver gives upbeat profiles of some denominations that are members of the National Council of Churches, with the hope of achieving better understanding between the member bodies. In her third section of *Having Gifts That Differ*,[7] which features "African-American Churches," Shriver, adapting my basic concept (which she calls self-distinction), gives positive, confident, and approving "profiles of the Black Baptist Churches." We consider here four black Baptist groups.

National Baptist Convention in America

As we have observed above, the National Baptist Convention in America owes its existence to the original National Baptist Convention, organized in 1895. However, a publishing house, established in 1897, proved to be a subject of dispute within the church (mainly over the subject of ultimate control and private ownership) and moved the young convention to the crucial stages of division. The attempt to establish a charter and to incorporate led to a separation in 1915. Those who opposed the incorporation combined to form the National Baptist Convention in America (NBCA, "the unincorporated"). Those who supported the incorporation became known as the National Baptist Convention of the U.S.A. (NBCUSA).

Shriver correctly notes that the NBCA holds to the basic Baptist tenets of the individual's ability to discern religious truth under the lordship of Christ over one's life. Shriver does point out, however, that the black churches take a somewhat different stance on the separation of church and state because, pragmatically, these churches are both the social center of black communities and the informer of political awareness and action.

The NBCA's polity (organizational system) is similar to the other major Baptist groups in the United States. The officers are quite standard, as are their major boards, commissions, and organization. The NBCA is the second largest body of black Baptists, with a membership that Shriver estimates to be as many as 3.5 million across the country.

The worship of the NBCA is similar to that of the mainstream of black Baptists as described above. Shriver describes the success of numerous black leaders, including Martin Luther King, Jr., as being "the power of worship and preaching in the Black Church."[8]

National Baptist Convention of the U.S.A.

The NBCUSA is the "remaining" body in the division of 1915 and is the largest black Baptist convention, with a membership, Shriver estimates, of 6.5 million. As with the NBCA, NBCUSA maintains the standard doctrines of the other major Baptist bodies, based on the fundamental belief of "theological individualism." This position allows differences on other beliefs, with one exception: the revelation of God's will in the Bible is the "supreme standard by which all hymns, conduct, creeds, and opinions must be tried."[9]

The polity of the NBCUSA is strongest at the level of the local congregation. As Shriver puts it, "Ecclesiastical structure and ecumenical relationships are approached cautiously."[10] The convention meets annually, and a board of directors functions between annual meetings. There are the usual boards and offices. As she did in the profile of the NCBA, Shriver comments positively on the importance of the special nature of NBCUSA's worship, agreeing that the black church has enabled black Christians to "sing the Lord's song in a strange land."[11] Her verdict thus differs greatly from that of Tucker.

National Primitive Baptist Convention

The origin of the National Primitive Baptist Convention (NPBC) as the Colored Primitive Baptist Church makes clear its difference from the three conventions of black Baptists discussed here. Actually, the NPBC is the black version of the white Primitive Baptist Church. It is basically the same in doctrine and polity as the white church and is almost as orthodox and exclusive as the white "primitives." One point of difference, however, is that the NPBC does have associations, societies, Sunday schools, and an annual convention, all of which have not yet seemed necessary to the white Primitive Baptists. Statistics from the mid-1970s report an estimated membership of 250,000 members and 606 churches.

Progressive National Baptist Convention

The Progressive National Baptist Convention (PNBC) came into existence as a result of a dispute within the NBCUSA over the matter of the tenure of its national officers, specifically over the issue of whether the office of executive secretary should be for life or for a limited tenure. A number of delegates favoring limited tenure, after experiencing what they perceived to be tyrannical treatment from NBCUSA officers, followed L. V. Booth of Zion Baptist Church, Cincinnati, who issued a call to a meeting to discuss the state of the church. After serious deliberation, the session voted to withdraw from NBCUSA and assert their recommitment to limited tenure, which they did in the preamble to the constitution of the PNBC.

> The people called Progressive Baptists believe in the principles, tenets, and doctrines proclaimed or advocated in the New Testament as sufficient for their polity and practices. In Church government Baptists believe in the rule of the people, by the people, and for the people, and in the vestment of the authority and power to act in the majority. Therefore, we the members of the Progressive National Convention, USA, Inc., federate ourselves together in the name of and under the direction and guidance of God, sharing our common faith in Jesus Christ and common activities, and establish this Constitution.[12]

The PNCB story is one of phenomenal success, growing from a small group of 30 charter members in 1961 to more than 1 million members in 1989 with over 1,000 churches.

Shriver notes "no significant doctrinal differences between the Progressive and other Baptist Conventions." Nor does Shriver find any difference between them on the subject of worship. The one "distinguishing feature of the Progressives is in its organizational structure,"[13] writes Shriver, and she proceeds to show a much fuller organization at the various levels than other conventions have. Each of the four regions meets annually. There are strong organizations of women (Women's Auxiliary), laymen, ushers, youth and Christian education, as well as two mission boards and a publishing board. The PNCB is more active in national and world ecumenical activities as well as in national and international Baptist fellowships. They also support numerous social programs, such as the NAACP and the Martin Luther King Center for Social Justice. King was one of the powerful voices of the PNCB, whose theology of hope inspired American blacks and whites to establish expanded civil rights.

Notes

1. Gunnar Myrdal, *An American Dilemma,* vol. 1 (New York: Harper & Brothers, 1944), p. xliii.

2. E. Franklin Frazier, *Negro Youth at the Crossways* (Washington, D.C.: American Council on Education, 1940), pp. 123–24.

3. Homer J. Tucker, "The Predicament of the Negro Baptist Church," mimeographed address, 1962.

4. H.A. Richardson, *Dark Glory* (New York: Friendship Press, 1947), p. 174.

5. Tucker, "The Predicament of the Negro Baptist Church," p. 30.

6. Ibid., p. 31.
7. Peggy L. Shriver, *Having Gifts That Differ* (New York: Friendship Press, 1989).
8. Ibid., p. 112.
9. Ibid., p. 115.
10. Ibid.
11. Ibid., p. 116
12. Quoted by Shriver on pp. 117–18.
13. Ibid., p. 118.

Bibliography
Booth, C. L. *Progressive Baptist Story.* N.p., n.d.
Fitts, LeRoy. *A History of Black Baptists.* Nashville: Broadman Press, 1985.
McCall, E. L. *The Black Christian Experience.* Nashville: Broadman Press, 1972.
——. *Black Church Life-Style.* Nashville: Broadman Press, 1986.
Sobel, Mechal. *Trabelin On: The Slave Journey to an Afro-Baptist Faith.* Westport, Conn.: Greenwood Press, 1988.
Washington, James M. *Frustrated Fellowship: The Black Baptist Quest for Social Power.* Macon, Ga.: Mercer University Press, 1986.
Wheeler, Edward. *Uplifting the Race: The Black Minister in the New South.* Lanham, Md.: University Press of America, 1986.

Prepared by the editor; the bibliography was provided by Dean Eric Ohlman, Eastern Baptist Theological Seminary, Philadelphia.

CONSERVATIVE BAPTIST ASSOCIATION

The section above entitled "Baptists" "fairly well represents our relationship to the Baptist denomination. We have an independent Baptist organization, tracing our beginnings to the same roots as shown [therein]."

Excerpts from a letter of February 28, 1989, from Rev. Walter Fricke, director of publications, Conservative Baptist Association, Wheaton, Illinois.

FREE WILL BAPTIST CHURCH

General Description
The Free Will Baptist denomination is not a movement that has sprung up within the past few years. History accords a place for our movement as far back as the early seventeenth century. Indeed, some scholars have said it is among the oldest denominations in the United States.

About 1701 an entire church, consisting of pastor and congregation, came from Wales and settled on the Delaware River on what was known as the Welsh Tract. From this group came several men who reacted strongly to the extreme Calvinistic doctrine of the day.

One these men, Paul Palmer, is credited with organizing the first Free Will Baptist church in 1727 in Perquimans County, North Carolina. The work in the Northeast was instituted under the leadership of Benjamin Randall, who organized the first Free Will Baptist church in that area at New Durham, New Hampshire, on June 30, 1780. The General Conference of Free Will Baptists was organized in 1827.

This movement has shown a steady growth. Today, the National Association of Free Will Baptists is active in all types of missionary and educational endeavors. Its work is promoted out of the Free Will Baptist National Office Building and the Sunday School Department in Nashville, Tennessee.

Beliefs and Doctrines

The Bible. The Scriptures of the Old and New Testaments were given by inspiration of God and are our infallible rule of faith and practice.

God. There is one living and true God, revealed in nature as the Creator, Preserver, and Righteous Governor of the universe; and in the Scriptures as Father, Son, and Holy Ghost; yet as one God, infinitely wise and good, whom all intelligent creatures are supremely to love, adore, and obey.

Christ. Christ is God manifest in flesh; in his divine nature truly God, in his human nature truly man. The mediator between God and man, once crucified, he is now risen and glorified, and is our ever-present Savior and Lord.

The Holy Spirit. The Scriptures assign to the Holy Spirit all the attributes of God.

The government of God. God exercises a wise and benevolent providence over all beings and all things by maintaining the constitution and laws of nature. He also performs special acts, not otherwise provided for, as the highest welfare of men requires.

The sinfulness of man. Man was created innocent but by disobedience fell into a state of sin and condemnation. His progeny, therefore, inherit a fallen nature of such tendencies that all who come to years of accountability in fact sin and become guilty before God.

The work of Christ. The Son of God by his incarnation, life, sufferings, death, and resurrection effected for all a redemption from sin that is full and free and that is the ground of salvation by faith.

The terms of salvation. The conditions of salvation are (1) repentance, or sincere sorrow for sin, and hearty renunciation of it; (2) faith, or the unreserved committal of one's self to Christ as Savior and Lord with the purpose to love and obey him in all things; in the exercise of saving faith, the soul is renewed by the Holy Spirit, freed from the dominion of sin, and becomes a child of God; (3) continuance in faith and obedience until death.

Election. God determined from the beginning to save all who should comply with the conditions of salvation. Hence, by faith in Christ, men become his elect.

Freedom of the will. The human will is free and self-controlled, having power to yield to the influence of the truth and the Spirit, or to resist them.

Salvation free. God desires the salvation of all, the gospel invites all, the Holy Spirit strives with all, and whosoever will may come and take of the water of life freely.

Perseverance. All believers in Christ, who through grace persevere in holiness to the end of life, have promise of eternal salvation.

Gospel ordinances. Baptism, or the immersion of believers in water, and the Lord's Supper are ordinances to be perpetuated under the gospel. Foot washing, an ordinance teaching humility, is of universal obligation and is to be ministered to all true believers.

Tithing. God commanded tithes and offerings in the Old Testament; Jesus Christ endorsed it in the Gospel (Matthew 23:23), and the apostle Paul said, "Upon the first day of the week let every one of you lay by him in store, as God hath prospered him" (1 Cor. 16:2).

The Christian Sabbath. The divine law requires that one day in seven be set apart from secular employments and amusements for rest, worship, holy works and activities, and personal communion with God.

Resurrection, judgment, and final retribution. The Scriptures teach the resurrection of all men at the last day. They that have done good will come forth to the resurrection of life, and they that have done evil unto the resurrection of damnation; then the wicked will "go away into eternal punishment, but the righteous into eternal life" (Matt. 25:46).

Organization

The Free Will Baptist denomination is Baptistic in government, recognizing the autonomy of each local church. Local churches are organized into quarterly meetings, which in turn are grouped into district associations. These district associations come together in state associations, and the various state associations compose the National Association.

The National Association meets annually for the purpose of carrying on its business and to formulate its program of work. Denominational ministries are represented through seven departments—Foreign Missions, Home Missions and Church Extension, Executive, Sunday School, Church Training Service, Retirement and Insurance, and the Free Will Baptist Bible College. The work of each department is projected through its board, which is elected by the National Association.

Activities

With a strong evangelistic ministry, the Free Will Baptist denomination has enjoyed a rapid development in recent years. Membership in the United States has now reached the 250,000 mark.

Through the efforts of the Home Missions Department, we continue to establish new churches. With the specific responsibility of the United States, Canada, Puerto Rico, Virgin Islands, and Mexico, this department now has sixty-eight home missionaries laboring in twenty-six fields.

The extension of this ministry around the world is through the Foreign Missions Department. We now have ninety-eight missionaries laboring in India, Japan, Brazil, Uruguay, Panama, Africa, France, and Spain. As soon as possible, other fields will be opened.

The educational interest of the denomination is represented by Free Will Baptist Bible College, located in Nashville, Tennessee. The college is accredited by the American Association of Bible Colleges and is approved by the Tennessee State Department of Education for teacher certification. The college offers the B.A. and the B.S. degrees. Standards are high, with a strong emphasis on spiritual values. There are other colleges and institutes in several states.

The Sunday School Department carries on an intensive program of training courses for teachers and Sunday school workers. In addition, this department is responsible for writing, editing, and printing all the literature used in Free Will Baptist Sunday schools. It has an expanding book-publishing ministry through Randall House Publications, its trade name. It also operates the denominational bookstore.

Through the Church Training Service Department, literature is provided for local Free Will Baptist churches. This organization affords the young people an excellent opportunity for training and wholesome Christian recreation.

The total work and ministry of the National Association is promoted by the Executive Department. This department also publishes the magazine *Contact* and provides the service of Executive Church Bonds, Inc., whereby funds may be secured for the building of churches.

The care of aged and retired ministers, missionaries, and other Christian workers is the concern of the Department of Retirement and Insurance. Excellent opportunities for provision of income at retirement are available.

The denomination has two auxiliary organizations—the Master's Men, and the Woman's National Auxiliary Convention. The Master's Men is composed of laymen in local churches who meet together for fellowship and to engage in spiritual ministries. The Woman's Auxiliary is composed of women from the various churches who join together for the purpose of helping the churches teach and support missions.

Significant Terms

Arminianism. A system of the theology named after Jacob Arminius, who strongly opposed Calvinism—more specifically, the dogmas of unconditional election and irresistible grace.

Backslider. One who, having made a credible profession of the Christian faith, ceases to trust in Christ for salvation and resorts to living in the practice of sin. However, the backslider in whose heart a desire arises to repent may do so and be restored to fellowship with God.

Church covenant. A statement of faith and practice according to which all Free Will Baptists agree to live. It begins, "Having given ourselves to God, by faith in Jesus Christ, and adopted the Word of God as our rule of faith and practice, we now give ourselves to one another by the will in this solemn covenant."

Free grace. An Arminian doctrine teaching that the grace of God, while indispensable to all good and salvation, is not irresistible. Those who choose Christ's help will be given God's grace.

Free salvation. An Arminian doctrine holding that those who are grafted into Christ by a true faith are abundantly supplied with power to overcome Satan and the world as well as to receive the gifts of regeneration, justification, sanctification, and eternal life.

Free will. An Arminian doctrine insisting that man possesses a faculty that enables him to choose between alternative choices of action. The opposite view is determinism, or Calvinistic predestinarianism.

Plenary, verbal inspiration (of the Bible). Inspiration that is "full and complete" and "extends to the very words of the Scriptures" and that inspires the Free Will Baptist Church to affirm the Bible to be "infallible and inerrant."

The gospel call. A gospel "call," coextensive with the atonement of all men by Christ, both from the world and by the strivings of the Spirit, so that salvation is rendered equally possible to all; and if there is any fault of eternal life, the fault is wholly man's own. Yet another opportunity for salvation is always offered.

Bibliography

Davidson, William F. *The Free Will Baptists in America, 1927–1984*. Nashville: Randall House Publications, 1985.

Dodd, Damon C. *The Free Will Baptist Story*. Nashville: Executive Office of the National Association of Free Will Baptists, 1956.

The 1989 Free Will Baptist Yearbook. Nashville: Executive Office of the National Association of Free Will Baptists, 1989.

Picirilli, Robert E., ed. *History of Free Will Baptist State Associations*. Nashville: Randall House Publications, 1976.

A Treatise of the Faith and Practices of Free Will Baptists. Nashville: Executive Office of the National Association of Free Will Baptists, 1981.

Wisehart, Mary, ed. *The Fifty-Year Record of the National Association of Free Will Baptists, 1935–1985*. Nashville: Randall House Publications, 1988.

Prepared by the editor from materials supplied by Melvin Worthington, Th.D., executive secretary, National Association of Free Will Baptists.

LIBERTY BAPTIST FELLOWSHIP
FOR CHURCH PLANTING

General Description

The Liberty Baptist Fellowship (LBF) originated as a means of fellowship among the pastors who were alumni of Liberty Baptist College (now Liberty University). The college was founded by Rev. Dr. Jerry Falwell in 1971 to complement his ministry both in the Thomas Road Baptist Church and in the evangelistic radio and TV programs he developed. The fellowship was an outreach of this ministry. Falwell is now the university and seminary chancellor.

It remained an informal fellowship until 1981, when a perceived need of having a national fellowship for Liberty Baptist College alumni who were clergymen was addressed. Thus the Liberty Baptist Fellowship emerged as a national religious organization with officers and a program. Its purpose was twofold: (1) to provide a means of fellowship for Liberty pastors and those of like ministry philosophy, (2) to provide an avenue of encouragement and support for other men who desired to become planters of Liberty type churches, i.e., autonomous, Baptistic, and congregational.

In 1985 the LBF was incorporated in the state of Virginia as a nonprofit organization. Funds were then committed to underwrite the church-planting pastors for a limited time and amount. It was not organized as a denomination, nor was that the intention. The LBF currently consists of more than 500 churches who have requested membership. Membership in the combined churches is more than 200,000.

Beliefs and Doctrines

LBF is a fellowship of like-minded clergymen who are described as fundamentalists, following the lead of their founder, who announced that his ministry was to call the United States back to God, back to the Bible, and back to moral sanity. With all fundamentalist Baptists, the LBF holds to "a triune God, three persons in one Godhead; Jesus Christ, true God, born of a virgin, who died and rose again and who is Lord of all our lives; sin that is real and leads to death and damnation; salvation by grace after repentance and faith; rewards of heaven for the saved or hell for the unsaved; the Bible as the authority, verbally inspired and absolutely infallible; and a law-oriented ethical point of view."

Forms of Worship

The Liberty Baptist Fellowship worships with the usual Baptist Sunday worship format. It is nonliturgical and contains prayers, Bible reading, gospel songs, preaching, and testimonies; it practices baptism by immersion.

Organization

The LBF officers, like those of most other fellowship groups, are a national president, an executive director, an executive secretary, and national committee members, with Falwell the national chairman.

Contributions and Influence

Under the leadership of Jerry Falwell, the loyal alumni of Liberty Baptist College (Liberty University) have presented a strong witness to absolute Christian morality, being definitely antiabortion, supporting prayer in the public schools, and so forth. But they have also exemplified a concern for social service to the poor, teenagers, senior citizens, and college students. In addition, the LBF has chaplains in each branch of the armed forces as well as the Veterans Administration and the Civil Air Patrol.

Bibliography

Falwell, Jerry. *Capturing a Town for Christ.* Old Tappan, N.J.: Fleming H. Revell, 1973.

Falwell, Jerry, and Elmer Towns. *Church Aflame.* Nashville: Impact Books, 1971.

Falwell, Jerry, ed., with E. Dobson and E. Hindu. *The Fundamentalist Phenomenon.* Garden City, N.Y.: Doubleday, 1981.

Towns, Elmer. *Getting a Church Started.* Nashville: Impact Books, 1975.

——. *Stepping Out on Faith.* Wheaton, Ill.: Tyndale House Publications, 1984.

Prepared by the editor from material provided by Dr. Dennis Fields, executive secretary.

SOUTHERN BAPTIST CONVENTION

General Description

The Southern Baptist Convention (SBC) is the largest Baptist group in the United States, numbering 14,727,770 in 1988. The SBC does not belong to either the National or the World Council of Churches, but Southern Baptist agencies do participate in some activities of those organizations. The Southern Baptist Convention originated in 1845 in Augusta, Georgia, after the American Baptist Home Missionary Society refused to appoint a slave-holder as a missionary. Southern Baptists share basic Baptist principles reflected in believer's baptism, religious liberty, separation of church and state, and voluntary association in missions, but differ from them as a result of regional (southern) influences. Intense evangelistic concern is an inheritance from American revivalism. (Fundamentalists frequently designate separation of church and state a heresy and look with suspicion on the affirmation of religious liberty.)

Founder and Leaders

Southern Baptists would not point to a single founder. Prominent in the organization of the convention were W. B. Johnson and Richard Furman. Notable later leaders include James P. Boyce, John A. Broadus, Basil Manly, Jr., William H. Whitsitt, E. Y. Mullins, W. O. Carver, A. T. Robertson, B. H. Carroll, George W. Truett, and J. M. Dawson. Some prominent living Southern Baptists are Duke K. McCall, Herschel Hobbs, Wayne E. Oates, Foy Valentine, James L. Sullivan, Roy L. Honeycutt, W. A. Criswell, Adrian Rogers, Charles Stanley, Paul Pressler, and Paige Patterson.

Beliefs and Doctrines

Southern Baptists are badly divided over doctrine. One group emphasizes "inerrancy" of the Scriptures as the key doctrine, while another group holds traditional Baptist views, such as the Bible as the sole rule of faith and practice, soul competency (priesthood of believers), religious liberty, separation of church and state, and autonomy of local congregations. The former group also has revived the Puritan vision for America as God's chosen people and participates actively in such nationalist groups as Moral Majority (Liberty Foundation), American Coalition for Traditional Values, and Christian Reconstructionism.

Southern Baptists prefer the term "ordinances" rather than "sacraments" for baptism and the Lord's Supper, ascribing no saving efficacy to either. Like other Baptists, they practice believer's baptism by immersion. Many, however, are influenced by a nineteenth-century "Baptist high-churchism" known as Landmarkism that recognizes only baptism by immersion. The Lord's Supper (the name preferred) is viewed by most as a "sign" rather than a "means" of grace and is practiced infrequently (monthly or less often).

Forms of Worship

Public worship usually includes prayers, hymn singing, Scripture reading, sermon, and invitation. The invitation distinguishes Southern Baptists from most other Baptists.

Organization

Because of the Landmark influence, Southern Baptists emphasize the local congregation, which they consider autonomous but voluntarily related to other congregations. Cooperation in various endeavors takes place through local associations, state conventions, and a national convention. A unified fund-raising effort, the Cooperative Program, funds much of the vast programming offered both nationally and internationally.

Contributions and Influence

In the past, Southern Baptists have had massive influence as a consequence of numerical dominance. In some areas, virtually every county is

Baptist, with Baptists repesenting anywhere from 25 to 100 percent of the religious population. By virtue of their sheer numbers, however, they can no longer be considered guarantors of religious liberty.

Significant Terms

Cooperative program. A unified fund-raising program that supports the majority of Southern Baptist ministries.

Local church autonomy. The teaching that local churches retain authority independent of the denominational organization and that the organization derives its authority from the churches.

Messenger. A representative of a local congregation sent to conduct business on the associational, state, or national level.

Ordinances. The term used in reference to baptism and the Lord's Supper to emphasize that the importance of these rites lies in their having been instituted by the Lord.

Priesthood of the believer. The teaching that the individual is not dependent upon any human mediator or institution in his or her relationship to God but only upon Christ's finished work.

Bibliography

(Except as noted, all items are published by Broadman Press, Nashville.)
Baker, R. A. *The Southern Baptist Convention and Its People, 1607–1972.* 1974.
Barnes, W. W. *The Southern Baptist Convention, 1845–1953.* 1954.
Barnhart, J. E. *The Southern Baptist Holy War.* Austin, Tex.: Monthly Press, 1986.
Encyclopedia of Southern Baptists. 4 vols. 1958–82.
Lumpkin, W. L. *Baptist Foundations in the South.* 1972.

Prepared by Prof. E. Glenn Hinson of the Southern Baptist Theological Seminary; terms and definitions by Myron C. Kauk.

Brethren in Christ

General Description

The Brethren in Christ Church is located in the United States and Canada and, as a result of missionary activities, in seventeen other countries, with congregations in all continents except Australia. Membership in North America is nearly 19,000 and over 22,000 in other countries combined.

The Brethren in Christ had their origin in the pietistic revival movement in Lancaster County, Pennsylvania, in the latter half of the eighteenth century. Most of those who formed the first group were from Anabaptist backgrounds, mainly Mennonites, whose church life at that time did not emphasize the conversion, new-birth experience. The founders all claimed this experience and shared a growing conviction that baptism should be by immersion. These were the leading issues that led the group to form a separate body around 1780. First calling themselves Brethren, they later accepted the name River Brethren (probably popularly given to them to distinguish their group from other Brethren groups in the area), but during the Civil War they registered as Brethren in Christ.

Founder

While the earliest Brethren disclaimed being founded by any one person, Jacob Engle was the leader of the group (at least in church tradition). The first baptism was conducted near his farm close to Mount Joy, Pennsylvania, and many of the first services were conducted in his house, which still stands today.

Typical of groups springing from Anabaptist and rural backgrounds, the Brethren in Christ have had few members who have gained national recognition. The exceptions are Ernest Boyer, whose birth and early years were spent in the group, and President Dwight Eisenhower, whose parents were members when he attended the Sunday school of the Brethren in Christ congregation in Abilene, Kansas. Members less well known but making significant contributions here and abroad are Samuel R. Smith, founder of Messiah College (a four-year liberal arts college in Pennsylvania), and Frances Davidson, a college teacher who went as a missionary to Africa in 1898, where she did significant work in education and translation. In more recent years, Arthur Climenhaga has served as president of two denominational colleges (including Messiah College), as an executive secretary of the National

Association of Evangelicals, and as dean of Western Evangelical Seminary. Ronald J. Snider, who writes widely on peace and social issues, is a minister in the denomination.

Beliefs and Doctrines

The Brethren in Christ accept the Bible as the Word of God, by which they mean it is the guide to faith and conduct. (They have not become involved in the dispute centering on the inerrancy of Scripture.) Given their Anabaptist and Pietist orientation, this has historically meant a rather biblicist approach to reading the Bible, resulting in attempts to practice in literal ways what they discern the Bible (particularly the New Testament) to be saying. Thus, the Brethren in Christ have practiced foot washing (John 13), the "holy kiss" (1 Cor. 16:20), and the wearing of the prayer veiling (1 Cor. 11). Within the last several decades, however, such practices are becoming muted as the group has become less separatist and as its understanding of the historical context of the Bible and of textual criticism has become more informed.

The Brethren in Christ are a believers' church, thus they practice adult baptism. At one time, their separatistic stance removed them from political activity; however, an increasing number are exercising their franchise, and a few have held local office.

Communion for the Brethren in Christ serves as a memorial to the suffering death of Jesus Christ and as a symbol of the fellowship that believers have because of Christ's death and resurrection. Fellowship (or brotherhood) is strongly emphasized in the life of the denomination.

Standing in the Anabaptist tradition, the Brethren in Christ are one of the historic peace churches. They consider their relief work, carried on nationally and internationally through the Mennonite Central Committee, to be a logical extension of their peace position.

Since the late 1800s, the Brethren in Christ have emphasized the work of the Holy Spirit in the life of the church and its members. This came from accepting the doctrine of Wesleyan holiness, particularly in its American holiness form with its emphasis on the purifying work of the Holy Spirit in an act of grace following conversion. In recent years, this once-strong American holiness emphasis has been modified, so that now the progressive nature of the work of the Holy Spirit is also taught. The denomination, for the most part, has not accepted the so-called tongues movement.

Forms of Worship

The worship of the Brethren in Christ is essentially nonliturgical. Largely because of their Anabaptist backgrounds, they have encouraged group participation, which includes much congregational singing, the "testimony meeting," and extemporaneous prayer. The preached word has always been and continues to be central to the worship services. In more recent years, lay participation has become less, particularly in the larger congregations with their choirs and "special singing" and with pastors conducting the various parts of the service.

Organization

The Brethren in Christ Church is connectional in nature and representative in government. Each congregation has considerable authority to decide its own affairs, but general decisions and policies are made on the regional and General Conference (North American) level by representatives from the congregations and by denominational officers and board members.

Contributions and Influence

The Brethren in Christ know that they are not sufficiently large to have a significant influence in the world or even in the countries where they are most strongly represented. Rather, they see themselves as helpful examples of what God intends for his people. Thus their peace testimony, their work in local and international relief, and their concern for brotherhood is given without fanfare. Such institutions as Messiah College and Messiah Village (a retirement home in Pennsylvania) are examples of specific denominational institutions that, it may be argued, have had some impact on a regional level beyond the denominational membership.

Significant Terms

Nonconformity. The doctrine that calls Brethren to be a separate ("peculiar") people who turn their backs as Christians to practicing ways of the world.

Nonresistance. Readiness to suffer attack and persecution rather than retaliate or resort to violence (Matt. 5:39).

Order of the Brethren. A term used during the nineteenth century in reference to the ordinances, polity, and attitudes of the Brethren.

Simple life. A twentieth-century term describing the Brethren concern to practice plainness in their daily living. This practice dates back to Brethren beginnings and is based on Matthew 6:25–34.

Bibliography

Sider, E. Morris. *The Brethren in Christ in Canada: Two Hundred Years of Tradition and Change*. Hamilton, Ontario, Canadian Conference of the Brethren in Christ Christian Church, 1988.

———. *Who Are the Brethren in Christ?* Nappanee, Ind.: Evangel Press, 1984.

Wittlinger, Carlton O. *Quest for Piety and Obedience: The Story of the Brethren in Christ.* Nappanee, Ind.: Evangel Press, 1978.

Prepared by E. Morris Sider, Ph.D., archivist and professor of history and English literature, Messiah College, Grantham, Pennsylvania.

BUDDHISM IN THE UNITED STATES

BUDDHIST CHURCHES OF AMERICA

General Description

The Buddhist Churches of America (BCA) has 62 temples/churches, 70 active ministers, and 100,000 adherents spread across the continental United States. The BCA is related to but not controlled by the Jodo Shinshu Honpa Hong-wanji-Ha, in Kyoto, Japan, and is within the family of Mahayana Buddhist denominations.

The BCA traces its history from the historical Buddha, Shakyamuni (565–486 B.C.), in Idai, through Shinran Shonin (1173–1263 A.D.) in Japan, through two priests, Shuei Sonoda and Kakuryo Nishijima, who came to San Francisco in 1889 at the request of Japanese immigrants who had pre-ceded them. (In 1889 Buddhists who were similarly affiliated with the Hong-wanji in Japan established Buddhism in the Kingdom of Hawaii.)

Buddhism, the major religion in many Asian countries, has hundreds of millions of adherents. Jodo Shinshu ("the pure land sect") is the largest Buddhist denomination in Japan. The religious head of Jodo Shinshu is His Eminence Koshin Ohtani, Monshu, whose headquarters are in Kyoto, Japan. Perhaps the best-known American follower of Jodo Shinshu is the late Lt. Col. Ellison Onizuka, USAF, one of the astronauts who died on January 28, 1986, in the *Challenger* disaster.

Beliefs and Doctrines

Jodo Shinshu followers share with all Buddhists the Four Noble Truths and the Eightfold Path. The Nembutsu (Namu Amida Butsu) distinguishes Jodo Shinshu from most other Buddhist groups. The Way of the Nembutsu is the way of the faith in the infinite wisdom and compassion of Amida Buddha, the Buddha of infinite light and life. The recitation of the Nembutsu is central to the religion and the services both in temples and homes.

Adherents profess Shinjin in the everlasting compassion of Amida, whose embrace will never let them go. Thus assured, Shin believers have confidence that they enter the pure land of enlightenment. This salvation, or rebirth, comes because of so-called other power (Tarikki), Amida's action, and not because of self-power (Jiriki), human will or action.

Forms of Worship

Shin services consist of chanting sutras (Scriptures) and reading them responsively, singing Gathas (hymns), hearing a sermon or homily, reciting the Three Treasures ("I take refuge in Buddha; I take refuge in Dharma; I take refuge in Sangha") and/or the Golden Chain ("I am a link in the Amida Buddha's golden chain of love that stretches around the world," etc.). The three primary sutras are the Larger (Sukhavativyuha) Sutra; the Smaller (Sukhavativyuha) Sutra, often called the "Amida Kyo"; and the Meditation (Amitayur Dhyana) Sutra.

Each family has an Obutsudan (altar/shrine) in the home for daily devotion. Special memorial services (Hoji) are held for the deceased every seventh day through the forty-ninth day as well as on the hundredth day and on certain year anniversaries: the first, third, seventh, thirteenth, and so forth.

Organization

The local temple/church is the basic unit. These are organized in the eight geographic districts, which meet monthly. Ministers and lay representatives are elected by the districts to the National Board, which meets three times a year. The senior minister and two lay representatives from each temple meet annually as the National Council, the primary legislative body of the BCA. A bishop, whose headquarters is in San Francisco, California, is elected for a five-year term. The current bishop is Seigen Yanoako.

Contributions and Influence

Buddhism is the primary non-Western, nontheistic religion in the United States and brings another perspective upon reality and the religious life. When and where invited, Buddhists enter into dialogue and interfaith discussion with all other faiths.

The BCA contributes to the United States' cultural diversity and religious pluralism and thereby promotes understanding, acceptance, and harmony among our citizens. As an Asian religion, it also contributes to international understanding and good will.

Significant Terms

Amida Buddha. The Buddha of immeasurable light (wisdom) and immeasurable life (compassion).

Dharma. The teaching.

Gassho. To hold the palms together in gratitude and respect.

Jodo Shinshu. True entrusting pure land.

Namu Amida Butsu. The Nembutsu.

Shinjin. True entrusting (faith).

Tariki. Other power (the working of Amida Buddha's primal vow).

Obutsudan. Altar/shrine.

Nembutsu. A synonym for the Name (Myogo), the fundamental reality.

In addition, many terms identify holidays observed: *Shushoe* is New Year's Day; *Honko,* a gathering to express gratitude, is Shinran Shoni's memorial day, January 16; *Nirvana* Day (literally, "blowing out the flame of personal desire") is February 15; *Higan,* which means the "other shore" of Nirvana, or enlightenment, is observed in the spring and autumn; *Hana Matsuri,* Buddha's birthday, is April 8; *Obon,* a time of reflection, is a joyous gathering when persons recall the compassionate embrace of Aimda Buddha and is celebrated on July 15; *Bodhi* Day, December 8, is the day of Buddha's enlightenment; and *Joya* is the year-end service, when Buddhists gather to express gratitude for the year ending and to hear the temple bell ring 108 times to remind them of the world's delusion. The *Eitaikyuo* (perpetual memorial service) is held, usually in the fall, to remember with gratitude the deceased.

Bibliography

Bloom, Alfred. *Tannisho.* San Francisco: Buddhist Study Center, 1981.

Notes on "Essentials of Earth Alone." A translation of Shinran's *Yunshisho-moni.* Kyoto, Japan: Hongwanji, International Center, 1979.

Shinsu Seiten, Jodo Shinshu Teaching. San Francisco: Buddhist Churches of America, 1978.

Prepared by Richard T. Shellhause, director of development.

ZEN BUDDHISM

General Description

Zen is a sect of Buddhism that developed as a result of the enlightenment of Shakyamuni Buddha five hundred years before Christ. Zen Buddhism is thought to have originated in India, as did Buddhism proper. It was taken to China by Bodhidharma in the sixth century A.D. Bodhidharma is considered to be the first patriarch of Zen. Zen's traditional form was established by the late seventh or eighth century. It was introduced into Japan by Esai and popularized by Dogan in the thirteenth century. Zen was relatively unknown to the Western world until the end of World War II, when the West became aware of it and its influence in Japanese culture.

Zen Buddhism itself consists of two sects: Soto and Rinzai, although some centers in the United States are an amalgam of both. Differences are largely in style of practice and in certain protocol.

Most of the early practitioners of Zen in the United States came from Japan or Korea. Shunryu Suzuki came to San Francisco in 1959 to lead a congregation of Japanese-Americans. Eventually, the San Francisco Zen Center—an American Zen Center—grew out of his efforts. In 1962 Joshu Sasaki used a small house in Los Angeles to teach and lead *sesshins*. He now has many American students in centers throughout the United States. In 1972 the Korean monk Seung Sahn arrived in Providence, Rhode Island, to teach.

Several Americans, foremost among them Philip Kapleau, Roshi, and Robert Atken, went to Japan for Zen training and returned to the United States as teachers. Kapleau, ordained a Zen monk during his years in the monasteries in Japan, authored what is now a classic on Zen training, *The Three Pillars of Zen,* as well as other books on the subject. Robert Wilken has also written several books on the subject. Several Zen centers sprang up in the late 1960s and early 1970s, including the Zen Center in Rochester, New York, founded by Kapleau and now led by his successor, Bodkin Kjolhede, Sensei.

Beliefs and Doctrines

Shakyamuni Buddha (also known as Gautama Buddha, or the Buddha) taught the Four Noble Truths: that pain and unsatisfactoriness (translation of the Sanskrit *dukkha*) exist, that there is a cause for this pain and unsatisfactoriness, that they can cease, and that the way Buddha taught leads to the cessation of this pain and unsatisfactoriness. Zen Buddhism follows this "Buddha Way"—the way to emancipation.

Zen is the Japanese pronunciation of the Chinese *chan,* which in turn is the Chinese pronunciation of the Sanskrit *dhyaa,* meaning "meditation." Meditation is the main emphasis in the following of the way. Through meditation Zen Buddhist adherents work to come to awakening, or enlightenment. Zen has been called paradoxical in that practitioners work toward enlightenment, when in reality they are already there. The practice must come from within; for this reason, Zen Buddhism does not proselytize. Once motivation for practice has risen to a certain level, a teacher is usually sought. The role of the teacher is to encourage the student and to act as guide in the student's search for self-realization. It is also said that the teacher has a duty to protect the student from undue influence of the teacher.

The Buddha also taught the doctrine of karma, or cause and effect: what I say or do in this moment will produce an effect at some future time. Another important feature of Zen Buddhism is the Bodhisavatta ideal, which is to work for emancipation not only for oneself but for all beings.

The doctrine of rebirth is another important teaching of Buddhism. This differs from transmigration or reincarnation in that there is no concept of a soul's being reborn. The process is often likened to that of walking in damp sand: an impression is made, yet what is there that passes over? Or to the cue ball in a game of billiards: when it strikes another ball, it stops, but the second ball—immobile when struck—moves forward.

Today in America, Zen Buddhism is producing second-generation teachers, those trained in the United states by teachers whose training was in the temples of Japan and Korea. Through these second-generation teachers, Zen

Buddhism is being adapted to the American culture in an ongoing, dynamic process in an effort to provide a "Western Zen" to Western students, just as Indian Buddhism was adapted to the Chinese culture, producing Chan Buddhism, which in turn became Zen, having been adapted to the Japanese culture. Today in America, there are well over a hundred Zen Buddhist centers and temples.

Worship and Ritualistic Practices

Periods of intense meditation called *sesshin*s are offered at Zen Buddhist temples and centers, in addition to scheduled daily "sittings," or shorter periods of formal meditation, and ceremonies. Ceremonies are held on the occasions of Thanksgiving; the Buddha's birth, enlightenment, and Parinirvana; the New Year; and at other times. They often involve sutra reading and chanting, as well as *zazen* (meditation) and *teisho* (a "Zen talk" that is a demonstration of Zen in action, given by a sanctioned teacher).

Contributions and Influence

Simplicity of life, respect for all beings, care and awareness in daily life, and greater clarity are the fruits of the practice of Zen. In the popular literature, a fascination with Zen has spawned many books such as *Zen and the Art of Motorcycle Maintenance* and *Zen and Flower Arranging*. And terms such as "karma" and "enlightenment" have made their way into popular language.

There is increasing dialogue among all Buddhist groups in the United States, and dialogue as well between Buddhists and Christians. Buddhists are active in such endeavors as the Buddhist Peace Fellowship (an activity group working toward world peace) and various animal-rights organizations, as well as being involved in the same sorts of activities as non-Buddhists. Zen Buddhism in America is evolving into more of an active lay practice than the mainly monastic emphasis of the Asian Zen Buddhist tradition. It thus is involved in the workday world and is becoming increasingly influential in the American culture as a whole.

Significant Terms

Bodhisattva. An enlightened being who dedicates himself or herself to helping others; such a person works on oneself for the sake of others.

Buddha. The historical figure, Gautama Buddha, also known as the Awakened One. *Buddha* also refers to the true nature of each of us.

Dokusan. A private encounter with the teacher, usually in the *dokusan* room.

Enlightenment. Self-realization; awakening to the true nature of reality. The term *kensho* is usually reserved for a shallow awakening; the word *satori* usually implies deeper awakening.

Gassho. The gesture of raising hands palm to palm to indicate respect, gratitude, and/or humility.

Inka shomei. Literally, "seal of approval," given by the Zen master acknowledging that his disciple has completed Zen training.

Karma. The law of causation on a personal level; the belief that what I say or do always has an effect. This means also that what happens to me is a result of actions I myself have set into motion at some prior time.

Koan. In Zen, this is a formulation in baffling language, insoluble by logical reasoning, pointing to ultimate truth and solved only by the awakening of a deeper level of the mind.

Lotus posture. A traditional meditation posture, in which one is seated with the right foot placed over the left thigh and the left foot placed over the right thigh, with both knees touching the floor or mat. The Buddha is often depicted in this posture.

Nirvana. Literally, "extinction." This is the state beyond birth and death after all ignorance and craving have been extinguished and all karma, which is the cause of rebirth, has been dissolved.

Parinirvana. A term used in reference to the Buddha's passing on at the end of his life.

Samadhi. In Zen, a state of intense absorption in which the mind has transcended all thought, visualizations, imaginings, and so on; an illumined awareness.

Sesshin. A period (often seven days) of silent, intensive meditation training held in seclusion.

Sutra. The Buddhist scriptures, said to be the dialogues and sermons of Shakyamuni Buddha.

Zazen. Literally, "sitting Zen," where the mind is "one-pointed," or stabilized and emptied of random thought.

Bibliography

Aitken, Robert. *Taking the Path of Zen.* San Francisco: North Point Press, 1982.

The Diamond Sutra and the Sutra of Hui Neng. Berkeley, Calif.: Shambala, The Clear Light Series, 1969.

Dumoulin, Heinrich. *The Mind of Cover.* San Francisco: North Point Press, 1976.

———. *Zen Buddhism: A History.* Vol. 1, *India and China.* New York: Macmillan, 1988.

Feibleman, James K. *Understanding Oriental Philosophy.* New York: Horizon Press, 1976.

Ikdea, Daisaku. *Buddhism, the First Millennium.* Translated by Buton Watson. New York: Kodansha International, 1977.

Kapleau, Philip. *The Three Pillars of Zen.* New York: Doubleday, Anchor Press, 1980.

Kraft, Kenneth. *Zen: Tradition and Transition.* New York: Grove Press, 1988.

Masunga, Reiho, trans. *A Primer of Soto Zen.* A translation of Dogen's *Shobogenzo Zuimonki.* Honolulu: University of Hawaii Press, 1971.

Ross, Nancy Wilson. *Buddhism: A Way of Life and Thought.* New York: Random House, Vintage Books, 1981.

Saddhatissa, H. *The Buddha's Way*. New York: George Braziller, 1971.
Sangharaktissa. *A Survey of Buddhism*. Boulder, Colo.: Shambhala, 1980.
Shibayama, Zekei. *Zen Comments on the Mumokan*. New York: Harper & Row, 1964.
Suzuki, Shunryu. *Zen Mind, Beginner's Mind*. New York: Weatherhill, 1970.

Prepared by the editor, with revisions by the Ven. Mitra Bishop, an ordained Zen Buddhist priest of the Zen Center in Rochester.

CHRISTIAN AND MISSIONARY ALLIANCE

General Information

The Christian and Missionary Alliance (C&MA) is an alliance of evangelical believers, joined together in local churches, committed to fulfilling the Great Commission of our Lord Jesus Christ. Matthew 28:19–20 instructs us, "Therefore go and make disciples of all nations." Our mission statement reads, "The Christian and Missionary Alliance is committed to world missions, stressing the fullness of Christ in personal experience, building the church and preaching the gospel to the ends of the earth."

As a missionary denomination committed to worldwide evangelism, we train and send into service only those who are sound in faith and filled with the Spirit of God and a passion for reaching those without Christ. The requirements include seminary training, several years of service in North America, and intense language training. The C&MA has not lost its passion for a deeper life for believers here in the United States. At our central council in 1987, we committed ourselves to planting many more churches by the year 2000.

History

We trace our roots to the ministry and vision of Albert B. Simpson, a Presbyterian clergyman. Motivated by the spiritual needs of multitudes in North America as well as unevangelized peoples in other lands, Simpson launched a vibrant ministry of evangelism and Bible teaching. He was joined by people from a variety of denominational backgrounds who were likewise compelled by Jesus' statement in Matthew 24:14, "This gospel of the kingdom will be preached in the whole world as a testimony to all nations, and then the end will come."

Simpson originally began two separate organizations in 1882. The "Evangelical Missionary Alliance" was commissioned to send missionaries to lands where there was not a witness. The "Christian Alliance" focused upon a teaching ministry to the existing churches in North America. In 1887 these two organizations merged to form the "Christian and Missionary Alliance."

Since our beginning in 1887, the alliance has grown to more that 2,000 churches in the United States and Canada and over 10,000 churches world-wide with a constituency of almost 2 million members in fifty-four nations.

Beliefs and Doctrines

The C&MA emphasizes the need for genuine spiritual conversion to Christ, a Spirit-filled life, and effective service. Our doctrinal statement was adopted in 1956. The following points were reaffirmed by councils in 1965, 1966, and 1975.

1. There is one God, who is infinitely perfect, existing eternally in three persons: Father, Son, and Holy Spirit.
2. Christ is true God and true man. He was conceived by the Holy Spirit and born of the Virgin Mary. He died upon the cross, the just for the unjust, and all who believe in him are justified by his shed blood. He arose from the dead and is now at the right hand of the Majesty on High as our great High Priest. He will come again to establish his kingdom of righteousness and peace.
3. The Holy Spirit is a divine person, sent to indwell, guide, teach, and empower the believer and to convince the world of sin, righteousness, and judgment.
4. The Old and New Testaments, inerrant as originally given, were verbally inspired by God and are a complete revelation of his will for the salvation of men. They constitute the rule of Christian faith and practice.
5. Man was originally created in the image and likeness of God: he fell through disobedience, incurring thereby both physical and spiritual death. All men are born with a sinful nature, are separated from God, and can be saved only through the atoning work of Jesus Christ. The prospect of the impenitent and unbelieving person is existence forever in conscious torment, and that of the believer in Christ is to have everlasting joy and bliss.
6. Salvation has been provided through Jesus Christ for all men, and those who repent and believe in him are born again of the Holy Spirit, receive the gift of eternal life, and become the children of God.
7. It is the will of God that each believer should be filled with the Holy Spirit and be sanctified wholly, being separated from sin and the world and fully dedicated to the will of God, thereby receiving power for holy living and effective service. This is both a crisis and a progressive experience wrought in the life of the believer subsequent to conversion.
8. Provision is made in the redemptive work of the Lord Jesus Christ for the healing of the mortal body. Prayer for the sick and anointing with oil are taught in the Scriptures and are privileges for the church in this present age.
9. The church consists of all those who believe in the Lord Jesus Christ, are redeemed through his blood, and are born again of the Holy Spirit. Christ

is the Head of the body, the church, which has been commissioned by him to go into all the world as a witness preaching the gospel to all nations. The local church is a body of believers in Christ who are joined together for the worship of God, edification through the Word of God, prayer, fellowship, the proclamation of the gospel, and observance of the ordinances of baptism and the Lord's Supper.

10. There shall be a bodily resurrection of the just and of the unjust; for the latter, a resurrection unto judgment.

11. The second coming of the Lord Jesus Christ is imminent and will be personal, visible, and premillennial. This is the believer's blessed hope and an incentive to holy living and faithful service.

Organization

The international headquarters of the C&MA is located in Colorado Springs, Colorado. The headquarters' administrative staff includes the president, four vice-presidents, general services, and finance. There are also a number of directors who administer the C&MA work.

Each year, pastors, administrators, and lay delegates from our local churches gather for our annual General Council, which is the highest legislative body in the alliance. The objective is to formulate policies for the coming years. The program of the General Council is administered by a twenty-eight-member board of managers and carried out by the staff of headquarters and that of each district office. Each local church sends its pastor and lay delegates to the council and to the district conference. The local church is governed by the "Constitution for Churches" found in the *Manual of the Christian and Missionary Alliance*.

Each church holds an annual missionary conference and receives faith promises, which are the bases for funding the worldwide work of the Christian and Missionary Alliance.

Contributions and Influence

The C&MA has had an impact on the consciousness of Christian missions among North American evangelical Christianity. A. B. Simpson had a passion for missions and was the first to produce a well-illustrated journal to communicate that passion. *The Word, the Work, and the World* was the forerunner of the present-day *Alliance Life*, whose focus is upon the work of missions overseas.

As the movement began, there was an evident need for workers to be trained for this expanding ministry. In 1882 the C&MA opened the Missionary Training Institute; this school, the oldest Bible college in existence today, is now known as Nyack College. Besides training missionaries, it had sparked other still-functioning missionary organizations.

The C&MA accomplishes so much in its mission and so effectively maximizes its resources because of the loyalty and commitment to the New

Testament principles of world evangelism and discipleship of faithful members of the alliance. Alliance people function as worthy stewards of God's resources. Their generosity in giving and loyal support of alliance ministries make the alliance what it is: an example to all churches.

Significant Terms

Bring back the King. Simpson encouraged the movement to preach the gospel with the motivation that when they have finished the job, Christ would return (Matt. 24:14).

District conference. This annual meeting of delegates from every alliance church within a specific district is held to elect members to the District Executive Committee, to review business concerning the district as a whole, and to worship and learn together.

Fourfold gospel. The preaching emphasis of A. B. Simpson, which emphasized the all-sufficiency of Christ for all of life: Christ as Savior, Sanctifier, Healer, and Coming King.

Healing in the atonement. This phrase was used to call Christians to trust in Christ for healing of their physical needs because of Christ's work upon the cross. It was based upon Matthew 8:16–17, which ties healing to the work of Christ on the cross.

Modified dichotomy. This missiological term was one of the major contributions of L. L. King, former president, and is a missionary statement of the alliance. The term describes the special partnership that exists between the alliance missions boards and other mission-minded churches in the United States.

Bibliography

Bailey, Keith. *Bringing Back the King: An Introduction to the History and Thought of the Christian and Missionary Alliance.* Nyack, N.Y.: Alliance Centers for Theological Study, 1985.

Hunter, J. H. *Beside All Waters.* Harrisburg, Pa.: Christian Publications, 1964.

Niklaus, Robert L., John S. Swain, and Samuel J. Stoesz. *All for Jesus: God at Work in the Christian and Missionary Alliance over One Hundred Years.* Camp Hill, Pa.: Christian Publications, 1986.

Simpson, Albert B. *The Fourfold Gospel.* Rev. ed. Camp Hill, Pa.: Christian Publications, 1984.

Tozer, A. W. *Wingspread: A. B. Simpson: A Study in Spiritual Altitude.* Camp Hill, Pa.: Christian Publications, 1943.

Prepared by the editor from materials furnished by Richard W. Bailey and revised by Rev. Mark Borda, a local C&MA pastor.

CHRISTIAN CHURCH
(Disciples of Christ)

General Description

The Christian Church (Disciples of Christ) was born on the American frontier in the early 1800s as a movement opposing the rigid denominations imported from Europe and seeking Christian unity on a simple New Testament basis.

Founders

Its founders were Alexander Campbell in western Pennsylvania and Virginia and Barton W. Stone in Kentucky. The basic principle was a fellowship built around the Lord's Table and tolerance of widely divergent viewpoints concerning nonessentials. Counting the Churches of Christ and the so-called independent Christian Churches, which gradually separated from the Disciples, the Campbell-Stone development represents an indigenous American religious movement second only to the Mormons in size. Both Campbell and Stone had been Presbyterians.

Beliefs and Doctrines

The Christian Church (Disciples of Christ) has no official creed that must be accepted by all. A simple confession of Jesus as the Christ is the basis of church membership. In 1809 Thomas Campbell wrote in his "Declaration and Address," "The Church upon earth is essentially, intentionally, and constitutionally one." Christian unity has been the Disciples' polestar. The Bible is the source of authority, with freedom of interpretation based on serious study.

The Lord's Supper is observed on each Lord's Day. Lay elders preside at the table along with ordained clergy, and lay deacons serve the congregation.

Organization

The Disciples have a history of congregational government, although in 1968 they adopted a structure that sees the church in congregational, regional, and general "manifestations." The manifestations are considered equal rather than pyramidal, and each has its protected rights and identified responsibilities. Each is in voluntary relation to the others and calls or dismisses its own staff and handles its own finances and property. The general manifestation is called general rather than national because both the United States and Canada are included in the structure. There are thirty-six regions, many of them encompassing all of a single state.

The General Assembly, the representative body of the church, meets biennially and may involve 8,000–10,000 participants, about half of them official voters from congregations and regions. All persons who register have the right to speak. The voters include all ministers, two laypersons from each congregation (more from a few larger congregations), some three hundred regional representatives, and the church's General Board. The General Board comprises 180 members and meets annually. A forty-four-member administrative committee meets twice annually.

Contributions and Influence

Disciples historically have been a leading force in the movement for Christian unity. Disciples' layman and industrialist J. Irwin Miller served as the first president of the National Council of Churches, and Paul A. Crow, Jr., was the first executive for the Consultation on Church Union.

Concern for issues affecting the lives of persons has led Disciples to work for peace, justice, and human rights. Alexander Campbell, Emily Tubman, and Preston Taylor were early Disciples who worked against slavery. U.S. presidents with Disciples background include James Garfield, Lyndon Johnson, and Ronald Reagan. The General Assembly speaks to issues of public policy, not as a test of fellowship, but as a way of seeking to be faithful to God's claim on life in the world.

Significant Terms

Campbellites. The name given to those Christians who followed Thomas Campbell and his son Alexander in the Disciples movement. It apparently gained worldwide usage in the western immigration of overland pioneers.

Covenant community. A description of the Christian Church (Disciples of Christ) that best reflects its origin and mission. The community is "individualistic, uncomplicated, free of corporate authority and unbound by tradition," yet its free members and congregations by agreement (covenant) hold to its main points of faith and practice.

No creed but Christ. An early slogan of the Disciples that expresses their belief that faith in Jesus Christ is a personal faith not dependent on manmade creeds. A good expression of this is the favorite recited perspective, "that the Church of Christ upon earth is essentially, intentionally, and constitutionally one."

Provisional design. A later document (covenant), adopted in 1967, which unified all the facets of the Christian Church (Disciples of Christ) into a common program of witness and service.

Stone-Campbell movement. The name given to the union of Barton Stone's

Christian group and Alexander Campbell's Disciples group in 1832 at Lexington, Kentucky, which gave impetus to the reform movement's expansion through all the United States.

Lord's Supper. The name for Holy Communion preferred by the Christian Church (Disciples of Christ). The Campbells sought to restore the New Testament practice offering the Lord's Supper every Sunday and on special days—and in fellowship with the entire church of Christ.

Bibliography

(Except as noted, all items are published by CBP Press, St. Louis.)
Cartwright, Colbert S. *People of the Chalice*. 1987.
Cummins, Duane D. *A Handbook for Today's Disciples*. St. Louis: Bethany Press, 1981.
Friedly, Robert L., and Duane D. Cummins. *The Search for Identity*. 1987.
McAllister, Lester G., and William E. Tucker. *Journey in Faith*. 1975.
Stemmler, Guin T. *A Mini History of the Christian Church (Disciples of Christ)*. 1987.

Prepared by Claude E. Grant, deputy general minister and president, with terms and definitions by the editor.

♦ ♦ ♦

CHRISTIAN CHURCHES AND CHURCHES OF CHRIST

General Description

The Christian Churches and Churches of Christ are an informal fellowship of independent congregations in the United States and Canada. The total constituency of this fellowship numbers just over 1 million members nationally, a majority of them in the states of the Ohio Valley.

These churches began early in the nineteenth century as a movement to restore the unity of the apostolic church by returning it to its pristine form and abandoning denominational divisions, sectarianism, and human theological formulations. The Bible is taken as the only creed, and human opinions are regarded as nonessential. These churches often refer to themselves as the Restoration movement—a movement to restore the apostolic church in its simplicity, doctrines, organization, and practices.

Major leaders include Barton W. Stone, who left the Presbyterians in Kentucky in 1804; Thomas and Alexander Campbell in western Pennsylvania in 1809; and Walter Scott, who began a career as an evangelist in northeastern Ohio in 1827. The movement grew steadily and significantly throughout the nineteenth century but then suffered two major divisions. In 1906 individuals who rejected the use of musical instruments in public worship secured a separate identity as "Churches of Christ." The development of theological liberalism led to doctrinal problems early in the twentieth century, and by 1927 these individuals had a separate existence, later choosing the name "Christian Church (Disciples of Christ)."

These name changes created a good deal of identity confusion, but the Christian Churches and Churches of Christ have a conservative theology, while still allowing musical instruments in public worship. They practice baptism by immersion for remission of sins. Weekly communion is a standard feature of worship services.

Organization

These churches are congregational in organization, refusing to give any organization authority over local congregations. The North American Christian Convention meets annually, drawing an attendance of about twenty thousand, but the gathering is for inspiration, challenge, and worship only.

No motions are passed or resolutions adopted. There are no business meetings. These churches do not consider themselves a denomination, since there is no central headquarters.

A publishing house in Cincinnati supplies much of the church literature. Thirty-five Bible colleges and three seminaries train the ministry. There are about 5,700 different congregations in the fellowship, supporting about 1,500 missionaries in fifty-three different countries throughout the world. There are numerous other church agencies of both an evangelistic and service nature.

Significant Terms

Autonomy. The commitment that each congregation is free and independent, that there is no agency that can have any authority over local congregations.

Bible only. The commitment to the Scriptures (specifically the New Testament) alone as the authoritative guide to the practices and doctrine of the church.

Elders. The conviction that the duly chosen elders of each congregation have the supreme governance of that body.

Noncreedal. The desire to abandon all human theological formulations (such as the Westminster Confession of Faith, Augsburg Confession, etc.) and follow the Scriptures only.

Opinion. Anything not taught specifically in the Scriptures is but human opinion and therefore ought never to be made a test of faith.

Restoration. The ideal of returning the church to its original New Testament format and function.

Bibliography

Garrett, Leroy. *The Stone-Campbell Movement*. Joplin, Mo.: College Press, 1981.

Hayden, Edwin V., ed. *North American Gold: The Story of Fifty North American Christian Conventions*. Joplin, Mo.: College Press, 1989.

Murch, James D. *Christian Only: A History of the Restoration Movement*. Cincinnati: Standard Publishing, 1962.

Richardson, Robert. *Memoirs of Alexander Campbell*. Cincinnati: Standard Publishing, 1969.

Rogers, John, ed. *The Biography of Eld. Barton Warren Stone*. Cincinnati: J. A. and U. P. James, 1847.

Prepared by Dr. James B. North, professor of church history, Cincinnati Bible College and Seminary.

◆ ◆ ◆

CHRISTIAN SCIENCE

General Description
The First Church of Christ, Scientist, in Boston, Massachusetts, is head-quarters for the Christian Science denomination. It has 2,700 branches in 166 countries. The Church of Christ, Scientist, was established to "commemorate the word and works of our Master, which should reinstate primitive Christianity and its lost element of healing" (*Church Manual*, p. 17).

Founder
Mary Baker Eddy discovered Christian Science after a spiritual healing in 1866 and founded the Church of Christ, Scientist, in 1879. Her major written work, *Science and Health with Key to the Scriptures*, is the denominational textbook.

Beliefs and Doctrines
As stated in *Science and Health*, p. 497, tenets of the church are as follows:

1. As adherents of Truth, we take the inspired Word of the Bible as our sufficient guide to eternal life.
2. We acknowledge and adore one supreme and infinite God. We acknowledge His son, one Christ; the Holy Ghost or divine Comforter; and man in God's image and likeness.
3. We acknowledge God's forgiveness of sin in the destruction of sin and the spiritual understanding that casts out evil as unreal. But the belief in sin is punished so long as the belief lasts.
4. We acknowledge Jesus' atonement as the evidence of divine, efficacious Love, unfolding man's unity with God through Christ Jesus the Way-shower; and we acknowledge that man is saved through Christ, through Truth, Life, and Love as demonstrated by the Galilean Prophet in healing the sick and overcoming sin and death.
5. We acknowledge that the crucifixion of Jesus and his resurrection served to uplift faith to understand eternal Life, even the allness of Soul, Spirit, and the nothingness of matter.
6. And we solemnly promise to watch and pray for that Mind to be in us

which was also in Christ Jesus; to do unto others as we would have them do unto us; and to be merciful, just and pure.

Forms of Worship

Sunday services include correlative passages from the Bible and *Science and Health*. Wednesday evening meetings include testimonies of Christian healing.

Organization

The Church Manual, by Mrs. Eddy, contains rules and bylaws that govern the First Church of Christ, Scientist. A five-member board of directors administers its affairs. Each branch is democratically self-governed.

Contributions and Influence

The Church of Christ, Scientist, has been a pioneer in the modern Christian church's revival of interest in spiritual healing. It has also, from its inception, acknowledged both the Fatherhood and Motherhood of God and the spiritual equality of men and women.

Significant Terms

Science and Health defines the following three key terms as follows:

God. Incorporeal, divine, supreme, infinite Mind, Spirit, Soul, Principle, Life, Truth, and Love.

Christ. The divine manifestation of God, which comes in the flesh to destroy incarnate error.

Man. The compound idea of infinite Spirit; the spiritual image and likeness of God; the full representation of Mind.

Bibliography

GENERAL ARTICLES

"Christian Science." *Encyclopedia Britannica*, 1984 ed.

"Christian Science" and "Eddy, Mary Baker." *Encyclopedia of Religion*, ed. Mircea Eliade. 1986.

BOOKS

Canham, Erwin D. *Commitment to Freedom: The Story of the Christian Science Monitor*. Boston: Houghton Mifflin, 1958.

A Century of Christian Science Healing. Boston: Christian Science Publishing Society, 1966.

Eddy, Mary Baker. *Science and Health with Key to the Scriptures*. Boston, Trustees under the Will of Mary Baker G. Eddy, 1934.

Gottschalk, Stephen. *The Emergence of Christian Science in American Religious Life*. Berkeley: University of California Press, 1973.

John, DeWitt. *The Christian Science Way of Life*. Boston: Christian Science Publishing Society, 1962.

Peel, Robert. *Mary Baker Eddy: The Years of Authority*. New York: Holt, Rinehart & Winston, 1977.

——. *Mary Baker Eddy: The Years of Discovery*. New York: Holt, Rinehart & Winston, 1966.

——. *Mary Baker Eddy: The Years of Trial*. New York: Holt, Rinehart & Winston, 1971.

——. *Spiritual Healing in a Scientific Age*. San Francisco: Harper & Row, 1987.

Revised from an earlier article by Nathan A. Talbot, manager, committee on publications.

◆ ◆ ◆

CHURCH OF CHRIST

General Description

The Church of Christ is a fellowship of autonomous congregations numbering approximately 2 million members. Its goal is a return to New Testament Christianity and the unity of all believers in Christ through a
renunciation of all creeds and confessions of faith, accepting the New Testament alone as its rule of faith and practice. The church accepts the Bible
as the inspired Word of God without error and wholly dependable for man's
spiritual welfare.

While congregations are independent entities, members cooperate as
individuals and as congregations in carrying on missions and in maintaining
educational institutions and homes for the aged and homeless children. Sometimes this is done under the oversight of some congregation while others
also participate. At other times, it may be done through a board of trustees.
Some congregations, however, refrain from cooperative efforts and maintain
their "good works" programs within the framework of their own congregation.

Organization

Each ecclesiastical unit is independently organized and recognizes no
one as head but Jesus Christ. The congregation appoints elders, or bishops,
as overseers in accordance with the directions given by the apostle Paul to
Timothy and Titus. There is always a plurality of elders who are selected
from among the men of the congregation. Deacons are also appointed to
assist the elders. Each congregation chooses its own minister or ministers,
usually done through the elders with the approval of the congregation. Under
the elders, a church functions through the work of the deacons, teachers,
ministers, and other workers.

When a church is too young or too small to have men who are considered
able to qualify according to the biblical standard, congregations function by
a consensus. Often a men's business meeting is granted the oversight. Or
certain committees may be formed to care for the congregation. This, however, is considered a temporary measure to function only until qualified men
have been recruited and trained.

Beliefs and Doctrines

Churches of Christ believe that the New Testament is complete in revealing God's will to man and that all religious matters must emanate from its message. The Bible, both Old and New Testaments, is held as inspired revelation from God. The New Testament is God's special message to the Christian to determine his Christian walk.

They hold that Jesus Christ was born of the Virgin Mary and is the Son of God. They believe that he was crucified for the sins of the whole world, was buried, and arose on the third day. They believe that he ascended to the Father and now is at his right hand. At the end of the world, he will return again. Then will come the judgment, when each person will be judged according to his works. They believe that there are two destinies: heaven and hell. Salvation, they believe, is by grace, through faith, upon one's obedience to the faith. This is accomplished through faith in Jesus Christ, repentance from sin, and baptism for the remission of sins, in keeping with the message at Pentecost. Baptism is the immersion of the penitent believer in the name of the Father, Son, and the Holy Spirit, upon which they believe that the Lord adds the individual to the church and that he receives the gift of the Holy Spirit as a guarantee of eternal life.

Churches of Christ commonly make the following general affirmations:

Bind nothing on the church except what is specifically taught or commended, necessarily inferred, or approved by scriptural example.
No creed but Christ, no book but the Bible, no law but God's (as revealed in the Bible, his inspired Word).
In faith, unity; in opinion, liberty; in all things, charity.

Forms of Worship

Following the New Testament example, the Church of Christ assembles on Sunday, the first day of each week. They take as their agenda that which occurred in New Testament assemblies. Their worship consists of teaching (preaching and reading Scripture), prayer, singing, communion (partaking of the Lord's Supper in memory of his death), and taking an offering. Their singing is without any instrument because they do not find it on the agenda of the New Testament church.

Another dimension to their worship is private, personal, and daily. The foundation for this is found in Paul's admonition in the Book of Romans to present one's body as a living sacrifice—or as an act of worship. This dimension includes one's daily responsibility to church work, constant commitment to Christian morality (exercising the fruit of the Spirit and refraining from the works of the flesh), and a continuing relationship of compassion and service to one's fellow man.

History

In the early 1800s Thomas Campbell and his son Alexander, clergymen in the Seceder Presbyterian Church, migrated from Ireland to America. They ran into difficulty when they crossed lines of communion even between segments of the Presbyterian Church. This led to an examination of the matter of religious disunity and gave rise to a movement to unite all Christians in unity through accepting the New Testament as the church's only rule of faith and practice. Others joined the Campbells, but all efforts to persuade denominations to unite on such a basis failed. Therefore, there emerged what was called the Restoration movement.

The movement's aim was to restore the church of the New Testament in doctrine, practice, government, and worship. The New Testament was to be the guiding document of the movement. Nothing was required of the members except what was expressly commanded, necessarily inferred, or approved in Scripture by example. The movement made use of three terms by which it was known: Disciples of Christ, Christian Church, and Church of Christ. One major controversy, which involved two issues, threatened the unity of the movement. Dispute arose over the organization of a missionary society as a means of spreading the gospel and over the use of instrumental music in the worship. A large segment within the movement held that neither of these was authorized by the New Testament. In the early 1900s the controversy became so intense that those who did not favor the missionary society and instrumental music became generally known as Churches of Christ and emerged as a separate fellowship of their own.

Contributions and Influence

Members of the Churches of Christ participate in a broad spectrum of American life. In addition to the general vocational and professional pursuits, they are often found in places of influence. The church has furnished the country with one president—James A. Garfield. Many of her members have served in both state and national legislatures. Her ministers serve frequently as military chaplains. Her members also serve as judges and mayors. Members are also active in both private and public education. Some have served as chief administrators of public universities. The congregations and members respond generously to tragedies and suffering around the world.

Although the church as a body does not generally take a political position, her impact on society is made through her members as they work and serve throughout the nation and the world.

Significant Terms

Church. The church is composed of all baptized believers.

Christian. A baptized believer.

Local congregation. It is composed of the baptized believers of a local community with their elders and deacons as directed in 1 Timothy 3 and

Titus 1, except where lack of qualified leadership prevents their appointment.

Christian unity. A concept of uniting all Christians into one body of believers without denominational division and based solely upon the teaching of the New Testament without humanly devised creeds and manuals.

Restoration movement. A movement among Christians to restore the church of Christ as described in the New Testament in name, doctrine, organization, worship, and practice.

Bibliography

Garrison, W.E., and A.T. DeGroot. *The Disciples of Christ.* St. Louis: Bethany Press, 1958.

Powell, J. M. *The Cause We Plead.* Nashville: Twentieth Century Christian, 1987.

West, Earl. *The Search for the Ancient Order.* 3 vols. Nashville: Gospel Advocate Press, 1948–79.

Prepared by Dr. Elza Hufford, president emeritus, Northeastern Christian Junior College, Villanova, Pennsylvania.

• • •

CHURCH OF GOD

Several denominations have in common the phrase "Church of God" in their name. We consider these together below, although at certain points they differ widely in their beliefs and history.

CHURCH OF GOD (ANDERSON, IND.)

History

The background of this religious movement relates generally to American frontier revivalism and specifically to the holiness movement of the last half of the nineteenth century. Religious antecedents include the radical reformers of the sixteenth century, the German Pietists, the English Puritans, and the Wesleyans, yet no generic ties with any of these groups persist.

No single individual could be regarded as the founder of the movement. Like-minded individuals were drawn together through a periodical called the *Gospel Trumpet*. Its editor, Daniel S. Warner, was most prominent among the pioneers. Warner (1842–95) was first associated with the Ohio Eldership of the Churches of God in North America. He later accepted the Wesleyan doctrine of perfection and became associated with the Holiness Association. In 1881 he and others declared themselves free from all human creeds and party names with adherence only to the apostolic church of the living God.

General Description

The church has an estimated constituency of around 470,000 members in approximately 5,200 congregations and mission stations on all five continents under the leadership of some 5,000 ministers. The church's publication agency is Warner Press, Anderson, Indiana. Periodicals are *Vital Christianity, Christianity Leadership, Church of God Missions,* and *The Shining Light*. It sponsors two liberal arts colleges—Anderson University and Warner Pacific College—plus three regionally supported schools. General offices are in Anderson, Indiana.

Beliefs and Doctrines

No formal creed has ever been adopted. An "open at the top" commitment to truth makes for considerable flexibility within the context of a basic biblicism. The following cardinal beliefs are emphasized.

To be a genuine Christian one must enter into a life-changing relationship with God. Personal conversion is the renewal of life at its deepest level through repentance and trust in the forgiveness of Christ.

The believer must "go on to perfection," that is, he must be made perfect in love, in intention, and in attitude. This infilling of the Holy Spirit brings the Christian an infusion of grace and power for belief and service.

The church is a divine institution composed only of true believers. Conversion places one in the church, and no church-joining formalities are necessary, either for the local congregation or the church universal.

God has only one church. Christian unity is an outgrowth of our common experience in Christ, which produces a solidarity with all true believers. Unity is realized basically in the oneness God gives, but man is under obligation to attain "to the unity of the faith."

Christ will come again, at a time of God's appointing, in judgment and without any millennial reign. He will dictate rewards and punishment.

Organization

The polity of the group is basically congregational, although there are elements of both presbyterial and episcopal patterns. The movement began with a basic fear of human ecclesiasticism and a firm conviction that the church should be governed by the Holy Spirit. For the first thirty-five years, there were no formal structures; even yet, behind the functional structures that growth has made necessary, there is the conviction that the Holy Spirit is the real determiner of policy and action in the church.

Contributions and Influence

Our contributions are probably most specific in two areas: Christian unity and the nature of the church. Although not an action leader in ecumenical organizations, the movement has been a strong witness to a valid undenominational Protestantism and has many interdenominational working relationships. With its avoidance of formal church-joining and its emphasis on rule by the Holy Spirit, the essentially divine character of the church is highlighted and demonstrated.

Significant Terms

Bible. The only creed of the Church of God. Hence, "Bible" became an adjective commonly used to describe matters of the movement's life, for example, "Bible doctrine," "Bible church," "worship in the Bible way."

Camp meeting. The principal expression of revivalism in the Church of God. More than twenty thousand people attend the largest of these: the

"Anderson Camp Meeting" (known more formally as "The International Convention of the Church of God").

Church. Composed of all those who believe unto God for salvation. The sole criterion of church membership is therefore the experience of salvation.

Holiness. The Christian's life of victory over the guilt and power of sin.

Holy Spirit. Understood largely as the divine agent of entire sanctification (i.e., holiness).

Movement. Church of God folk prefer this term over "denomination" as a self-description. Denominations divide the church, whereas the Church of God movement seeks to call the church back to its lost unity.

Bibliography

(All items are published by Warner Press, Anderson, Ind.)

Callen, Barry L. *The First Century: Church of God Reformation Movement.* 2 vols. 1979. Selected portions of representative materials that identify the setting in which the Church of God emerged. It tells the story of its growth and maturing.

——. *Preparing for Service.* 1988. A history of higher education in the Church of God.

Crose, Lester A. *Passport for a Reformation.* 1981. The story of the worldwide missionary work for the Church of God.

Massey, James Earl, ed. *Educating for Service.* 1984. A volume showing the thought of the second- and third-generation Church of God leaders in focusing Church of God ideals on contemporary concerns, written in honor of a leading Church of God educator.

Newell, Arlo F. *The Church of God As Revealed in Scripture.* 1893. Religious beliefs that have helped to shape and mold the Church of God.

Smith, John W. V. *I Will Build My Church.* 1985. Biblical insights on distinguishing doctrines of the Church of God.

——. *The Quest for Holiness and Unity.* 1980. A history of the beginning and the first hundred years of development of the Church of God.

Prepared by Dr. John W. V. Smith, historian, and revised by Dr. Paul A. Tanner and Dr. Edward L. Foggs, successive executive secretaries.

CHURCH OF GOD (CLEVELAND, TENN.)

History

The Church of God began as a people movement in 1886 among the common folk in the Unicoi Mountains in North Carolina and eastern Tennessee. Those who had a deep desire for a holy life based upon the principles of Christ as they are revealed in the Bible, the Word of God, banded together for prayer and Bible study. This small group of believers had developed into a number of congregations when early leaders decided to move across the mountains to Cleveland, Tennessee.

From early in its history, the church has emphasized home evangelism and world missions. By 1910 it had launched its educational systems, one of the earliest support ministries to develop and one that emphasized both practical and academic preparation. Other ministries grew as the denomination progressed and realized its obligations to nurture as well as to evangelize.

General Description

The evangelistic, missionary emphasis of the Church of God is a response to Christ's command to go into all the world and make disciples. The world mission enterprise is aimed at taking the gospel of Christ into near and distant parts of the world. Church of God congregations are located in every state and in 115 countries around the world. These missions are administered by 149 Americans, 43 others, and 257 national missionaries. Furthermore, there are 12,000 national ministers and pastors serving the Church of God outside the United States and Canada. The 1990 missions budget is $10.2 million.

An aggressive effort to win converts to Christ has always been essential to the Church of God. Every program of the church reflects this evangelistic attitude: revivalism, youth camps, camp meetings, congregational services, and its missionary efforts.

The Church of God is affiliated with the Pentecostal Fellowship of North America, the National Association of Evangelicals, and the Pentecostal World Conference.

Beliefs and Doctrines

Christian. First and foremost, the Church of God is a determinedly Christian church. It is built upon the person of Jesus Christ, not as a good man alone or a great teacher alone or a worthy example alone, but as the Son of God. The doctrines and practices of the church are based upon his teachings, just as its hope is based upon the fact that he was and is exactly what he is recorded to be in the Scriptures.

Protestant. The Church of God is founded upon the principles of Protestantism, although it is not a traditional follower of Martin Luther, John Calvin, John Knox, Jacob Arminius, or any other specific leader of the Protestant Reformation. The denomination stands firmly for religious freedom, the separation of church and state, and the priesthood of believers. It stands equally against abuses and extravagances of ecclesiastical ritualism and dogmatism.

Evangelical. An evangelical denomination, the Church of God stands for the whole Bible rightly divided. The New Testament is the only rule for government and discipline.

The Church of God began at a time when the Christian world was split into two schools of persuasion: liberalism and fundamentalism. The classical difference between the two was the fundamentalists' belief in and the liberals' denial of five basic Christian doctrines: (1) the inerrancy and infallibility of the Scriptures, (2) the Virgin Birth and complete deity of Christ, (3) the atoning sacrifice of Christ's death for the sins of the world, (4) the literal resurrection of the body, and (5) Christ's second coming in bodily form to earth. The Church of God officially and earnestly accepts these positions of fundamentalism as being the teachings of Scripture.

Holiness. The doctrine of holiness, one of the key doctrines of the Church of God, asserts that Christ both forgives man of his sins and thereafter lives in his heart. With Christ's life within him, the Christian should follow the example of Christ in purity, love, forgiveness, mercy, and devotion to God. Holiness is viewed as the nature, the spirit, and the essence of Christ within the heart of the believer.

Pentecostal. In 1896 people of the Church of God had a spiritual experience that they identified as the baptism of the Holy Spirit. Because it was so similar to the experience of the early Christians on the Day of Pentecost, it came to be called a Pentecostal experience, an enlightenment of the Christian life that made the people more effective witnesses for Christ. The Church of God is therefore known as a Pentecostal church.

Charismatic. The Greek word *charisma* refers to the spiritual gifts listed in 1 Corinthians 12: a word of wisdom, a word of knowledge, faith, healing, miracles, prophecy, discerning of spirits, tongues, and the interpretation of tongues. Christians who accept these gifts as being valid for this day are therefore called Charismatic. The Church of God believes staunchly in the gifts of the Spirit and encourages its members to be subject to them.

Organization

The episcopal form of government is hierarchical in character. Pastors are appointed by state or territorial overseers, who are themselves appointed by the Executive Committee. The Executive Committee consists of the general overseer, the three assistant overseers, and the general secretary-treasurer, all of whom are nominated by the General Council and elected by the General Assembly.

The general church holds title to all church property, and local churches regularly support church programs through a percentage of tithes given to the local church. The combined strength of the local churches makes possible many ministries that would otherwise be impossible.

Although the state or territorial overseer appoints pastors, the congregations express their preference by ballot. A church council assists the pastor in local business matters between quarterly conferences, which are open to all church members. Local churches are grouped geographically into districts within the state boundaries for area projects and fellowship.

The Executive Council conducts general church business when the General Assembly is not in session. It is composed of the Executive Committee and eighteen members elected by the General Council. It meets three times a year.

Contributions and Influence

From the beginning, in the mountains of eastern Tennessee, western North Carolina, and northern Georgia, the Church of God has felt its responsibility to the poor, the homeless, and the orphaned. It is a caring church. It belongs to interdenominational agencies that specialize in this ministry and sponsors numerous programs of its own. It operates three homes for children in the United States, scores of such homes in its mission work, numerous centers for servicemen and women in the States and abroad, and other ministries that express care for those in need.

Bibliography

(All items are published by Pathway Press, Cleveland, Tenn.)
Conn, Charles W. *Like a Mighty Army: A History of the Church of God.* 1977.
Horton, Wade H. *Pentecost Yesterday and Today.* 1964.
Hughs, Ray H. *Church of God Distinctives.* 1989.
Lemons, Frank W. *Our Pentecostal Heritage.* 1963.
Slay, James L. *This We Believe.* 1963.

Prepared by the Office of Public Relations, with the assistance of the editor.

CHURCH OF GOD IN CHRIST

General Description

The Church of God in Christ (COGIC) is an extensive network of primarily black congregations composing the largest black Pentecostal body in North America. While the denomination is international in scope, its origins can be traced to an abandoned gin house in Lexington, Mississippi, in the year 1897. This movement, which numbers approximately 1.7 million members (some sources claim as many as 3.7 million) has roots deep within the nineteenth-century holiness movement in America and the adopting of the Wesleyan view of entire sanctification and holiness of life, with an emphasis on the baptism of the Holy Ghost, with signs following.

Founder

Bishop Charles Harrison Mason (1866–1961) is the founder of the Church of God in Christ. He was born in an area just beyond Memphis, Tennessee. His parents, Jerry and Eliza Mason, former slaves, were members of the Missionary Baptist Church. Mason was licensed and ordained to preach in 1891, at Preston, Arkansas. In 1895 Mason met Charles Price Jones, new pastor of the Mount Helms Baptist Church in Jackson, Mississippi. The quest of both men for a "deeper way of life" led to Mason's pilgrimage to the Los Angeles Azusa Street Revival in 1906 at the request of Jones, who was his pastor. Mason's newfound Pentecostal experience of the baptism of the Spirit accompanied by glossolalia (speaking in tongues) bore the seeds of dissension. After intensive debate, Jones continued with the Church of Christ, Holiness, U.S.A., while in 1907 Mason formally organized the Church of God in Christ, in Memphis, Tennessee.

Beliefs and Doctrines

Doctrinally, the COGIC identifies with the Wesleyan view of entire sanctification (subsequent to justification) evidenced by holiness of life, with the total blessing of the baptism of the Holy Ghost, with signs following and experience subsequent to and distinct from conversion. The denomination adheres to the basic ordinances of the faith, such as baptism by immersion, foot washing, and the Lord's Supper. Fasting standards, personal conduct, and moderation in dress codes continue to be values worthy of esteem. The Bible is the inspired library for faith and practice. COGIC believes in the imminent and blessed return of our Lord for his church.

Organization

COGIC is episcopal in organizational structure, with bishops (Greek *episkopos*) as chief administrative officers, but with increasingly more autonomy within individual congregations, which has engaged the church in a creative tension. Bishops are appointed by the presiding bishop and General Board, which oversees the administrative and executive functions of the church. The twelve-man General Board presidium recommends, but the bishop designates, appointments to the General Assembly (the only law-making body of the church) for ratification. Jurisdictional bishops appoint ordained ministers as pastors of local congregations, all supervised by superintendents. General Board members are elected every four years; bishops and pastors are appointed indefinitely. Women are appointed as licensed missionaries without churches, a trend that is under debate, protest, and revision.

Forms of Worship

Worship style varies throughout the church from traditional to modified contemporary expression. The church's first hymnal, entitled "Yes Lord," was published in 1984. The COGIC *Manual* contains instruction for initiating a local church in the use of the hymnal. It contains instructions for worship, administering sacraments of baptism and communion, marriage, funerals, dedication of a church, and the discipline of members. The average worship includes testimonies, prayers for renewal, proclamation of the Word of God, the ministry of stewardship, an altar call to discipleship, and a benediction. COGIC worship is esteemed of great value when punctuated and characterized by spontaneity of expression. Organ music and gospel choirs with full musical accompaniment usually combine to enhance worship services, which help to achieve the anointing of the Spirit, embellished by the presence of the joy of the Lord.

Contributions and Influence

COGIC has been the catalyst in providing a broader dimension of spirituality to the black religious experience in America. Its strong emphasis on the necessity of the empowering presence of the Holy Spirit for witnessing and transforming society has made a profound statement throughout the world. Martin Luther King, Jr., delivered his final, "Mountain Top" address at Mason Temple, historic headquarters of COGIC, the evening preceding his death. In 1970 the COGIC founded the first fully accredited Pentecostal Theological Seminary in North America (the Charles Harrison Mason Seminary, affiliate of the International Theological Center, Atlanta, Ga.). COGIC is testimony to a God who can initiate a movement in a cotton gin bar and demonstrate once again how he can in a "saving moment" choose the foolish things of this world to confound the wise.

Significant Terms

Presiding bishop. The chief leader of the church, elected by a majority vote of the General Assembly to conduct and implement the executive affairs of the church in a close relationship with the eleven-member General Board.

Jurisdictional bishop. The top executive of a state jurisdiction, appointed by the presiding bishop to supervise pastors for the ministry to the denomination.

State supervisor. A female administrator appointed by the national supervisor of women to supervise and coordinate the ministry of women in state jurisdictions.

Superintendent. An administrator appointed by jurisdictional bishops to supervise districts and the pastors they include.

Elder. An ordained minister with or without charge whose ministry assignment is to a local church.

Licensed minister. The first level of ministry; the designate receives a license acknowledging one's call to ministry. This step precedes ordination.

Jurisdiction. An administratively designated area that includes pastors under the supervision of a bishop.

Sanctification. The act of being set apart or consecrated to the Lord to cleanse and purify oneself for the Lord's purpose. One is consecrated by the Lord, the blood, and the Spirit.

Saved. A term used to describe the saving moment when a person believes in Jesus Christ as Savior and accepts him as Lord and lives under his lordship.

Spiritual anointing. The spiritual effusion created by the presence of the Holy Spirit that imbues the individual for a special task of ministry.

Bibliography

"Black Holiness-Pentecostalism." In *Dictionary of Pentecostal and Charismatic Movements,* ed. S. M. Burgess, G. B. McGee, and P. H. Alexander. Grand Rapids, Mich.: Zondervan, 1988.

Cornelius, L. J. *The Pioneer History of the Church of God in Christ.* Privately published, 1975.

Lovett, L. "Aspects of the Spiritual Legacy of the Church of God in Christ: Ecumenical Implications." *Midstream* 24, no. 4 (1985): 389–97.

Mason, M. E. *The History and Life Work of Elder C. H. Mason and His Co-Laborers.* Privately published, 1934.

Nelson, D. J. *A Brief History of the Church of God in Christ.* Privately published, 1934.

Please, C. H. *Fifty Years of Achievement: The Church of God in Christ.* Privately published, 1975.

Ross, G. *History and Formative Years of the Church of God in Christ.* Memphis, Tenn.: Church of God in Christ Publishing House, 1969.

Prepared by Leonard Lovett, Ph.D., senior pastor, the Church at the Crossroads, Los Angeles.

WORLDWIDE CHURCH OF GOD

General Description

The Worldwide Church of God has congregations in 120 countries and a membership of 94,000. The weekly attendance, in 780 congregations, averages 135,000, which includes members, prospective members, and their families.

Beliefs and Doctrines

The church accepts the Virgin Birth, the deity of Jesus, his atoning death and resurrection, new life by baptism, the immersion in God's Holy Spirit of sinful lives, the inspiration of the Scriptures, both Old and New Testaments (it rejects the Apocrypha, except as a historical document), and teaches obedience to God's laws, including the Ten Commandments, but always in the spirit in which Christ had magnified the law.

The Christian life begins at baptism (which follows repentance of one's sins) and culminates in the kingdom of God. In the present life, the Christian must develop God's character by transforming himself through the help of God's Holy Spirit, with all diligence and sincerity. He supports the mission of the church with his prayers, time and knowledge, tithes and offerings, and tries to follow Christ's example in his personal and family life.

The church accepts the biblical account of creation as accurate. It teaches salvation by faith through grace after repentance, baptism, and the laying on of hands. It considers smoking and drunkenness to be sins, but it does not prohibit the use of alcohol in moderation.

Organization

Each congregation is led by a pastor and served by elders (who pray for the sick) and deacons and deaconesses (who plan and organize church activities). All ministers are directed by the pastor general, who communicates with the ministry through an official bulletin, the *Pastor General's Report*. He also oversees various church publications (*Plain Truth* and *Good News*, the Ambassador College Bible correspondence courses, the *Worldwide News*, telecasts, and all youth literature, such as *Youth '90* and Youth Bible Lessons) and heads committees that examine various facets of the activities of the church. The pastor general is advised by the Council of Elders, which meets regularly to discuss various major issues.

Founder

The present structure of the church was initially developed by Herbert W. Armstrong, whose background was in a small Church of God with headquarters in Stanberry, Missouri. Because of a regular radio broadcast, the Church of God was first called "The Radio Church of God" and was so incorporated in 1933.

In 1947 the church headquarters moved to Pasadena, California, and in 1968 the name of the church was changed to the Worldwide Church of God, so as to reflect its international character. Armstrong died in January 1986, at the age of ninety-four, having led the church for more than fifty years. He was succeeded by Joseph W. Tkach, who previously had headed the Church Administration Department under Armstrong.

Forms of Worship

The church does not use statues or pictures of Christ, Mary, or the saints; neither do the ministers wear special clothing. The church worships in rented halls, in central locations easily accessible to the majority of members in each area. Apart from regular Sabbath (Saturday) services, members have the opportunity to attend Bible studies, social functions, and dances organized by the church.

The service consists of opening and closing prayers, a short message, special music, and a sermon of about one hour. The service lasts a total of two hours.

The church encourages family attendance and fellowship. These are officially promoted through afterservice gatherings, and special functions, with emphasis on cultural activities for senior citizens and the youth.

Contributions and Influence

The church has an outreach program for the immediate community and a large-scale involvement in philanthropic projects around the world. It cooperates with the Red Cross, for example, in providing relief for the victims of the Armenian disaster, hurricane Hugo, and the San Francisco earthquake.

Through the Ambassador Foundation, the church has assisted disadvantaged people in Jordan, Sri Lanka, Thailand, Haiti, Kenya, the Philippines, and other countries. It has also played an active role in promoting projects of a cultural nature, such as in the establishment of the International Shakespeare Globe Center in London.

The church sponsors Ambassador College, with campuses in California and Texas, and a renowned performing-arts season in the prestigious Ambassador Auditorium. Among the events, these art seasons have included performances by the late Artur Rubinstein and Vladimir Horowitz and by the Berlin Philharmonic. It also sponsors Imperial Schools in Pasadena, where student enrollment is more than 375 in grades K–12.

The church produces "The World Tomorrow," a television and radio program that airs in Australia, Canada, the Caribbean, and Europe, as well as the United States. In addition to the magazines previously mentioned, the church publishes books, booklets, and various brochures. The literature of the church discusses biblical, theological, and current local and global issues. Readers of the church literature also have the opportunity to write to a Personal Correspondence Department for answers to specific questions. The literature and social services of the church are available to all and are rendered free of charge or obligation.

Significant Terms

Pastor general. Chief administrative and ecclesiastical authority over the Worldwide Church of God.

Council of elders. A group of senior ministers who comment and provide advice on doctrinal and other matters of the church.

Bibliography

Dart, John. "Two TV Ministers Rise above Bible Belt." *Los Angeles Times*, April 1, 1989, sec. 2, p. 6.

De Groot, Paul. "Focus on Issues Propels 'World Tomorrow.'" *Edmonton Journal*, October 7, 1989, p. 76.

Melton, Gorgon J. "Worldwide Church of God." *Encyclopedia of American Religions*. 3d ed. Detroit: Gale Research, 1988.

Recapturing True Values: The Story of the Worldwide Church of God. Pasadena, Calif.: Ambassador Publishing, 1990.

The Plain Truth. Pasadena, Calif.: Worldwide Church of God (monthly).

Prepared by Michael A. Snyder, APR, assistant director, Public Affairs.

• • •

CHURCH OF THE BRETHREN

General Information

The Church of the Brethren is an American Protestant denomination with approximately 155,000 members and 1,050 congregations. Before 1908 their official name was German Baptist Brethren, but they were sometimes referred to by nicknames such as Dunkars, Tunkers, and Dunkards. The highest governing authority in the denomination is the Annual Conference, which consists of delegates from local congregations. The Annual Conference determines policy for the church and elects the twenty-five members of the General Board to carry out its policies. The board, in turn, employs staff members, some of whom work in Elgin, Illinois, and some at the Brethren Service Center in New Windsor, Maryland. Both the Brethren Press and the Brethren Historical Library and Archives are located at the Elgin address. The two major periodicals of the Brethren are *Messenger* (formerly *Gospel Messenger*), which operates out of the Elgin offices, and *Brethren Life and Thought,* a journal published jointly by the Brethren Journal Association and Bethany Theological Seminary.

History

The church was founded in 1708 in Schwarzenau, Germany, by a group of eight persons dissatisfied with the existing German churches. While this group of people was part of the Pietist movement, they were also strongly influenced by the Anabaptists. The leader of this group of eight was Alexander Mack, Sr. (1679–1735). Other major leaders during the eighteenth century were Peter Becker, Alexander Mack, Jr., John Naas, and Christopher Sauer, Jr. Between 1719 and 1733 the Brethren migrated to the colony of Pennsylvania and settled in the area around Germantown. Over the next 150 years, the Brethren spread southward and westward. Currently, the heaviest concentrations of Brethren are in Pennsylvania, Maryland, Virginia, Ohio, Indiana, Illinois, Kansas, and California.

Divisions among the Brethren have not been unusual. As early as 1723, Johann Conrad Biessell separated himself from the Conestoga congregation in order to found the Ephrata Cloister. During the early 1800s, major divisions occurred with the separation of a conservative and a progressive group from the larger body. As a result of these divisions and later divisions, there are now several major branches of the Brethren, in addition to the Church of the Brethren. These branches include the Old German Baptist Brethren (1881), the Brethren Church (1833), the Fellowship of Grace Brethren Church (1939), and the Dunkard Brethren (1926).

Beliefs and Doctrines

The Brethren have many doctrines in common with mainstream Protestants. Unlike many Protestant groups, however, they do not have a creed. Instead of a creed, they claim the New Testament as the rule of their faith and practice. In addition, the Brethren give a special emphasis to the following: pacifism, the simple life, nonconformity to the world, temperance, and service to others.

Forms of Worship

The Brethren practice baptism by threefold immersion, anointing for healing, laying on of hands for special commissioning, and the love feast. The love feast, which is uniquely Brethren, consists of an examination period, the practice of foot washing as described in John 13, a fellowship meal, and the Eucharist.

Contributions and Influence

Because of the Brethren doctrine of pacifism, they have become known as one of the three historic peace churches in the United States. This peace emphasis has led them to call their members to object conscientiously to participation in military service as well as to work to promote peace among the nations of the world. Their concern for Christian service has led them to many relief projects and service programs in the twentieth century. Of particular note are (1) Heifer Project International, which was begun in 1938 by a Brethren, Dan West, and became an official program of the Brethren Service Committee in 1942; (2) Sales Exchange for Refuge Rehabilitation Vocations (SERV), a nonprofit program to market handcrafts made by artisans around the world; and (3) Brethren Volunteer Service (BVS), which challenges young men and women to give a year of service in projects around the world.

In light of the gospel call to evangelism, since 1876 Brethren have been involved in foreign mission activities. The countries in which the Brethren have done extensive mission work are China, India, Nigeria, and Ecuador. Because of the Brethren's concern for the ecumenical church and the need for Christians to serve others, they participate in both the National Council of the Churches of Christ and the World Council of Churches.

Significant Terms

Anointing. The practice, based on James 5:14-16, whereby the sick are anointed with oil for healing.

Avoidance. A term used to describe the former practice of having no interaction (religious, social, or business) with an erring member.

Foot washing. An element of the love feast whereby members wash the feet of other members following the example of Jesus Christ.

Nonconformity. The doctrine that calls Brethren to be a separate ("peculiar") people who turn their backs on the non-Christian ways of the world.

Nonresistance. Readiness to suffer attack and persecution rather than retaliate or resort to violence (Matt. 5:39).

Order of the Brethren. A term used during the nineteenth century in reference to the ordinances, polity, and attitudes of the Brethren.

Simple life. A twentieth-century term used to describe the Brethren's concern to practice plainness in their daily living. This practice dates back to Brethren beginnings and is based on Matthew 6:25–34.

Bibliography

(All items are published by Brethren Press, Elgin, Ill.)
Durnbaugh, Donald F., ed. *Church of the Brethren: Yesterday and Today.* 1986.
——. *European Origins of the Brethren.* 1958.
Sappington, Roger E. *The Brethren in the New Nation.* 1976.
——, ed. *The Brethren in Industrial America.* 1985.

Prepared by Kenneth M. Shaffer, Jr., director, Brethren Historical Library and Archives.

CHURCH OF THE
NEW JERUSALEM

General Description

The General Convention of the New Jerusalem Church in the U.S.A. is the sister of the General Conference of the New Church in Great Britain, with missionary interests throughout the Far East, Egypt, Nigeria, and South Africa and branches in Europe, Australia, and New Zealand. Its teachings are based on theological writings of Swedenborg.

Swedenborg founded no sect per se. The organized New Church was first established by his readers in 1788. The General Convention of the New Jerusalem in America first met in 1817, and was incorporated in 1981. It now has some 5,000 members in 62 churches throughout the United States and Canada. There are 50 ordained ministers (with 10 overseas), and a theological school in Cambridge, Massachusetts.

Founder

Emanuel Swedenborg (1688–1772), was an eminent Swedish scientist, philosopher, and theologian with an encyclopedic mind. Swedenborg made original contributions in the areas of astronomy (nebula hypothesis) and physiology (brain and ductless glands) and on the relationship between life and matter. From the age of fifty-five he experienced psychic changes, leading to the opening of spiritual sight. During the last twenty-five years of his life, Swedenborg was actively conscious in both heaven and hell and aware of the philosophical principles underlying life after death, which showed the relationship between spiritual and natural worlds.

Swedenborg produced commentaries on the Bible, expanding the "science of correspondence" and giving the inner meaning of Genesis, Exodus, and Revelation. He wrote on providence, marital love, and other topics. His central doctrine, however, is the sole divinity of the glorified Jesus Christ, whose soul is "God-in-Father," whose body (or humanity) is "God-the-Son," and whose outflowing life is "the Holy Spirit." He insisted on the primacy of love and the need for practical application of religion to life. Swedenborg believed himself to be the herald of a new age, called the New Church, foreseen in Revelation 21–22 and the New Jerusalem. He asserted that the former age, or "church," was terminated by the Last Judgment in the spiritual world, witnessed by him in 1757. The increased flow of spiritual life into the world following that event is "the Lord's second coming," which has come through the opening of the divine word.

Forms of Worship and Organization

The Church of the New Jerusalem follows the conventional Protestant tradition, with liturgical forms of worship. The emphasis is placed on the spiritual nature of man and his survival after death. Its church government is focused on congregations, with a national president (a minister) and a vice-president (a layman). Between annual conventions, the church's affairs on a national level are handled by an elected general council.

Secessionist Group

The General Church of the New Jerusalem is a secessionist group and has an episcopal government. They accept the theological writings of Swedenborg as part of the Word of God. They have a community at Bryn Athyn, Pennsylvania, with a cathedral and schools ("the Academy"). There are also centers in Chicago, in Kitchener, Ontario, and elsewhere. The secession group now has some 4,200 members in the United States, Canada, England, and Australia, and scattered members in other countries. There are 75 ordained ministers.

Contributions and Influence

The church's impact is admittedly out of all proportion to its size, mostly because of the influence of Swedenborg on Carlyle, Coleridge, the Brownings, Blake, Balzac, Goethe, and others and, in the United States, on Emerson, Whittier, Phillips Brooks, Joseph Fort Newton, Edwin Markham, and Helen Keller, to mention a few. Many changes in religious thought since Swedenborg's day have been harmonious with his teachings.

Significant Terms

Conjugal. A translation of Swedenborg's Latin word *conjugialis,* meaning "lover; pertaining to marriage." When Swedenborg says, "Love truly conjugal," the meaning is an eternal relationship intended by the Lord between men and women.

Correspondence. A concept basic to Swedenborgianism, correspondence is both a causal and a functional relation between the divine and all lower degrees of life. It is the law or mode of divine inflow of creation.

Divine-human. The central idea in the theology of the New Church. This term applies to the Lord Jesus Christ after his glorification and thus refers to divine love in human form, "All the fullness of living deity in bodily form" (Col. 2:9).

Grand-man. Refers to the entire heavens and the "body" of the Lord, or the Lord's kingdom, including heaven and the church on earth.

Proprium. This word means "selfhood" and is simply a Latin word Swedenborg employed. A key concept in this faith is that man is not life but a receiver of life. And yet God grants to him the feeling that he has a wholly independent life. This is proprium. If man insists arrogantly that he lives of himself instead of from God, this proprium is folly.

Remains. This refers to the impression of love and truth implanted in a person by the Lord in ways unknown and "remaining" with the person from infancy through the rest of life, serving as a basis for rebirth.

Wisdom. Seldom used to refer to possession of great knowledge, this term is usually predicated only of life. It consists of perceiving, willing, and doing what is true from love. A wise person has a constant desire for doing good that is based on truth.

Bibliography

Keller, Helen. *My Religion.* New York: Swedenborg Foundation, 1986.

Scalding, J. H. *Introduction to Swedenborg's Religious Thought.* New York: Swedenborg Publishing Company, 1956.

Sigstedt, C. *Swedenborg Epic.* New York: Bookman Associates, 1952; London, Swedenborg Society, 1981.

Toksvig, Signe. *Emanuel Swedenborg: Scientist and Mystic.* Yale University Press, Newsletter, 1948.

Prepared by Don L. Rose, assistant pastor, Bryn Athyn Church of the New Jerusalem, Bryn Athyn, Pennsylvania.

• • •
CONGREGATIONALISTS
EVANGELICAL CONGREGATIONAL CHURCH

General Description

The Evangelical Congregational (EC) Church is a denomination that dates back to an evangelical movement in the United States as early as the Civil War. The church is Wesleyan in structure and originated as the Evangelical Association. As the church grew, its constituency began to be polarized over church polity, which was autocratic and dictatorial, and over the erosion of basic doctrines. In 1894 a minority group formed that was designated the United Evangelical Church. In 1922 an effort was made to reunite the Evangelical Association and the United Evangelical Church, but the effort was largely unsuccessful. The United Evangelical Church, which was very democratic in character, grew rapidly from 1894 until 1922. Two features distinguished the United Evangelical Church from the Evangelical Association: (1) the members of each church elected a lay delegate along with the pastor as members of the Annual Conference, which determined the policies of the entire ecclesiastical body; and (2) the local congregation held ownership of its property and determined its own membership. It was a spiritual church with a strong emphasis on conversion and growth in the grace of God through Jesus Christ. The United Evangelical Church later changed its name to Evangelical Congregational Church.

The denomination consists of approximately 37,000 members in the United States, exercising ministries primarily in New Jersey, Pennsylvania, Ohio, Indiana, Illinois, Kentucky, Texas, and Mexico. The EC missionary work covers the entire globe via independent faith mission boards. There is never a moment day or night in which someone is not ministering the gospel throughout the world.

Founder

The EC Church shares its founder with the one element of the current United Methodist Church conglomerate. The Evangelical Association later merged with the United Brethren to form the Evangelical United Brethren, which later merged with the Methodist Church to become the present United Methodist Church. Jacob Albright, born of Pennsylvania German parentage in 1759, is the founder of this entire movement. Albright was a drummer in the Revolutionary War. In addition to farming in Lancaster County, Pennsylvania, Albright was a tile maker—he made an orange-red type of ceramic tile that formed the roofs of many buildings of his day. Albright was an honest, hardworking businessman with all of the elements of secular success, but he was not happy or at peace within himself. In 1790 Albright's internal unrest was tested when he lost several children in a dysentery epidemic.

Through a reformed pietistic minister, Anthony Houtz, Albright was confronted with his deep spiritual lack, convicted by the Holy Spirit, and eventually was converted to Jesus Christ. He immediately began studying the Word of God, and he began to grow spiritually. This newfound love for God evidenced itself in a concern for the spiritual welfare of his neighbors and friends. As his friends accepted the finished work of Christ as payment for their redemption, they also wanted to study God's Word. The result was that Bible classes sprang up, and Albright gave less and less of his time to tile making and more and more to teaching and disciplining people. He originally worked within the framework of his home Methodist Church. The Methodist Church, however, was moving away from German-speaking worship to the mother tongue of their newly occupied country, namely, English. The new immigrants, however, did not understand English sufficiently to read and study the Bible and wanted to use their native German. Since the Methodist Church had little or no interest in perpetuating the German language, Albright and the Methodists had a friendly parting of the ways. But he used the Methodist discipline to formulate doctrines and polity for the Evangelical Association. Albright's early ministry involved circuit riding to lead Bible class groups. Once the groups were formed into a denomination, Bishop John Seybert became the first bishop to be elected to that office.

Beliefs and Doctrines

The EC Church today continues to adhere to the basic doctrines of early Methodism. It embraces a conservative, Bible-centered, evangelical interpretation of the fundamentals of Scripture. The church endorses the Apostle's Creed; it holds to one true and living God who is eternal and consists of three unified persons—Father, Son, and Holy Spirit; it declares that Jesus Christ is God's only begotten Son and that he enacted God's plan of redemption via his sacrificial death on the cross (man has no other means of eternal salvation). The church claims that the Holy Spirit convicts and seals the work of salvation, gives peace, joy, and so forth to all who come to God via Jesus Christ, and it holds that the Father enacts the official work of this transaction.

The EC Church teaches that the Bible is God's holy Word as recorded in the canon of sixty-six books that form the Old and New Testaments—therein only is contained God's way of redemption. Extrabiblical information is not an equal of Scripture in that the Bible originates from God and is fully inspired by God through human, godly authorship. The EC Church embraces the second coming of Jesus Christ, the resurrection of Jesus Christ, and eternal life only through Jesus Christ. Outside of Jesus Christ all men are eternally lost and in need of redemption. Man cannot redeem himself; without redemption, he would be eternally lost in hell. The sacraments of the church are baptism and the Lord's Supper (known as the Holy Communion or Eucharist). The basic doctrinal position of the EC Church is both Reformed and Arminian.

Forms of Worship

The EC Church has no written standard for liturgy, although there is an unwritten worship order. The service of worship on Sunday morning is usually more formal than the Sunday evening worship. A flexibility allows for the inclusion of alternate forms into the service. Worship basically includes the announcement time, offering, friendship time, a choir anthem, and a children's message or children's church. The main core of the worship is the preaching/teaching of the Word of God and a benediction. Sunday evenings may be more an informal Bible study and discussion time.

Organization

The EC Church has both congregational and episcopal elements in its structure. The church is congregational in that it determines its own membership and owns its own property. It is democratic in church spirit, but its polity also includes a bishop and district superintendents, a general conference every four years, the Annual Conference, and a local conference that presides over the local church. The local church has an official board that presides over all subdivisions and committees under it. Trustees form the property committee, and stewards form the finance committee. Each pastor is appointed to a church by a supervisory committee of the Annual Conference.

The bishop and district superintendents are elected by the Annual Conference and may serve a total of two four-year terms. The selection of one lay delegate and one ministerial delegate per church protects the balance of power within the denomination.

Contributions and Influence

The EC Church is a member denomination of the National Association of Evangelicals. This involvement allows the church to have a voice in all social, moral, and spiritual issues in Washington, D.C., and on the state level. Several of its ministers have served in the chaplaincy of the armed forces, and numerous constituents have served in local, county, state, and federal political capacities. Evangelical Congregationalists have influenced a number of important issues in the United States, such as abortion, drugs, education, literature, the entertainment field, and philanthropic giving.

Significant Terms

Bishop. The episcopal leader who presides over the entire denomination, including the General Conference and the annual conferences; he is an ex officio member of all boards and agencies of the denomination and presides over the placement of all ministers.

Conferences. The EC Church comprises two conferences, known as the Eastern and Western Conference of the Evangelical Congregational Church.

District superintendents. These leaders serve districts within the conference areas of the EC Church.

Official board. The chief decision-making body of the local church.

Minister. The person who serves a local church or charge.

Charge. One of several churches under one minister.

Bibliography

Albright, Raymond W. *A History of the Evangelical Church.* Harrisburg, Pa.: Evangelical Press, 1956.

Wilson, Robert S. *History of the Evangelical Congregational Church.* Myerstown, Pa. (personally published), 1976.

Prepared by Glenn A. Miller, pastor, Plymouth Meeting Evangelical Congregational Church, Plymouth Meeting, Pennsylvania.

NATIONAL ASSOCIATION OF CONGREGATIONAL CHRISTIAN CHURCHES OF THE UNITED STATES

General Description

The Congregational Christian Churches are a fellowship of 400 churches, an association that is independent of any other larger religious body or area. Following seventeen years of discussions, arguments, legal suits, and name calling, 150 persons met in Detroit, Michigan, in 1955 to form our Association of Free Congregational Churches, determined that they did not want to join with the Evangelical and Reformed Church to form the United Church of Christ.

Our association, through its autonomous churches, its 800 ministers and 90,000 laypersons, emphasizes faith, freedom, and fellowship. We are a fellowship of self-governing churches, voluntarily working together in area associations, state conferences, and various national council and mission bodies, with control and authority reserved to the local church.

Founder

The first moderator of this association was John H. Alexander. Neither he nor anyone else, however, can be considered the founder, or even a major leader. In accordance with the Free Congregational tradition, Alexander served for a term of one year and presided at the meetings of the newly formed association in 1955, the first year of its existence.

Beliefs and Doctrines

As a fellowship of convenantal churches, there are no formal doctrinal statements within our association. Mary Woolsey, editor of *The Congregationalist*, wrote, "You may describe Congregationalists as Christ-following people who have the responsibility to remain alert to the ideology and teaching of Christ as it is revealed to us through prayer, meditation, Bible study and fellowship."

Forms of Worship

In our 400 member churches, the typical form of worship includes the commonly practiced Bible readings, prayers, music, sermon, and collection.

Organization

The unique feature of our fellowship (we prefer not to use the word "organization") is that there is no hierarchy. The autonomous, member churches are the ultimate authority. This is congregationalism in action.

Serving as the association, ad interim, is the twelve-member Executive Committee, which comprises both ministers and laypersons. Each year, four members complete their four-year terms, and four new persons are elected to this committee. The chairmen serve for one year.

Contributions and Influence

Pilgrims belonging to the so-called Free Congregational Way strengthened the purpose of the settlers of America, who came to this country seeking life, liberty, and the pursuit of happiness. A specific contribution to life in the United States comes from the Congregational insistence on a highly educated ministry. In England, there were colleges at London, Cambridge, Oxford, and elsewhere. In the United States, both Yale and Harvard were established by Congregationalists as well as numerous other ministries of higher learning.

Significant Terms

Congregational. Literally, "of or relating to a congregation" (an organized local group meeting regularly for worship and other religious purposes), the fundamental unit of congregational polity.

Congregational polity. Sometimes said simply to be "independence"; it refers to the governance of local religious groups autonomously and to the administration of their affairs by congregational decision. Congregational polity is also found among the Baptists, Unitarians, Disciples of Christ, and others. The National Association of Congregational Christian Churches is one of the viable symbols of a free Christian Church in America.

Congregational theology. Although it began within the fold of New England theology, with the Westminster Confession and the Savoy Declaration, which are Calvinistic, Congregationalists have debated most of the Calvinistic issues (e.g., freedom and moral responsibility), all of which mitigated Calvinistic severity and allowed Congregational theology to be more liberal.

Covenantal. Literally, "relating to promises, or a covenant," an agreement made by two or more parties or naming members of a church to hold to points of doctrine, faith, and so forth, as they promised in the covenant.

Liberty (of conscience). The freedom of choice in relation to religion and its practices, including the interpretation of the Scriptures, a freedom that is guaranteed by the Congregational Christian Churches.

The Congregational Way. The name given to one group of New England Pilgrims, who ultimately led to the compromise between Presbyterians and Congregationalists. The Congregational Christians are the custodians of the Pilgrim heritage; although this heritage is cherished, the Congregational Christian Churches do not worship their noble past.

National Association of Congregational Christian Churches of the United States. A national fellowship of self-governing churches voluntarily working together. Control and authority rest with the local church. This makes it possible to provide fellowship and service for everyone.

Pilgrim ideals. A continued expression of three simple truths: (1) each individual is free to follow Christ according to his or her conscience; (2) each church is a complete ecclesiastical organization with the right to self-government in all matters; and (3) each church, while autonomous, may choose to be part of a fellowship of churches bound together by love rather than legal or ecclesiastical authority.

Bibliography

Abercrombie, A. V. *The Congregational Christian Way of Inter-Church Fellowship*. Oak Creek, Wis.: National Association of Congregational Christian Churches, 1988.

Atkins, G. C., and F. L. Fegley. *History of American Congregationalism*. Boston: Pilgrim Press, 1942.

Gray, H. D. *Congregational Handbook*. Phoenix: Seven Seas Publications, 1984.

Kohl, M. W. *Congregationalism in America*. Oak Creek, Wis.: Congregational Press, 1977.

Rouner, A. A. *The Congregational Way of Life*. Englewood Cliffs, N.J.: Prentice-Hall, 1960.

Prepared by J. Fred Rennebohm, executive secretary, with the assistance of Rev. Dr. Henry Gray, Rev. Dr. Harry Butman, and Rev. Dr. Arthur Rouner, Jr.

UNITED CHURCH OF CHRIST

General Description

The United Church of Christ (UCC) was formed in 1957 by the union of the Congregational Christian Churches and the Evangelical and Reformed

Church. Each of these was itself a union of two groups. The Congregational Churches of the English Reformation with Puritan New England roots in America and the Christian Church with American frontier beginnings were both concerned for freedom of religious expression and local autonomy.

The Evangelical Synod of North America, a nineteenth-century German-American church of the frontier Mississippi Valley, and the Reformed Church in the United States, initially composed of early eighteenth-century churches in Pennsylvania and neighboring colonies, were of German and Swiss heritage, conscientious carriers of the Reformed and Lutheran traditions of Reformation. They united in 1934.

The United Church of Christ—passionate in its impulse to unity, committed to "liberty of conscience inherent in the gospel," biblical people under a mutual covenant for responsible freedom in Christ—seeks to complement freedom with order. At present, the UCC comprises 1,400 congregations and over 1.6 million members. Its greatest strength is in the northeast part of the United States.

Leaders

Among the leaders of antecedent bodies of the United Church of Christ were Philip Schaff, John Nevin, Louis Aduard Nollau, Adolph Baltzer, Robert Browne, John Robinson, John Cotton, Jonathan Edwards, John Eliot, Henry Ward Beecher, and Barton W. Stone. Among leaders of the United Church of Christ since its formation have been James Wagner, Fred Hoskins, Louis Goebel, George Hastings, Sheldon Mackey, Fred Buschmeyer, Truman Douglass, Howard Spragg, Alford Carlton, David Stowe, Ben Herbster, Robert V. Moss, Joseph Evans, Avery D. Post, Everett C. Parker, Roger Shinn, Shelby Rooks, Scott Libbey, Carol Joyce, Yvonne Delk, and Reuben Sheares.

Beliefs and Doctrines

The doctrines of the UCC are essentially those of the several streams of its heritage, with emphasis given to "in essentials, unity; in nonessentials, liberty; in all things, charity." The church honors the historic creeds and confessions of the church, but as testimonies rather than as tests of faith. The UCC has, both in its national and its regional and local settings, laid emphasis upon "doing" as well as "hearing" and "speaking" the gospel.

Organization

The General Synod of the United Church meets every two years. Its 675 to 725 delegates are elected by the thirty-nine conferences that encompass the congregations of the UCC. The General Synod, a representative body, approves the budget of the UCC and nominates and elects the officers of the church: the corporate members of the instrumentalities and the Executive

Council. In maintains the treasury of the UCC, determines ecumenical relationships, and adopts and amends the UCC Constitution and Bylaws.

The Executive Council is the General Synod ad interim and is the focal point of decision making and national overall planning, evaluating, and budgeting. It serves as the Business Committee of Reference of the General Synod and maintains an open channel for minority and dissenting opinions.

National instrumentalities and other national bodies include the United Church Board for World Ministries, the United Church Board for Homeland Ministries, the Pension Boards, the Office for Church Life and Leadership, the Office for Church in Society, the Center for Women in Church and Society, and the Commission for Racial Justice. The boards are responsible to directories that are elected by their corporate bodies. The directories of other bodies are responsible to the General Synod.

The Council for Racial and Ethnic Ministries coordinates the activities for the Pacific Islands and Asian American Ministries, Council for Hispanic Ministries, American Indian Ministry, United Black Christians, and Ministers for Racial and Social Justice. A broad spectrum of special interest groups are approved each biennium to give voice to persons and groups that otherwise might not be heard by the General Synod.

Local congregations and ministers hold their standing in associations, each of which is related to one of the thirty-nine conferences of the UCC.

Contributions and Influence

The UCC is a uniting church. It is related to the Christian Church (Disciples of Christ) in an ecumenical partnership relationship and to other Protestant denominations through the Consultation on Church Union, the National Council of Churches of Christ in the U.S.A., and the World Council of Churches. The UCC is among the most liberal and socially active denominations in the United States. It is not because all of its members are of one mind on individual issues; they are not. Rather, the UCC has traditionally affirmed a pluralism that allows for a variety of individual and common witnesses, including such diverse perspectives as the Biblical Witness Fellowship, the Gay and Lesbian Caucus, UCC Military Chaplains, and Conscientious Objectors. The church, especially its national expression, has endorsed many liberal causes and opposed politically conservative ones.

The UCC has an indirect influence upon U.S. religious life that is beyond its proportionate strength in the general population. The Washington Office of the Office for Church in Society carries on efforts to inform and influence the federal government on policies endorsed by the General Synod.

Significant Terms

Associations of the United Church of Christ (within a conference of the UCC).
The bodies composed of all local churches in a geographic area, all ordained

ministers holding standing therein, and so on. Associations typically meet once or twice each year for fellowship and business.

Conference. The bodies of the UCC that are composed of all local churches in a geographic area, all ordained ministers, and its associations and licensed ministers. Conferences generally meet annually and include lay delegates selected by and representing local churches of the conference or ordained ministers holding standing.

General Synod. The representative body of the UCC, composed of delegates chosen by the conference and former officers. It meets every two years.

Local autonomy. The UCC defines itself as having as its base unit of life and organization the local church; of this we say, "The autonomy of the local church is inherent and modifiable only by its own action." The UCC constitutionally protects this right, limiting the conferences and synod to "describing and recommending."

Our church's wider mission. A phrase referring to the total work of the UCC's conferences, national agencies, and related institutions. It is the entity that inspires giving by local congregations to the general work of the church.

Bibliography

Gunneman, Louis H. *The Shaping of the United Church of Christ.* New York: United Church Press, 1977.

——. *United and Uniting.* New York: United Church Press, 1987.

Horton, Douglas. *The United Church of Christ.* New York: Thomas Nelson & Sons, 1962.

Paul, Robert S. *Freedom with Order.* New York: United Church Press, 1987.

United Church of Christ: History and Program. 4th ed. New York: United Church Press, 1982.

Zikmund, Barbara Brown, ed. *Hidden Histories in the United Church of Christ.* New York: Pilgrim Press, 1984.

Prepared by Charles W. Cooper, Jr., assistant to the president.

EASTERN ORTHODOX
(GREEK) CHURCH

General Description

The Eastern Orthodox Church is a historical church founded by Jesus Christ and established by his holy apostles, embracing some 280 million members of diverse national and linguistic groups. It is the original church from which the Roman Catholic Church severed her unity and in turn from which Protestantism broke away. It was founded and exists for the redemption of all members of the human race.

Founder

The true founder is the coeternal and consubstantial Son and Logos of God, who "became flesh" and walked the face of the earth—Jesus Christ. Christ commissioned twelve disciples and apostles to establish his church and carry his gospel of salvation "to the uttermost parts of the earth," hence the designation "apostolic" church. The holy fathers and doctors are the immediate successors by ordination of the apostles, who continued their apostolic ministry of preaching the word, administering the sacraments, and shepherding the church.

Jesus Christ is the only head of the church. All the apostles are equal in authority, and all bishops, who follow the apostles in succession of ordination, perpetuate this equality. No single authoritative head over the entire church exists.

Beliefs and Doctrines

The divine Logos is the eternal principle of true religion, true government, respectively as absolute Priest, Prophet (Professor), and King.

Christ is both true God and true man, born of the Virgin Mary and of the Holy Spirit, and declared for three years the revelation of God the Father. He was delivered into the hands of wicked men, suffered, died upon the cross, was buried, arose on the third day, and ascended into heaven on the fortieth day. The fullness of the Godhead was disclosed by Christ as divine, consubstantial, and undivided Trinity—Father, Son, and Holy Spirit: three persons (hypostases) with a common essence or nature *(homoousios)*.

The Bible (Old and New Testaments) is the divinely inspired writing through which God reveals his will to men of all generations, speaking through the prophets and apostles.

Redemption is experienced in the life of the church, in which the Holy Spirit indwells, leading the chosen people of God "into all truth."

Baptism, confirmation, and Holy Communion are administered together in the initiatory rite of regeneration. Infants are always recipients of this threefold redemptive sacrament. Baptism is by triple immersion, and the Communion is administered as blessed leavened bread and wine.

Apostolic succession is essential to the authenticity of the church, including tactual succession of ordinations traceable to the apostles in an unbroken continuity, coupled always with the purity of apostolic doctrine and conforming to the doctrines and canons of the first seven ecumenical councils.

Worship

The Holy Eucharist is the chief corporate act of worship. It is the reexperiencing of the death and resurrection of Christ by sharing in his body and blood offered on the table of the Last Supper. It is the renewal of union with Christ, the forgiveness of sins, and the reassurance of eternal life. The church, as the body of Christ, thereby renews her identity with her divine Head.

Organization

The Eastern Orthodox Church in her totality is a federation of self-governing churches, with the Ecumenical Patriarchate of Constantinople as the primus inter pares—first in authority of honor by reason of being originally in the capital city of the Roman Empire. Each patriarch, archbishop, or bishop is the chief shepherd of each self-governing church, with the priests in his jurisdiction as pastors of the flocks entrusted to them and deacons to assist the priests in worship and pastoral administration.

The Holy Spirit remains the final authority within the church, in accordance with the promises of her divine Founder. The conscience of the church is the manifestation of the Spirit of Christ, which becomes articulated as regards dogma and discipline in ecumenical councils, where the total aggregate of the episcopate serves as the authoritative voice of the church universal. The first seven ecumenical councils are those that govern the church.

Contributions and Influence

Orthodoxy stands as the fourth major faith, along with the Roman Catholic and Protestant churches and Judaism. Its contribution to religious life in the United States is increasing, with all national jurisdictions, numbering about 10 million, uniting mainly on social and moral issues confronting U.S. society. The Standing Conference of Bishops is the administrative body effectively promoting this unity. The Orthodox share in the National Council of Churches is proving significant, asserting itself as the major form of historical Christianity and witnessing to the purity of the faith and polity of the ancient undivided church in its ecumenical contacts.

Orthodoxy represents the embodiment of an entire cultural continuum and is not only a religion in the narrow sense. It is associated essentially and inseparably with unity in a world torn by pluralism and holds the key to the recovery of the religious and intellectual unity of Western society, which now faces extinction. It makes a contribution to the strengthening of the moral and spiritual fiber of American culture, assuming that a nation cannot hope to survive long without sustaining moral and spiritual values, and it reminds all that Western civilization needs reconversion.

Significant Terms

Catholic. Actually or potentially universal.

Orthodox. True belief.

Divine liturgy. Holy Eucharist or Communion service, the oldest recorded form of Christian worship.

Byzantine. Pertaining to the Christian Roman Empire centered in Byzantium, or to the imperial Constantinople.

Bibliography

Benz, Ernst. *The Eastern Orthodox Church: Its Thoughts and Life*. Translated by Richard Winston and Clara Winston. New York: Anchor Press, 1963.

Bulgakov, S. *The Orthodox Church*. London: Centenary Press, 1935.

Callinicos, C. *The Greek Orthodox Catechism*. New York: Greek Orthodox Church Diocese, 1953.

Efthimiou, Milton, ed. *History of the Greek Orthodox Church*. New York: Greek Orthodox Church Diocese, 1984.

Gavin, F. *Some Aspects of Contemporary Greek Orthodox Thought*. Milwaukee: Morehouse, 1923.

Lossky, V. *The Mystical Theology of the Eastern Church*. London: J. Clarke Publishing, 1957.

Makrakis, Apotles. *Divine and Sacred Catechism*. New York: Hellenistic Christian Education Board, 1946.

Ware, Kaloistos. *The Orthodox Church*. Baltimore: Penguin, 1963.

Prepared by Rev. Dr. Milton B. Efthimiou, Greek Orthodox Archdiocese of North and South America.

ARMENIAN ORTHODOX CHURCH

General Description

The Armenian Orthodox Church, also known as the Armenian Church, or the Church of Armenia, is called both apostolic and Orthodox, the latter being the commonly used adjective in Muslim countries.

The first Armenian parish in the United States was organized in 1889 in Worcester, Massachusetts, and ten years later the Diocese of the Armenian Church in America was established by order of His Holiness Catholicos Mkrtich Khrimian, who sent a bishop to Worcester, where headquarters were set up in the Church of Our Savior. The present diocesan headquarters of the eastern diocese is located in New York City, with St. Cartan as center of the diocesan complex. The California parishes were formed into a separate diocese in 1928, and the Canadian region in 1984.

The geographic areas of concentration are eastern Massachusetts and Rhode Island; metropolitan New York and New Jersey; Philadelphia and vicinity; greater Detroit; Chicago and its suburbs; in California, the San Joaquin and San Fernando valleys, Los Angeles and vicinity, and the San Francisco Bay area; and Toronto and Montreal in Canada. There are roughly 500,000 communicants in North America and 75 clergymen, bishops, and priests.

The Armenian Church is a member of the World Council of Churches, which it joined in 1963. In 1970 His Holiness Vazken, Catholicos of all Armenians, visited Pope Paul VI at the Vatican. The Armenian Orthodox Church is in communion with all members of the Oriental Orthodox Church family: Coptic, Ethiopian, Indian, and Syrian Orthodox churches.

Founder

The Church of Armenia traces its origins to Sts. Thaddeus and Bartholomew, two of the twelve apostles, who are referred to as the first enlighteners of Armenia, to distinguish them from the second enlightener, St. Gregory (c. 251–333; also called the illuminator), who established the Church of Armenia and brought it into touch with Christendom. Gregory was ordained a bishop soon after he had brought about the conversion of King Trinidates. Gregory built the first cathedral in 303 in Vagharshapat. It is still the official seat of the supreme head of the Armenian Orthodox Church. In 325 Aristakes, the son of Gregory, participated in the first ecumenical council at Nicea.

History

A major turning point in the history of the Armenian Church was the devising of the characters of the Armenian alphabet in 406, which made possible the translation of patristic works. A Synod of Armenian, Georgian, and Caspio-Albanian bishops was called in 506 at Dvin, the seat of the Armenian catholicos since 485, where the third ecumenical council of Ephesus (431) was proclaimed as faith, and Nestorianism and the acts of the Council of Chalcedon (451) rejected. Attempts at reunion first with the Greek Church, then with the Latin Church, and finally with the Byzantine Church were initiated by Catholicos St. Nersess the Gracious in the twelfth century, but he died before responses could reach him.

The Armenian Patriarchate of Turkey was created by the Ottoman rulers in 1461, soon after the conquest of Constantinople. A statute setting up the general administration of the patriarchate by the Armenian Church was proposed and approved by the Ottoman government in the nineteenth century, but it was annulled by the Turkish secular government in the 1920s. This was the same Turkish government that carried out genocide and deportations against the Christian population of the provinces during World War I, which dealt a severe blow to the Armenian Church. For instance, of the five thousand clergymen living in 1915, only four hundred were alive in 1923. Furthermore, with the Sovietization of the tiny Armenian Republic, the statute for the patriarchate was abrogated. However, in 1929, with the help of the Armenian patriarch of Jerusalem, Catholicos Sahak II established his seat at Antelias, north of Beirut, Lebanon, under French mandate.

Structure, Teachings, and Worship

The Armenian Church considers Holy Etchmiadzin, Armenia (USSR), as its hierarchical center, where His Holiness Catholicos Vasken I is the supreme patriarch catholicos, the 130th pontiff since St. Gregory the Enlightener. The central seminary is also at Holy Etchmiadzin, with three branches in Bikfaya (Lebanon), Jerusalem, and New Rochelle, New York (named after St. Nersess). Candidates to the priesthood may be chosen from among married men, but marriage may not follow ordination. Celibate priests are required to make perpetual vows, and candidates to the episcopate must be celibate. The supreme patriarch catholicos is elected in the General Assembly, composed of clerical and lay delegates from all the dioceses and the patriarchates.

The Armenian Church adopted the Gregorian calendar in 1922, which was introduced everywhere except in the Patriarchate of Jerusalem and in some dioceses in the Soviet Union. Theophany (Epiphany) and Christmas is still celebrated on January 6; the Armenian calendar is the only one that has kept the original usage, in spite of the popularity in the West of celebrating the Nativity on December 25.

The Armenian Church recognizes seven sacraments. The three traditional sacraments of Christian initiation—*baptism, confirmation,* and *Holy Communion*—are administered together. Baptism is usually by submersion, and confirmation follows immediately. Holy Communion is administered under both species by intinction, with the priest placing a broken portion of the wafer soaked in wine on the tongue of the communicant. The wafer is unleavened bread, baked by the priest on the day of the liturgy. It is circular in form and stamped with the sign of the cross. The wine must be undiluted by water. The divine liturgy is chanted in classical Armenian, with priest, deacon, and choir participating. (When unconfirmed members of other denominations request admission into the Armenian Church, they are not rebaptized, provided they show proof of having received a baptism in the Trinitarian formula. Their admission merely follows confirmation.)

The sacrament of *penance* includes confession and is treated as preparation for communion. *Ordination* up to the rank of deacon is performed by the imposition of hands. Priests, bishops, and the catholicos are ordained and anointed. Bishops may confer orders up to the rank of priests. The episcopate is conferred by the catholicos, with the assistance of two bishops. The catholicos is conferred by twelve bishops. *Marriage* is known as the sacrament of the crowning, for crowns are placed on the heads of the bride and groom by the priest, officiating under the authority of the bishop. *Anointing of the sick* is rarely administered, and the reason for its inclusion among the sacraments is not clear.

Contributions and Influence

The Armenian Church's stated goal in the United States is to serve as a "mother and father" to the Armenian community, as it has in other parts of the world for eight centuries. Despite their loss of political independence and of their recognition as citizens of a kingdom, the Armenian people have survived as both an ethnic and religious group down through the centuries. The Armenian Church serves as a spiritual and cultural center for American Armenians of all generations, thereby helping to preserve their rich identity.

Significant Terms

The Catholicos of all Armenians. The Catholicos, residing at Holy Etchmiadzin (Soviet Armenia), is known as Supreme Patriarch. He has the right to consecrate bishops, whereas the patriarchs have no such right. The catholicos of the House of Cilicia (Lebanon) has similar rights for the communities in his territorial jurisdiction.

Deaconess. There is historical evidence that ordained Armenian deaconesses served at the altar and performed all functions pertaining to deacons within the confines of convents, but not in parish churches. There were nunneries in Tiflis (Georgia), Ispaha (Iran), and Constantinople.

Mount Ararat. The most important geographic symbol of Armenian identity. Armenians call it the Mother of the World, and some say the Garden of Eden was located there; others say it was the resting place of Noah's ark after the great flood. It represents the fatherland to Armenians around the world.

Patriarch. The title reserved to the hierarch heading the Brotherhood of St. James in Jerusalem. This is an elective position with life tenure. The Armenian patriarch of Jerusalem is the custodian of Armenian rights in the main Christian shrines in the West Bank of Jerusalem. The jurisdiction of this position includes the Armenian Orthodox communities in Israel and Jordan. Its history dates from the Arab conquest in the seventh century.

The term "patriarch" also is reserved to the elected hierarch who attends to the religious needs of the Armenian churches in Istanbul and the interior provinces of Turkey. This is a lifetime position. The patriarchs of Armenians in Turkey began by an act of the Ottoman Turkish ruler soon after the fall of Byzantine Constantinople in the fifteenth century.

Bibliography

Arpee, Leon. *A History of Armenian Christianity.* New York: Armenian Mission Association of America, 1946.

Atiya, Aziz S. *History of Eastern Christianity.* South Bend, Ind.: University of Notre Dame Press, 1968.

Fortescue, E. F. K. *The Armenian Church.* New York: AMS Press, 1970.

Nersession, Sirarpie Der. *The Armenians.* New York: Praeger Publishers, 1970.

Ormania, Malachia. *The Church of Armenia.* 2d rev. ed. London: Mowbray, 1955.

Prepared by the editor from an article by Fr. Arten Ashjian, diocesan director of ecumenical relations, and other materials furnished by him.

COPTIC ORTHODOX CHURCH

General Description

The Coptic Orthodox Church was also known as the Church of Alexandria, named for the city of its origin. The words "Copt" and "Egyptian" are identical in meaning, derived from the Greek word *aigyptios.* The Copts are neither Semitic nor Hamitic, but rather Mediterranean.

The first parish in North America was organized in Toronto, Canada, in 1965, and the Diocese of North America was established with the Coptic pope as its bishop. Later, in 1970, parishes were organized in New York and New Jersey, with St. Mark's Church as the diocesan headquarters in Jersey City, New Jersey. Geographic areas of concentration of the Coptic Church in the United States are Metropolitan New York and New Jersey, Washington, D.C., Los Angeles, San Francisco, Chicago, Troy (Minnesota), Cleveland, Houston, and Philadelphia; in Canada, concentrations are in Toronto and Montreal.

The Coptic Pope Shenouda III visited the Roman Catholic Pope Paul VI in 1973 and both signed a common declaration that in the essentials of faith, both churches are one; they encouraged theologians to study ways of reconciling some differences of dogmas and rituals. The Coptic Church is also a member of the World Council of Churches, the National Council of Churches, and the All Africa Conference of Churches. The Coptic Church is in communion with all the members of the Oriental Orthodox Family: the Syrian, Armenian, Ethiopian, and Indian Orthodox churches.

Founder

The Copts identify the Evangelist St. Mark as the founder of their national church. It is believed that Mark came to Alexandria between 49 and

55 A.D., where he made many converts and ordained several priests and deacons. He also established the first catechetical school, which became the highest center of theological education in the Middle East. The church in Alexandria became so strong that a cathedral was built during one of Mark's voyages to Rome. He was martyred in 68, when the pagans attacked the cathedral, where later he was buried.

History

The church underwent various ages of persecution under the Romans from 69 to 639, but the persecution of Diocletian was the most disastrous. Indeed, the Coptic Calendar of Martyrs begins with this event in 284 A.D., the year of Diocletian's accession. Despite this long period of Roman persecution, Alexandrine Christianity became the light of the world.

Several great thinkers and writers emerged as the heads of the catechetical school of Alexandria, notably Clement (c. 150–c. 213) and Origen (185–c. 251). Clement wrote abundantly and has been called a witness to the virtual completion of the New Testament. Clement was succeeded by his brilliant student Origen about 215. Origen has been called one of the world's greatest exegetical scholars of all time. The Coptic School contributed greatly to the shaping of Christian doctrine and theological scholarship during the first four centuries. The reign of Constantine the Great (c. 274–337) ushered in the triumph of Christianity over paganism and the reversal of the policy of persecution.

The first three church councils—Nicea (325), Constantinople (381), and Ephesus (431)—received spiritual and intellectual leadership from the Coptic Church, mainly St. Athanasius and St. Cyril I the Great, who were patriarchs. Coptic monasticism and cenobitism were truly the gifts of Egypt to Christendom. Most writers ascribe the origins of monasticism to St. Anthony (c. 251–356), whose fame was spread by a biography written by Athanasius, who incidentally introduced monasticism to the Western church. The Coptic Church also suffered under the Arab conquest of Egypt in 640, yet while continuing their unwavering loyalty to their church, they managed to adapt themselves to the conditions of Islamic rule without the loss of their way of life. The Crusades, however, brought a new agonizing chapter of persecution toward all "worshipers of the cross."

Structure, Teachings, and Worship

The Coptic Church considers Cairo, Egypt, as its hierarchical center and calls it the see of St. Mark. Pope Shenonda III is pope of Alexandria. (Many documents affirm that the first prelate in Christendom to bear the title "pope" was Hercules the Copt, who was called "papa" to distinguish him from the rest of the bishops in the early part of the third century—long before this term was used in Rome.) The central seminary is also at Cairo, with several branches in seven dioceses in Egypt.

Candidates to the priesthood may be chosen from among married men, although marriage may not follow ordination. If a person chooses to become a monk, he must be celibate. A monk is eligible for promotion to all ranks of the priesthood, up to patriarch, the official who presides over all clergy, deacons, priests, and bishops.

The Coptic Church uses her own ecclesiastical calendar—the Martyrs' Calendar, which is a solar one that started from 284 A.D. Christmas is celebrated on January 7.

The Coptic Church recognizes seven sacraments. *Baptism* is usually by submersion; mothers are advised to baptize their babies forty (for boys) or eighty (for girls) days after birth, in order to give the mothers the canonical time required for cleansing to be ready for Holy Communion. Baptized infants take communion on the day of baptism. *Confirmation* is by oil, or holy mayron, on the same day as baptism.

Holy Eucharist is administered in the two elements: holy bread (Korban) and wine. The bread should be leavened and should be prepared on the same day of the divine liturgy. It is circular in form with a round stamp bearing the sign of the cross and the Trisagion on it. The wine must be fresh and undiluted. The divine liturgy is celebrated in Egypt in both Coptic and Arabic languages, while in other countries both Coptic and locally spoken languages are used by priests, deacons, and people, who all take their particular part in the service.

The remaining sacraments are *penance* (required before Holy Communion), *holy unction of the sick* (anointing), *holy matrimony,* and *holy orders.*

Contributions and Influence

His Holiness Pope Shenonda III, pope of Alexandria and patriarch of the see of St. Mark, in responding to an interview in 1987 noted a number of opportunities and obligations of the Coptic Church to Christians in the lands of immigration. The church provides Sunday schools and youth classes. The spiritual principles and the spiritual meanings of the rites of the church need to be translated into modern settings. The new generation should have a deeper knowledge of the history of the Coptic Church, its apostolic origin, and its role in ecumenical councils, monasticism, and Christian education; they also should study the history of the heroes of faith, the famous martyrs, and the great antiquities of the Coptic Church.

In addition to all these points, they also need to have an idea about the church today in detail. Visits to the mother church in Egypt may be of great profit to the new generation and will deepen the relation between the Coptic churches in the West and the mother church. Our priests should pay great care to keep our sons in deep spiritual life through the sacrament of confession, which should be practiced thoughtfully. We should provide the facilities needed to keep children and youth in the bosom of the church. Finally, we need to have Coptic magazines for the children and youth and also to have libraries for them supplied with books for every age.

Significant Terms

Cenebotism. From "cenobite," a member of a religious monastic community. The so-called Father of Cenobites is St. Pachomius, who with St. Anthony, the Father of monks, led the spread of monasticism through all Christianity.

Chrismation. A confirmatory sacrament of the Eastern Orthodox Church in which a baptized member is anointed with chrism (consecrated oil usually mixed with balm of spices), which corresponds to confirmation in the West.

Coptic. Of or relating to the Copts, from the Greek *aegyptios,* "Egyptian," who were either Egyptians or members of the ancient Monophysite Christian Church of Egypt. The Coptic Orthodox Church is also known as the Church of Alexandria.

Eutychianism. From the Alexandrian monk Eutyches, who denied the human nature of Christ in favor of the divine. The Coptic Church held this view to be heretical, maintaining that there are two natures, distinct yet not separate.

Holy mayron. The name for holy oil (chrism) blessed by the bishop and used in the ceremony directly following baptism (the chrismation). It is also used in the rites of ordination and extreme unction (the anointing of the dying).

Monophysite. Literally, "one nature" (e.g., that the human and divine in Jesus Christ constitute really only one nature). While the Coptic Church is correctly called monophysite, it is only because they do not believe in a separation of the two natures in one person—Christ.

Martyrs' Calendar. The Coptic calendar, which begins with 284 A.D., the year Diocletian's persecution began. This year is 1 A.M. (Anno Martyri). Christmas is celebrated January 7, according to the Julian calendar.

Trisagion. The opening words in Greek (meaning "thrice holy") of an invocation, doxology, or hymn, frequently used in the Greek liturgy. It was used as early as 576 in the Gallican liturgy.

Bibliography

Atiya, Aziz S. *History of Eastern Christianity.* South Bend, Ind.: University of Notre Dame Press, 1968.

Coptologia: An International Journal of Coptology and Egyptology. Toronto, Ontario, n.d.

El-Masri, Iris H. *Introduction to the Coptic Church.* N.p.: Dar el Alamel Arabi, 1977.

———. *The Story of the Copts.* N.p.: Middle East Council of Churches, 1978.

Marlow, John. *The Golden Age of Alexandria.* London: Victor Gollancz, 1971.

Parsons, Edward A. *The Alexandria Library.* Amsterdam: Elsevier Press, 1951.

Prepared by the editor from an article on the Coptic Orthodox Church by Rev. Fr. Gabriel Abdelsayed, Ph.D., and an interview (article) with His Holiness Pope Shenonda III, published in Coptologia.

RUSSIAN ORTHODOX CHURCH

"The outline regarding Greek Orthodoxy would be substantially the same for Russian Orthodoxy. . . . The Orthodox Church and faith is identical for Greeks and Russians—except for language, culture, and 'style.' "

Excerpts from a letter of September 25, 1987, from Prof. Thomas Hopko of St. Vladimir's Orthodox Theological Seminary, Crestwood, New York.

ECKANKAR

General Description

Eckankar is a worldwide religion with followers in over ninety-six countries. In the United States there are over two hundred Eckankar centers where members (ECKists) gather to study monthly discourses that come with membership.

The aim and purpose of Eckankar is to link one up directly with the Holy Spirit, which can be seen as divine Light and heard as inner Sound. This is done through daily practice of simple twenty-minute exercises, which combine unique visualizations, dream exercise, "soul travel" techniques, and simply listening within.

Founder

There is no fixed date when we can say the Eckankar teachings began, because the path of Light and Sound far predates man's recorded history. But for our purposes, Paul Twitchell first brought the modern ECK teachings to the Western world in 1965, after years of study under various Vairagi ECK masters such as Rebazar Tarz, his predecessor.

Today, Sri Harold Klemp, another American, is the spiritual leader responsible for the continued evolution of the Eckankar teachings. His title is the mahanta, the 973d living ECK master.

Beliefs and Doctrines

Eckankar teaches that one can develop one's own relationship with the Life Force, or Holy Spirit, also known as ECK. The easiest way to begin to establish this relationship is through a study of one's dreams and their spiritual meanings. The first two years of membership include *The ECK Dream Disclosures,* which aim to replace gradually the member's jumbled dreams and to understand spiritual insight. Topics include how to remember and understand one's dreams, methods to find one's inner dream guide, and how to make the transition from dream travel to soul travel.

Eckankar is also known as the Ancient Science of Soul Travel. Soul travel is a natural ability of the individual to move in awareness beyond the human senses. This happens in moments when one is most engaged in life and is the next step beyond dream study.

The ECK, or Holy Spirit, as taught in Eckankar, can be perceived as sparkling pinpoints of Light on the inner screen of the mind. One may also perceive the divine Spirit as the Audible Sound Current, or Music of God. Students sometimes report a ringing sound in the ears or a heavy wind in their inner hearing. Other sounds might include a single note of a flute, the buzzing of bees, or even the humming of high-tension wires.

Another unique aspect is the spiritual capacity of the living ECK master to serve as both inner and outer guide. Much as a student learns from a teacher in school, the living ECK master is an adept guide to spiritual experiences in the realms of heaven. He teaches the student about his five spiritual bodies, or sheaths, which include the physical, emotional, causal, mental, and soul bodies. The student strives for harmony and balance among all these parts of himself in order to be a clear vehicle for the Light and Sound of God, or the Holy Spirit.

Forms of Worship

Many Eckankar centers hold worship services, in which attendees sing "Hu" (pronounced like the man's name Hugh). This ancient name for God attunes one to the ECK, or Holy Spirit. It is one of the daily spiritual exercises given in the discourses and teachings of Eckankar. A passage is then read from the ECK scriptures, the *Shariyat-Ki-Sugmad,* book 1 or 2. A brief small-group discussion among attendees concludes the service.

Other forms of worship are individual. Personal scriptural exercises are performed daily by members. Four major seminars are held around the world each year for ECKists to gather and share insights via workshops, talks, and roundtable forums. The living ECK master speaks at these seminars.

Organization

Eckankar is a nonprofit religious organization. The Eckankar centers are staffed entirely by volunteers. The international headquarters for Eckankar are in Chanhassen, Minnesota, where a temple for ECK is currently being built.

Contributions and Influence

Eckankar members have been noted for their disciplines of the five passions of the mind: lust, anger, greed, attachment, and vanity. They do not believe in proselytizing; information about Eckankar is shared when friends or family inquire about it. Public introductory talks on the teachings are offered as a public service. Eckankar is one of the few religions today that teaches how to connect with the Light and Sound of God—as Saul of Tarsus experienced on the road to Damascus. This experience is accompanied by a warm feeling of love or joy that uplifts the ECKists and those around them. It is a path that values the freedom of the individual above all.

Significant Terms

ECK. The Life Force, or Holy Spirit; the Audible Sound Current, which sustains all life.

Living ECK masters. The current spiritual leader of Eckankar in a long line of Vairagi ECK masters. As the inner and outer master, it is his duty to lead the soul back to God. As the inner master, he is known by his spiritual name, Wah Z.

Shariyat-Ki-Sugmad. The two volumes of sacred scriptures in ECK. There are twelve volumes on the inner places; the first two were transcribed by Paul Twitchell and are currently available from Eckankar.

Sugmad. A sacred name for God, the source of all life, as is the word "Hu." It is neither masculine nor feminine.

Arahata. An experienced and qualified instructor for local Eckankar classes, called *satsangs.*

Bibliography

(All items are published by Eckankar, Minneapolis.)
Klemp, Harold. *Child in the Wilderness.* 1989.
——. *How to Find God.* 1988.
——. *Journey of Soul.* 1988.
——. *Soul Travelers of the Far Country.* 1987.
Twitchell, Paul. *ECKANKAR: The Key to Secret Words.* 1969.
——. *Stranger by the River.* 1970.
——. *The Tiger's Fang.* 1967.

Prepared by Suzanne Alexander, Communication Services.

• • •
EPISCOPALIANS
(PROTESTANT EPISCOPAL
CHURCH IN THE U.S.A.)

General Description

Episcopalians (those led by bishops) are part of the Anglican Communion—a worldwide Christian fellowship of churches 40 million strong and in communion with the Church of England. The church in the United States is called the Protestant Episcopal Church in the U.S.A. and has over 3 million members. Others who consider themselves Episcopalians, such as the Reformed Episcopal Church (1873) and several Anglican, Catholic, Orthodox, or Episcopal churches (formed between the early 1960s and the late 1980s) have separated from the American church.

Episcopalians/Anglicans have their origin in the English Reformation, which was marked by a return to ancient Christian beliefs, worship, and discipline. At this time, during the reign of Elizabeth I, "the Church in England" became "the Church of England." Roman Catholics, by papal decree, were therefore ordered to withdraw from the Church of England.

Founder

There is no founder per se. During the reign of Henry VIII, which preceded that of Elizabeth I, Henry, acting in council with the bishops of the Church of England and the Parliament, issued a declaration denying the right of the pope to exercise authority over the Church of England. The most influential figure of the English Reformation was Thomas Cranmer, a man of masterful literary skill. Under his guidance, the *Book of Common Prayer* was developed as a unique and unifying ecclesiastical instrument and one of England's great cultural achievements.

Two-thirds of the signers of the Declaration of Independence were Anglicans, as were George Washington, Alexander Hamilton, James Madison, and Patrick Henry, to name just a few. Samuel Seabury, William White, and Samuel Provoost were elected the first bishops of the Episcopal Church, but because of postwar missionary tensions, they were consecrated in Great Britain. In 1785, after the Revolutionary War, Anglican missionary work in America led to the establishment of a native church in Philadelphia.

Beliefs and Doctrines

There is no separate "Episcopalian doctrine." Episcopalians adhere to the Christian Apostles' and Nicene creeds and to the Holy Scriptures, which are said to be "profitable for doctrine." Yet while the creeds and Scripture are considered to be the bulwark of doctrine, Episcopalians also believe that individual Christians and the dynamic fellowship of the Christian family, the church, must study and interpret these resources in order to live out the new life of love and brotherhood in Christ. In addition, Episcopalians/Anglicans affirm two other doctrinal elements: "There are two sacraments ordained by Christ our Lord in the Gospel . . . Baptism and the Supper of the Lord" (*Book of Common Prayer*, p. 607) and "the historic Episcopate, a continuous line . . . coming down to us from the original apostles" (*Handbook for Episcopalians*, p. 76).

Forms of Worship

The *Book of Common Prayer* is Anglicanism's great contribution to the life, faith, and worship of Episcopalians and to many other national Episcopal churches. First used in England in 1549, it has been revised numerous times and printed in many languages. In the United States, the first prayer book was published in 1789, and the most recent revision was approved in 1979. The prayer book speaks to all aspects of human life. It gives structure and guidance for the services of morning and evening prayer, the sacraments of Holy Baptism and Holy Communion and for such sacramental rites as matrimony and ordination. The prayer book also includes other rites such as the burial of the dead, the consecration of a church, and prayers. The *Book of Common Prayer* provides for a continual sharing of the universal Christian heritage, from the Psalms of Judaism to the widely varied prayers and rites of Roman Catholic, Orthodox, and Protestant origin, and remains a rich resource for worship, public and private.

Organization

As the name suggests, the Episcopal Church is a church where bishops (Greek *episkopos*) are chief officers. However, true to the democratic spirit of the United States and its new constitution, the framers of the constitution of the Episcopal Church (some of whom were the same men) established a federal system of church government patterned after that of the United States. The parish church is the basic unit, and the dioceses are the states of a two-house General Convention, or legislative body (House of Bishops and House of Deputies). Bishops are elected as "governors"—or, more accurately, as presiding officers of the dioceses, or "states"—and a presiding bishop was ultimately elected as presiding officer of the General Convention. Each parish elects a rector (head priest) to be both spiritual leader and presiding officer of the parish meeting and the vestry (an elected lay governing body). Episcopalian uniqueness lies in its utilization of both local autonomy and central unity in organization and function.

Contributions and Influence

Episcopalians have been noted for their tolerant, accepting attitudes toward other faiths and practices. Sometimes called the bridge church, the Episcopal Church has always been in the forefront of the ecumenical movement. Episcopalians' firm emphasis on the democratic nature of American society has led to positions of leadership in government, literature, and philanthropy in the United States.

Significant Terms

Archbishop. A bishop who presides over a province (several dioceses).

Bishop coadjutor. A bishop elected to assist and eventually to succeed the bishop of a diocese.

Bishop suffragan. A bishop elected only to assist a bishop of a diocese.

Communicant. A baptized member of a parish church.

Deacon. An ordained order in the church, whose focus is the servant ministry and who serves under the direction and guidance of the bishop.

Priest. An ordained order in the church with responsibility and authority for sacramental administration and the declaration of absolution and blessing.

Rector. A priest who is in charge of a parish church.

Vicar. A minister who has charge of a mission representing the bishop.

Bibliography

(Except as noted, all items are published by Morehouse-Barlow, Wilton, Conn.)

Booty, John E. *What Makes Us Episcopalians?* 1982.

Holloway, Richard. *The Anglican Tradition*. 1984.

Norris, Richard A. *Understanding the Faith of the Church*. New York: Seabury, 1979.

Synder, William. *Looking at the Episcopalian Church*. 1981.

Williamson, William B. *A Handbook for Episcopalians*. 1961.

Prepared by William B. Williamson, editor and Episcopal clergyman.

◆ ◆ ◆
ETHICAL CULTURAL MOVEMENT

General Description

The following statement of purpose was adopted by delegates at the 1980 Assembly of the American Ethical Union, the Federation of the Ethical Culture Societies.

> Ethical Culture is a humanistic religious and an educational movement inspired by the ideal that the supreme aim of human life is working to create a more humane society.
>
> Our faith is in the capacity and responsibility of human beings to act in their personal relationships and in the larger community to help create a better world.
>
> Our commitment is to the worth and dignity of the individual and to treating each human being as to bring out the best in him or her.
>
> Members join together in ethical societies to assist each other in developing ethical ideas and ideals . . . to celebrate life's joys and support each other through life's crises . . . to work together to improve our world and the world of our children.

Beliefs and Doctrines

Ethical Culture is a philosophy of life dedicated to the concepts that the highest value on earth is human worth, that we must strive to protect the mother earth upon which we are solely dependent, and that every person on earth has an equal right to live with dignity and in harmony with one another.

Ethical Culture has kept its nontheistic religious position, neither affirming nor denying the existence of a Supreme Being by focusing on the centrality of ethics in daily living in our interpersonal relationships and our relationship to all life on this planet.

History

The American Ethical movement, one hundred years old in 1976, began with the founding of the Ethical Society of New York by Felix Adler in St. Louis; in 1889 it became a federation under the American Ethical Union (AEU).

AEU's dedication to improving our way of life has led to the establishment of committees through the years, including those that counsel former convicts and their families, help refugees settle in the United States, make clothing for poor children, provide coffeehouses in poor areas, and open Ethical Culture schools.

Historically, AEU members and societies have been instrumental in the formation and support of organizations and projects in the interest of human rights, world peace, health, education, welfare, and civil liberties.

Founder

The founder of Ethical Culture was Felix Adler (1851–1933), born in Alzey, Rhenish Hesse, in southwestern Germany. He was the son of Samuel Adler, a rabbi, and Henrietta Feibisch (Phoebus) Frankfurter.

Felix's father, Samuel Adler, had been ordained in the Orthodox Jewish faith, but he gradually established himself as a proponent of the Reform movement and, during his appointment in Alzey, introduced significant changes, such as holding confirmation ceremonies for boys and girls and removing the rampart from the part of the gallery where women sat. He labored for Jewish civil equality, and his efforts resulted in equal time being given to the teaching of the Jewish faith together with the two Christian confessions in the school district of Alzey, thereby ensuring the Jewish community an equal voice in school matters as a whole.

Felix's mother, Henrietta Frankfurter, was the daughter of Rabbi Feibisch (Phoebus). She was described as "a kind, gentle, yet dependable and practical human being, a loving mother who mediated between her husband and the outside world, and who complemented her husband's more stern intellectual posture, with her own example of warmth and personal goodness" (Kraut, 1979). However, it was his father who exposed Felix to the urban poor.

Samuel Adler accepted an invitation to become rabbi at Temple Emanuel in New York City, the wealthiest Jewish congregation in the United States. On February 22, 1857, he and his wife and their two sons, set sail for New York.

Felix was educated at Columbia Grammar School and then Columbia College. In the fall of 1870 Felix enrolled at Berlin University, studying natural science, Greek philosophy, modern philosophy, philosophy of education and pedagogy, Bible criticism, Semitics, linguistics, philology, and psychology with the outstanding university faculty. In addition to his formal education, Felix studied Arabic, Aramaic, and Halakic literature with Moritz Steinschneider, at the Royal Library in Berlin. In addition, he privately studied Kantian philosophy with Hermann Cohen.

From 1874 to 1876 Adler was visiting professor in Hebrew and Oriental literature at Cornell University. On May 24, 1880, Felix Adler and Helen (Nellie) Goldmark were married.

From 1902 to 1921, Felix Adler continued his academic career as professor of political and social ethics at Columbia University, which, along with his continuous work to further Ethical Culture and his leadership at the New York Society for Ethical Culture, filled both his days and nights.

The Sunday closest to May 15 is Founder's Day in Ethical Culture. It was on this date in 1876 that Felix Adler delivered his address in Standard Hall in New York City outlining the Ethical Culture movement. The following are excerpts from that address:

> On the face of it, our age exhibits certain distinct traits in which it excels all of its predecessors. Eulogies on the nineteenth century are familiar to our ears, and orators delight to descant upon all the glorious things which it has achieved. Its railways, its printing presses, its increased comforts and refined luxuries—all these are undeniable facts, and yet it is true none the less, that great and unexpected evils have followed in the train of our successes and that the moral improvement of nations and their individual components has not kept pace with the march of intellect and the advance of industry. . . .
>
> . . . freedom of thought is a sacred right of every individual man; diversity will continue to increase with the progress, refinement, and differentiation of the human intellect. But if differences be inevitable, nay, welcome in thought, there is a sphere in which unanimity and fellowship are above all things needful. Believe or disbelieve as ye list—we shall at all times respect every honest conviction. But be one with us where there is nothing to divide—in action. Diversity in the creed, unanimity in the deed! (S. Burns Weston, *Twenty Years of the Ethical Culture Movement*, Philadelphia, 1305 Arch Street, 1896, pp. 2, 14)

Organization

At present, the Ethical Culture movement has 21 societies and approximately 4,000 members nationwide. The recent organizational restructuring of the America Ethical Union into regions is an attempt to move from an hierarchical institution to one that is more participatory and willing to share power, encouraging regional networking and thinking. Each society, however, has its distinct flavor and history, very often traceable to the influence and personality of its early leaders. Each society elects its own board of trustees and functions under its own bylaws. Ethical Culture leaders perform all the duties of a minister, priest, or rabbi. They speak from an ethical platform, teach and serve actively in the community, conduct weddings, officiate at funerals and memorial services, and welcome infants into the human family.

Contributions and Influence

It did not take long for the newly created religious organization to begin its rich and varied influence on social reform. In 1877, for example, it established the first free kindergartens in New York and San Francisco; in 1879 the United Relief Works of the New York Society were incorporated, which consolidated the society's social welfare work into one organization; in 1888 the New York Society started the Mother's Society to Study Child Nature, which later become the Child Study Association. In the same year, the Chicago Society organized the Bureau of Justice, the organization that preceded the Legal Aid Society, and the St. Louis Society established the Self-Culture Halls Association, pioneering adult education.

Bibliography

Kraut, Benny. *From Reform Judaism to Ethical Culture: The Religious Evolution of Felix Adler*. Cincinnati: Hebrew Union College Press, 1979.
Radest, Howard B. *Toward Common Ground*. New York: Ungar, 1969.
Religious Education with AEU. New York: AEU, n.d.

Prepared by Margaretha E. Jones, administrator, with assistance by the editor.

FELLOWSHIP OF RELIGIOUS HUMANISTS

General Description

The Fellowship of Religious Humanists was organized in 1963 by a group of liberal religious leaders, mainly Unitarians and Ethical Culturalists, and is principally concerned with the practice and philosophy of humanism as a religion.

Religious Humanism is an affirmation based on insights into the world as it is, not as wish-inspired fancies would imagine it. Its commitment is to the world as accumulated finds of the human spirit have revealed it. Religious Humanism aims to explore the religious implications and perennial values available to the world, forever old and yet forever new, and to draw from the various faiths and philosophies of mankind whatever enduring gains we may.

Purpose

1. To provide fellowship in association devoted to the cultivation of humanistic religious living which springs from the insights of inner experience that is circumscribed neither by creed nor by ecclesiastical or political authority. In this endeavor, the disciplines are such as are required by the pursuit of truth.
2. To state and restate from time to time, without dogmatism or compromise of the free-mind principle, the basic tenets of humanism as philosophy, ethics and religion.
3. To support and preserve the pluralistic character of modern humanism through understanding other emphases in humanism than the

religious (rationalist, scientific, secular, etc.) and to help relate the various facets of the movement, including the organized liberal religious, ethical and humanistic societies in co-operative endeavors.

4. To defend and protect freedom of thought in religion.

5. To develop and apply the scientific spirit and methods in the study of religion.

6. To encourage among humanists writing that will give voice to those values of religion which can only evolve where there is freedom.

7. To meet the particular needs of religious humanists by providing the inspirational materials, arranging seminars and conferences, and if possible, publishing in economical form some of the basic writings, past and present, of religious humanism.

Although we are not primarily structured as are many other groups, to promote social action programs, we stand for racial equality, freedom of speech, separation of church and state, an end to slaughter and destruction through war and for evenhanded, peaceful, wholesome, and zestful living for people, men and women everywhere. (*Religious Humanism* 23, no. 2 [Spring 1989], inside back cover)

A Testimonial

Lester Mondale, past president of the Fellowship of Religious Humanists, has commented as follows about Religious Humanism:

Humanism is a point of view, an attitude, of many facets. There are Christian Humanism, Ethical Humanism, Scientific Humanism, and how many others?

Each has its following and vigorous advocates. Humanists agree in general (for all their several differences) on emphasizing the idea of man as measure. They stress the importance of man's making the most of his life on earth. All Humanists place the highest value on thinking that is scholarly, scientific, insightful. Most Humanists perceive in man a spirit that is not necessarily a hapless victim of the ups and downs of untoward cause and effect.

Among the general facets of humanism is one specifically that stands between the extremes of Christian Humanism on one side, and secularistic, Ethical Humanism on the other. This is my brand: Religious Humanism.

Like most persons of this persuasion, I regard myself as a Religious Humanist not because of having been converted to a creed or faith; not because of having signed a membership card in a crusading fraternity of believers. The term, "Religious Humanism," is more descriptive of a state of mind, of an attitude with respect to philosophy, religion, ethics, than it is a label for another "ism." Basic to the attitude is a questing openness to an ever enlarging perspective on man, on one's own self, on the universe; there is a commitment to developing an ever more adequate adjustment to that perspective.

Man's chief claim to dignity, as I see it as a Religious Humanist, lies in his most basic responses to life and death.

In contrast to the immortals of mythology, whether Greek, Christian or oriental, man is very much the mortal. Since he is mortal and weaker in mind and body, he was regarded by the immortals as an inferior being. Man, nevertheless, could do one thing that the immortals could not do. He could give his most prized possession, his existence, if need be, to enhance or save the life of another.

As with his dying, so with his living. He has the wherewithal of selfhood to refuse to quail before misfortune and danger, to refuse to die many times before his death. He can go on to live with high abandon. Thus, in his living as in his dying, he can rise to heights of courage and heroism that are not to be topped by the gods themselves.

For me, the concept of deity—polytheistic or monotheistic—answers none of man's ultimate questions. Among these questions is eminently, "Why something rather than nothing?" The deity concept enlightens neither life nor non-life, nor does it reduce the cosmic infinitude to anything that even begins to approximate neighborhood familiarity.

When all things visible and conceivable begin to take on an aspect of strangeness—even to the degree of appearing positively eerie—a Religious Humanist is not likely to panic. He knows that this unmasking of the familiar is not necessarily symptomatic of mental disease. Actually, it is the awesome disclosure that the world we customarily see is fixed only by culture and habit and state of feeling, not by the law of nature or the accuracy of scientific measurement. The dissolving of the familiar at times into amorphous unfamiliarity is man's opening to things and persons and their intermingling in their essential differentness and hence to new avenues of coping with problems, to new approaches, to achievement and creativity.

As I can see the religious situation, this awareness of the universe of strangeness beyond the habit-structured appearances of the commonplace is one of man's most distinguishing marks as man.

And for him to accept with courage and expectation, rather than with dread, openings of the mysterium that is in fact the source of most of that which is creative and new, is to measure up to the full stature of his dignity as man.

As a Religious Humanist, I am not unaware of the unsettling effects of one's first encounter with the engulfing strangeness of all things, animate and inanimate. I hope that I am not lacking in appreciation of the brevity of the days of our years, of the perils of time and chance all along the way. But rather than let things untoward dampen one's spirits, lay one low with moods of self-pity and defeat, how much more dignified to take them as a defiance and testing of that in one which most distinguishes one as man: one's prowess of selfhood. ("A Testimonial," *Religious Humanism* 14, no. 3 [Summer 1970]: 126–27)

Significant Terms

Empirical philosophy of religion. The interpretation of religion from experience given in language that will not conflict with that of the world of science.

Humanist Manifesto I and II. Statement of beliefs and goals of humanists.

The first was issued in 1933 and signed by 34 people, mostly professors, writers, and ministers. The second was issued in 1973 and signed by 114 individuals of prominence and distinction.

Naturalistic Humanism. A humanistic theory that holds that mankind secures meaning from nature not from the supernatural. Also, the universe is self-existing, and man is an emerging part of nature; both are revealed only by natural (scientific) process and methods.

Realization of human personality. The only end of human life, which humanism seeks in the here and now, and which will be achieved only by attaining social well-being for all humans.

Religion without god. A slogan by opponents of humanism as well as by some adherents, to describe a nonsupernaturalistic, nontheistic religious humanism.

Unitarian birthplace. Prior to World War I, John H. Dietrich, a Unitarian minister, preached sermons in which he used "humanism" to describe the message he was preaching. Also Curtis W. Reese, a Unitarian, joined Dietrich in proclaiming his humanism. (See his book *Humanist Religion.*)

Bibliography

Auer, J. A. C. F. *Humanism States Its Case*. Boston: Beacon Press, 1933.

Kurtz, Paul. *Humanist Manifesto I and II*. Buffalo, N.Y.: Prometheus Books, 1973.

Lamont, Corliss. *The Philosophy of Humanism*. New York: Ungar, 1967.

Mason, Leonard. *Roots of Religious Humanism*. Yellow Springs, Ohio: Fellowship of Religious Humanists, 1978.

Mondale, Lester. *New Man of Religious Humanism*. Peterhead, Scotland: Voltunna Press, 1973.

Olds, Mason. *Religious Humanism in America*. Washington, D.C.: University Press of America, 1978.

Potter, Charles F. *Humanism: A New Religion*. New York: Simon & Schuster, 1930.

———. *Humanizing Religion*. New York: Harper & Brothers, 1933.

Reese, Curtis W. *Humanist Religion*. New York: Macmillan, 1931.

Sellars, Roy W. *The Next Step in Religion*. New York: Macmillan, 1918.

———. *Religion Coming of Age*. New York: Macmillan, 1928.

Prepared by the editor from articles in Religious Humanism, *with the approval of the acting editor, J. Harold Hadley.*

FREEDOM FROM RELIGION FOUNDATION

Free Thought: Atheism and Agnosticism

(Editor's note: Atheism is not a religion, but since it does make a statement *about* religion, and since nonreligious people represent a significant portion of the world's population, it is included in this book.)

Significant Terms

Freethinker. A person who forms an opinion about religion on the basis of reason, not tradition, authority, or established belief. Modern freethinkers include atheists, agnostics, secular humanists, and rationalists. The eighteenth-century Deists, such as Thomas Paine and some of the Founding Fathers, were freethinkers of their day, though most believed in an impersonal "God of Nature."

Atheism. Some dictionaries define "atheism" as a "denial" of a god or a "belief" that there is no god, while others define it as a "disbelief," or rather a lack of belief in a deity. They seem to have consulted theologians rather than atheists. Historic and contemporary atheistic literature is in almost complete agreement that atheism is an absence of belief in a god or gods. It is not a belief system. The term "atheism" is formed by attaching the Greek prefix *a-* ("not" or "without") to the word "theism." The prefix does not mean "against." Since theism is a belief, "atheism" means "without belief."

Since theists are convinced that a god exists, it is difficult for many of them to imagine that a person could actually not believe, so they define atheists as people who are resisting or denying a fact. Many wrongly view atheism as an antireligion, or natural religion standing in opposition to their own. Other than a respect for the principles of reason, however, atheism has no creed. It has none of the trappings associated with religion: no god; no holy book; no sacraments, symbols, rituals, or prayers; no ministers, prophets, missionaries, or Sunday schools; no explicit moral code; no doctrine of anything that transcends nature, such as ideas of spirit, sin, salvation, evil, or damnation.

Though atheism does not pretend to offer a philosophy for living, freethinkers find a basis for morality, purpose, and joy outside of religion, finding meaning in things like humanism, feminism, pacifism, and other social and moral causes. Atheism is positive, in the sense that freedom from superstition is a very precious thing—like having a large debt canceled.

Theists and atheists agree about the existence of the natural universe. The theist, however, asserts something additional: that there is a realm that transcends nature. The burden of proof lies with the one who makes the assertion. Atheists simply notice that god has been unproved, not disproved.

Convinced that theistic arguments are illogical or unsupported, atheists feel confident enough to justify their continuing lack of belief, or to make such informal statements as, "There is no God." This is no different from saying, "There is no Santa Claus."

Atheists may deny the existence of a particular god, if such a god has been sufficiently defined. The Judeo-Christian Yahweh, for example, has been adorned with the self-contradictory attributes of omniscience and omnipotence. Atheists join Christians in positively denying Allah, Hera, Mithra, Zeus, and a multitude of ancient deities. It can be said that an atheist simply believes in one less god than a Christian does.

The definition of agnosticism is somewhat more difficult than that of atheism. Yet agnosticism and atheism are not mutually exclusive. Neither are agnosticism and theism. Either one does have a belief in a god (theist), or one does not (atheist). There is no middle ground.

The term "agnostic" was invented by Thomas Huxley in 1869, prefixing *a-* to *gnostos* ("knowing"). " 'Agnosticism,' in fact, is not a creed," he wrote, "but a method . . . ." The principle may be expressed positively: in matters of intellect follow your reason as far as it can take you, without regard to any other considerations; negatively: in matters of the intellect, do not pretend conclusions are certain which are not demonstrated or demonstrable" ("Agnosticism [1889]," *Science and Christian Tradition: Essays* by Thomas H. Huxley [New York: Appleton & Co., 1893], pp. 245, 246). Virtually synonymous with rationalism and skepticism, agnosticism is a broad and useful concept that today usually is erroneously taken as a halfway house between atheism and theism and that has been adopted as a label by nontheists who may be uncomfortable with the social stigma attached to the word "atheism."

Since atheism deals with belief and agnosticism deals with knowledge, their spheres of application overlap. Every atheist is an agnostic, and some believers (such as philosopher Blaise Pascal) are theistic agnostics—people who claim that they do not (or cannot) know that a god exists but who choose to believe anyway.

Religion. A system of thought or practice that claims to transcend our natural world and that demands conformity to a creed, bible, or savior. Freethinkers understand that some use the term more generally, such as anything that addresses "ultimate questions" or that unites people in a common bond. Such people may prefer to avoid the common supernaturalistic connotation by using naturalistic synonyms such as "culture" or "society." In this case, however, stamp collecting or kindergarten might be called a religion.

God. A transcendent being who created and/or governs the universe. Normally, it contains personal aspects such as intelligence, will, wisdom, love, and hatred as well as supernatural aspects such as omnipotence, omniscience, immortality, omnibenevolence, and omnipresence. It is most often pictured with humanity, but it is sometimes held to be an impersonal force or nature itself.

Rationalism. The idea that all beliefs should be subject to the proven methods of rational injury. Special concessions, such as to faith and authority, that are taboo in other disciplines are not acceptable for analyzing religion.

Truth. The degree to which a statement corresponds with reality; or simple correspondence with reality.

Reality. That which is directly perceived through our natural senses, or indirectly ascertained through the proper use of reason.

Reason. A tool of critical thought that limits the truth of a proposition by the tests of *verification* (what evidence or repeatable observations confirm it?), *falsifiability* (what, in theory, would disprove it? and have all such attempts failed?), and *logic* (is it free of contradictions and non sequiturs?).

Secular Humanism. A rationalistic natural outlook that makes humanity the measure of values.

History

The history of Western civilization shows that most social and moral progress has been brought about by persons free from religion. In modern times, the first to speak out for social reforms such as women's rights have been freethinkers and religious rebels, just as they were the first to call for the end of slavery. Nineteenth-century American feminist Elizabeth Cady Stanton, author of *The Women's Bible*, wrote, "The Bible and the Church have been the greatest stumbling blocks in the way of women's emancipation" (*Free Thought Magazine*, vol. 14, September 1896, n.p.). Twentieth-century British philosopher Bertrand Russell noted, "The Christian religion has been and still is the principal enemy of moral progress in the world" (*Why I Am Not a Christian* [New York: Simon & Schuster, 1957], p. 21).

Free thought flowered during the Enlightenment, influenced by skeptical Deists such as Voltaire (1694–1778), French atheists such as Paul Henri d'Holbach (1723–89) and Dennis Diderot (1713–84), British philosopher David Hume (1711–76), who authored *Dialogues concerning Natural Religion,* and American revolutionary Ethan Allen (1738–89). Allen wrote the first atheist book published in the United States: *Reason the Only Miracle of Man* (1784).

The most widely read critic of the Bible has been patriot Thomas Paine. A Deist, Paine wrote in *The Age of Reason* (1794), "Whenever we read the obscene stories, the voluptuous debaucheries, the cruel and tortuous executions, the unrelenting vindictiveness with which more than half the Bible is filled, it would be more consistent that we call it the word of a demon than the Word of God. It is a history of wickedness that has served to corrupt and brutalize mankind."

Free thought's most eloquent spokesperson in the nineteenth century was the orator Robert G. Ingersoll (1833–99), known as the Great Agnostic. "All religions are inconsistent with mental freedom," Ingersoll believed. His life philosophy was summed up in the maxim, "One world at a time," and he was known for family devotion, generosity, and joie de vivre. He commanded speaking fees as high as seven thousand dollars, in an era of low wages and no income tax. The personal friend of three presidents, he was known and admired by the intellectuals and activists of his day, including freethinker Thomas Edison (who once said, "Religion is all bunk").

Prominent twentieth-century freethinkers include the celebrated attorney Clarence Darrow ("I don't believe in God, because I don't believe in Mother Goose"), American journalist H. L. Mencken, and British philosopher Bertrand Russell, whose brilliant logic, humanitarian compassion, and lucid prose have attracted many readers to free thought.

Other well-known freethinkers include America Red Cross founder Clara Barton; birth control proponent Margaret Sanger; physicists Albert Einstein and Marie Curie; entrepreneur and philanthropist Andrew Carnegie; abolitionist William Lloyd Garrison; feminist Emma F. Goldman; labor activist Joe Hill; reformer Jane Addams; philosopher John Stuart Mill; painters Joseph Turner, Rosa Bonheur, and Pablo Picasso; poets Robert Burns, Robert Louis Stevenson, Walt Whitman, James Russell Lowell, Percy Shelley, Henry David Thoreau, and Mary McCarthy; dancer Isadora Duncan; biologist Charles Darwin; psychologist Sigmund Freud; composers Johannes Brahms, Claude Debussy, and Robert Schumann; authors Isaac Asimov and Carl Sagan; and botanist Luther Burbank, to name a few. Early Deist freethinkers included Thomas Jefferson, Benjamin Franklin, and John Adams.

The Importance of State/Church Separation

The United States was the first nation to establish the complete separation of church and state. Following a colonial period fraught with religious intolerance and in the shadow of the bloody European crusades, inquisitions, and witch-hunts, the Founding Fathers wanted no continuation of religious warfare. The U.S. constitution is a godless document. Its only references to religion are exclusionary, such as that there shall be no religious test for public office (art. 6, sec. 3). The First Amendment mandates that "Congress shall make no law respecting an establishment of religion, or prohibiting the free exercise thereof."

Jefferson described the Establishment Clause as erecting "a wall of separation between church and state." His Virginia Statute for Religious Freedom (1786) is replicated in differing versions in the state constitutions. This unique American principle gradually has been adopted in other nations. Under state/church separation, religion has flourished, and the rights of dissidents and freethinkers have been equally protected. As Thomas Paine noted, "Persecution is not an original feature in any religion; but it is always the strongly marked feature of all religions established by law." There can be no religious freedom without the freedom to dissent.

General Description

The Catholic News Service and *Encyclopedia Book of the Year* (1989) show that there are 1.1 billion "nonbelievers" in the world. This is one out of every five people, a group second in size only to Christianity, which can count 1.7 billion. According to the *World Christian Encyclopedia* (1985), "more than a billion of the world's people consider themselves non-religious (agnostic about religious claims) or atheistic (actively opposed to religion)." The *Universal Almanac* (1990) reports that 20 million nonreligious/atheists live in North America.

The Freedom from Religion Foundation (FFRF) is an example of a modern group of freethinkers. Founded in 1978 as a national organization and based in Madison, Wisconsin, its primary purposes are to protect the constitutional principle of separation of church and state and to educate the public about monotheism. It serves as an association for people of like-minded belief, with approximately 4,000 supporters in 1990. *Freethought Today,* the only free-thought newspaper in North America, with more than 7,000 readers in 1990, is FFRF's publication, regularly covering state/church news, criticism of religion and other free-thought concerns, and a dissemination of free-thought books.

The foundation's legal actions have included a lawsuit challenging Ronald Reagan's declaration of 1983 as the year of the Bible and lawsuits against governmental bodies that display religious symbols on public property, against public money going to the support of religion, and against violations of the First Amendment.

In 1989 FFRF conducted a survey of freethinkers. Most were raised religious (18 percent had been Catholic, 12 percent Methodist, 12 percent other mainstream Protestant, 10 percent Baptist, 7 percent Lutheran, 6 percent Episcopalian, 3 percent Unitarian). Only 6 percent cited fundamentalist or Pentecostal backgrounds. Of the 12 percent raised without religion, two-thirds were second-generation freethinkers, and the rest between third and sixth generation. (Obviously 14 percent did not respond.)

Those from religious backgrounds credit their reaction mainly to intellectual factors ("it doesn't make sense," "trusting my own mind over authority," "religion contradicts science," "the Bible is discrepant," "comparative religion shows natural origins of myth"). In the survey, 4 percent became atheists after reading the Bible. Three-quarters indicated that reading authors such as Russell, Paine, Mencken, Ingersoll, and Stanton had had a major impact on their views.

Debunking the "selfish atheist" stereotype were the results showing that an overwhelming majority (94 percent) were actively involved in charitable activity. Atheists work to save the environment, to gain civil rights and women's rights, to control population, and to bring about peace. And many do service or volunteer work in their local communities.

Conclusion

Atheism is a straightforward concept—a reasonable, thoughtful, benign point of view. Atheists hold that universally accepted laws for ethical behavior are based on the value of life, human rights and dignity, and the need for cooperation and preservation of life on earth. They also maintain that reason is a better basis for ethics than faith. The hallmark of some religious groups is their insistence that conduct be governed by guilt and fear—an irrational basis for ethics. Religious morality ("righteousness") depends on an abolitionist, authoritarian moral code handed down "from on high." History shows that appeals to divine authority often cause strife, bloodshed, intolerance, and bigotry. Basing actions on reason and kindness, an individual stands on firmer moral ground.

Bibliography

Barker, Dan. *Just Pretend: A Freedom Thought Book for Children*. Madison, Wis.: FFRF, 1988.

Gaylor, Anne Laurie. *Woe to the Women! The Bible Tells Me So*. Madison, Wis.: FFRF, 1988.

Green, Ruth. *The Born Again Skeptic's Guide to the Bible*. Madison, Wis.: FFRF, 1982.

Neilson, Kai. *Ethics without God*. Buffalo, N.Y.: Prometheus Books, 1989.

Paine, Thomas. *The Age of Reason*. Seacaucus, N.J.: Citadel Press, 1974.

Pfeffer, Leo. *Church, State, and Freedom*. Boston: Beacon Press, 1967.

Russell, Bertrand. *Why I Am Not a Christian*. New York: Simon & Schuster, 1957.

Smith, George. *Atheism: The Case against God*. Buffalo, N.Y.: Prometheus Books, 1989.

Stein, Gordon. *Anthologies of Atheism and Rationalism*. 2 vols. Buffalo, N.Y.: Prometheus Books, 1980–87.

Prepared by Dan Barker, director of public relations, Freedom from Religion Foundation.

SOCIETY OF NATURAL SCIENCE

General Description

The Society of Natural Science is a scientific religion. It holds an evolving body of postulates and tenets outlining our views of the nature of humanity, how we fit into the natural world, how we should conduct our lives, and what happens to us when we die. To the best of our ability, these beliefs have been drawn from our study of natural objects and events. As such, they are subject to modification, refinement, or rejection as required by increasing knowledge. Our religion is oriented to constitute the most effective approach to the world's current pressing problems.

The Society of Natural Science maintains that *we are what we believe*. To the extent that people believe in that which is not real, their ability to cope with life in impaired. The society addresses this fundamental impairment with a process of deep psychotherapy, that is, conversion, whereby people learn not only a new belief system but also how to apply it to the problems of their lives.

We practice religion that adheres to the principle of nature and whose system of beliefs is based on observation rather than myth. It is a major departure from traditional religions. We offer a psychotherapy that intends to assist people in correcting and revising their basic belief system, and that is a major departure from traditional psychotherapy. These two departures are united in the organic whole of a major, new religion—the Society of Natural Science.

Founder and History

The Society of Natural Science was formally organized and incorporated in 1985 by Peter Lawrence Gill, Ph.D., and several of his student-colleagues. Its creation was the natural consequence of the recognition by Gill that his most basic beliefs—those that were developed from and underlay his thirty-year practice of psychotherapy—dealt with the same issues that are basic to all comprehensive religions.

Lynne Feldman, a colleague of Gill, later described the founding process as an evolution occurring

> over a period of approximately twenty years as an outgrowth of a training institute for psychotherapists under the direction of Dr. Peter Gill. As we did our work as therapists, we found ourselves talking to our patients about their beliefs, values and how to lead their lives. It occurred to us that we were dealing with basic religious questions. We depart from traditional psychotherapy in that we attempt to change the patient's fundamental belief system. We depart from traditional religion by our dedication to the scientific method as the means of seeking truth. We encourage skepticism and view all beliefs as subject to change and modification. (*The Society News* [no date available])

On the subject of religion, Gill points out that the Random House *American College Dictionary* presents as its first and most basic definition of religion: "The quest for the values of the ideal life, involving three phases: the ideal, the practices for attaining the values of the ideal, and the theology or world view relating to the quest to the environing universe." Clearly this definition is broad enough to cover all the myriad religions now extant—some several hundred—and presents not the slightest problem for seriously including scientific religion.

The Society of Natural Science is similar to our conventional, present-day religions in terms of both its aim to guide man from birth to death and its concern with the most basic issues. The society differs from conventional religions in its resolution to maintain scientific ideals and processes. That is, the society eschews the concepts of revealed, absolute, and uncriticizable truths. The society has its beliefs based on faith, as well as beliefs resulting from evidence gathered and interpreted according to the principles of modern science. But all these beliefs are subject to review, open to question and criticism, and regarded as improvable or replaceable should the evidence require.

As far as the difference between conventional psychotherapy and the work performed at the Society of Natural Science is concerned, it is primarily that conventional psychotherapy ignores and avoids the crucial, basic, religious issues. The quality of therapy is sacrificed by conventional therapists in order to avoid controversy by appealing to the broadest public and offending no one.

Beliefs and Doctrines

The Society of Natural Science believes not only that there is a desperate need for much greater quality both in conventional religion and in conventional therapy but also that the public is hungry for such quality. The society suffers the attacks typically mounted on the pioneers of life, but the pursuit of excellence is rich in its own rewards.

The society holds five fundamental postulates:

1. We believe in the principles of the scientific process as the only reliable and acceptable methodology in the attempt to discover and clarify the truths of man's existence.
2. It therefore follows that the tenets of the Society of Natural Science are not absolute and not fixed but rather are the hypotheses of science. These tenets may be most firmly held but are still subject to intelligent skepticism, modification or even rejection should future evidence so require.
3. Mother Nature is our god. She is to be worshiped in the sense of cultivating a profound understanding and appreciation of her laws. She is not to be prayed to or begged for favors. It is in the understanding of her laws that we will find the truths of man's existence.
4. We reject as unacceptable methodology the literal acceptance of mythology, folklore, accounts of so-called visions or miracles, and all other non-scientific approaches used by the primitive psychologies.
5. We reject all concepts of personal life after death and thus we also reject all concepts of heaven and hell, purgatory, limbo, and the like.

The basic religious beliefs of the Society of Natural Science are the following:

All children are born innocent. All persons are totally respectworthy. There are no bad persons, only those with greater or lesser degrees of health.

The purpose of life is the pursuit of happiness. There is no life of the personality after death, only a recycling of constituent chemicals.

There is no anthropomorphic god with a knowledge of, concern, and plan for individual organisms. Human behavior, unless physically forced, is always in response to one's own motivation (i.e., selfishness). One of man's strongest and most important motivations is to seek the approval and love of one's fellows.

Healthy behavior is social, equitable, tolerant, cooperative, and respecting of all. As with Shakespeare, in *King Lear*, "Mother Nature is our God."

Purpose

The purpose of the Society of Natural Science is to conduct research into the realities of human nature and conduct, to disseminate our best understanding of these realities, to train members to minister to the public, and then to minister directly to the needs of the public.

Conditions are such that the world is crying out for a new religion. Existing religions have been required to help us to cope in a world replete with overpopulation; abuse of and discrimination against women, children, minorities, the ill, and the aged; international hostilities on the verge of nuclear world war; violence in families and on the street; inadequate and cruel treatment of criminals and the mentally ill; destruction of our natural environment; and disease.

Other religions tend to favor the ancient, primitive views and ignorance of the nature of man and the world, and they view humanity's problems in ancient rather than modern terms. Other religions tend to consider their primitive beliefs to be immutable "truths." This has prevented these religions from growing with science and thus from being able to address and cope with the current world problems.

The world needs a new religion that reflects current scientific knowledge and research methodology and that addresses current world problems. It needs one that has a flexible, scientific set of fundamental postulates that can adapt as man's knowledge and scientific understanding improves, as scientific research methodology expands and improves, and as world conditions change. Finally, the world needs a religion that will repair the condition of the world through individual health and happiness.

(All of the above was taken from *The Society News*, Nos. 1, 2, 3 and 4, 1988–1989.)

Significant Terms

Gregariousness. The behavior that describes one of man's central needs, the love of others.

Psycho-religious issues. Issues basic to both religion and psychology.

Respect and innocence. Respect is a key concept in our thinking and denotes a state that all humans deserve, since we are all innocent in terms of what we are and what we do. We paraphrase humanistically the biblical expression to read, "There but for the grace of our determinants go I." It means that there are no perfect persons, only persons more or less healthy or sick.

Scientific methodology. The technique basic to the ascertaining of reality.

Scientific religion. Religious explanation based on empirical phenomena stemming from natural and behavioral sciences as available to human experience.

Selfishness. A neutral term characterizing most of all human behavior.

Bibliography
(Dr. Peter Gill refers "the interested reader to the vast library of the natural sciences—
   biology, psychology, anthropology, etc.")
The Society News. Chestnut Hill, Mass.: Society of Natural Science.

*Prepared by the editor from the writings of Peter Lawrence Gill, founder of the Society of
Natural Science, and from* The Society News *(the principal source of the writings of Dr.
Gill)*.

UNITED CHURCH OF RELIGIOUS SCIENCE

General Description

The United Church of Religious Science describes itself as a spiritual movement dedicated to the awakening and supporting of the conscious experience and expression of every person's inherent divine nature. What Religious Science teaches us is known as Science of Mind. It draws upon the wisdom of the ages as well as the frontiers of modern science and philosophy to bring together the highest reaches of the human mind for practical use in daily life.

Universal in its appeal to all people, it seeks to follow the threefold pattern of preaching, teaching, and healing. Preaching involves the presentation of great truths; teaching concerns how to use them; and through their use, healing becomes evident and tangible by changes in human lives.

Founder and History

The United Church of Religious Science was founded by Dr. Ernest Holmes and is based on his study of the great spiritual teachings of all ages and his investigation of the scientific and philosophical principles that correlated with those spiritual truths. He is quoted as saying, "Religious Science is a correlation of laws of science, opinions of philosophy, and revelations of religion applied to human needs and the aspirations of man."

Holmes was born January 21, 1887, in rural Maine and came to California in 1912 on an exploratory visit. Speaking to audiences who responded to his practical spirituality, he made progressive moves to a larger ministry and in February 1927 incorporated the Institute of Religious Science and School of Philosophy. The purpose of the school was to teach classes and offer lectures on the Science of Mind, as his philosophy had come to be called.

In October 1929 the *Science of Mind* magazine was first printed. It now has a worldwide circulation of several million readers. It offers articles, interviews, and excerpts from the writings of famous authors in positive living and the relationship of mind and matter.

Education

A major part of the message of the Science of Mind to the world lies in the area of education. The primary purpose of the Ernest Holmes College School of Ministry is to educate ministers who can carry that message to the world with clarity and love.

The school continually graduates ministers who not only are committing their time but are dedicating their lives to be of service to humankind, to assist in creating a world where love, prosperity, peace, and happiness are commonplace.

The Ernest Holmes College School of Ministry is the educational arm of the Church of Religious Science. The School of Ministry, a division of the Ernest Holmes College, provides the education and training necessary to become a Religious Science minister.

Continuing in the direction set by its founder, the Home Office of United Church of Religious Science is located in the heart of Los Angeles. Member churches are spread across the United States and in some other countries. Study groups are also internationally located to bring together in small groups people who are interested in using in daily life the universal practice of the church.

In 1989 there were approximately 184 churches worldwide and approximately 110 study groups. There are approximately 400 licensed and ordained ministers. This number includes retired, inactive, or candidating ministers as well as those who hold a letter of call. There are five regional schools of ministry known collectively as Ernest Holmes College. They are located in Los Angeles and Huntington Beach, California; Denver, Colorado; Seattle, Washington; and Orlando, Florida.

Bibliography

Holmes, Ernest. *The Base Idea of Science of Mind.* Los Angeles: Institute of Religious Science, 1957.
——. *How to Use the Science of Mind.* New York: Dodd, Mead, 1948.
——. *Religious Science.* Los Angeles: Institute of Religious Science, 1932.
Holmes, Ernest, and Fenwickel Holmes. *What Religious Science Teaches.* Los Angeles: Institute of Religious Science, 1944.
Kinnear, Willis H., ed. *The Coaching Power of Mind.* New York: Prentice-Hall, 1957.

Prepared by the editor from materials furnished by Rev. Linda McNamar, dean of Ernest Holmes College.

◆ ◆ ◆
EVANGELICAL
FREE CHURCH

General Description and Distinctives
The Evangelical Free Church is inclusive not exclusive. It is evangelical in spirit though not in structure; it believes in liberty with responsibility. The Evangelical Free Church believes in both the rational and relational dimensions of Christianity and is congregational in government.

History
The Evangelical Free Church of America is the result of a merger between the Swedish Evangelical Free Church and the Norwegian-Danish Evangelical Free Church Association. This merger took place in 1950 at Medicine Lake, Minnesota. At the time of the merger, the Swedish Evangelical Free Church had 175 congregations, and the Norwegian-Danish Evangelical Free Church Association had 90 churches. Together, they had a constituency of 20,000.

The Evangelical Free Church movement began in Europe and the Scandinavian countries. On the Continent, it goes back to 1816, when Robert Haldane, a layman, began meeting and studying the Book of Romans along with some local pastors and seminary students in Geneva, Switzerland. The ultimate result of this study produced a "new reformation" in which churches united that were free from state control. This Free Church movement spread through many of the countries on the continent of Europe.

In the Scandinavian countries, a similar movement, primarily among laymen, began in the 1800s. It was called the Readers movement. Laymen gathered for the reading of God's Word, the singing of hymns, and sharing of a time of prayer. Persecution forced them outside the state church, which resulted in a Free Church movement in the Scandinavian countries generally called the Mission Covenant Churches.

The great waves of migration from the Scandinavian countries from 1880 to 1920 produced Mission Churches here in the United States. These, along with some others begun by the ministry of Fredrik Franson, resulted in the establishment of the Swedish Evangelical Free Church in 1884. In that same year, two Norwegian-Danish churches began in this country—one in Boston and one in Tacoma, Washington. As the Swedish and Norwegian churches grew and as the Scandinavian languages diminished in their importance, they found it possible to join together at the merger conference in 1950.

Early leaders of the Evangelical Free Church include John Joseph Princell, a scholar and educator, and Fredrik Franson, an evangelist and revivalist. In addition to these, there were many other scholars, ministers, and laymen who were part of the early establishment of the Free Church movement here in the United States.

The Evangelical Free Church of America has now grown to a denomination of more than 1,000 churches throughout the United States and more than 600 churches overseas. A new Evangelical Free Church is being formed at the rate of one church each week somewhere in the United States. We have almost 400 missionaries serving in 15 fields of the world. Special concern is now focused on some great world-class cities of America and other places around the world.

Beliefs and Doctrines

The official doctrinal position of the Evangelical Free Church includes twelve points.

We believe:

1. The Scriptures, both Old and New Testaments, to be the inspired Word of God, without error in the original writings, the complete revelation of His will for the salvation of men and the Divine and final authority for Christian faith and life.
2. In one God, Creator of all things, infinitely perfect and eternally existing in three persons, Father, Son, and Holy Spirit.
3. That Jesus Christ is true God and true man, having been conceived of the Holy Ghost and born of the Virgin Mary. He died on the cross a sacrifice for our sins according to the Scriptures. Further, He arose bodily from the dead, ascended into heaven, where at the right hand of the Majesty on High, He is now our High Priest and Advocate.
4. That the ministry of the Holy Spirit is to glorify the Lord Jesus Christ, and during this age to convict men, regenerate the believing sinner, indwell, guide, instruct, and empower the believer for godly living and service.
5. That man was created in the image of God but fell into sin and is therefore lost and only through regeneration by the Holy Spirit can salvation and spiritual life be obtained.
6. That the shed blood of Jesus Christ and His resurrection provide the only ground for justification and salvation for all who believe, and only such as receive Jesus Christ are born of the Holy Spirit, and thus become children of God.
7. That water baptism and the Lord's Supper are ordinances to be observed

by the Church during the present age. They are, however, not to be regarded as means of salvation.

8. That the true Church is composed of all such persons who through saving faith in Jesus Christ have been regenerated by the Holy Spirit and are united together in the body of Christ of which He is the Head.
9. That only those who are thus members of the true Church shall be eligible for membership in the local church.
10. That Jesus Christ is the Lord and Head of the Church, and that every local church has the right under Christ to decide and govern its own affairs.
11. In the personal premillennial and imminent coming of our Lord Jesus Christ and that this "Blessed Hope" has a vital bearing on the personal life and the service of the believer.
12. In the bodily resurrection of the dead; of the believer to everlasting blessedness and joy with the Lord, of the unbeliever to judgment and everlasting conscious punishment.

Organization

Our constitution states that our primary purpose is the evangelization of the nonbeliever. In other words, we are charged with the responsibility of fulfilling Christ's Great Commission by "making disciples of all nations." We are also charged with fulfilling the "great commandment," in which our Lord challenges us to love God and love our neighbor. These purposes and responsibilities are carried out by training ministers and missionaries, by establishing churches at home and overseas, by nurturing the believer in the Christian faith, and by training the Christian to minister to others to fulfill the mandates of our Lord.

The Evangelical Free Church is an association of churches joined together in bonds of love for the purpose of developing and maintaining ministries best accomplished by mutual cooperation. The focal point of these ministries is the evangelization of lost humanity and the edification of believers. Outreach ministries in the United States and around the world are accomplished through the efforts of our Church Ministries and Overseas departments. Denomination-sponsored facilities of higher education not only train Christian leadership for missions or ministry but also train and equip laypeople for effective Christian living in the secular marketplaces of life.

Various ministries of the Home Office serve the needs of the local church in children, youth, and adult curriculum programming, publishing, and stewardship. Auxiliary organizations, such as Free Church Women's Ministries and Free Church Laymen's Fellowship, significantly contribute to the expansion of our ministries at home and overseas. The compassion of Christ is demonstrated through homes for children and facilities for the aging.

The denomination as such does not hold title to the property of the local congregation and recognizes the right of every church under Christ to decide and govern its own affairs.

Each year, a general conference is held of delegates and ministers from local churches throughout the United States to elect members to the administrative boards and the board of directors of the denomination. It also elects the following full-time, salaried executives: president, executive director of Church Ministries, presidents of the schools, and the editor of the *Evangelical Beacon,* the official magazine of the denomination. The board of directors is responsible for dealing with the entire organization of the Evangelical Free Church between general conference sessions. All boards, organizations, institutions, and departments, however, are in existence to serve the local church. They seek to carry out the wishes of the general conference between the annual meetings of the denomination.

Contributions and Influence

The Evangelical Free Church of America has made a unique contribution to the religious life in America by providing some of the outstanding evangelical leaders at the forefront of the evangelical movement. Such a person was Arnold T. Olsen, former president, author, and president of the National Association of Evangelicals, and a leader recognized in the United States, Europe, Israel, and other nations.

The Evangelical Free Church has been named by the American Institute of Church Growth as one of the fastest-growing denominations in America today. Our goals for the year 2000 include more than doubling the number of our churches and more than doubling the number of our missionaries.

The Evangelical Free Church of America is a founding member of the National Association of Evangelicals. The NAE is composed of many denominations across North America and is part of the World Evangelical Fellowship, which is a worldwide fellowship of evangelical movements.

Significant Terms

Evangelical. Refers to our commitment to the authority of Scripture as being inerrant in the original autographs and the only safe and sufficient guide to faith and practice.

Free. Refers to our form of church government as being congregational. Free Churches depend upon the active participation of laypeople in the decisions and directions of the local church.

Associate/Assistant pastor. A licensed or ordained minister serving as a part of a pastoral team.

Deacon. A layman who serves on a board of deacons, who may be responsible for the overall ministry of the local church.

Elder. A layman who has been elected by the congregation to serve on a board of elders, who are responsible for the spiritual welfare of the congregation.

Member. A member of the local church is one who has officially joined a local church by meeting the qualifications for membership.

President. The chief full-time administrative officer of the Evangelical Free Church of America.

President of theological seminaries or colleges/universities. The chief executive officer of a particular institution.

Senior pastor. An ordained minister who is the senior, or head, pastor in a local church.

Bibliography
(All items are published by Free Church Publications, Minneapolis.)

THE HERITAGE SERIES
Vol. 1, *Search for Identity,* by Arnold T. Olsen. 1980.
Vol. 2, *The Significance of Silence,* by Arnold T. Olsen. 1981.
Vol. 3, *Stumbling toward Maturity,* by Arnold T. Olsen. 1981.
Vol. 4, *The Dynamic of the Printed Page,* by Roy A. Thompson. 1982.
Vol. 5, *Light a Small Candle,* by Bernard Palmer. 1983.
Vol. 6, *The Trinity Story,* by Calvin Hanson. 1983.
Vol. 7, *While the Sun Is High,* by Bernard Palmer. 1984.
Vol. 8, *Care and Concern of Churches,* by Edwin Groenhoff. 1984.

OTHER WORKS
Believers Only. 1962.
This We Believe. 1961.

Prepared by Dr. Thomas A. McDill, president of the Evangelical Free Church.

HINDUISM IN
THE UNITED STATES

INTERNATIONAL SIVANANDA
YOGA VEDANTA CENTER

General Description

The International Sivananda Yoga Vedanta Center (ISYVC) and ashrams were founded by Swami Vishnu Devananda, a Hindu swami (monk) and direct disciple of the late Swami Sivananda. Swami Sivananda belongs to the Sarasvati lineage of monks, one of the ten lineages started in India in the eighth century A.D. by Sankaracarya, who himself belonged to an interrupted lineage of monks started in the Vedic times by the great Rishis (seers). The Rishis had direct experience of the divine and started passing on their divine knowledge to their disciples.

These great seers, whose religious authority is absolute for Hindus, expressed their authentic experience of God in esoteric hymns called the Vedas, which are the source of the most important philosophical and religious system of Hinduism, called Vedanta ("the end of the Veda"). The second most important system among the six branches of Hinduism is called Yoga (in a restrictive meaning), which is a complete system in itself, aiming to reach the state of Yoga—the union of the individual soul with the supreme divine soul.

The ISYVC follows and spreads the teachings of Swami Sivananda, who realized a synthesis of these two branches (Vedanta and Yoga).

Swami Vishnu Devananda was sent by his master to the West in 1957 to spread the Yoga Vedanta. He has created all the Sivananda ashrams and centers and since then has trained five thousand teachers and has written books published throughout the world. Centers in the United States include those in New York, Los Angeles, Chicago, and San Francisco; there are Ashrams in Grass Valley, California; Woodbourne, New York; and the Bahamas. Centers and ashrams are also in Canada, South America, India, and in all main cities of Europe. Their aim is to spread the Yoga Vedanta and to train spiritual leaders to promote self-discipline and very high spiritual values and so to lead the world to peace and harmony.

Founder

Swami Vishnu Devananda was born in South India in 1927. He spent ten years in the service of his master at Svarg Ashram, Rishikesh, Himalayas.

He was sent to the West by the Swami Sivananda to spread Yoga Vedanta. Swami Sivananda is recognized in India as a saint, continuing the very ancient spiritual tradition started by the Rishis.

Beliefs and Doctrines

Vedanta is a nondualistic religion. Its basic principles are the following: (1) everything is Brahma (God, the Absolute); (2) the phenomenal world is an illusion; (3) the individual soul is nothing but our false identification with limiting agents—the body and mind. This false identification is our main impurity, and we have to engage in intense practice to purify all the different levels of our personality in order to regain our divinity.

Swami Sivananda thus emphasized integral practice, which he called the Yoga of synthesis. It consists of the following four kinds of yoga:

1. Jnana Yoga, the intellectual part of yoga, is based on the Vedantic philosophy. It is an inquiry of our true nature (divine) by the intellect, ceaselessly raising in the mind the fundamental question, "Who am I?"
2. Raja Yoga, the scientific path of yoga, aims at a complete control of body and mind through physical disciplines (asanas, pranayama), ethical disciplines (yamas and niyamas), and mental disciplines (meditation), the latter being the central practice for realizing our unity with God.
3. Karma Yoga, the yoga of selfless service to others, develops awareness of the presence of the divine in all beings one is serving. The goal is to give up the fruit of one's actions to God and to act as an instrument of God.
4. Bhakti Yoga, the yoga of devotion, aims to realize our unity with the Lord through devotional practices.

Forms of Worship

Worship forms include meditation, prayers, repetition of sacred words (mantras), study of sacred scriptures, chants in Sanskrit, pujas (a traditional Hindu ceremony), and the celebration of Hindu religious festivals and spiritual marriages.

Organization

The international headquarters of ISYVC is in Quebec, Canada. It coordinates and supervises the different branches throughout the world. The various organizations work like one unit, being in constant communication with the headquarters.

Contributions and Influence

Swami Vishnu Devananda was one of the first swamis to spread the teaching of Yoga Vedanta in the United States. He published several books in New York City, including *Complete Illustrated Book of Yoga* (which sold over 1 million copies), *Meditation and Mantras, The Sivananda Companion* to *Yoga,* and *Commentary to the Hatha Yoga Pradipika.* A video was recently released, illustrating *The Sivananda Companion to Yoga.* The ISYVC has trained over five thousand teachers, many at the Sivananda Yoga Ranch, in Woodbourne, New York, and Sivananda Vrindavan Yoga Farm, in Grass Valley, California. The swami has toured the United States often during the last thirty years, teaching and lecturing, all of which was done to make the people aware of the necessity to develop self-discipline and to follow high ethical and spiritual values, which in turn allows one to reach a universal vision of life in which the divinity hidden in each being is revealed. This universal vision enables men to see the unity of all religions beyond the superficial differences of names and cults.

Significant Terms

Yoga. Union between individual and universal consciousness.

Vedanta. The most important philosophical and spiritual system of Hinduism. Its basic principle is unity (or nondualism), multiplicity being only an appearance.

Self-realization. The aim of the Yoga Vedanta practice, which is realization of our divine nature (also called *samadhi* in the Raja Yoga path).

Brahma. The Absolute, the infinite God without name or form.

Mantra. A sacred word revealed to a Rishi (seer) in the Vedic time when in a supraconscious state. Its repetition leads eventually to God-consciousness.

Dyhana (meditation). A technique to reach God-consciousness by stilling completely all the mental modifications (as defined by Patanjai in the Yoga Sutras).

Asanas. A steady posture, which the body should be able to hold for a long time in order for the mind to reach the state of meditation.

Pranayama. Breathing techniques to control one's vital energy.

Yamas and Niyamas. Ethical rules of Raja Yoga.

Guru. One who has reached God-consciousness and is thus entitled to teach spiritual seekers the way to reach the same spiritual development.

Ashram. A place dedicated to spiritual practices, usually in a natural setting away from cities, where spiritual seekers live together following a specific discipline, having the common goal to reach God-consciousness.

Swami (also *sannyasin*). One who takes the vow of complete renunciation (chastity, poverty, service to the guru), having for a goal to reach the highest spiritual state and to help others to do it. He is initiated into sannyas by a guru.

Summary

The charitable religious organization founded by Swami Vishnu Devananda, an authority recognized worldwide in Yoga Vedanta, does not teach any new religion or philosophy but wants to spread the message of the late

Swami Sivananda, an authentic master carrying on the teachings of the great Rishis. Swami Vishnu Devananda brought credibility to Yoga in the West. He continues to do his great work through his centers, ashrams, world tours, peace missions (including flights over designated trouble spots of the world, dropping leaflets and flowers for peace, for instance, over the Berlin Wall in 1983 and over the Suez Canal in 1971, visiting in Belfast with the late Peter Sellers), lectures, teacher training courses (with an average increase of about 7 percent per year since 1969), book publishing, and training of close disciples. The message of Swami Vishnu Devananda is a personal example of compassion, of a person ready to risk his life for peace, with love to encounter war and nationalistic or fanatic religious hatred. He has beautifully said, "Serve, love, give, purify, meditate, realize." To realize this means to realize unity in diversity—the unity of all religions and all beings.

Bibliography

Devananda, Swami Vishnu. *The Complete Illustrated Book of Yoga.* New York: Julian Press, 1960, 1988; pocketbook edition, New York: Simon & Schuster, 1972.
——. *The Hatha Yoga Pradipika: A Commentary.* New York: Om Lotus, 1987.
——. *Meditation and Mantra.* New York: Om Lotus, 1978.
——. *The Sivananda Upanishad.* New York: Om Lotus, 1987.
Sivananda, Swami. [34 books, published by Divine Life Society, U.P., Himalayas, India].
Sivananda Yoga Centre. *The Sivananda Companion to Yoga.* New York: Simon & Schuster, 1983.

Prepared by Uma Chatanya, Sivananda Yoga Center.

KRISHNA CONSCIOUSNESS

Origins and History

At the time of creation, Krishna, the Supreme Lord, imparted knowledge directly into the heart of Brahma, the first created being in the universe. Brahma taught his son, Narada. Narada taught Vyasa, and Vyasa taught Madhava. In this way the science of God was handed from master to disciple in an unbroken chain, coming to Sri Chaitanya Mahaprabhu in India in the fifteenth century.

Sri Chaitanya Mahaprabhu is Krishna himself in the guise of a devotee, come to this world to teach the principles of Krishna Consciousness. He emphasized the chanting of the holy names of God, particularly the Hare Krishna Maha-mantra: Hare Krishna, Hare Krishna, Hare Hare, Hare Rama, Hare Rama, Rama Rama, Hare Hare.

In 1965 His Divine Grace A. C. Bhaktivedanta Swami Prabhupada brought the teachings of the original succession of disciples to the West and founded the International Society for Krishna Consciousness in New York.

Beliefs and Doctrines

The basic principles of Krishna Consciousness are given in the Bhagavad Gita, spoken five thousand years ago by Krishna to his friend and disciple Arjuna. The principles are elaborated in the Sprimad Bhagavatam, and further in the Chaitanya Charitamrita. These are the main works in the vast body of Krishna Consciousness writings.

Krishna Consciousness is love of God, and the first principle is that God is a person. He has a body and a name. He lives somewhere, does things, and has friends. Still, he is unlimited and omnipresent. Thus, he can be simultaneously in his abode and in the hearts of all living beings.

All living beings originally share in the eternal, knowledgeable, and blissful nature of God, but those who have fallen into this world, out of a desire to imitate God rather than love him, are covered by illusion and transmigrate from body to body, species to species, in a vain search for satisfaction. From time to time, God comes into this world to reclaim these fallen souls and bring them back to the spiritual world.

God may appear in different ways—as Rama, the great king; as Nrshimas, the protector of the devotee; as Krishna, the beautiful youth—but he is always the same Lord. Therefore, Krishna Consciousness agrees with any religion that teaches the love of God, but it must be based on Scripture, with no tinge of invention or speculation. The love of any form of God is perfect, but the Scriptures teach that the love of Krishna is the fullest development of this love.

Forms of Worship

Krishna Consciousness has both individual and congregational worship. Both forms center on the chanting of the Hare Krishna Mahamantra. Individually, the devotees repeat the Mahamantra, counting the repetitions on a string of 108 prayer beads. The devotee goes through the whole string at least sixteen times each day.

Congregationally, the devotees gather every morning before sunrise and every evening to sing the Mahamantra to the accompaniment of musical instruments and to hold classes on the Scriptures.

Spiritual Master

The Scriptures teach that worship of the spiritual master is as important as the worship of God himself. Thus, every morning, the devotees also worship His Divine Grace A. C. Bhaktivedanta Swami Prabhupada, the great teacher who brought Krishna Consciousness to the West.

The spiritual master is called "His Divine Grace" because he delivers the mercy of Krishna by teaching Krishna Consciousness. This system is ordained by Scripture and is the surest way to spiritual perfection. However, the spiritual master must be a devotee of Krishna.

Practices

Devotees of Krishna abstain from certain foods (meat, fish, eggs), from intoxication (including refraining from drugs, alcohol, coffee, tea, and tobacco), from illicit sex, and from gambling. The devotees encourage everyone to follow the same principles. They also encourage everyone to attain the perfection of human life, which is love of God, and they work constantly for the benefit of society.

Significant Terms

Avatara. "One who descends," a fully or partially empowered incarnation of God who descends from the spiritual realm for a particular mission.

Bhagavad Gita. The scripture that records the spiritual instructions given by Lord Krishna to his friend Arjuna on the battlefield of Kurukshetra.

Bhagavan. "He who possess all opulences," the Supreme Lord, who is the reservoir of all beauty, strength, fame, wealth, knowledge, and renunciation.

Bhakti Yoga. Linking with the Supreme Lord through devotional service.

Chaitanya Charitamrita. The biography of Sri Chaitanya Mahaprabhu, composed in Bengali in the late sixteenth century by Krishnadesa Kaviraja.

Deva. A demigod or godly person.

Goloka (also *Krishnaloka*). The eternal abode of Lord Krishna.

Guru. A spiritual master.

Jiva. The eternal individual soul.

Karma. Material activities, for which one incurs subsequent reactions.

Mantra. A transcendental sound of a Vedic hymn.

Maha-mantra. The great mantra: Hare Krishna, Hare Krishna, Krishna Krishna, Hare Hare, Hare Rama, Hare Rama, Rama Rama, Hare Hare.

Maya. Appearance. As the external energy of the Supreme Lord, maya covers the conditioned soul and keeps him from understanding the supreme personality of the Godhead.

Samsara. The cycle of repeated birth and death in the material world.

Srimad Bhagavatam. The authoritative Vedic scripture that deals exclusively with the pastimes of the supreme personality of the Godhead and his devotees.

Vaishnava. A devotee of Krishna.

Vedas. The four original Scriptures (Rig, Sama, Atharva, and Yajur).

Vyasa. The compiler of the Vedas, Srimad Bhagavatan, Bhagavad Gita, and many other Scriptures.

Bibliography

A. C. Bhaktivedanta Swami Prabhupada. *Bhagavad Gita As It Is*. Los Angeles: Bhaktivedanta Book Trust, 1983.

Brooks, Charles R. *The Hare Krishnas in India*. Princeton, N.J.: Princeton University Press, 1989.

Gelberg, Steven J. *Hare Krishna, Hare Krishna: Five Distinguished Scholars on the Krishna Movement in the West*. New York: Grove Press, 1983.

Stillson, Judah J. *Hare Krishna and the Counterculture*. New York: John Wiley & Sons, 1974.

Prepared by Umpati Swami, director of educational services.

VEDANTA SOCIETY

General Description

The Vedanta philosophy is the thread that connects all the various sects of Hinduism. The philosophy is thousands of years old, originating from the mystic experiences of ancient saints and seers and transmitted from generation to generation. Eventually, the doctrines of Vedanta were recorded in the Vedas. The Sanskrit word "vedanta" literally means "the end of the Vedas" and refers to the body of literature known as the Upanishads.

Through the ages, the eternal truths of Vedanta have been expressed through the lives of many saints and exemplars. Foremost among them was the great Indian saint Sri Ramakrishna (1836–86). Swami Vivekananda, his chief disciple, introduced Vedanta to America in 1893, when he attended the World's Parliament of Religions in Chicago as a representative of Hinduism. After extensive lecturing in the West, the swami returned to India and founded the Ramakrishna Mission in 1898.

The Ramakrishna Order of India, with headquarters at Belur Math in Calcutta, maintains ninety centers in India and thirty-five centers throughout the rest of the world. There are thirteen Vedanta Societies in the United States, all of which are affiliated with the Ramakrishna Order.

Beliefs and Doctrines

There are four basic tenets of Vedanta.

1. God, or Brahma, is the underlying reality, the essence of all existence.
2. Brahma is one, appearing as many. There is unity in variety.
3. The true nature of man is divine.
4. Each person can directly experience this divinity within and, in doing so, becomes one with the Infinite. This is the ultimate goal of life.

Ramakrishna gave new dimension to these tenets by emphasizing the harmony of religions and service to God in man. All religions are but different paths to the same goal—the realization of God. External methods may differ, but all religions lead to God. Each person is encouraged to find the path most suitable to him and then pursue it.

Since God exists in all beings, the highest worship is to worship him in man; thus we serve God. In this way, social service is transformed into a spiritual practice.

It is not possible to define God as being only this or that. The term "God" can indeed be confusing, for in the West the word is most frequently thought of only in the sense of a personal God. To a Vedantin, however, God can be with or without form. God can be personal or impersonal. It is like water, which can be completely formless as water vapor, relatively formless as liquid water, or with form as ice. We conceive of God according to our state of mind. God has form when called Christ, Buddha, Krishna, or Rama, and again is without form when thought of as Divine Force, Pure Consciousness, or Awareness.

All ethics are a means to the end of finding God within ourselves or expanding our awareness. "Right" action is action that expands our awareness and brings us closer to self-knowledge. "Wrong" action leads us away from that knowledge. Our ideas of "good" and "evil" are therefore only relative values by which we judge others. Each member of an orchestra has a different score suited to the instrument that he plays. But the scores are all for the same piece of music, and the goal is the harmonious playing of that composition. Similarly, each of us has individual problems and an individual path of development. But the goal is the same for all. This is another aspect of the harmony of religions taught by Vedanta.

Forms of Worship

Three forms of worship are practiced. First is *external, ritualistic worship,* which consists of invoking the presence of God at the altar and worshiping him with various articles (flowers, incense, food, etc.). Next is *internal worship,* or meditation, which is the act of concentrating the mind on God, either with form or without. Finally is *worship of God in man,* which is achieved through various social services. In India, where the physical need is great, social services include feeding the poor, nursing the sick, and educating those in need. In America, however, the service is more on the spiritual level, where the poverty is greatest.

Organization

Every branch of the Ramakrishna Order is headed by an Indian monk who serves as a spiritual guide to the members. Several of the centers have a monastery or convent. Each center is independent and self-supporting. Financial matters are coordinated by a board of directors, which usually includes both monastic and lay members. While Americans are free to adapt the Vedanta philosophy to their Western culture, the spiritual connection to the order's headquarters in India remains open and vital.

Contributions and Influence

The teachings of Vedanta do not contradict science or reason. In fact, Vedanta encourages questioning and rational, scientific scrutiny. As a result, it has attracted great thinkers from all walks of life such as Ralph Waldo Emerson, Albert Einstein, Aldous Huxley, and Joseph Campbell. One of the fundamental tenets of Vedanta, the concept of "unity in diversity," is now attracting theoretical physicists, who have come to the same conclusion using scientific methods.

Other concepts of Eastern thought have entered into the mainstream of American culture. Words such as "karma," "yoga," and "guru" are now commonplace. There has been a growing interest in meditation, along with the awareness that peace comes from within. Even in corporate America, meditation techniques are being used to reduce stress.

America is predominately a Protestant country. Those Americans who have adopted Eastern monasticism are treading new waters and are introducing a new way of life into the mainstream of American religious tradition. Their life is one of renunciation, contemplation, and service to God in man. They strive to perfect themselves rather than change the world, because they know that only the one who has achieved peace can give it to others.

In the melting pot of America, it is important that all religions of the world not only be represented but also coexist in harmony. The ideas of harmony and universality are inherent in the teachings of Vedanta and appeal to progressive thinkers who are trying to liberalize religious thought. Such liberality can be seen in various faiths emphasizing the harmony of religions. Vedanta Societies in this country often represent Hinduism or Vedanta at these councils.

Vedanta has helped many people find new meaning and interest in religion. Some have come to a greater understanding of their own religious heritage. Others, who had previously denied all religious beliefs, have found a philosophy they can accept. The beauty of Vedanta is its appeal to a wide variety of people with different approaches to religion.

Significant Terms

Brahma. Absolute consciousness, the eternal underlying reality.

Atman. The indwelling spirit, Brahma within man.

Samadhi. The ultimate experience of Brahma.

Yoga. A path or method of achieving union with God.

Guru. A teacher or spiritual guide.

Mantra. Sacred words imparted to the disciple by the guru, to be repeated throughout the day.

Swami. The name given to a monk who has taken the final vows.

Bibliography

The Gospel of Sri Ramakrishna. Translated by Swami Nikhilananda. Ramakrishna-Vivekananda Center, 1984.

How to Know God: The Yoga Aphorisms of Patanjai. Translated by Swami Prabhavananda and Christopher Isherwood. Hollywood, Calif.: Vedanta Press, 1983.

Isherwood, Christopher. *RamaKrishna and His Disciples.* Hollywood, Calif.: Vedanta Press, 1980.

Nikhilananda, Swami. *Self-Knowledge.* Ramakrishna-Vivekananda Center, 1980.

The Song of God: Bhagavad-Gita. Translated by Swami Prabhavananda and Christopher Isherwood. New York: New American Library, 1972.

Vedanta for the Western World. Edited by Christopher Isherwood. Hollywood, Calif.: Vedanta Press, 1946.

Vivekananda, Swami. *Vivekananda: The Yogas and Other Works.* Edited by Swami Nikhilananda. Ramakrishna-Vivekananda Center, 1984.

(All books published by or available from the Vedanta Society and Vedanta Press, Hollywood, Calif.)

Prepared by Nancy Kenny, the Vedanta Society of Southern California.

INDEPENDENT
FUNDAMENTAL
CHURCHES OF AMERICA

General Description
The Independent Fundamental Churches of America (IFCA) is a voluntary organization of independent churches and vocational Christian workers joined together by a common doctrinal position. There are approximately 800 organizations in the fellowship, with an additional 300,000 individual fellowships under the auspices of the IFCA. The IFCA includes North America and adjacent territories. Our objectives are to promote fellowship among God's people of like precious faith, to put forth every possible effort to disseminate the gospel, and to proclaim the whole counsel of God.

The feature that is probably most unique to us is the autonomy of the local church. It is not unique to our fellowship but is far different than in most denominations that uphold this principle. Each local church is an autonomous, independent organization in which Jesus Christ is considered to be the only head; there is no denominational hierarchy in our fellowship.

The IFCA simply provides fellowship among local churches with doctrinal unity. It offers services such as counseling, pastoral placement, assistance in ordination, referral of IFCA churches when members are traveling under the membership directory, information on missions and educational institutions, representation in governmental matters regarding tax-exempt status and military chaplains, and it gives assistance in the matter of Christian education and cooperative fellowship. For the individual, the IFCA provides opportunity for fellowship around a common doctrine, reinforces sound doctrinal conviction, and offers ministers a recommendation by a nationally recognized movement. We serve as a source of information on current affairs that affect independent churches and provide a basis for cooperative financial ventures in the matter of church development and extension.

History and Founders
The development of secularism and the liberal religious movement during the last quarter of the nineteenth century and first quarter of the twentieth were the catalysts to the development of the Independent movement. In 1909 the first concerted effort to rebuff these two errors surfaced through the publication of a twelve-volume work entitled *The Fundamentals*. Historians

have identified the beginning of the fundamentalist movement with the impact of these books. The hermeneutical basis of this movement rests upon a dispensational understanding of the Scriptures.

Two men were instrumental in the beginning and development of the IFCA—Mr. O. B. Bottorff and Dr. William McCarrell. Bottorff was the leader of a movement begun in 1867 called the American Conference of Undenominational Churches, the forerunner of the IFCA. In January 1930 McCarrell, pastor of the Cicero Bible Church, and several associated Congregational churches voted unanimously to sever their denominational affiliations and adopted a policy to associate themselves with any group of Congregationalists agreeing with the fundamental doctrines that they had identified. Bottorff's and McCarrell's groups joined to begin the IFCA.

Beliefs and Doctrines

The IFCA was formed in days of intense doctrinal controversy by a group of Bible-believing pastors and churches. The fellowship was officially organized in 1930 and adopted its doctrinal position as a distinctive statement of faith. There are sixteen definitive doctrinal positions identified in the constitution of the IFCA; they deal with the Scriptures, the Godhead, the person and work of Christ, the person and work of the Spirit, the total depravity of man, salvation, eternal security and the assurance of the believer, the two natures of the believer, separation, missions, the ministry and spiritual gifts, the church, dispensationalism, the personality of Satan, the second advent of Christ, and the eternal state.

In subscribing to these articles of faith, we by no means set aside or undervalue the Scriptures of the Old and New Testaments; but we deem the knowledge, belief, and acceptance of the truth as set forth in our doctrinal statement to be essential to sound faith and fruitful practice, and therefore they are requisites for fellowship in the IFCA.

Forms of Worship

Each church determines its specific form of worship. Common practices, however, include congregational singing, choral selections, Scripture reading, prayer, and special emphasis on the exposition of the Scriptures with practical application and opportunity for personal response and decision.

Organization

Membership in the IFCA is available to both organizations and individuals. Organizations include churches, missions, missionary agencies, gospel tabernacles, centers, and Christian educational institutions that have accepted the constitution, bylaws, and articles of faith of the IFCA. Individual membership is open to vocational workers and lay individuals who are members of IFCA organizations.

The IFCA is a fellowship of individual, independent, autonomous churches who have entered fellowship together on the basis of a common doctrinal statement and an understanding of common cause. We exist in order to provide a sense of interdependency for the local churches and services such as a national chaplaincy and representation with the government. We publish a national magazine, *Voice* (the name of IFCA's journal), which is the only unified mouthpiece of our fellowship. We have about forty different regional conferences around the nation that meet together for common cause, fellowship, and mutual encouragement. We provide counseling services for our churches and also a common cause in terms of church-planting and church-extension efforts. We also provide arbitrators for church disputes and provide counsel in solving church problems.

Contributions and Influence

The IFCA is one of the few fellowships that provides a sense of inter-dependence for the independent church movement. The independent church is a sleeping giant in the United States; nobody knows how many there are, and yet we have gathered together into one fellowship a mutual commitment for interdependence a good number of them.

Our people in the IFCA churches are committed to holiness in life and to reflecting the life of Christ in the community in which they live. In that sense, we believe in personal involvement in religious life simply on the part of individual people living it out in everyday life.

Significant Terms

Dispensational. A hermeneutical governing of the teaching and perception of the Word of God, as contrasted with a conventional, allegorical, or mystical interpretation. Dispensationalism interprets the Bible with a literal, historical, grammatical, and contextual slant applied to all sections. It does recognize the use of grammatical devices.

Fundamental. This term denotes a conscientious adherence to the integrity of the Word of God. It has direct correlation to specific doctrinal positions regarding God (Father, Son, and Spirit), Jesus Christ (his birth, life, and death), and the Bible. "Fundamental" should be distinguished from "fundamentalist," which is used as a derogatory term.

Independent. This term relates to polity. Our churches are self-governing but not isolated. Independence also carries the idea of interdependence: we need to be accountable to each other as well as to be available to provide assistance when needed.

Inspiration. The inspiration of the Scriptures is concerned with the recording of the truth. Revelation is the communication of that truth. Inspiration guarantees the absolute perfectness of the recorded information of the Bible, extending to the words and syntax employed by the original authors, via the inexplicable power of the Holy Spirit. The original authors were preserved from all error and from all omissions. In the Bible we therefore have the verbally inspired Word of God.

Justification. A benefit of the death of Christ, provided by God's grace and appropriated by faith (Rom. 5:1–11). A judicial term declaring one righteous. Justification assures the believer of peace with God. The cost for our justification was paid when Jesus Christ shed his blood and died.

Salvation. The great work of God in respect to man. Because of sin, man is separated from God and destined to eternal damnation (Rom. 3:23; 5:12ff.; 6:23). There is nothing within man that merits God's favor. However, because of God's mercy, grace, and love, he provided a means of spiritual restoration through the death of Jesus Christ. Christ, the sinless one, took upon himself our sin and died in our place. He was buried and rose from the grave on the third day according to Scripture. The resurrection validated him. Salvation is available to all mankind via faith (Eph. 2:8–9; Rom. 10:9–13). Once received, it is eternally valid.

Sanctification. Akin to the word "holy," sanctification is concerned with the matter of being removed from sin and set apart unto God. Sanctification is both a process and an act. As a process, it is experienced prior to salvation as the Holy Spirit of God works in a person's life toward salvation (2 Thess. 2:13). At conversion, sanctification is experienced as a complete act (1 Cor. 1:1–2; Heb. 10:10). The child of God should daily practice a life of sanctification (1 Thess. 4:3; 2 Tim. 2:21; 1 Peter 3:15). The final or complete act of sanctification will transpire when the believer meets the Lord at either death or translation (Heb. 9:28; 12:23; 1 John 3:2; 1 Thess. 3:13).

Bibliography

Cole. S. G. *History of Fundamentalism.* Westport, Conn.: Greenwood Press, 1971.

Dollar, George. *A History of Fundamentalism.* Greenville, N.C.: Bob Jones University Press, 1973.

Hebert, A. G. *Fundamentalism and the Church of God.* London: SCM, 1957.

Henry, J. O. *For Such a Time as This.* Wheaton, Ill.: IFCA, 1983.

Pickering, Ernest. *Biblical Separation.* Schaumberg, Ill.: Baptist Press, 1979.

Sandeen, Ernest. *The Origins of Fundamentalism.* Philadelphia: Fortress Press, 1968.

Wells, D. F., and J. D. Woodbridge. *The Evangelicals.* Grand Rapids, Mich.: Baker Books, 1977.

Prepared by Paul J. Dollaske, editor, IFCA.

INTERNATIONAL CHURCH OF THE FOURSQUARE GOSPEL

Founder

No discussion of the International Church of the Foursquare Gospel is possible without reference to its founder, Aimee Semple McPherson. Born in Ontario in 1890, Aimee Semple McPherson was converted under the preaching of her first husband, Robert Semple, a Pentecostal evangelist. In 1910 the couple traveled to China as missionaries, and while serving there, Robert died of malaria. Aimee returned to the United States in 1911, where she answered the call of God to conduct evangelistic crusades throughout North America.

In 1918 Mrs. McPherson and her children, Roberta and Rolf, settled in Los Angeles. With the help of those who had been blessed with her ministry, she built Angelus Temple, dedicating it on January 1, 1923. This lady evangelist was gifted with great oratorical ability in writing religious drama, presenting illustrated messages, and asking prayers for the sick. She had great interest in the poor; more than a million and a half people are said to have been fed by Angelus Temple during her ministry.

An evangelistic and training institute was created almost simultaneously with Angelus Temple and began training leaders, who in turn established branch churches. The creation of some thirty-two churches in southern California by 1921 had spurred steps toward the formal organization of the Echo Park Evangelistic Association. On December 30, 1927, the International Church of the Foursquare Gospel was incorporated and registered in the state of California.

Beliefs and Doctrines

Doctrinally, the Foursquare Gospel represents Jesus Christ as Savior of the world, the Baptizer with the Holy Spirit, the Great Physician and the soon-coming King. The teaching of the church is set forth in its twenty-one-paragraph Declaration of Faith. Strongly fundamental, it is premillennialist, holiness, and Trinitarian, advocating the Bible as "true, immutable, steadfast, unchangeable, as its author, the Lord Jehovah." The baptism with the Holy Spirit, with the initial evidence of speaking in other tongues, is subsequent to conversion, and there is power to heal in answer to believing prayer. There are the usual doctrines on the imminent return of Christ "in clouds of glory," with rewards for the righteous at the judgment and eternal punishment for the wicked. Water baptism by immersion and the Lord's Supper are observed.

Organization

McPherson served as president of the church during her lifetime and oversaw the denomination's expansion together with a board of directors. Upon her death in 1944, her son, Rolf Kennedy McPherson, became president and faithfully presided in the position until May 31, 1988. Upon Rolf McPherson's retirement from the presidency, the position was filled by John R. Holland, who continues to serve to the present.

The official business of the church is conducted by the Board of Directors, the Church Cabinet, and the Executive Council. The highest seat of authority is the convention body, which alone has the power to make or amend the bylaws of the church. District supervisors are appointed for nine districts in the United States and are ratified by the pastors of the respective districts every four years. Each local congregation is governed by a church council and contributes monthly to home and foreign missionary work.

Communication had been a major concern, and thus a periodical, *Bridal Call*, was begun in 1917. This magazine is now known as the *Foursquare World Advance*, reaching into over eighty-five thousand homes, churches, and institutions. The denomination operates KFSG-FM, the first church radio station in America owned by a woman, and the third station commissioned in Los Angeles. The Foursquare movement also operates KHIS-AM/FM Bakersfield, California, and its churches are involved in various TV ministries throughout the nation.

A missionary program established early in the church's life now ministers in over sixty countries around the world, with over 1.2 million members and adherents meeting in 20,000 churches. Membership in the United states is 201,198, meeting in 1,363 churches. Today, there are ninety-four foreign Bible schools and two Bible colleges in the United States: L.I.F.E. Bible College in Los Angeles, and L.I.F.E. Bible College East in Christianburg, Virginia.

Significant Terms

Interdenominational. We believe in the unity of all believers who have accepted Jesus Christ as their personal Savior. In obedience to the ordinances, we welcome all believers to receive communion and water baptism by immersion.

Moreover, we believe the term "denomination" refers to the commonness of a cause—in our case, the Foursquare Gospel. This should in no way separate us from other parts of the body of Christ, and we are very much involved in interdenominational functions. Many of our members have even founded other movements and organizations with our blessing and continue in fellowship with us until this present time.

Foursquare Gospel. This term appeared during an intensive revival that touched the city of Oakland, California, in July 1922. As thousands had gathered to hear the gospel, the evangelist, Aimee Semple McPherson, described a vision that God had given her, taken from the Book of Ezekiel, chapter 1. In the vision he had received from God, Ezekiel saw the revelation of the omnipotent God. He perceived four faces—those of a man, a lion, an ox, and an eagle.

To Aimee Semple McPherson, those four faces were likened unto the four phases of the gospel of Jesus Christ. In the face of the man, she saw the "Man of Sorrows"—Jesus our Savior according to Isaiah 53:3. In the face of the lion, she saw the mighty Baptizer with the Holy Spirit and fire—Jesus the Baptizer who sent to us the Holy Spirit, giving us strength and power for godliness and witness. In the face of the ox, she saw the great Burden Bearer—Jesus, who himself took our infirmities and carried our sicknesses. In the face of the eagle, she saw reflected the coming King—Jesus the Bridegroom, who is returning in power for the church, his bride. It was a perfect, complete gospel for body, soul, spirit, and eternity. It was a gospel that faces squarely in every direction, thus, the name was "Foursquare."

Foursquare symbols. The four symbols of our Foursquare faith are *a cross,* which represents Jesus, the Savior; *the dove,* which represents Jesus, the Baptizer with the Holy Spirit; *the cup,* which represents Jesus, the great Healer; and *the crown,* which represents Jesus, the soon-coming King.

Foursquare flag. The colors of the Foursquare flag represent our four main teachings: *red,* the color of Christ's blood, which was shed for men; *gold,* the power of the Holy Spirit; *blue,* the promise of divine healing; and *purple,* the royal, kingdom ministry of Jesus.

The "Four" on the "Square" reminds of us the balance and stability Jesus brings into our lives, based on the Word of God and made available to each of us as we believe in the power of his cross. The Foursquare Gospel is scriptural, based on God's Word. The name "Foursquare" is used ten times in the Bible, beginning with God's "tabernacle with man" in the Book of Exodus and continuing to the Book of Revelation with heaven, where we shall "tabernacle with God" forever.

Bibliography

Burgess, Stanley M., and Gary B. McGee. *Dictionary of Pentecostal and Charismatic Movements.* Grand Rapids, Mich.: Zondervan, 1988.

Cox, Raymond L. *The Foursquare Gospel.* Los Angeles: Foursquare Publications, 1969.

Foursquare World Advance. Los Angeles. Edited by Ronald D. Williams.

McPherson, Aimee Semple. *Aimee.* Los Angeles: Foursquare Publications, 1979.

———. *This Is That.* Los Angeles: Echo Park Evangelistic Association, 1923.

Prepared by Ronald D. Williams, editor, Foursquare World Advance.

◆ ◆ ◆
ISLAM IN THE UNITED STATES
AL-HANIF, HANAFI MADH-HAB CENTER

General Description
(Al-Hanif) Hanafi Madh-hab means "upright (or standard) of the faith of Islam." All of the 124,000 prophets, both major and minor, were Al-Hanif Muslims. This is the prophet's side of Islam.

> Abraham was not a Jew
> Nor yet a Christian,
> But he was true [Arabic *hanif*] in faith
> And bowed his will to Allah's
> (Which is Islam),
> And he joined no gods with Allah.
> (surah 3, ayat 67, of the Holy Quran)

The true Muslims follow the Sunnah. Our guides are the two standards: the Holy Quran and the Hadiths, which are the same for the over 1 billion Sunni Muslims the world over.

Founder
Allah is the author of Islam. There are over ninety-nine other attributes of Allah the Supreme. The seal of all of the prophets and prophecy is the Holy Prophet Muhammad Rasulallah (Salallahu Alaihi wa Salaam). He was born in Mecca in 570 A.C. (after Christ) and returned to Allah in 632.

Beliefs and Doctrines
The Holy Quran is the book of salvation for mankind.
Islam is the perfect faith, perfected by Allah the Supreme Being, and the Sunnah of our Holy Prophet Muhammad (Salallahu Alaihi wa Salaam) is the perfect example for all mankind.

Forms of Worship
All Sunni Muslims who follow the Prophet's side of Islam pray five times a day and recognize all of the spiritual holy days of the Sunni Muslims.
All Sunni Muslims bear witness to the five principles:

1. The profession of faith (or Kalima: La ilaha ilallah Muhammad ur Rasullah).
2. Prayer (or Salat).
3. Alms to the poor (or Zakat).
4. Fasting.
5. Pilgrimage to Mecca (or Hajj), if physically and financially able, once in one's lifetime.

All Sunni Muslims bear witness also to the seven cardinal articles of faith: to believe in the oneness of Allah; to believe in all his angels; to believe in all his books; to believe in all his prophets; to believe in the day of resurrection; to believe in the day of judgement; to believe in the predestination of good and evil, and the fact that we are all responsible for our own actions.

Organization

The basic principle is to obey the Shariat, or Islamic law, the fundamental principles of Islam, and the 130 principles of Hiqmat or (Hikmat, from "Hikma," meaning "wisdom," but also "science" and "philosophy"—*Encyclopedia of Islam*).

Contributions and Influence

Sunni Muslims strive to practice Islam in its pristine purity to save our souls on the judgment day from hellfire and to save our country from Allah's wrath. Allah has blessed our community to spread this message all over the United States and throughout the world through persecution, harassment, imprisonment, and martyrdom. We hope to continue to work in our country America, as American Muslims, to build a bridge of trust and friendship in all affairs with other peoples of the world that are non-Muslims.

Significant Terms

Hadith. Arabic "tradition," or writings on the life and teaching of Mohammed. It is the whole corpus of the Sunnah, which with the Quran forms the basis of Islamic religion and law.

Imam. The person who leads others in prayer.

Inan. Faith, belief.

Khalifa. An overall leader of a community in Islam.

Madh-hab. One of four schools of the Sunnah of the Holy Prophet Muhammad (Salallahu Alaihi wa Salaam).

Maulana (Maulvi). A scholar in the faith of Islam.

Mullah (Mawla). One who teaches Islamic law.

Murid. A disciple of a Murshid.

Murshid. A guide or leader; one who has attained perfection and is able to help others attain it.

Muslim (Mussulman). One who submits to the will of Allah.
Sheikh. A respectable man, a man of authority, a leader, a learned man.

Bibliography
The Holy Quran. Annotated version of Yusef Ali.
Khalifa Hamaas Abdul Khaalis. *Look and See*.
Sahih Al-Bukhari Sahih Muslim. *The Hadiths*. There are many other genuine Hadiths accepted by true Muslims as well as many other works written by Sunni scholars in the Islamic faith.

Prepared by the Al-Hanif, Hanafi Madh-hab Center staff.

SUFI ORDER FOUNDED BY PIR-O-MURSHID INAYAT KHAN

An Interfaith Approach to Spiritual Growth
History
The Sufi Order founded by Pir-O-Murshid Inayat Khan in 1910 is descended from the Chishti order of Sufis, one of the four major branches of classical Sufism. As an order for initiates, the initiate (or *mureed*) accepts individualized spiritual training under the direction and counsel of a spiritual guide. With an emphasis on prayer, contemplation, and meditative techniques, conducted privately in classes and in individual and group retreats, as well as in the course of one's everyday activities, the *mureed* gradually awakens to a deeper awareness of the soul's eternity and the divinity of collective humanity as a single body.

In 1910 the Indian musician, poet, and mystic Inayat Khan (1882–1927), upon the request of his teacher Abu Hashism Madani Chisti of Hyderabad, India, arrived in Europe to introduce the ethics, philosophy, psychology, and mysticism of Sufism to the Western world. Traveling throughout Europe and the United States, Inayat Khan presented the essence of Sufism in a language and symbolism that was comprehensible to Western audiences.

In 1917 the Sufi movement was formally incorporated in London, England. Today, under the name Sufi Order, Inayat Khan's spiritual legacy continues under the guidance of his son Pir Vilayat Inayat Khan, who further develops and offers instruction in meditation techniques and is an active participant in the current dialogue between the world's religions and between spirituality and the modern sciences. Over one hundred Sufi Order centers currently exist throughout the United States and Western Europe as well as in Australia, India, Japan, and Poland.

Beliefs and Doctrines

The focus of the Sufi Order's teaching is the Message, which is regarded as the essential truth underlying all world religions. All faiths are viewed as forms and expressions of a single, transcendent, and personal religion carrying God's word and spirit to humanity; no single religious body or spiritual group is regarded as its sole custodian and promulgator.

Consequently, there is no conversion, and members are never requested to leave their religion of origin or preference. In Sufism, this one faith is also referred to as "the religion of the heart" and may be personally discovered and experienced as the living presence of the divine inheritance unfolding in every man and woman. The Message also addresses the individual man and woman as a divine expression of God. By seeing the world from God's point of view, to the best of our abilities, all vision becomes a single vision of God's beauty and love.

The Sufi Order does not promote or hold to a distinct, fixed doctrine and therefore is outside the common definitions of an organized religion. Properly speaking, the order is a school of wisdom and spiritual instruction for helping one live a mystical life of harmony and balance while functioning within society. Members strive to worship God constantly throughout life's activities: in all houses of worship, in nature, in relationships, through active service, and in the privacy of their own solitude. The purpose thereby is to awaken one's inherent spiritual faculties and activities; ideally, the *mureed*'s heart becomes the temple of God, and one regards all persons not only as brothers or sisters but as oneself.

Besides the compilation of Inayat Khan's sayings and his written work, *Gayan Vadan Nirtan,* the scriptures of all the world's religions are equally valued and studied as sources of wisdom and inspiration. More important, however, is the manuscript of nature—all phenomena and things in the heaven, the cosmos, and on earth—and is regarded as God's signs instructing one in the divine law and love.

Organization

Religious organization and the institutionalization of the Sufi Order's teachings is secondary to the more important personal teacher-pupil relationship of spiritual instruction and guidance. Consequently, the organization maintains a structural flexibility based on democratic organization (involving a series of decision-making assemblies) as well as hierarchical principles. Since the time of its inception, the order has affirmed the spiritual and social equality between the sexes; men and women worship, pray, and engage in spiritual activities together and are equal in their leadership role.

Practices

Under the aegis of the Sufi Order are four major concentrations or specific trainings in which members may voluntarily participate. The *Healing*

Order concentrates on the awakening of one's inherited divine power of healing through prayer and applied meditation methods. The *School of the Universal Worship* trains ministers (or *cherags*) to perform universal worship services, which offer an opportunity for those belonging to different religions to worship together and to generate greater understanding and respect toward each other. *Brotherhood/Sisterhood* work emphasizes a mature social conscience toward selfless service in acts of love for the improvement of human conditions. Finally, *Ziraat* focuses on the development of an active ecological awareness of the planet's sacredness and service toward her preservation.

In summary, although the Sufi Order serves to assist one's personal experience of the soul's yearnings, a spiritual yearning inherent in everyone, its ultimate purpose is to enable us better to look after the welfare of others. With this intention, the order hopes that when reciprocity, love, and goodness toward one another and between races, nations, and religions is achieved, humanity and the planet as a whole will enjoy greater harmony and peace.

Significant Terms

Fana (annihilation). The state of surrendering the false self and giving rise to the true self.

Akhlak Allah (divine manner). Harmonizing and tuning oneself in a regal and beautiful manner, whereby God becomes reflected in everything one thinks, says, and does.

Wajad (ecstasy). An experienced state of bliss, peace, and wholeness that simultaneously embraces joy and suffering.

Gathas and *Githas*. A series of private teachings by Hazrat Inayat Khan giving instruction and practices on how to live a spiritual life.

Byat (initiation). To become a disciple of a *murshid;* the creation of mutual trust between a teacher and the disciple, which establishes a spiritual bond.

Pir Murshid, Pir-O-Murshid. Titles for a spiritual teacher who, by being receptive to the Word of God from within, serves as a bridge between the disciple and God.

Ziker (to remember). The praise and glorification of God in one's heart; a meditation technique for enhancing the *mureed*'s affirmation of God's oneness.

Bibliography

Hazrat Inayat Khan. *Gyan, Vadan, Nirtan.* Lebanon Springs, N.Y.: Sufi Order Publications, 1980.

——. *The Sufi Message of Hazrat Inayat Khan.* 12 vols. Franam, England: Service Publishing, 1978.

Islamic Spirituality, Vol. 1: *Foundations,* ed. Seyyed Hossein Nasr. New York: Crossroad Publishing, 1987.

Schimmel, Annemarie. *Mystical Dimension of Islam*. Chapel Hill: University of North
    Carolina Press, 1975.
Vilayat Inayat Khan. *Introducing Spirituality into Counseling and Therapy*. Lebanon
    Springs, N.Y.: Omega Press, 1982.
———. *The Message in Our Time*. San Francisco: Harper & Row, 1987.

Prepared by Richard Gale, National Secretariat.

AN AMERICAN MUSLIM'S
PILGRIMAGE TO MECCA

(Editor's note: The reader will recognize that this chapter, which is rich with
the lore and the practices of Islam, is not a self-description of a religious
group but an account of one person's experience of an important element of
Islam. I include this fine article by Idris M. Diaz only after two years of
fruitless efforts to solicit an article from several active mosques and Islamic
schools in Philadelphia. The Hajj that Diaz describes includes references to
the other four of the so-called five pillars of Islam: the Creed, Prayer, Alms-
giving, and Fasting. I reprint this account from the *Philadelphia Inquirer
Magazine*, April 2, 1989, pp. 24–30; I have shortened it with the author's
permission.)

Nearly two million Muslims from more than 130 countries descended
on Mecca in July for the annual rites of pilgrimage. As Muslims have done
for more than 1,400 years—as many will do in July of this year—the pilgrims
come to re-enact a journey first performed by a simple, uneducated man, the
Prophet Muhammed.

The Saudi government has occasionally referred to the Hajj as the largest
non-military logistical operation in the world and it's hard to argue with the
claim. For the Saudi government, the task of providing food, shelter, and
transportation for the pilgrims virtually cripples all other activities.

The Hajj has been a tremendous unifying element in the Muslim world.
From the earliest days of Islam, the Hajj brought together scholars and
merchants from around the Islamic world and helped to create a sense of
unity among the disparate Islamic regions. The Hajj is also the stuff that
legends, like the story of Mansa Musa, a 14th-century West African King
who performed the pilgrimage by trekking across the continent with hordes
of camels and servants and a fortune in gold.

But what unites all the pilgrims, rich and poor, is their collective belief
in the oneness of Allah, as they perform the few relatively simple rites of the
pilgrimage. During the five days of Hajj, pilgrims visit the Grand Mosque
in Mecca, where they circle the Ka'ba (pronounced "ka-bah"), a shrine of
black stone that all Muslims throughout the world face when praying. The
visit to the Grand Mosque is a prelude to the day when all of the hajjis gather

at the foot of Mount Arafat, where Muhammed delivered his last sermon. They also visit Minia, the site where Muslims believe Abraham was ordered to slay his son; there, they hurl rocks at three stone pillars, an act that recalls the prophet Abraham's rejection of Satan, and they run between the ancient hills of Safa and Marwa, ritually re-enacting the story of Hagar, Abraham's handmaiden. The Hajj ends with the Id al-Adha, or Festival of Sacrifice, when all pilgrims who can afford it slaughter an animal, and the food is delivered to poor Muslims around the world.

Few Americans have had the opportunity to encounter the Muslim world except through the media. The ranks of American Muslims grow stronger every day—they now number nearly five million, by one recent estimate. Yet most people's impressions of Islam and its adherents are largely influenced by reports of hostages, or by pictures on the evening news of the rubble left by the 1983 suicide truck bombing of the U.S. Marine barracks in Beirut. Or by accounts of the Ayatollah Khomeini's calling for the death of author Salman Rushdie.

Unfortunately, such political events often overshadow Islam and its essential message of peace and brotherhood. But during the annual pilgrimage to Mecca, the politics that seems to outsiders to dominate so much of life in the Islamic world largely takes a back seat to the religious sincerity of millions of people coming from all over the globe to fulfill a principal requirement of their faith.

The fundamental credo of Islam is that there is no God but Allah and that Muhammed is his prophet. Allah is simply another name for the same God in which Christians and Jews believe. In fact, Muslims see Muhammed, who died in the year 632, as the last in a long line of prophets that include Adam, Abraham, Moses, David and Jesus, all of whom are discussed at some length in the *Quran,* the Muslim holy book. While Westerners frequently speak of a Judeo-Christian tradition, most Muslims would prefer to speak of a Judeo-Christian-Islamic tradition.

Aside from the basic tenet, the other requirements of Islam are regular prayer, charity, fasting and the pilgrimage to Mecca.

The actual rite of Hajj occurs five days during Dhul-Hiji, the 12th month of the Muslim calendar. While all of the rites are performed in the vicinity of Mecca, a city of about a half a million people, most pilgrims also visit Medina, whether before or after the days of Hajj. Medina has a special status in Islam because its citizens sheltered Muhammed during the early days of his ministry when he came under attack from the tribes of Mecca.

Before Muhammed began preaching Islam early in the seventh century, Mecca had been a center for the polytheistic religion that so dominated the region. Pilgrims came from all over to trade and to visit the Ka'ba, which was then a haven for idol worshippers. Muhammed's teaching—with its central tenet that there is no god but Allah—threatened the rich trade that flowered in the city. Fearing for their livelihoods, Mecca leaders first tried to persuade Muhammed to stop his teaching. When that failed, they tried to kill him.

Eventually, Muhammed left the city for Medina, and the Muslim calendar begins the year of his flight. Medina was the base from which Muhammed repelled the continued attacks of the Meccan tribes and eventually defeated them. Even after that visit, however, Muhammed continued to live at Medina and administered the first Islamic state from there.

Several years after the Meccan tribes had been subdued, Muhammed announced a plan to make a pilgrimage to the city. He was joined by several thousand of his supporters. The rites performed by Muhammed during that first trip in the year 629 are repeated today by Muslims when they journey to Mecca for Hajj.

Outside the Mosque of the Prophet in Medina, heavily armed Saudi police officers keep a stern-faced watch. Other security guards, wearing ankle-length robes, or jallabriyahs, work swiftly to search each of the entering pilgrims. The military and the police are visible everywhere. But in the press of the thousands that converge on Medina and the even larger crowds that eventually gather in Mecca, the security forces seem irrelevant.

The goal of pilgrims during Hajj is to keep their minds focused on Allah, and for many, the security forces are just one more annoyance to be ignored.

I first visited the mosque, an enormous building of pink marble, late one afternoon with Syed Husain, a native of India who now works as an architect in San Francisco and who befriended me shortly after my arrival in Medina. The mosque is built on the rise where Muhammed lived and taught, and his tomb lies inside. The building has been enlarged several times since Muhammed's day, and around the mosque, construction workers were busy with the government's current expansion project. When the project is completed, the mosque should be able to accommodate more than 600,000 worshippers.

After emptying our pockets and submitting to a frisk, we entered the mosque at the front near the tomb of Prophet Muhammed. The tomb was barely visible behind wrought-iron gates bent in places to form Arabic letters. Saudi police surrounded the tomb, some bearing machine guns, as they tried to keep the crowd moving.

Mosques are not equipped with chairs, so worshippers sat on the floor, which was covered with elaborate rugs, in neat rows. Women are kept separate; so far as the eye could see, there were hundreds of thousands of men waiting patiently for the Maghrib, or evening prayer. A few lay curled up asleep on the rugs.

The mosque's tile walls were covered with verse from the *Quran* written in Arabic calligraphy. Bright ceiling lights danced off hundreds of glass and brass chandeliers. My ears were filled with the constant whir of fans and the deafening hum of thousands of pilgrims chanting from the *Quran*.

Muhammed once told his followers that on the Day of Judgment, he would plead with Allah on behalf of any Muslim who visited his tomb, so pilgrims try to spend as much time there as they possibly can. As we began to make our way past the tomb, the passageway was blocked by scores of pilgrims who stood with their hands outstretched in prayer. Some were crying, others stood with glassy-eyed stares. All seemed impervious to the nudges of the security officers who tried to keep them moving.

The aisle which runs past the tomb and across the front of the mosque was about five feet wide. But it was approaching prayer time, and the mosque had become so crowded that people simply began to sit down in the aisle. All around, Islamic scholars held impromptu lectures. Our walking space was reduced in each direction.

Eventually, we reached the mosque's exit. Since we had come too late to find a place to sit inside for the Maghrib prayer, we had to spread our prayer rugs down on the sidewalk outside the mosque along with scores of other Muslims in our predicament. Within a few minutes, the *adhan,* or call to prayer, rang out from the mosque's loudspeakers. "Allah Akbar." Allah is the Greatest. Shortly afterward, the prayer began, and we, along with thousands of Muslims from all over the world, bowed down.

A born Catholic, I was first exposed to Islam in the late 1960s while still in elementary school in New York City. I vividly remember the sight of clean-cut members of the Nation of Islam selling *Muhammed Speaks,* the organization's newspaper, on the streets of my neighborhood in Jamaica, Queens. The organization had been founded decades earlier by Elijah Muhammed, who claimed to be a prophet. Elijah's message contained elements of Islam combined with large doses of black nationalism. He claimed that white people were devils and advocated a separate black nation for America's blacks.

I recall being attracted to the Nation of Islam's message even at that young age. I admired the organization's efforts to build business among its members and to combat drug abuse in the black community. But even then I knew I was not prepared to accept the notion that whites, despite the war some of them were waging against black Americans at the time, were devils.

Several years later, my interest in Islam heightened when I read the *Autobiography of Malcolm X.* Many Americans know Malcolm X, who later adopted the name El-Hajj Malik El Shabazz, only as the one-time street hustler and pimp who rose to become the leading exponent of Elijah Muhammed's brand of Islam before being assassinated in Harlem in 1965. But I was touched by Malcolm's account of his own pilgrimage to Mecca in 1964—of his feelings of ignorance at not knowing the proper way to pray, which was not emphasized in Elijah Muhammed's National Islam. More importantly, I felt moved by Malcolm's description of the kindness poured on him in Mecca by people from all over the world, including light-skinned people whom he believed in America would have been considered white.

That experience eventually led Malcolm to revise his thinking on race relations in America and to believe that there could someday be harmony between whites and blacks.

I also realized that if ever I became a Muslim, the Islam that taught the kind of brotherhood Malcolm had experienced in Mecca was the Islam for me.

Eventually, I encountered a group of orthodox Muslims in New York and decided to convert to Islam. That was in the summer of 1975, a few weeks before my 16th birthday.

After slightly more than a week in Medina, the group I had been traveling with was finally ready to depart for Mecca. In my hotel room, I laid out the *ihram* that I had purchased in the market in Medina.

For Muslims making the Hajj, adopting the *ihram* involves more than putting on an outfit. It symbolizes the eradication of national, racial or class barriers that is the goal of Islam. *Ihram* also refers to a state pilgrims enter into in which they are totally focused on Allah and leave all worldly vanities behind.

Later that evening, we headed for Mecca's Grand Mosque, for the first rites of Hajj. The mosque is a three-story building of gray marble topped with seven minarets that pierce the sky like swords. In an unroofed courtyard inside the mosque sits the Ka'ba, a 50-foot cube of black stone covered with a shroud of silk.

The Ka'ba is the subject of many stories. Some believe the first Ka'ba was built by Adam shortly after his expulsion from the Garden of Eden. It is also said that the Ka'ba is an exact replica of a shrine that the angels circumambulate in praise of Allah.

The *Quran* states that the Ka'ba was originally built by Abraham with the help of his first son, Ishmael. Years after Abraham, the inhabitants of the Arabian peninsula continued to make pilgrimages to the Ka'ba, even though, by then, the shrine had degenerated into a center for idol worship. Muslims believe that with the arrival of the Prophet Muhammed, the Ka'ba was purified as a center for the worship of Allah.

After entering the mosque, we began the *tawaf,* or the rite of walking around the Ka'ba seven times. The rite begins at the Black Stone, a rock about 12 inches in diameter that is set in silver in a corner of the Ka'ba. The stone is believed to be the only remaining relic from the original Ka'ba built by Abraham.

People pressed against me from all sides and I was pushed helplessly back and forth. There was no point in resisting. The crowd, men and women together, continued to chant prayers as we walked in the shadow of the Ka'ba.

The Ka'ba was surrounded with police, who struggled to keep the crowd moving as pilgrims lunged forward in an effort to touch the Ka'ba or kiss the Black Stone.

As religious symbols go, the Ka'ba is remarkably simple. Yet it remains the central symbol of the unity of Allah and his creation, and as I performed the *tawaf,* I felt moved by the sight of the thousands of pilgrims who had journeyed so far to visit it.

On one level, the Hajj is something of an Islamic boot camp. It is a religious endurance test that provides pilgrims with a vivid reminder of what each soul must face on the Day of Judgment, the day on which Muslims believe Allah will call all the souls to account for their actions in this life.

As I walked away from the shrines, I noticed a small black-haired boy dressed in a dirty green robe leading a bearded blind man. The old man held onto the boy with one hand and carried a white umbrella in the other.

Watching the old man, it suddenly seemed appropriate to me at the shrine: the Ka'ba is really no more than a cubelike building made of stone. Like the test of Abraham centuries ago, the Hajj is a latter-day test of obedience. The rituals are less significant than the sincerity of an old blind man and millions like him who are willing to travel thousands of miles and endure the heat and cramped conditions so they can throw rocks at three stone pillars, in the middle of the desert, because they believe this is what their creator commands.

On my return to Mecca, I made the required farewell visit to the Grand Mosque and once again circled the Ka'ba, this time in the afternoon sun. As I walked away from the mosque, I turned and took one last look at its glistening gray walls and watched the pilgrims still struggling for a place inside.

◆ ◆ ◆
JEHOVAH'S WITNESSES

General Description
Jehovah's Witnesses is the worldwide Christian society of people noted for their use of God's name, Jehovah, who bear witness regarding God and his purposes before mankind. Their purpose is to do God's will as revealed in the Bible.

History
In the Bible, all faithful worshipers such as Abel, Noah, Abraham, and Jesus were called witnesses of God (Heb. 11:1–12:1; Rev. 3:14). A prominent witness in modern times was Charles Russell, who in 1870 organized a Bible study group in Pittsburgh, Pennsylvania, for the purpose of promoting the basic teachings of the Bible. In 1879 he began to publish the *Watchtower*, and in 1884 he incorporated the Watch Tower Bible and Tract Society (WTB & TS) for legal purposes. Russell was the first president of this legal body, and he was followed in 1916 by Joseph Rutherford and then by Nathan Knorr. The current president is Frederick Franz. Previously called Bible Students, in 1931 they adopted the name Jehovah's Witnesses, based on Isaiah 43:10.

Organization
Their worldwide activities are coordinated by the Governing Body, located at their world headquarters in Brooklyn, New York. Under this Governing Body, 93 branch offices supervise activities in 212 countries (as of 1988). Worldwide, there are 58,000 congregations, each cared for by a body of elders. Bibles and Bible-study aids are published by the WTB & TS in 289 languages. In 1989 some 13 million copies of each issue of the *Watchtower* were printed in 105 languages, and 11 million copies of *Awake!* were printed in 54 languages. This is the largest worldwide circulation of any religious magazine.

Beliefs and Doctrines
Jehovah's Witnesses accept the entire Bible as the inspired word of truth. Not Trinitarians, they believe that God, "whose name alone is JEHOVAH," is the Most High (Ps. 83:18 King James Version). Jesus, who said, "My Father

is greater than I," is his son and the redeemer of believing mankind (John 14:28). The Holy Spirit is God's active force for accomplishing his will. God's kingdom is a heavenly government of which Jesus Christ has been installed as King (Isa. 9:6). The 3.5 million Witnesses worldwide (1988) proclaim that we are living in the "last days" of this present system (2 Tim. 3:1–15; Matt. 24). This kingdom, or heavenly government, will soon remove wickedness from the earth and convert it into a paradise wherein worshipers will live forever. There will be resurrection of the dead into that paradise (Rev. 7; 20:11–13; 21:3–4; Ps. 37:9–11). Five meetings for Bible study and worship are held weekly in each congregation. Larger assemblies and conventions are also held regularly each year.

Practices

In response to Jesus' command "go, therefore, and teach all nations," all Witnesses accept the responsibility to share their beliefs with their neighbors, especially preaching "from house to house" (Matt. 28:19–20; Acts 20:20). According to C. S. Braden, they "have literally covered the earth with their witnessing. . . . It may truly be said that no single religious group in the world displayed more zeal and their allegiance in group [activities] to spread the good news of kingdom than the Jehovah's Witnesses."

Because of their allegiance to God's kingdom, they do not become involved in political affairs. One sociological study reported that the Witnesses "have consistently maintained their stand of nonviolent 'Christian Neutrality' through two major world wars and the subsequent military clashes of the 'Cold War' period. Their continuing stand . . . [has] resulted in periods of prosecution, imprisonment, and mob action throughout the world. . . . The Witnesses, however, have never responded with violence."

Contributions and Influence

By conducting weekly Bible-study sessions in over 3 million households (1988), Witnesses have helped many apply Bible standards of honesty, morality, and family life. Law professor W. S. McAninch also adds, "The Jehovah's Witnesses have had a profound impact on the evolution of constitutional law, particularly by expanding the parameters of the protection for free speech and religion . . . [they have] caused the Court to reconsider and reshape basic guarantees of speech, press, and religion" (1076–77). This has been true not only in the United States, where they have won forty-three cases before the Supreme Court, but also in other countries, including Canada, where court cases involving Witnesses helped to demonstrate the need for a Bill of Rights, which was adopted in 1960.

Significant Terms

Armageddon. God's war against the wicked as described in Revelation 19:11–12. In Revelation 16:14, it is called "the war of the great day of God the Almighty."

Disfellowshipping. The arrangement by which unrepentant wrongdoers are expelled from the congregation in harmony with the apostolic command to "quit mixing in company with anyone called a [spiritual] brother that is a fornicator or greedy person or an idolater or a reviler or a drunkard or an extortioner, not even eating with such a man. . . . Remove the wicked man from among yourselves" (1 Cor. 5:11–13).

Elder. One of a group of men in each congregation who meet scriptural qualifications and who oversee the activities of the local congregations.

Kingdom Hall. The building in which Jehovah's Witnesses meet to receive Bible instruction (equivalent to "church" in other religions).

Ministry. The activity in which Jehovah's Witnesses engage in door-to-door or other forms of preaching, making return visits to impart further Bible knowledge and conducting Bible studies in groups or with individuals. This is all done free of charge, and none of the Jehovah's Witnesses are paid for their ministerial activities.

Pioneer. One who spends at least one thousand hours a year engaging in the preaching work.

Publisher. One who regularly participates in some part of the work outlined by Jesus to make disciples and preach the gospel, or good news (Matt. 24:14).

Bibliography

Blumenthal, Monica, et al. *More about Justifying Violence: Methodological Studies of Attitudes and Behavior.* Ann Arbor: University of Michigan Press, 1975.

Braden, C. S. *These Also Believe.* New York: Macmillan, 1950.

McAninch, W. S. "A Catalyst for the Evolution of Constitutional Law: Jehovah's Witnesses in the Supreme Court." *University of Cincinnati Law Review* 55, no. 4 (1987), pp. 997–1077.

You Can Live Forever in Paradise on Earth. New York: WTB & TS, 1982.

Prepared by the Watchtower Bible & Tract Society of New York.

• • •
JUDAISM
CONSERVATIVE JUDAISM

Institutions

Conservative Judaism is one of three major movements in contemporary Jewish religious life, generally understood as occupying the middle ground between Reform Judaism on the religious left and Orthodox Judaism on the religious right. The movement is centered in the United States but is also represented in Canada, South America, Europe, and Israel. Institutionally, it is composed of (1) the Jewish Theological Seminary of America, an academy for higher Jewish studies that trains rabbis, cantors, academicians, social workers, and educators and, jointly with Columbia University and Barnard College, its neighbors in New York City, sponsors undergraduate programs in Jewish studies; (2) the Rabbinical Assembly, an association of over 1,200 rabbis, most of them ordained at the seminary; and (3) the United Synagogue of America, an association of over 800 congregations. The World Council of Synagogues extends movement affiliation to congregations outside North America, and the Masorti (or "traditional") movement coordinates a wide range of academic, congregational, and political activities on behalf of the movement in Israel.

Within the general organizational structure of the United Synagogue are, among other bodies, the United Synagogue Youth, an association of adolescents from Conservative synagogues who meet for social, recreational, and informal educational purposes; the Commission on Jewish Education, which supervises the educational policies of supplementary schools affiliated with Conservative congregations; and the Solomon Schechter Day School Association. The Women's League for Conservative Judaism and the Federation of Jewish Men's Clubs are independent national bodies that coordinate a wide range of activities on behalf of adult female and male members of Conservative synagogues.

The Jewish Museum, which now occupies its own home on New York City's Fifth Avenue, and which houses the most comprehensive collection of Jewish ceremonial art and objects, was initially launched by the seminary in 1904.

History

Although in its present form, Conservative Judaism is a thoroughly American phenomenon, its roots lie in a conservative reaction to the increasing radicalization of Reform Judaism in mid-nineteenth-century Europe. The break was symbolized by the decision of Rabbi Zechariah Frankel (1801–75) to resign from a conference of Reform rabbis in Frankfort (1845), following that conference's refusal to endorse the indispensability of Hebrew as the language of the synagogue liturgy. Frankel acknowledged that though the use of Hebrew was not mandated by Jewish law, it had nevertheless been sanctified by history and tradition—in effect, by the community itself. Frankel later became the first head of the Jewish Theological Seminary of Breslau (1854), an academy of higher Jewish studies that propounded a moderately traditionalist approach to Jewish observance while at the same time encouraging an open, critical stance toward the study of Jewish texts, institutions, and history.

A parallel, American version of this conservative reaction took place after the publication of American Reform Judaism's Pittsburgh Platform (1885). This statement, which came to be recognized as the first formal articulation of the principles of American Reform, among other claims, rejected the binding quality of Jewish rituals such as the dietary laws, denied Jewish nationhood, and repudiated the traditional Jewish dream of a return to Zion. The reaction against this statement was led by Rabbi Sabato Morais of Philadelphia, who became president of the Jewish Theological Seminary of New York (later "of America") upon its founding in 1886. This school, modeled on Frankel's Breslau Seminary, remains, both chronologically and structurally, the fountainhead of Conservative Judaism.

After a relatively desultory early history, the movement's period of rapid growth began under the aegis of Solomon Schechter (1847–1915), who left Cambridge University to become president of the seminary in 1902. Schechter appointed a faculty of renowned, European-trained scholars that quickly established the seminary's international reputation as a leading center of modern Jewish scholarship. He began to assemble the collection of books, manuscripts, and incunabula that makes the seminary library one of the most exhaustive collections of Judaica in the world. Schechter's writings (some of which are collected in his *Seminary Addresses and Other Papers*) spelled out the early ideology of the movement, and in 1913 he founded the United Synagogue, with an initial membership of twenty-one congregations, as its congregational arm.

Following Schechter's death, the leadership of the seminary (and, implicitly, of the movement) was assumed by Dr. Cyrus Adler (1863–1940) and then by Rabbi Louis Finkelstein (b. 1895), who was also appointed the seminary's first chancellor in 1951. Finkelstein was responsible for the creation of many of the seminary's most notable nonacademic programs, such as Camp Ramah, a network of Hebrew-speaking, educational summer camps (1947); "The Eternal Light," a series of radio (and later, television) programs that disseminated Jewish teachings to the country at large; and the Institute for Religious and Social Studies (1938) and Conference on Science, Philosophy, and Religion (1940), which pioneered in opening lines of communication between different American religious communities and academicians in the humanities and the sciences. The University of Judaism, which serves both as a school and as the West Coast center for the movement, was established in Los Angeles in 1947.

Though the seminary's scholarly eminence remains unchallenged to this day, the 1940s saw the gradual emergence of the Rabbinical Assembly as the body that defined the distinctive style of Conservative Judaism as a congregational movement in American Judaism. It was this body's Committee on Law and Standards that initiated and implemented a wide-ranging body of legal responses that, to take some notable and controversial examples, permitted driving to the synagogue, when necessary, on the Sabbath, the use of the organ in the synagogue on the Sabbath, the marriage of a *kohen* (or member of a priestly family) to a divorcee or a convert, and the equalization of male and female roles in synagogue rituals.

The Rabbinical Assembly, together with the United Synagogue, published the *Sabbath and Festival Prayerbook* (1946), which introduced some significant modifications in the traditional liturgy while preserving its classical format and its traditional Hebrew, and which became omnipresent in Conservative synagogues throughout the country. Among the other liturgical publications produced by this body are the *Mahzor* (the liturgy for the high holidays), published in 1972; and (again together with the United Synagogue) *Siddur Sim Shalom* (1985), a prayer book for the Sabbath, festivals, and weekdays.

Upon Rabbi Finkelstein's retirement in 1972, the presidency and chancellorship of the seminary was assumed by Rabbi Gerson D. Cohen (to 1986) and currently by Rabbi Ismar Schorsch. In 1983, under Chancellor Cohen's aggressive leadership, the seminary's faculty voted to admit women to training for the Conservative rabbinate. In 1987 that policy was extended to training for the cantorate. However, in a reaffirmation of the traditional position, at its 1987 convention the Rabbinical Assembly voted to retain the movement's commitment to the principle of matrilineal descent as the sole determinant (apart from conversion) of Jewish legal identity, in contrast to Reform Judaism, which has accepted the legitimacy of patrilineal descent as well.

The seminary's decision to ordain women led to the formation of the Union for Traditional Conservative Judaism, a coalition of members of the seminary faculty, the Conservative rabbinate, and the lay community, which continues to serve as a lobby for a more conservative posture on matters of belief and practice facing the movement.

Ideology

Conservative Judaism's first formal statement of principles was published in 1988 in a pamphlet entitled *Emet Ve-emunah* ("Truth and Faithfulness").

This statement, three years in the making, was composed by a commission of seminary and University of Judaism academicians, Conservative rabbis, and lay representatives from the movement at large.

The century-long delay in formulating an ideological platform can be attributed to several factors. First, from the outset, the movement served as a broad coalition of anti-Reform tendencies within the community; any sharp ideological statement could be potentially divisive. Furthermore, the leadership of the movement saw itself as representing classical, normative Judaism, which, in contrast to Reform, needed no justification or defense. Finally, the seminary, and to a lesser extent, the movement as well, inherited the ideological tensions of its European predecessor, the Breslau Seminary, in that it tried to combine a Western, modern, critical stance toward Jewish observance. It acknowledged the possibility that Jewish law could be accommodated to modernity and to an American setting but viewed this process as gradualist and evolutionary and as touching upon only peripheral areas of the life of the community.

However, as noted above, the evolution of a more distinctive style in Conservative congregations "in the field," toward the middle of this century, and the increasingly aggressive stance of Conservative rabbis toward modifying Jewish law led to a growing sense of ideological fragmentation within the movement. That, together with the more stridently ideological posture of American Orthodoxy—a reflection of the rise of religious fundamentalism in the world at large within the past decades—impelled the formation of the commission that produced *Emet Ve-emunah*.

This forty-page pamphlet is divided into three parts, dealing respectively with the themes "God in the World," "The Jewish People," and "Living a Life of Torah." Among its more notable claims are that when human beings speak of God, they must resort to metaphors; that revelation must "admit a human component"; that Jewish law is "what the Jewish community understands God's will to be"; that change in Jewish law is both "traditional" and "necessary"; that the doctrine of the Chosen People should be affirmed as teaching that the Jewish people "emerged on the stage of history to be a people dedicated to the service of God"; that Judaism has been "land-centered but never land-bound"; that Israel and the Diaspora serve complementary roles in Jewish life; that "God may well have seen fit to enter covenants with many nations"; that the Jewish home is "the principal center for Jewish religious life"; and that the conservative approach to Jewish study "combines traditional exegesis with modern, historical methods."

Despite the controversial nature of many of the claims, *Emet Ve-emunah* has been distributed widely throughout the movement and is being studied in congregational and school settings.

As it enters its second century, Conservative Judaism confronts two major challenges. First, it must confirm the viability of a middle-of-the-road religious movement in an age of religious fundamentalism and in the face of the increasing polarization among religious Jews in America and in Israel. Second, in order to achieve this goal, it must continue to address its own internal ideological agenda in an open and forthright way. *Emet Ve-emunah* is a promising beginning, but only that. Whether or not a movement that flourished for the better part of a century largely because of its ideological openness can continue to flourish in a sharply ideological culture remains open.

Significant Terms

Diaspora. Any Jewish residence outside the State of Israel.

Halakah. Literally, "the path" or "the way." The Orthodox view is that the revealed Torah (Bible) and its laws must be obeyed as written. The Reform view is that only the moral laws are mandatory. And the Conservative view is that basic and fundamental laws—for example, Sabbath and holy day observance; dietary, marriage, and divorce laws; education; Hebrew language; and ethical values—should be obeyed. However, laws should be evaluated by the social situation and evolve thereby.

Marriage of a kohen to a divorcee or convert. Biblically prohibited under Leviticus 21:7. This precept is largely ignored, since the priesthood has been relegated to only symbolic status in modern Jewish life.

Matrilineal and patrilineal descent. Jewish identity since Talmudic days has been determined by the status of the birth mother, regardless of the father's religion. This principle has helped preserve the Jewish family throughout eras of adversity and has recognized the traditional importance of the Jewish mother. Several years ago the Reform movement established the ability of the biological father to pass down Jewish status; even if the mother is not Jewish. While Reform Rabbinical practice in determining Jewish status is generally accepted in such areas as marriage (between two Jews only) and conversion (even if all traditional requirements are not scrupulously attended to), the patrilineal principle has been overwhelmingly rejected by Conservative and Orthodox Judaism. The persistence of this dual standard could create a fractured Jewish community where Jewish status (heretofore usually unquestioned) could be suspect if claims to Jewish identity are based on patrilinealism.

Rabbinical Assembly. The international, professional association of Conservative rabbis. All ordained at the Jewish Theological Seminary Rabbinical School are automatically admitted as members. Ordained rabbis of other institutions are eligible for membership if they agree to profess and practice beliefs and ritual standards acceptable within the continuum of Conservative Judaism's parameters.

Responsa. The traditional system of specific rabbinic decision making based primarily on actual cases or events. Written questions and subsequent written replies have provided contemporary solutions to problems unforeseen by biblical (written) or Talmudic (oral) law. This process has continued for over one thousand years. Thousands of sages have published replies to questions numbering in the millions, pertaining to almost every topic conceivable to the human mind and condition.

Siddur Sim Shalom. "May God establish peace"—the name of the Conservative prayer book.

Tradition and change. Two words often used to describe Conservative Judaism. "Tradition" addresses the restoration of valued Jewish beliefs and practices neglected by Reform Judaism; "change" denotes an evolving adaptation of Judaism to the American environment and culture.

Bibliography

Dorff, Elliott N. *Conservative Judaism: Our Ancestors to Our Descendants.* New York: Youth Commission, United Synagogue of America, 1977.

Emet Ve-emunah: Statement of Principles of Conservative Judaism. New York: Jewish Theological Seminary of America, the Rabbinical Assembly, United Synagogue of America, Women's League for Conservative Judaism, Federation of Jewish Men's Clubs, 1988.

Schechter, Solomon. *Seminary Addresses and Other Papers.* New York: Burning Bush Press, 1959.

Sklare, Marshall. *Conservative Judaism: An American Religious Movement.* New York: Schocken Books, 1972.

Waxman, Mordecai, ed. *Tradition and Change: The Development of Conservative Judaism.* New York: Burning Bush Press, 1958.

Prepared by Rabbi Neil Gillman of the Jewish Theological Seminary of America; terms and definitions by Rabbi David Maharam, Tiferet Bet Israel Synagogue, Blue Bell, Pennsylvania.

ORTHODOX JUDAISM

General Description

Orthodox Jews look upon their version of Judaism as the continuation of the traditional Judaism of the ages. They view it as part of the stream with the Jewish experience that began when God made a covenant with the Jewish people at Mount Sinai and commanded them to be a "kingdom of priests and a holy nation" (Exod. 19:6).

History

Traditional Jews (those who observed all rules and regulations of the Shulhan Aruch) were shocked by the developments in Reform Judaism. They could not regard ethical monotheism stripped of law and traditional ritual as sufficient for the Jews, and they viewed the shift in emphasis from the

Torah and the Halakah (Jewish law) to the prophets as a mistake. They were opposed to the elimination of references to the Land of Israel and the ancient temple in Jerusalem and viewed the changes that the Reform movement introduced in Jewish ritual, such as adding an organ and a mixed choir, the uncovering of the head, and the use of German in the synagogues and the confirmation ceremony, as sins against divine tradition. Most important of all, they could not accept the Reform substitution of reason for faith in what they believed was the perfect revelation of God.

But while all the traditionalists opposed the Reform, they were not of one mind in their attitude to the changes, or the so-called Emancipation. The stricter traditionalists insisted that all contact with European culture should be avoided. If Judaism was to be preserved, the Jewish people must be kept free of outside influences. They must continue to be separated and isolated from non-Jews. Traditionalist Jews who hold this view are still found in the large cities of Israel, Europe, the United States, and Canada. Many of them would like to see the creation of traditionalist Jewish communities where the Sabbath and other Jewish observances may be enforced strictly.

Some traditionalist Jews, especially in Germany, felt that it would be possible for the Jews to continue to resist Christianity and escape the negative influences of European culture in spite of Emancipation. The Emancipation, they reasoned, might even make it easier for Jews to observe all the traditional regulations concerning ethics, worship, and ritual. Without the medieval restrictions, the Jewish people would be able to serve God joyfully and spread the teachings of his Torah among non-Jews. This group even favored slight changes in worship services, including preaching in the language of the country instead of using Yiddish. They also sought to strengthen decorum in the synagogues along the Western lines. They wanted Jews to be loyal citizens and parties of their respective nations. But they agreed with the stricter traditionalists that the Torah, including both the written and oral laws, should be accepted without question. They viewed the Torah and its traditional interpretation as divine and felt that Jews are duty bound to follow all of the rules set down in it. Their point of view came to be known variously as Orthodox, Neo-Orthodox, and Modern Orthodox Judaism.

Ideology

"The essence of traditional Judaism," writes Rabbi Samuel Belkin, "is the indisputable faith that the Torah, the revealed word of God, is not a mere constitution of code but that, as the law of God, it represents divine authority and contains the highest wisdom and truths, and that divine law should guide the entire life and destiny of our people" (pp. 56–57 [See Bibliography on p. 186]).

"The Torah," writes Rabbi Oscar Z. Fasman, "is not only the written law but also the oral law; and the oral law is the authoritative and binding interpretation of the written law. To fulfill the commandments of Judaism properly, according to the teachings of Orthodox Judaism, a Jew must observe the written precepts in the Bible according to the explanation and instruction of the Talmudic sages and the great scholars who continued their work in every age" (pp. 18–19).

In Orthodox Judaism, the Torah is considered to be God's perfect revelation of his will to the Jewish people. Orthodox Jews thus are obedient to study the Torah in the traditional spirit and to reject any criticism that casts a doubt on the divinity of the biblical text.

Rabbi Samson Raphael Hirsch (1808–88), the founder of Orthodoxy, stated the case for the Orthodox approach to the Torah when he wrote, "We must keep and carry out this Torah without omission and without carping, in all circumstances and at all times. This word of God must be our eternal rule superior to all human judgement, and instead of complaining that it no longer is suitable to the times, our only complaint must be that the times are no longer suitable to it" (2:213–14).

Orthodox Judaism, in stressing Halakah and mitzot ma'asiyot ("action mitzot"), emphasizes the ritual aspect of Jewish religion as well as ethics. A characteristic Orthodox definition of Judaism is that of Rabbi Emanuel Rackman, who views Judaism as a legal order. Judaism, he writes,

> always was and still is an international legal order for Jews. . . . Essentially the Law is codified in the Shaulhan Arukh [and] is the guide for Jewish practice in the synagogue and the home. Dietary laws are prescribed in this code. The order and manner of prayer are also set forth there. The strictest Sabbath and festival observance is ordained as well as a multitude of commandments applicable to man's behavior from the cradle to the grave. There is hardly a theme in philosophy, political science, economics, sociology and psychology upon which the Law does not touch. ("What Is Orthodox Judaism?" pp. 4, 9)

"The basic credo of traditional Judaism," says Rabbi Belkin, "is its belief that all the ideals of the Torah, such as the universalism and fatherhood of God, the brotherhood of man, the sanctity of our own lives, can become meaningful only when they are integrated with Torah observances, with a Judaism which is practiced in accordance with the basic principles of the Shulhan Arukh" (p. 46).

Rabbi Joseph Soloveitchik (b. 1903), the leading exponent of Orthodox Judaism in America today, has emphasized in his writing that Halakah involves both a way of living and a way of thinking. He believes that by following the rules of Jewish tradition in daily life, Jews can come to sense the nearness of God.

In the Orthodox view of God, he has the ability to perform miracles and answer prayer. Since God is the creator of nature, it is in his power to change the course of nature. Thus all miracles are but an extension of the one great miracle of creation. Orthodox Jews believe that prayer is meaningless unless one has faith that God can and does intervene in nature to answer human supplications. Therefore, prayer is not merely introspection or a self-conscious attempt at self-improvement, but a communication between God and His people.

Orthodoxy looks upon the Jewish people as a spiritual group with a divine mission. It is the Jewish people's destiny to fulfill a divine role. It must serve as an example of ideal humanity by fulfilling the rules of the Torah and thus become the teacher of all mankind. While most Orthodox Jews questioned Zionism in its early years because the secular Zionist leaders seemed to be "forcing the hand of God," many of them gradually came to accept it and formed Zionist groups of their own. The Orthodox "Religious Zionists" have played a great role in the establishment and rebuilding of Israel. Rabbi Abraham Isaac Kuk (1868–1935), the first chief rabbi of Palestine, was largely responsible for winning Orthodox Jews to the Zionist cause.

In stressing the importance of Torah, Orthodox Jewry has made an important contribution to Judaism as a whole. It has made all Jews aware of the central role that the Pentateuch, or Five Books of Moses, plays in Jewish religion and of the significance of law and discipline in religious life. Through its day-school system, Orthodoxy has proved that the traditional commitment to study Torah can be fulfilled even in this day.

According to Rabbi Isidore Epstein, "Orthodox Judaism is a blending of the old with the new, and of its strict adherence to tradition, with a full participation in the science and culture of the age" (p. 295).

"I believe that Orthodoxy or Traditional Judaism can succeed in converting a great majority of our people to our cause," writes Rabbi Belkin (p. 42). "Orthodoxy's future in America," according to Rabbi Rackman, "depends upon its ability to mobilize more devotees of the Law in every generation so that the legal order which it is will be applicable to many. . . . None can gainsay that the Law and its guardians have many problems. But for Orthodox Jews, the faith is eternal that the written and oral tradition has the answer" ("What Is Orthodox Judaism?" p. 11).

We may summarize Orthodoxy by describing its method in Judaism as the preservation of the totality of Jewish religious tradition in the modern world.

Institutions

In the United States, the principal institutions of Orthodox Judaism are the Isaac Elchanan Rabbinical Seminary of Yeshiva University in New York, the Hebrew Theological College of Chicago, the Union of Orthodox Jewish Congregations of America, the Rabbinical Council of America, the Union of Orthodox Rabbis, and the Rabbinical Alliance of America. Many Orthodox youths are part of the National Conference of Synagogue Youth.

Significant Terms

Brit. A covenant.

Halachic. Adverb or adjective for Halacha, the term for Jewish law.

Mechitza/Mehitzah. The physical partition separating the sexes in the synagogue.

Milah. Circumcision.

Mitzvot. Commandments.

Mohel. A professional person who is trained and licensed to perform the ritual of circumcision.

RIETS. Rabbi Isaac Elhanan Theological Seminary—the rabbinic school affiliated with Yeshiva University that is the foremost (but not the only) institution of higher learning and training for modern Orthodox communities throughout North America and the world.

Shulhan Aruch. The most important Jewish law code, edited in the sixteenth century.

Talit. Prayer shawl with fringes on the four corners of the garb, worn by the observant Jew in keeping with the commandment recorded in Numbers 15:37–41.

Tevillah. Ritual immersion in a specially designed pool of water known as the mitveh (purification and conversion ritual).

UOJCA. Union of Jewish Orthodox Congregations of America—also popularly referred to as the UO or OU (Orthodox Union).

Bibliography

Belkin, Samuel. *Essays in Traditional Thought*. New York: Philosophical Library, 1956.

Epstein, Isidore. *Judaism*. Harmondsworth, England: Penguin Books, 1959.

Fasman, Oscar Z. "Orthodox Judaism." In *Meet the American Jew,* ed. Belden Menkus. Nashville: Broadman Press, 1963.

Hirsch, Samson R. *Judaism Eternal*. London: Socino Press, 1956.

Rackman, Emanuel. *One Man's Judaism*. New York: Philosophical Library, 1970.

——. "What Is Orthodox Judaism?" *Jewish Heritage*, Winter 1959–60, pp. 4, 9.

Prepared by Rabbi Ira Samuel Grussgott, Congregation Shaarg Shamayim, GNJC, Philadelphia.

RECONSTRUCTIONIST JUDAISM

History

A religious ideology and movement that has emerged in twentieth-century American Jewish life, Reconstructionism was initiated by the teachings and writings of Rabbi Mordecai M. Kaplan. Reconstructionists view Judaism as the evolving religious civilization of the Jewish people and therefore seek to adapt inherited Jewish belief and practice to the needs of the contemporary world.

The movement's beginnings can be dated to 1922, when Kaplan founded the Society for the Advancement of Judaism (SAJ), a synagogue in New York City. The congregation experimented with changes in the traditional liturgy, with the inclusion of women (including the introduction of the first bat mitzvah ceremony in 1922) and with the reinterpretation of Jewish ritual. The *SAJ Review* was published to disseminate the ideas of Kaplan and his disciples to a wider audience of Jewish leaders.

In 1934 Kaplan published *Judaism as a Civilization,* a comprehensive analysis of the condition of modern Judaism and a program for its reconstruction. The book had an immediate and significant impact in the Jewish world and is regarded as one of the major works of Jewish thought in this century. In 1935, in the aftermath of the book's enthusiastic reception, the *Reconstructionist* magazine was published. Ever since, it has been an important forum for forward-looking and controversial ideas and programs and is read widely beyond Reconstructionist circles.

In 1940 the Jewish Reconstructionist Foundation was established to support works promoting the Reconstructionist program. Kaplan and his disciples, Rabbis Ira Eisenstein and Eugene Kohn, then published a series of liturgical texts that created a storm in the traditional Jewish world because they altered the wording of the Hebrew text to eliminate references to chosenness, resurrection, and the messiah.

In 1954 the SAJ joined with three other synagogues to form the Federation of Reconstructionist Congregations. In 1960 the federation introduced the idea of *havurot*—small, lay-led participatory groups of Jews that meet for study, worship, and celebration. The federation grew rapidly in size in the early 1980s under the leadership of Rabbi David Teutsch, doubling in size to over sixty affiliates. In 1989 the federation published a new prayer book, *Kol Haneshamah,* which embodies many of the new currents in the movement.

In 1968 the Reconstructionist Rabbinical College (RRC) was founded in Philadelphia by Eisenstein. This event marked a definitive turn in the growth of the movement, which has ever since produced its own leaders. The rabbinic curriculum reflects the movement's philosophy, representing Judaism as ever evolving, encouraging lay participation in decision making, pioneering new ritual and theological innovations, and training rabbis to lead in other areas besides the synagogue. In the 1980s the college has experienced a dramatic rise in reputation and size under the leadership of Dr. Arthur Green.

The Reconstructionist Rabbinical Association was founded in 1974 by RRC alumni and has grown in 1989 to a membership of 165, which also includes rabbis trained at other seminaries. Pioneering in developing guidelines for conversion, divorce, and intermarriage, it has emerged as part of the movement's leadership and is now a voice heard on the American Jewish scene.

Ideology

Kaplan's program for Jewish life remains the single most dominant influence on Reconstructionist thinking. With the emergence of the federation as a full-fledged synagogue body that encourages lay participation and with the ordination of a new and ever-growing generation of rabbis, Kaplan's ideas are themselves in the process of ongoing reconstruction.

In defining Judaism as the evolving religious civilization of the Jewish people, Kaplan embraced the perspective of modern historians of Judaism. He rejected the traditional claim that Torah had literally been revealed by God at Sinai and the consequent claim that *halakah* (Jewish law) is binding. Rather, he viewed the development of Jewish belief and practice as having undergone a process of continuous evolution as successive generations of Jews adapted to ever-changing social circumstances, political challenges, and cultural influences. Thus, Jewish traditions are treasured because evolution has distilled the most lasting and compelling insights by previous generations about the ultimate meaning and sanctity of life.

By defining Judaism as a civilization, Kaplan emphasized the all-embracing character of the Jewish ways of life, which transcends modern definitions of religion. He argued that the exclusive religious definition is inimical to Jewish survival, which depends on a broader acculturation that comes from the adoption by Jewish families and communities of rituals, customs, language, literature, folklore, and all other aspects of Jewish civilization. He saw Jewish people as the constant that has run through Jewish history, and he interpreted all aspects of the Jewish legacy as refractions of revelation through the eyes of Jews.

The need for reconstruction arises out of the radical dislocations in Jewish life caused by the Enlightenment, the political emancipation of the Jewish people, and the technological revolution. Prior to 1800, Jews lived in autonomous Jewish communities that governed their members in accordance with Jewish law. People were born into Jewish communities that established enforceable norms and provided a comprehensive set of social, economic, and cultural services and that were surrounded by religious cultures that did not undercut traditional Jewish belief claims.

Kaplan was the first to note that the Jewish crisis of modernity is a consequence of the alteration of these circumstances. Jews no longer live in autonomous communities, but rather as citizens of larger societies that may choose to identify Jewishly. Halakah is no longer the law. Jewish teachings about such things as revelation, miracles, chosenness, and messianism are undercut by dominant societal beliefs. Thus, a new mode for establishing community norms is needed that does not depend on rabbinic authority.

In response to the loss of rabbinic authority, Kaplan sought to initiate a reevaluation of Jewish ritual that seeks to infuse old ritual forms with meaning expressed in a contemporary idiom. Hence, the introduction of the conventional naming and bat mitzvah ceremonies for girls, and the inclusion of women in all aspects of Jewish life—in the rabbinate and cantorate, as witnesses, as equal partners in marriage and divorce. In response to modern naturalism, Kaplan departed from personal and supernatural descriptions of God, whom he defined as the Power or Process inherent in the world that makes salvation, or the sources of the human impulse to virtue.

Out of these original teachings, the current Reconstructionist movement has emerged as a vibrant source of Jewish creativity and renewal. Its religious naturalism has attracted Jews who now transcend Kaplan's pragmatism and are interested in exploring the sources in Jewish *kabbalah* (mysticism) and Hasidism as maps of the inner spiritual quest. Its emphasis on Judaism as a civilization has made it fertile ground for a Jew's rediscovery of ritual and culture, so that large numbers of those who affiliate are highly traditional in their practice even as they entertain progressive theological ideas. Its emphasis on lay participation and partnership with rabbinic leaders has cast Reconstructionist congregations and havurot as communities in which members are energized and enthusiastic about their personal and collective Jewish odysseys. The movement has thus attracted both Jews interested in maximizing the Jewish content of their lives and Jews who feel alienated from other Jewish organizations, but who are made comfortable by the nonjudgmental Reconstructionist approach. It has also attracted many Jewish feminists, who see in Kaplan's reconstruction a model of how Jewish traditions ought to be recast to right the injustices of previous generations.

Significant Terms

Bat mitzvah. Literally, "daughter of the Commandments." An initiation rite of Judaism formerly limited to boys *(bar)* but opened to girls by Reconstructionism as part of its inclusion of women in all aspects of Jewish life.

Halakah. A general word used as a name for authoritative Jewish law. It may also be used to refer to the parts of the rabbinic literature that deal with any phase of Jewish law. Reconstructionists, however, do not accept its absolutionist, universal status.

Hasidism. Literally, "pious" *(hasid)*. A mystical movement in modern Judaism that emphasizes constant communion with God in thought and in proper devotion or spirituality.

Havurot. The name for a small, lay-led participatory group of Jews who meet for study, worship, and celebration; an innovation introduced by Reconstructionist Judaism.

Kabbalah. A word taken from the Hebrew *kabel* (to receive), which has come to mean "tradition." It is important to the mystic lore of medieval Judaism and is based upon an occult interpretation of the Bible maintained through the handing down of secret documents and notes.

Mordecai M. Kaplan. The founder of Reconstructionism, a graduate and professor of the Jewish Theological Seminary, the school of Conservative Judaism. He organized his own congregation in New York, which he called the Society for the Advancement of Judaism, the pioneer congregation of Reconstructionism.

Reconstructionism. A movement of Jews who view Judaism as the evolving religious civilization of the Jewish people and therefore seek to adapt inherited Jewish beliefs and practices to the needs of the contemporary world.

Bibliography

Alpert, Rebecca T., and Jacob J. Straub. *Exploring Judaism: A Reconstructionist Approach.* New York: Reconstructionist Press, 1985.

Goldsmith, Emmanuel S., and Mel Scult, eds. *Dynamic Judaism: The Essential Writings of Mordecai M. Kaplan.* New York: Schocken Books, 1985.

Kaplan, Mordecai M. *The Future of the American Jew.* New York: Reconstructionist Press, 1949.

——. *Judaism as a Civilization.* Philadelphia: Jewish Publication Society of America, 1981.

——. *The Meaning of God in Modern Jewish Religion.* New York: Reconstructionist Press, 1936.

Teutsch, David A., ed. *Kol Haneshamah.* Philadelphia: Reconstructionist Press, 1989.

Prepared by Rabbi Jacob J. Straub, dean, Reconstructionist Rabbinical College, Wyncote, Pennsylvania.

REFORM JUDAISM

General Description

Reform Judaism is one of the three major branches of the Jewish faith in the United States and in the world today. As a product of Judaism in the last two hundred years and as a result of its own evolution since the early nineteenth century, Reform Judaism today stands for the principles of openness to religious change and the necessity for choice and responsibility in the individual Jew's relation with God.

History

The Jews of Europe faced a religious and cultural crisis at the end of the eighteenth century. Political and social developments were bringing about the end of the traditional isolation and independence of Jewish communities in western and central Europe. At the same time, the Enlightenment was undermining traditional ideas about religion in the Christian world and therefore also in the increasingly open Jewish world. Jewish leaders were faced with the challenges of dealing with the increasing integration of the Jews into a non-Jewish society with the concomitant erosion of traditional Judaism, of forming a Judaism capable of retaining the loyalty of Jews, and of satisfying their spiritual needs in a changing environment.

Reform Judaism was one response to this challenge. Moses Mendelssohn (1729–86), though not a Reform Jew, helped open the way by emphasizing the harmony of Judaism with natural religion and showing that some traditional Jewish practices could be changed. Saul Ascher (1767–1822) saw Judaism as a matter of faith more than as a collection of laws. Under the impact of the thought of Immanuel Kant, Jews began to regard religion as a means leading to personal spiritual fulfillment instead of (as in the traditional conception of Judaism) as service to God through the observance of divinely ordained rituals.

Israel Jacobson (1768–1828) began to refashion Jewish worship and practice in accordance with this view. He stressed decorum and order in the worship service, introduced confirmation, and encouraged the use of instrumental music (primarily the organ) in the synagogue. Sermons in the vernacular on moral and contemporary themes were introduced and made a centerpiece of the liturgy. Later reformers issued new prayer books that removed such elements as the longing for return to Zion, substituted the vernacular for some of the Hebrew in prayers, and shortened the service.

Abraham Geiger (1810–74) helped to provide the theological and scholarly underpinning for these reforms. By elaborating a concept of progressive revelation, Geiger made it possible for Jews to admit the possibility and validity of change in their practices and beliefs. This doctrine implied that religious practices must be congruent with the needs and forms of the present and that the individual Jew must judge for himself the relevance of the tradition to his own spiritual development. Ethical monotheism as taught by the biblical prophets was the essence of Judaism; it gave Reform Jews a justification for their continuing identification with Judaism and a new pride and purpose stemming from the mission of Israel to spread this truth to all humanity. In this way, the message of Reform Judaism was in the nineteenth century, and still is today, a simplified ritual that emphasizes an individual's religiously based moral responsibility.

In America

Reform Judaism came to America with the immigration of German Jews in the middle third of the nineteenth century. American religious pluralism and separation of church and state were conducive to the growth of a form of Judaism that stressed integration into general society and personal religious commitment. David Einhorn (1809–79) was a spokesman for Reform thought in America. Einhorn brought to America Geiger's interest in the mission of Judaism to spread ethical monotheism and his belief in the continued vitality of Judaism in the modern world. He was opposed to traditional Jewish liturgical and ritual forms and emphasized belief over practice. Isaac Mayer Wise (1819–1900) of Cincinnati represented a more practical orientation. It was Wise who successfully brought together congregations throughout the United States to form the Union of American Hebrew Congregations (1873) as a support for a school to train American rabbis (Hebrew Union College, founded in 1875).

In 1885 a rabbinic conference formulated what became known as the Pittsburgh Platform—an expression of classic Reform Judaism. The platform's emphasis on morality, progress, the Bible, universalism, and a religious definition of the Jewish community expressed the sum of a century of Reform Jewish development.

At the end of the nineteenth century, large numbers of Jews from Eastern Europe with no experience of Reform Judaism migrated to America. Their traditional Jewish practices and adherence to Jewish ethnicity began to change the religious climate of American Jewry. The weakening of extreme rationalism in philosophy and renewed interest in religion in Western thought at the beginning of the twentieth century also laid the groundwork for a shift in Reform Judaism ideology. By the 1930s, Eastern European Jews were bringing their desire for familiar rituals and ethnic identification into American Reform Judaism at the same time that the rise of Nazism was stirring concern for other Jews as members of a people instead of merely as coreligionists. The Columbus Platform of 1937 reflected these changes in its increased openness to a personal concept of God, the rebuilding of Palestine as the Jewish homeland, concern for oppressed Jews in Europe, and the importance of ritual in religious life. At the same time, the platform did not retreat from the by now familiar commitment to social justice and social action implied in the concept "Mission of Israel."

Contributions and Influence

Reform Judaism shared in the American religious revival of the 1950s with a growth in membership and number of congregations. The centrality of the universalist message of the prophets to Reform Judaism led to continued commitment to social concerns, which was expressed in participation in the civil rights and antiwar movements of the 1960s. Reform Jews were active in interfaith endeavors and contacts. In the 1970s and 1980s, Reform has shown great interest in outreach to Christians interested in Judaism and to the Christian spouses of Jews, thereby involving itself deeply in questions about conversion and Jewish identity. The trend toward more traditional religious practices has led to increased use of Hebrew in services and the addition of formerly rejected or neglected observances to the long-standing Reform observance of Friday night candle lighting, the Passover seder, and Hanukkah. Ethnic consciousness heightened by the Holocaust and commitment to the existence and cultural growth of Israel as a Jewish state are witnesses to Reform's greater openness to Jewish particularity.

Theological developments reflect the diversity of Reform, ranging from religious existentialism to renewed questions about the authority of the *halach* (religious law) for Reform Jews, to humanistic and Polydex Judaism (philosophies with followings within the Reform movement). The diversity of

Reform beliefs and practices is reflected in the 1976 platform "Reform Judaism—a Centenary Perspective." While it has been criticized by some Reform Jews for failing to take definitive stands on many issues of belief and practice, the 1976 platform is revealing in the acceptance of its own ambiguities as an expression of the openness and individuality that Reform Judaism considers among its most important contributions to modern Judaism.

Today, Reform Judaism counts more than 1 million adherents concentrated predominantly in North America but including congregations in Latin America, Europe, Israel, and Australia. The Union of American Hebrew Congregations and the World Union for Progressive Judaism are the American and international guiding lay institutions of Reform Judaism. The Central Conference of American Rabbis and the Union College–Jewish Institute of Religion provide rabbinic and intellectual leadership. The Reform movement today continues to develop as a dynamic expression of the interaction of a centuries-old faith with the ever-changing world.

Significant Terms

Ethical monotheism. The concept, first found in the writings of the biblical prophets, of one universal God who desires mankind to work to create a moral world.

Mission of Israel. The Jewish religion and people were created to serve as examples and leaders in the struggle for a moral world.

Progressive revelation. God has revealed his will to each generation in terms meaningful to that generation, thus allowing for change in Jewish practice.

Classical Reform. American Reform Judaism of the late nineteenth and early twentieth centuries, which stressed English language and congregational reading in worship and rationalism in theology. Its chief document was the Pittsburgh Platform in 1885.

Temple. The common Reform name for a congregational building, a place of worship and religious education.

Rabbi. Literally "teacher." The spiritual leader of a congregation; a trained clergy, man or woman.

Bibliography

Borowitz, Eugene B. *Reform Judaism Today*. New York: Behrman House, 1977–78.
Martin, Bernard, ed. *Contemporary Reform Jewish Thought*. Chicago: Quadrangle Books, 1968.
Meyer, Michael A. *Response to Modernity: A History of the Reform Movement in Judaism*. New York: Oxford University Press, 1988.
Plaut, W. Gunther. *The Growth of Reform Judaism*. New York: World Union for Progressive Judaism, 1965.

———. *The Rise of Reform Judaism*. New York: World Union for Progressive Judaism, 1963.

Prepared by Allan D. Satin, librarian, Hebrew Union College, Cincinnati.

SECULAR HUMANISTIC JUDAISM

General Description

Secular Humanistic Judaism is a worldwide movement with organizations on five continents that have organized to form the International Federation of Secular Humanistic Jews. It is a voice for Jews who value their Jewish identity and who seek an alternative to conventional Judaism. Humanistic Judaism affirms the right of individuals to shape their own lives independent of supernatural authority.

Humanistic Judaism is an alternative to Orthodox, Conservative, Reform, and Reconstructionist Judaism. It embraces many Jews who identify as secular, in addition to those who identify as humanistic. It offers many Jews today the opportunity to express and celebrate their identity consistent with their belief system.

Humanistic Judaism exists in order to enable Humanistic Jews throughout the world to communicate with one another; create celebrational, inspirational, and educational materials; help to organize Secular Humanistic Jewish communities (congregations, chapters, and havurot); and serve the needs of the individual Humanistic Jews who cannot find communities that espouse their beliefs.

Founder and Later Leaders

The founder of organized Humanistic Judaism is Sherwin T. Wine. He was born January 25, 1928, in Detroit, Michigan. He received an A.B. and A.M. in philosophy from the University of Michigan and was ordained as a Reform rabbi and graduated from Hebrew Union College in Cincinnati in 1956. He began the first congregation for Humanistic Judaism in 1963, when he also established the Society for Humanistic Judaism. In 1986 he organized the International Federation of Secular Humanistic Jews.

Rabbi Daniel Friedman, leader of Congregation Beth Or, Deerfield, Illinois, joined the movement in 1966. Miriam Jerris is the executive director of the Society for Humanistic Judaism, a *madrikha* (leader of the Secular Humanistic Jewish Movement) and on the executive boards of the International Institute for Secular Humanism, International Federation of Secular Humanistic Jews, the North American Federation of Secular Humanistic Jews, and the Leadership of Secular Humanistic Jews.

M. Bonnie Cousins is the assistant director of the Society for Humanistic Judaism and the managing editor of the journal *Humanistic Judaism*. Ruth Duskin Feldman is creative editor of *Humanistic Judaism*.

Marilyn Rowens is a *madrikha,* a member of the Board of Directors of the Society for Humanistic Judaism and the executive boards of the North American Federation of Secular Humanistic Jews and the Leadership Conference of Secular Humanistic Jews.

Barbara Brandt is a *madrikha,* western region coordinator of the Society for Humanistic Judaism, board member of the Society for Humanistic Judaism, and leader of the San Diego Society for Humanistic Judaism.

Len Cherlin is a *madrikh,* eastern region coordinator of the Society for Humanistic Judaism, past president of the Society for Humanistic Judaism, and leader of the Long Island Havurot for Humanistic Judaism.

Geraldyne Revzin is a *madrikha,* executive director of the Congress of Secular Jewish Organizations, vice-president of the International Federation of Secular Humanistic Jews, chairperson of the North American Federation of Secular Humanistic Jews, and on the Executive Board of the International Institute for Secular Humanistic Judaism and the Leadership Conference of Secular Humanistic Jews.

Beliefs and Doctrines

A Jew is someone who identifies with the history, culture, struggles, triumphs, and future of the Jewish people. Judaism is the historic culture of the Jewish people. It is the historical, cultural, and ethnic experience of the people.

Ethics and morality should serve human needs. The goals of humanist morality are the preservation of human dignity and integrity for ourselves and for others. Moral decisions are based on the circumstances of the situation and evaluated on the consequences of behavior. Humanistic Jews believe that behavior should be consistent with stated beliefs.

Forms of Worship

Humanistic Jewish celebrations emphasize the human value of holiday and life-cycle events. The universal value of holidays and life cycles are utilized in the creation of celebrations. For example, the themes of spring and freedom are celebrated at Passover; at memorial services, we acknowledge the reality of grief and sadness or tragedy while celebrating the life of the deceased and the triumph of the human spirit.

Holiday celebrations are rooted in the historic reality and origin of the holidays. Creative nontheistic liturgy is used. Hebrew, Yiddish, and English (also Spanish and French) songs that have human meaning in the here and now while still connecting the participants to their heritage are sung.

Organization

Groups are organized as congregations, society chapters, or havurot, depending on the needs of the membership. Individuals may join the Society for Humanistic Judaism and celebrate their Jewish identity in that manner.

Contributions and Influence

A voice for Jews who identify as secularists, agnostics, and atheists is provided for those who want to identify with a Jewish group and celebrate their identity in a nontheistic format. The point of view of Secular Humanistic Jews ensures the pluralistic nature of the Jewish community and of the United States generally. People are provided an opportunity to identify with their culture in a way that is consistent with their behavior in their daily lives. Secular Humanistic Judaism avoids hypocrisy and provides integration for many Jews who would have no organizational alternative.

As more and more people learn about Secular Humanistic Judaism, this alternative and its views become more widely known. The positions of Secular humanist Jews on issues such as "Who is a Jew?" and intermarriage are inclusive and promote a broader and more open alternative. Individual Jews who would not normally participate in the ethnic and cultural experience of their people have become affiliated.

Significant Terms

Jew. Someone who identifies with the history, culture, and fate of the Jewish people.

Judaism. The cultivation of the Jews, created by the Jewish people and including Jewish language, ethical traditions, historic memories, cultural heritage, and a commitment to the State of Israel.

Madrikh (m), *madrikha* (f). A Hebrew word denoting a leader in the Secular Humanistic Jewish movement.

Bibliography

Humanistic Judaism. The quarterly journal of the Society for Humanistic Judaism, Farmington Hills, Mich.

Humanistic Judaism: An Anthology. A collection of articles from the pages of the journal *Humanistic Judaism.* Farmington Hills, Mich.: Society for Humanistic Judaism, n.d.

Wine, Sherman T. *Celebration.* Buffalo, N.Y.: Prometheus Books, 1988.

——. *Humanistic Judaism.* Buffalo, N.Y.: Prometheus Books, 1978.

——. *Judaism beyond God.* Farmington Hills, Mich.: Society for Humanistic Judaism, 1985.

——. *The Real History of the Jews.* Farmington Hills, Mich.: [Society for Humanistic Judaism], n.d.

Prepared by M. Bonnie Cousins, assistant director of the Society for Humanistic Judaism.

LUTHERANS

Founder
Lutheranism traces its origins to the activity of Martin Luther (1483–1546), the leading figure of the Protestant Reformation. In criticizing certain doctrines and practices of the Roman Catholic Church, Luther attempted to restore a scripturally based understanding of the gospel as the prime treasure and message of the church. Lutheranism became particularly strong in parts of Germany and in the Scandinavian countries.

History
America's Lutherans began arriving during the seventeenth century from Holland, Sweden, and Germany, settling in the Hudson and Delaware valleys. With the arrival of Henry M. Muhlenberg in Pennsylvania, the first permanent synod of congregations was organized in 1748. Lutheran strength, enhanced by successive immigrations to the United States during the nineteenth century, kept much of immigrant character (organized by national backgrounds, use of native languages, etc.) until the early twentieth century, when a full transition to English and American ways took hold.

Mergers of Lutheran bodies have consolidated but not eliminated all divisions. The two major Lutheran church bodies in the United States are the Evangelical Lutheran Church in America and the Lutheran Church—Missouri Synod (1847). Total membership exceeds 9 million, making Lutherans the third largest Protestant denomination.

Roots of Lutheran Theology
The most basic beliefs are (1) belief in Jesus Christ as the incarnate revelation of God and the bearer of God's promise of salvation and (2) an acceptance of the Bible as the norm for the faith and life of the church.

Lutherans hold the ecumenical creeds—the Apostles', Nicene, and Athanasian—as true declarations of the faith of the church. They take the Augsburg Confession (1530) and Luther's Small Catechism (1529) as true witnesses of the church's faith; in addition, the Apology of the Augsburg Confession (1531), the Schmalkaldic Articles (1537), Luther's Large Catechism (1529), and the Formula of Concord (1577) are taken as aids. All these statements together make up the _Book of Concord,_ first issued in 1580.

Organization

Lutheran polity, or government structure, based as it was on a national church, developed in the United States into synods or districts, usually corresponding to state or sectional boundaries. The local congregation was the foundation for the whole structure. The levels thus became: national body, synod, and congregation; all had authority to act in different matters, carefully distributed among these three agents.

Most American Lutheran bodies have been affiliated loosely with one another in the National Lutheran Council (1918–66), which in 1967 became the Lutheran Council in the U.S.A., and with other Lutheran churches in the Lutheran World Federation.

Forms of Worship

Lutheran worship follows the traditional liturgical order of the mass, including the confession of sins, a series of elements of prayer and praise, a lectionary of readings from the Bible, the confession of faith (creed), the sermon, and the offertory.

Other traditional orders are found in such services as matins and vespers. Lutherans acknowledge two sacraments—baptism and the Lord's Supper. Each is regarded as a special bearer of God's grace to the church.

Influence

Largely restricted for many years to particular immigrant groups, Lutheranism in America in recent years has exerted a wider influence through a broader outreach and increasing cooperation with other communions. Ecumenical dialogue with Reformed, Roman Catholic, Anglican, Orthodox, and other bodies has also played an important part in the enhancement of Lutheranism's prestige.

Significant Terms

Justification by grace through faith. A more explicit version of the familiar "justification by faith" (Rom. 1:16–17). It means that God's righteousness brings the sinner into a right relation with himself. God in his own being, through redemptive action in Christ and beyond all power of the law, brings about justification, which is a declaration of God's favor, of his grace, toward the sinner whose faith centers in Christ. Hence, the phrases made famous by Luther, as drawn from the Bible: faith alone _(sola fide),_ grace alone _(sola gratia),_ Christ alone _(solus Christus),_ and the Word alone _(sola Scriptura)._

Law and gospel. In terms of precept and promise, as found in the Scriptures, law and gospel are contrasting and combining factors that describe a twofold relation between God and humankind. The human predicament, as

Paul, Augustine, and Luther later spelled out, lies in the human impossibility of fulfilling the law meritoriously by good works. Only Christ is the perfect fulfillment of the law, which is the good news, the gospel. Luther sees God's promise in the Old Testament—a promise expressed in connection with obedience to the law as precept—as fulfilled in Christ's salvific life, death, and resurrection. With Paul, Luther sees the law as a schoolmaster (custodian) bringing the believer to Christ (Gal. 3:24–25).

Means of grace. The instrumentalities (means) through which a gracious God, in Christ, pursues the redemption of humankind through the vivifying Holy Spirit—who calls, gathers, enlightens, and sanctifies the whole Christian church on earth, doing so through the gospel in Word and sacrament (the audible and the visible Word). In practice, this means the faithful preaching of the Word and the scripturally faithful administration of the two sacraments: baptism and the Lord's Supper (Eucharist), all of which is gathered up in the liturgical worship of the congregation and is set in modes rooted in the early church. Thus, "for the true unity of the church it is enough to agree concerning the teaching of the gospel and the administration of the sacraments" (Augsburg Confession [1530], art. 7).

Ninety-five theses. Topics for debate on the faith and life of the church in the early 1500s, calling attention to abuses then corrupting the church and to Christocentric doctrines of Scripture then being ignored. In 1517, on the eve of All Saints' Day (October 31), Martin Luther posted the theses on the door of the Castle Church (the town bulletin board) in Wittenburg, near the university where he taught. Though originally written in Latin, the theses (in translation) soon awakened a widening response among the people, touching them at their deepest anxieties about eternal life or damnation. In contrast to the corrupting sale of papal indulgences (purchasing reduced time in purgatory), Luther's Thesis 62, for example, asserted that "the true treasure of the church is the most holy gospel of the glory and grace of God" (*Luther's Works* 31:31). To the faithful, this treasure cannot be bought but is free.

Pietism. True piety has been in all ages a life of faithful devotion to Jesus Christ and a sharing of the gospel through loving service. The four books entitled *True Christianity* (by Johann Arnd, about 1612) fostered piety among generations of Lutherans and others. For a new edition, Philip Jacob Spener, then head pastor in Frankfurt am Main, Germany, wrote a lengthy introduction in 1675 entitled "Pia Desideris" (Devout Desires). Therein, he criticized the corruption of the church and proposed correctives, such as meetings (conventicles) of the world-be devout at some time other than the regular public worship. Spener called them "collegia pietatis" and saw them as carrying out what Luther had once suggested as "a third form of the church." Despite often stern opposition from the doctrinally rigid or orthodox Lutherans, this Christ-centered piety—or Pietism, as the opponents dubbed it—persisted. It found ways of partnership with similar movements in other communions (confessional bodies), thus helping to make Pietism perhaps the earliest form of international as well as ecumenical Protestantism. Pietism continues in many parts of Lutheranism to this day, still with critics.

Priesthood of all believers. This term, popularized by Luther, denotes the church as the people of God. It is derived from the Scriptures, notably from a passage such as 1 Peter 2:5, 9: "You are a spiritual house . . . a royal priesthood." Accordingly, laity and clergy are bound together with common responsibilities in living and spreading the gospel.

Sovereignty of the Word. The creative Word (God the Creator), the incarnate Word (God the Redeemer), the inspired Word (God the Holy Spirit)—this Trinitarian understanding sees the Scriptures as a whole but with Jesus Christ at the center. In terms of function, Lutherans, like most other communions, regard the Scriptures of the Old and New Testaments as the authority and the norm by which all Christian teaching and practice is to be judged. Ironically, disagreements over practice have at times been divisive among Lutherans, most noticeably in North America.

Muhlenberg, Henry Melchoir. Called the patriarch of the Lutheran Church in America by virtue of his leading position in organizing in 1748 the first permanent synod (soon known as the Ministerium of Pennsylvania and Adjacent States) and in influencing in manifold ways the development of congregational formation and Christian nurture. Born in 1711 in Germany (Einbeck, Hanover), Muhlenberg graduated from Göttingen University and began a ministry in association with the Halle Institutions (founded by August Hermann Francke, the dynamic leader of Lutheran Pietism).

In 1742 he came to America. His ensuing forty-five-year ministry bore the marks of his Pietism as well as of the Small Catechism. By personal journeys and extensive correspondence, his influence extended from Georgia to Nova Scotia, while his residence and local pastorate was at Trappe (New Hanover), near Philadelphia. Although critical of German and other sectarians (including Quakers), his position was churchly and ecumenical toward Episcopalians, German Reformeds, Presbyterians, and the forerunners of Methodism. His motto was *ecclesia plantanda* ("the church must be planted"), and he urged the Halle fathers to send more pastors as well as encouraged others already present to join forces. The descendent of this colonially rooted "Muhlenberg tradition" was the United Lutheran Church in America (1918–62), later the major part of the Lutheran Church in America (1952–88), and since then of the Evangelical Lutheran Church in America, a body combining two-thirds of American Lutherans.

Bibliography

Bachman, E. Theodore. *Lutheran Churches of the World*. Minneapolis: Augsburg, 1988.

Elert, Werner. *The Structure of Lutheranism*. Vol. 1. St. Louis: Concordia, 1962.

Letts, H. C., ed. *The Lutheran Heritage*. Philadelphia: Muhlenberg, 1957.

Nelson, E. C., ed. *The Lutherans in America*. Philadelphia: Fortress Press, 1975.
Wentz, A. R. *A Basic History of Lutheranism in America*. Philadelphia: Muhlenberg, 1955.

Prepared by Dale Johnson and revised by E. Theodore Bachman, visiting fellow, Princeton Theological Seminary.

EVANGELICAL LUTHERAN CHURCH IN AMERICA

General Description

The year 1988 marked a time of gigantic change for the Evangelical Lutheran Church in America. Through what occurred at the start of that historic year, the landscape of Lutheranism throughout the United States was dramatically altered. On January 1, 1988, the Evangelical Lutheran Church in America (ELCA) officially came into existence. This church body is the youngest of the two large Lutheran churches in North America. At the same time, it is the oldest, tracing its history through its predecessors to the mid-1600s in the area now known as New York.

The ELCA was created by the uniting of the Lutheran Church in America (2.9 million members), the American Lutheran Church (2.3 million), and the Association of Evangelical Lutheran Churches (about 100,000). The Evangelical Lutheran Church in America thus includes 5.3 million members, in about 11,000 congregations. Serving in the ELCA are nearly 17,000 clergy.

The ELCA's main office is located near O'Hare International Airport in Chicago.

History and Organization

Intense efforts to form the ELCA began in 1982, when the three uniting churches made a commitment to come together and elected a commission of seventy people to draft the constitution and other documents for this new church. Even that significant step had been preceded by many years of co-operative efforts. It also reflected the long-held dream of numerous members and leaders for greater Lutheran unity.

In August 1986 the conventions of the three uniting churches approved the ELCA's constitution, articles of merger, and other documents. Then came the historic moment of the ELCA constituting convention, held April 30 through May 3, 1987, in Columbus, Ohio. Herbert W. Chilstrom was elected the ELCA's first bishop. Then followed the election of Lowell G. Almen as secretary, Christine H. Grumm as vice-president, and the members of the Church Council and various boards. In the succeeding weeks, the ELCA's sixty-five synods held their constituting conventions to elect synodic bishops and other officers.

On June 1-3, 1987, the ELCA Church Council held its first meeting and elected the fourth officer. Named ELCA treasurer was George E. Aker. On June 29 through July 1 the ELCA boards first met and named their executive directors. The ELCA Conference of Bishops—which include the sixty-five synodic bishops, plus the churchwide bishop and secretary—gathered for the first time on August 1–3. From September through December 1987, the second meetings of the boards, the Church Council, and the Conference of Bishops took place. Meanwhile, some initial staff persons began work in Chicago preparing for the official start of the ELCA.

The four churchwide officers were installed on October 10, 1987, in Chicago at a service of Holy Communion attended by numerous international guests. Among the participants in the service was the distinguished president of the Lutheran World Federation, Johannes Hanselmann.

While January 1, 1988, was the official beginning of the ELCA, much work had been done to prepare for that moment. The first official workday for most of the churchwide staff was Monday, January 4, 1988. At 8:30 A.M. on that day, the staff gathered at the entrance to the church's office for a service. How appropriate that the service began with this dialogue: "Sing to the Lord a new song; let God's praise fill the assembly of the faithful."

Vivid signs of renewed hope and grand expectation abound throughout the ELCA's congregations—renewed hope through the power of the gospel and grand expectation that God's Spirit will lead us with vision and strength into the years ahead.

Prepared by David L. Alderfor, executive assistant for rosters and statistics.

LUTHERAN CHURCH—MISSOURI SYNOD

General Description

The Lutheran Church—Missouri Synod (LC-MS) is one of the historical Christian churches frequently identified with evangelical denominations because of its evangelistic and missionary emphasis. It is liturgical and contemporary in worship, faithful to the material principle of faith in Jesus Christ as Lord and Savior, and faithful to the formal principle of authority in the Scriptures alone as God's truth for today.

The LC-MS is the second largest Lutheran body in the United States (behind the Evangelical Lutheran Church in America), with 2.6 million members, making it among the ten largest denominations in this country. It is related to the worldwide family of Lutheran churches (55 million members), which is the largest Protestant denomination in the world, or the third largest Christian denomination (behind Roman Catholicism and Eastern

Orthodoxy). In the United States, Lutheranism is the third largest Protestant denomination (behind Baptists and Methodists), with about 9 million members.

The LC-MS has been identified by Richard Quebedeaux, author of *Evangelical-Unification Dialogue,* and others as one of the two major evangelical denominations in the United States (together with the Southern Baptists), while other mainline denominations have been identified with liberal or moderate theology. Consequently, the LC-MS is a historical church body with liturgical and contemporary worship, committed to the truth of the Scripture and a willingness to share the redemption of Jesus Christ with others. Because the LC-MS does not belong to the Lutheran World Federation or other national or international Lutheran organizations, it usually does not participate in doctrinal pronouncements or social action statements of those organizations.

Founder and Major Leaders

The founder of Lutheranism is Jesus Christ, Lord and Savior of the world, for whom Christianity is named; also crucial are the actions of the Holy Spirit, by which orthodox Christianity exists. When Martin Luther (1483–1546) suggested reforms for the Roman Catholic Church in the sixteenth century, he was expelled from the church, resulting in the Lutheran denomination, which later expanded rapidly in northern European countries. The LC-MS also draws heavily on confessional Lutheran leaders of the seventeenth century, for example, Johann Gerhard (1582–1637).

In the United States, C. F. W. Walther (1822–87) was the founding president of the Missouri Synod and first president of Concordia Seminary, St. Louis. Franz A. O. Pieper (1852–1931), also a president of the Missouri Synod and Concordia Seminary, is chiefly remembered by the three-volume edition stating the beliefs of the denomination entitled *Christian Dogmatics.* The current president of the LC-MS is Ralph Bohlmann, who previously served as the president of Concordia Seminary.

Beliefs and Doctrines

The doctrines of the Lutheran Church are derived alone from the sixty-six books of the Old and New Testaments. The LC-MS believes that these doctrines are correctly interpreted in the confessional writings gathered in the *Book of Concord,* first issued in 1580.

The "object of faith," or the material principle of the LC-MS, is "faith alone by grace in Jesus Christ," who is the only Lord and Savior of the world, fulfilling the Old Testament prophecies about the Messiah. The "basis of authority," or the formal principle of the LC-MS, is "Scripture alone," which indicates that only Scripture (not tradition or ecclesiastical authority) is the true and only inerrant record of God's will for our time.

The gospel of Jesus Christ is that God sent him into the world as true

God and true man to die on the cross for the forgiveness of sins and that he rose from the dead and was proclaimed by the disciples as the Savior of the world.

Sin is found not only in the wrong or bad actions of human beings (actual sin) but more fundamentally in the self-centered will of mankind, which is known as original sin and is linked with Adam's rebellion against God. Luther and Calvin would subscribe to the idea that "we are what we are because we do what we do." Christians are redeemed by Christ but are never free from the self-centeredness of original sin; they are, therefore, *simul justus et peccator* (simultaneously justified and a sinner).

The attitude toward culture is "Christ and culture in paradox" (see H. Richard Niebuhr, *Christ and Culture*), or as defined in Luther's two-kingdom theory. A person works in two different worlds—one is the kingdom of power, owned by God through creation, which includes Christians and non-Christians working with reason toward justice; the other is the kingdom of grace, owned by God through Jesus Christ in salvation, which includes the universal invisible Christian church, where Christians practice *agape* love.

Forms of Worship

The LC-MS practices the liturgical worship forms of the Western branch of Christianity and thus shares a liturgical tradition with Roman Catholics, Anglicans, and other Lutherans. A Sunday worship service usually contains a Trinitarian invocation, confession and absolution of sins, the designated scriptural readings of the day, hymns, sermon, thanksgiving, Lord's Supper, and benediction. Other liturgical holy days are celebrated, including Easter, Lent, Epiphany, Ascension, Advent, Christmas, and Pentecost.

There are many contemporary or folk worship songs in services for youth or at retreat sites, which draw heavily on the evangelical and Roman Catholic contemporary tradition.

Organization

The LC-MS holds that the final authority of the church resides in the individual congregations, which call pastors. Each district presides in an advisory way to between one hundred and three hundred congregations, and the thirty-seven districts are part of the national LC-MS. While the Evangelical Lutheran Church in America and the various European organizations elect regional or national bishops, the LC-MS uses the designation "president" rather than "bishop." The national church body meets in national convention every three years, with equal numbers of delegates from the clergy and laity.

Contributions and Influence

The LC-MS has been a major influence in American religious life, with chief concentrations of membership in the upper Midwest states. It has had the largest Protestant elementary school system in the United States, second only in religious systems to that of the Roman Catholics. It has a significant number of Lutheran high schools as well as twelve Lutheran colleges or universities and two Lutheran seminaries.

The deaf ministry of the LC-MS is larger than that of any other Protestant group. In the last twenty-five years it has established a large media ministry with probably the largest Protestant radio and TV ministry, namely, "The Lutheran Hour," with about 1,700 radio stations worldwide, and "This Is the Life," with about 300 TV stations. Although it has taken positions on various social issues such as equality in race relations, poverty, church and government, public morals, world hunger, fairness in business, employment, and housing, the most noticed public stance has been that taken against abortion.

Significant Terms

Means of grace. Faith is created by the Word of God and the two sacraments, namely, baptism (including for infants) and the Lord's Supper.

Ninety-five theses of 1517. These mark the beginning date of the Reformation.

Priesthood of all believers. Clergy or full-time workers are not a special class before God. Christian "priesthood" includes all believers.

The Lord's Supper. Involves partaking the body and blood of Christ through the bread and wine for the forgiveness of sins.

Lutheran Church—Missouri Synod. Often called "Missouri Synod" or just "Missouri Lutherans."

Ordination of women. The LC-MS, unlike the ELCA, does not practice such ordination.

Second coming of Christ.. This is defined without a rapture or millennium.

The uses of the law. Other Lutherans specify two uses (the civil use and the theological use); the LC-MS in addition includes as a minor motif a third use of the law (its didactic use, for sanctification).

Bibliography

Althaus, Paul. *The Ethics of Martin Luther.* Philadelphia: Fortress Press, 1972.

Book of Concord. Edited by T. G. Tappert. Philadelphia: Fortress Press, 1959. This work includes the authoritative confessions of the Lutheran Church.

Luther, Martin. *Luther's Works.* 55 vols. St. Louis: Concordia Press; Philadelphia: Fortress Press, 1955.

Mundinger, Carl S. *Government in the Missouri Synod.* St. Louis: Concordia, 1980.

Pieper, F. *Christian Dogmatics.* 4 vols. St. Louis: Concordia, 1955.

Piepkorn, Arthur Ross. *Profiles in Belief.* 4 vols. New York: Harper & Row, 1977.

Wentz, Abdel Ross. *A Basic History of Lutheranism in America.* Philadelphia: Fortress Press, 1955.

Prepared by Charles L. Manske, Ph.D., Christ College, Irvine, California

WISCONSIN EVANGELICAL LUTHERAN SYNOD

General Description

The Wisconsin Evangelical Lutheran Synod (WELS) has some 420,000 members in 1,200 congregations in all fifty states. Because of its uncompromising commitment to scriptural inerrancy and to a fellowship practice that presupposes doctrinal agreement, the WELS is viewed as a "strict" or "conservative" Lutheran body. From 1879 to 1893 it was a member of the Evangelical Lutheran Synodical Conference.

Founder and Leaders

Under the leadership of Pastor John Muehlaeuser, three emissaries of German mission societies in 1850 organized the church body that aimed to serve German immigrants pouring into Wisconsin at that time. In 1892 a federation was formed with similar groups in Michigan, and in 1917 with groups in Nebraska. The result was a body with its present form of a synod, with headquarters in Milwaukee and twelve geographic districts.

President Muehlaeuser's successor, John Bading (served 1860–64 and 1868–89), solidified the confessional-theological stance of the church body, which was subsequently headed by Philip Von Rohr (1889–1908). Other presidents have been Gustav E. Bergemann (1908–33), John Brenner (1933–53), Oscar J. Naumann (1953–79), and Carl Mischke (1979–present).

Theological leadership has been provided by Adolph Hoenecke, longtime head of the Wisconsin Lutheran Seminary, presently located in Mequon, Wisconsin, and by teachers there: John P. Koehler, August Pieper, John Schaller, John Meyer, and Carl Lawrenz. Leaders at Northwestern College, Watertown, Wisconsin, the preseminary ministerial school, have been August Ernest, William Notz, Erwin Kowalke, and Carleton Toppe. The teacher training school, Doctor Martin Luther College at New Ulm, Minnesota, has had as school heads such men as Christian J. Albrecht, E. R. Bliefernicht, and Carl Schweppe.

Beliefs and Doctrines

The canonical books of the Old and New Testaments are regarded as the inspired, inerrant, and authoritative Word of God. The basic confessional writing, subscribed to because it is a correct exposition of Bible doctrine, is the Lutheran *Book of Concord* (1580), consisting of the three ecumenical creeds (Apostles', Nicene, and Athanasian) and the distinctively Lutheran confessions: the unaltered Augsburg Confession and its Apology, Luther's Large and Small catechisms, the Schmalkald Articles, Melanchthon's tract on the papacy, and the Formula of Concord in its longer and shorter forms.

Orthodox Lutheran doctrine has been summarized into three *solas*: Scripture alone, grace alone, faith alone. These are also the *solas* of the WELS, which upholds biblical creation, limits pastoral ordination to males, and opposes abortion on demand.

Forms of Worship

The liturgical tradition set down in the Reformation era espouses decent order in worship services but also allows for sufficient variety to express area and era preferences. Congregational hymn singing is stressed, as a current hymnbook revision indicates.

Organization

Local congregations are grouped into area districts, twelve in all, that exercise supervision over the doctrine and practice of pastors and congregations. The twelve districts are joined into the central structure, which carries out synodically controlled foreign and stateside mission efforts; worker-training programs to supply missionaries, pastors, and teachers; and other joint endeavors such as evangelism, publication, and charities.

Contributions and Influence

The WELS has always exhibited concern for religious education. The worker-training program has three synodic prep schools, two colleges, and the theological seminary. In addition, local groups maintain Wisconsin Lutheran College in Milwaukee and twenty area high schools.

A synodic feature is the elementary school system. Some 3,754 elementary schools are maintained, enrolling over 30,000 pupils and staffed by over 1,000 teachers, most of them trained at the teachers college at New Ulm, Minnesota.

Significant Terms

Book of Concord of 1580. The collected confessional documents of Lutheranism, consisting of the three ecumenical creeds, the Augsburg Confession and Apology of the Augsburg Confession, the Schmalkald Articles, Luther's Small and Large catechisms, and the Formula of Concord. It was published by joint agreement of the Lutheran potentates of Germany to commemorate the fiftieth anniversary of the Augsburg Confession and to put an end to internal doctrinal controversies. The Wisconsin Synod accepts it without qualification as a true exposition of the church fathers' beliefs. This is a significant departure from the views of most other Lutheran theologies today.

Ecumenical unity. The Wisconsin Synod believes that there can be no cooperation or union between church bodies unless there is complete unity of faith and practice. For this reason, the synod is not a participant in bodies such as the Lutheran World Federation or the World Council of Churches.

Evangelical. Derived from the Greek word *euangelion,* meaning "gospel," or "good news." That which pertains to the gospel is evangelical. It is currently used for expressions of Christianity that stress the need of atonement for sin and the rebirth (in Christ) of the individual.

The Bible as inspired, infallible, and inerrant. The Wisconsin Synod believes that the Bible is literally the Word of God—inspired, infallible, and inerrant in every word. It believes, for example, in the literal historicity of Genesis 1–12.

Bibliography

Koehler, J. P. *History of the Wisconsin Synod.* Sauk Rapids, Minn.: Protestant Conferences by Sentinel Printing, 1981. A denomination history.

This We Believe. Milwaukee: Northwestern Publishing House (A church pamphlet), n.d. A summary statement of belief.

Wisconsin Lutheran Quarterly and *Northwestern Lutheran.* Theological journals published by Northwestern Publishing House, Milwaukee.

Prepared by James P. Schaefer, public relations director.

MENNONITES

General Description

Beginning in 1525, the Radical Reformation had an ongoing legacy throughout much of Europe within the various Anabaptist groups that survived the turmoil and persecutions of that century and beyond. In the main, these groups are the Mennonites (from 1525), the Hutterites (from 1528), and the Amish (from 1693). The Brethren in Christ—since the eighteenth century—is another group that is affiliated with this religious stream. With the Quakers and the Brethren in Christ, the Mennonites constitute the three historic peace churches.

The Mennonites have roots in Swiss and South German Anabaptism, but also in Low Country Anabaptism (from 1530). The former is foundational for the largest North American Mennonite group (the Mennonite Church), and the latter, foundational for the General Conference Mennonite Church and the Mennonite Brethren (the second and third largest Mennonite groups in North America). By and large, the Hutterites and the Amish also have their roots in the Swiss and South German tradition. Although they come from at least two different cultural backgrounds, which can explain certain differences in religious practice, a common faith binds all the groups.

The Anabaptists came into existence in 1525 primarily in the attempt to remain true to the spirit and teachings of Jesus Christ and to his body, the church. They saw themselves as disciples called to live out Christ's gospel of peace, as defined in the Sermon on the Mount, knowing that this calling is impossible except within the gathered church, where the Spirit of Jesus Christ lives on. Such a gathered church, they felt, could have no connection with the political world of general society, and so they were the first Reformation group to break formally with the state-church configuration, establishing in its stead a free church of believers, based upon believer's (adult) baptism.

Founder and Major Leaders

The birth of the Anabaptist movement in Zurich was the result of acts of faith on the part of a number of leaders, including George Blaurock,

Conrad Grebel, and Menno Simons. Jacob Ammann was a founding leader for the Amish. A few examples of later leaders are Johann Cornies (1789–1848) from Russia and Orie O. Miller and Harold S. Bender from North America, the last two working in many contexts in relief work and peace concerns since the time of the First World War and into the 1960s.

Beliefs and Doctrines

Mennonites practice believer's (adult) baptism and view the church as the gathering of baptized believers. They stand for the nonswearing of oaths and for nonviolence and the way of peace, rooted in Jesus and his spirit of love, seen in times of conflict and warfare.

Forms of Worship

A tradition of simplicity, also in worship, defines Mennonite worship forms. Believers, who enjoy being together, gather in the name of Christ, in song (often in four-part a cappella singing), in prayer, and around the proclaimed living Word of God in Christ. Simplicity of the meetinghouse building is part and parcel of an emphasis on attempted simplicity in all things.

Organization

Mennonites follow a congregational polity, modified by synodal elements. Most Mennonite groups are part of the Mennonite World Conference, a worldwide body representing some 750,000 Mennonites. The Mennonite Central Committee, a relief organization begun in 1920, is a unique program that most Mennonite groups support and are active in. Mennonites Disaster Service, set up to act quickly in times of crisis (e.g., caused by tornadoes, earthquakes, or fires), is an example of inter-Mennonite outreach in times of human need.

Contributions

In the area of a peace witness the Mennonites have labored long, as well as in the reaching out in relief work and in responding to human suffering, in the name of Christ, no matter what religious orientation the individual or group may have.

Significant Terms

The term "Anabaptist" generally designates the Radical Reformation movement from 1525 to 1630. After 1630 the term "Mennonite" is often used, for both Low Country as well as Swiss and South German Mennonites. In recent times, "Anabaptist" has been used for any group originating in the sixteenth century, such as the Hutterites, the Amish, the Brethren in Christ, and the Church of the Brethren.

Bibliography

(Except as noted, all items are published by Herald Press, Scottdale, Pa.)

Bender, Harold S. *The Anabaptist Vision*. 1944.

Dyck, Cornelius J. *Introduction to Mennonite History*. 1981.

Friedmann, Robert. *Theology of Anabaptism*. 1973.

Klaassen, Walter. *Anabaptism in Outline*. 1981.

Mennonite Encyclopedia. 4 vols. Edited by Harold S. Bender and C. Henry Smith. 1956–69.

The Schleitheim Confession. 1977. Originally published 1527.

Weaver, George H. *The Radical Reformation*. Philadelphia: Westminster Press, 1962.

Prepared by Leonard Gross, executive secretary, Historical Committee of the Mennonite Church; copyright © 1989 by Leonard Gross.

◆ ◆ ◆

METHODISTS

General Description

A variety of Christian denominations are included in the Methodist family of churches. Methodists number approximately 25 million worldwide and are found in 101 countries. Membership in the United States is about 15 million. The World Methodist Council, the World Council of Churches, and the National Council of the Churches of Christ are actively supported by many of the Methodist churches.

Methodism originated as a renewal movement within the Church of England in the mid-eighteenth century. It sought to bring genuine evangelical fervor and social reform to England. The movement later spread to Ireland, the American colonies, and other parts of the world. Methodists began to organize into churches in 1784 with the formation of the Methodist Episcopal Church in America.

Founder

Methodists acknowledge John Wesley (1703–91) as their founder. They also recognize his younger brother, Charles (1707–88), as an important personality in the origins of Methodism. The Wesleys were born in Epworth, England, educated at Oxford University, became priests in the Church of England, and were missionaries to the colony of Georgia. Both had transforming religious experiences in May 1738.

Later Methodist leaders include Robert Strawbridge, Barbara Heck, Phillip William Otterbein, Martin Boehm, Jacob Albright, Francis Asbury, Thomas Coke, Richard Allen, Orange Scott, Matthew Simpson, Frances E. Willard, Adam Clarke, John William Fletcher, Edgar S. Brightman, Georgia Harkness, Charles Albert Tindley, Marjorie Swank Matthews, G. Bromley Oxnam, and D. T. Niles.

Beliefs and Doctrines

Following the theological direction of John Wesley, Methodists hold to the primacy of the Bible in the formation of their beliefs and practices. They also acknowledge tradition, reason, and experience as important sources for their doctrine and life. Historically, the Wesleys emphasized original sin, prevenient grace, justification by faith, the new birth, assurance, and holiness of heart and life to be central to an understanding of Christianity. They advocated an approach to the faith that included a balance between the personal and the social, experience and reason, preaching and sacrament, and evangelism and social action. The sacraments recognized among Methodists are baptism and the Lord's Supper. Baptism may be by immersion, sprinkling, or pouring. The Lord's Supper is viewed as a memorial of Christ's death, an anticipation of future blessing, and a means by which God conveys grace to the recipient.

The historic doctrinal positions of Methodism are usually to be found in the sermons of John Wesley, in his *Notes on the New Testament,* and in the Articles of Religion, which he sent to America in 1784. It is generally accepted that the hymn texts of Charles Wesley, of which there are about six thousand, also contain the marrow of Methodist theology.

Forms of Worship

Many Methodist churches use a very simple form of liturgy for their worship. Many others use a more formalized liturgical form. In almost every case, the components of worship include hymns, prayers, readings from the Scripture, a creed (such as the Apostles' Creed), a sermon, and a benediction. Some churches also include an invitation to Christian faith and discipleship in their worship.

Organization

Methodists refer to their structure as a connection. In many of the Methodist churches, this connectional form includes a general conference that sets the policy for the church, annual conferences presided over by bishops that meet yearly to appoint preachers to the churches, districts headed by district superintendents, and local churches. The local church is not autonomous as in some other Protestant denominations.

Contributions and Influence

Methodism was organized in the United States at the same time the nation was born. It thrived and grew as the nation matured. For that reason, some have said that Methodism has been "the most American of all churches" in the land. Methodists have advocated freedom and have been enthusiastic in their support of ecumenicity.

The size of the Methodist community and its geographic spread across the nation have made it an influential force in the life of the nation. In its evangelical thrust and in its pronouncements and actions on social problems, Methodism has been an important factor in national affairs. The largest Methodist body, the United Methodist Church, has a formal statement of social principles and a social creed that seeks to address various questions facing society.

Significant Terms

Articles of Religion. Wesley's abridgment of the Articles of Religion of the Church of England, which he sent to America in 1784 as doctrinal standards for the Methodist people.

Assurance. The scriptural promise that believers can expect to receive assurance regarding their present salvation.

Bishop. The office of a general superintendent in many of the churches of the Methodist family.

Christian perfection. Increasing in the knowledge and love of God and in the love of one's neighbor by the presence and the power of the Holy Spirit.

Connection. The relation of Methodist churches to each other; all are connected in a network of relationships that involve both advisory and legal responsibilities.

Discipline. A word often used to refer to the *Book of Discipline,* which is the official published statement of the church's organization and procedures.

Prevenient grace. The divine love that surrounds all of humanity and precedes any and all of our conscious impulses; it awakens the sinner and prompts our desire to please God.

Bibliography

Green, V. H. *John Wesley.* Lanham, Md.: University Press of America, 1987.

McEllhenney, John G. *Proclaiming Grace and Freedom: The Story of United Methodism in America.* New York: Abingdon Press, 1982.

Norwood, Frederick A. *The Story of American Methodism.* New York: Abingdon Press, 1974.

Piepkorn, Arthur C. *Profiles in Belief.* Vol. 2. New York: Harper & Row, 1978.

Prepared by Charles Yrigoyen, Jr., General Commission on Archives and History, United Methodist Church.

AFRICAN METHODIST EPISCOPAL CHURCH

General Description

The African Methodist Episcopal Church is a church in the true tradition of Wesleyan Methodism. The twenty-five articles of the Articles of Religion embraced by the mainstream of Methodist bodies are also the basis of doctrine of the African Methodist Episcopal Church. Founded as the result of discrimination in St. George Methodist Episcopal Church of Philadelphia, a group of African worshipers left the church in a body. They formed the Free African Society, out of which two congregations were born.

The church called Bethel adopted the distinctive title "African Methodist

Episcopal Church of Philadelphia." It was not the intent or purpose of this body of Christians to be anything other than Methodist. They embraced the doctrines and discipline of the Methodist Episcopal Church except that portion dealing with property rights, which were to be vested in the Bethel congregation and not the Conference of the Methodist Episcopal Church. For a short while the pulpit was supplied by the appointed elders of the Methodist Conference.

The first church building, a converted blacksmith shop, was dedicated in 1794 by Methodist Bishop Francis Asbury, who also ordained Richard Allen in 1799. Allen, Bethel's first pastor, later was elected and consecrated the first bishop of the new church when a number of African congregations united to form a new denomination.

Founder

Richard Allen, the founder of the African Methodist Episcopal Church in Philadelphia, was born February 14, 1760. As a slave to Benjamin Chew, he was later sold with his brother to the Stockley Strugess plantation in Delaware. He was allowed to hire himself out after work was done on the plantation. From this extra labor he saved two thousand dollars in Continental money, with which he bought his freedom and that of his brother. As a freeman, Allen moved back to Philadelphia in 1786, where he became a successful businessman. He worked as a teamster, shoemaker, and chimney-sweep and was a local preacher at St. George Methodist Episcopal Church.

Richard Allen was a prime mover in the life of the African people not only of Philadelphia but also in the nation, where he was a leader in the quest for a quality life for all people. He took the lead in providing social services during the yellow fever epidemic. He was among the conveners of the first national convention for African people. Allen opposed the back-to-Africa movement. Although he was well known, he was once captured by slave catchers. They were observed, however, and were later arrested, and Allen was freed.

Richard Allen died March 26, 1831, in Philadelphia. The inscription on his tombstone declares that he was "vox populi, vox Dei" (voice of the people, voice of God). Richard Allen is buried in a crypt in his beloved Mother Bethel African Episcopal Church in Philadelphia.

Beliefs and Doctrines

The doctrines of the African Methodist Episcopal Church are the same as those expressed by the major branches of Methodism. The Articles of Religion expresses the full scope of the body of beliefs of this church. The Apostles' Creed embodies the belief of the church as it relates to the doctrine of God. The entire canon of Scripture is embraced as the Word of God. The church believes that there are two sacraments—baptism and the Lord's Supper, both of which were ordained by Christ himself.

Forms of Worship

The forms of worship of the African Methodist Episcopal Church provide for simple but orderly expression of religion. The music ranges from anthems to hymns, spirituals, and gospel expression. Music is both choral and congregational. Preaching is central to the African Methodist worship experience. Worship also includes reading of the Holy Scriptures, the Decalogue, the Apostles' Creed, and a benediction. Participation of the entire congregation is central to all African Methodist worship.

Organization

The African Methodist Episcopal Church's organization mirrors, to a large degree, that of the Wesleyan Methodist tradition. The body is known as a connection of congregations. The chief officers are the bishops, who are elected to be general superintendents of the church. They preside over "episcopal districts," or areas that are made up of "annual conferences." The annual conference is composed of "presiding elder districts," which are in turn constituted by local congregations supervised by a presiding elder appointed by the bishop. Each church, or congregation, is under the care of a pastor appointed by the bishop.

Contributions and Influence

The African Methodist Episcopal Church is the oldest African-American institution in the United States. It is the result of the first civil rights expression and has played a major role in the process of liberation and reconciliation of African people in this country. Out of the church has come Wilberforce University, the oldest African institution of higher learning in the nation. This church produced many of the most outstanding leaders of our race, including Richard Allen, Daniel A. Payne, Henry McNeil Turner, B. Tucker Tanner, Morris Brown, and Rosa Parks, to name just a few. It has been at the forefront of every major movement for the advance of African-American people.

Significant Terms

Bishop. General superintendent of the African Methodist Episcopal Church, charged with general oversight of the connection. He presides over the general annual conferences, makes appointments of pastors and presiding elders, ordains clergy, and consecrates deaconesses.

Class leader. Subpastor appointed by the pastor to assist in the discharge of ministry to the membership.

General officer. Person elected by the General Conference every four years to administer the departments of the connection, including publications, pensions, evangelism, and missions.

Pastor. A minister assigned by the bishop to the spiritual and administrative responsibility of a church or churches.

Presiding elder. A minister assigned to travel through an appointed district to oversee the spiritual and temporal affairs of the church. The presiding elder presides over the quarterly and district conferences.

Steward. One of the spiritual officers of the church, charged with some temporal responsibilities. They are charged with provision of the elements of the Lord's Supper, support and expenses of the ministry, and social outreach to the poor and the needy.

Trustee. One of the officers elected by a congregation to administer the temporal affairs of the church, holding in trust the property.

Bibliography

Nash, Gary B. *Forging Freedom.* Cambridge: Harvard University Press, 1988.

Payne, Daniel A. *History of the African Methodist Episcopal Church.* Nashville: A.M.E. Sunday School Union, 1891.

——. *Recollections of Seventy Years.* Nashville: A.M.E. Sunday School Union, 1888.

Turner, Henry McNeil. *The Genius and Theory of Methodist Polity.* Philadelphia: A.M.E. Book Concern, 1885.

Wesley, Charles H. *Richard Allen: Apostle of Freedom.* Washington, D.C.: Association Publishers, 1969.

Winch, Julie. *Philadelphia's Black Elite.* Philadelphia: Temple University Press, 1988.

Prepared by Richard Norris, pastor, Mother Bethel AME Church, Philadelphia.

AFRICAN METHODIST EPISCOPAL ZION CHURCH

General Description

The African Methodist Episcopal (AME) Zion Church is one of several denominational bodies following the Wesleyan tradition. Historically, it was born out of slavery, injustice, and the struggle for freedom and has continued in the struggle for improved conditions and civil rights for persons of African descent and others.

Approaching its bicentennial in 1996, the denomination has grown from one congregation in the state of New York to 2,200 congregations, 59 conferences, and approximately 1.5 million members. The body spans the United States with churches in 37 states and the Virgin Islands, plus England, the Bahamas, Guyana, Ghana, Jamaica, Trinidad-Tobago, Liberia, India, and Nigeria.

The denomination is a member of the World Council of Churches, the National Council of the Churches of Christ in the USA, the World Methodist Council, the World Federation of Methodist Women, the Commission on Pan-Methodist Cooperation, Church Women United, the American Bible

Society, the International Society of Christian Endeavor, and the Consultation on Church Union. Merger is currently being considered with the Christian Methodist Episcopal Church.

History

Dissatisfaction arose regarding restrictions in public worship, failure to ordain black clergy, religious deprivation, including problems with burial of the dead and racial proscription within the John Street Methodist Episcopal Church in New York City in the late 1700s and early 1800s. This caused some members of African descent to seek an audience with Bishop Francis Asbury in 1795. The group included James Varick, Abraham Thompson, William Miller, William Hamilton, Francis Jacobs, Thomas Miller, George Moore, George White, Thomas Cook, David Bias, and Samuel Pontier. Still dissatisfied, the above group began meeting in the home of James Varick and finally decided to seek permission to become a separate Methodist society. Peter Williams, June Scott, and William Brown were also pioneers in this new experience. In August 1796 the group met with Bishop Asbury and requested permission to hold separate meetings. This request was granted, and the group began meeting at a house on Cross Street in October 1796. James Varick, Abraham Thompson, and June Scott were the first three blacks to be ordained by the Methodist Church in New York State and led the development of the denomination. Since 1925, after several moves and turmoil, the historic mother church has been located at West 137th Street in New York City.

James Varick emerged as the leader to hold the group together during turbulent times and was elected the first bishop of the newly formed denomination in 1822. In 1820 the group voted to disconnect officially with the Methodist Episcopal Church and published its first *Discipline*. James Varick led one congregation into a denomination that became known as the Freedom Church.

Among its ranks are key persons of the abolition movement such as Frederick Douglass, Harriet Tubman, Sojouner Truth, Jermain Wesley Lougen, William Howard Day, Eliza Ann Gardner, and Catherine Harris. The denomination's mission has been to share the gospel of Jesus Christ, be concerned about the wholeness of persons, and fight for justice and equality for all persons.

Bishop Alexander Walters was one of the founders of the National Association for the Advancement of Colored People in 1909 and served as one of its three vice-presidents. Bishop Stephen Gill Spottswood served as chairman of the National Board of Directors from 1960 to 1974, and Bishop William Milton Smith continues the legacy. The denomination has also been actively involved in the National Urban League, the Southern Christian Leadership Conference, and the Student Nonviolent Coordinating Committee. Many members, both clergy and lay, fought for justice during the

1960s and were involved in boycotts, sit-ins, and marches across the United States. In 1987 members marched against apartheid on the South African Embassy in Washington, D.C.

Beliefs and Doctrines

The basic doctrines of Methodism and the Christian faith are held within the denomination, including the Articles of Religion as established by John Wesley. The Apostles' Creed was adopted as the formal creed, and the sacraments of Holy Communion (the Lord's Supper) and baptism are recognized. Other major doctrinal themes include sanctification, the witness of the Spirit, a life of joy and obedience, Christian experience, and the means of grace and conversion. Rituals are used for holy matrimony, the burial of the dead, ordination of deacons and elders, consecration of bishops and local church deaconesses, cornerstone laying, dedications of church buildings, furnishings, and other essentials.

Organization

The denomination is divided into thirteen episcopal districts, each presided over by a bishop. Congregations are led by pastors and divided into classes following John Wesley's class system for nurturing and ministering to the needs of the membership. Two levels of ordination, deacon and elder, are recognized, and an internal ministry is practiced. Persons may become members by profession of faith, transfer, or restoration.

Twelve general officers administer the denominational affairs, and a publishing house is maintained in Charlotte, North Carolina. The General Conference is the highest governing and legislative body and is a delegated body composed of equal clergy and lay representation from conferences. "It enacts the laws for governing the church on every level, including the episcopacy. It elects all bishops, general officers (and members of the Judicial Council) and assigns them to their fields of operation, appoints the connectional boards, and regulates all spiritual and temporal matters of the connection. The bishops and general officers report to this body on their four years' labor in their field of operation. The bishops preside . . . in rotation" (Walls, p. 109). The Board of Bishops supervises the AME Zion Church in the interim of the General Conference. The Connectional Council is composed of all bishops, general officers, and Administrative Board members and meets annually to assess denominational affairs.

The Connectional Lay Council serves to deepen the spiritual life of the laity, disseminate information and cultivate denominational loyalty, expand the denomination through education and evangelism, and promote any other interests of the kingdom of God. The Woman's Home and Overseas Missionary Society was organized in 1880 to promote world evangelism and raise funds systematically. The Christian Education Component exists for the promotion and supervision of the Christian training and development of the entire membership.

Forms of Worship

The AME Zion Church uses the basic Methodist style of worship, flavored with the traditions of the African-American experience. Simplicity is emphasized, yet the Christian year is observed, and flexibility exists for the use of the talents of the membership in worship. Music used in worship includes anthems, hymns, chants, spirituals, and contemporary gospel.

Contributions and Influence

The struggle for education and improvement of the race has always been on the agenda of the AME Zion Church. Several schools and institutes were established, with Livingstone College, Hood Theological Seminary, and Clinton Junior College operating today. Livingstone College was founded in 1879 in Concord, North Carolina, as Zion Wesley Institute and was for the purpose of training persons for the ministry. It was moved to Salisbury, North Carolina, with Joseph Charles Price becoming its first president. In 1885 the name was changed to Livingstone College, in memory of the explorer and missionary to Africa, David Livingstone. Hood Theological Seminary was officially established by the 1888 General Conference and is located adjacent to Livingstone College. Clinton Junior College, located in Rock Hill, South Carolina, was founded in 1894 by Presiding Elder Nero A. Crockett and Rev. W. M. Robinson.

Tuskegee Institute was born in Butler Street AME Zion Church. Lewis Adams was Sunday school superintendent and operated a prosperous crafts school. Booker T. Washington, who contacted the American Missionary Association in 1868, was sent as a teacher, and the school was housed in the church for two years.

Other schools were organized in the states of Alabama, Tennessee, Kentucky, Arkansas, Virginia, Mississippi, and Pennsylvania. In Africa, schools were established in Liberia, Ghana, and Nigeria.

Women have always played a major role in the life of the church. The denomination was the first in Methodism to ordain a woman, May J. Small, as elder in May 1865. The first female general officer, Madie Simpson, was elected financial secretary in 1976.

Many congregations are providing low-income housing, apartments for the elderly, day care, senior citizens' programs, and substance abuse programs to minster to the physical needs of others. Politically, members of the AME Zion Church have served in local government, on city councils and school boards, as mayors and congressmen, and in the White House as aides to the president.

Significant Terms

Deacon. The first level of ordination of clergy. One is elected by a majority of the Annual Conference and the imposition of the hands of a bishop and elders.

Elder. The second level of ordination of clergy (same process as described above).

Bishop. An elder who has been elected by two-thirds of the General Conference and consecrated for the episcopacy.

Conference. A grouping of presiding elder districts in the same geographic area that holds an annual meeting.

Episcopal district. A number of conferences presided over by a bishop.

Presiding elder. Clergy members assigned by a bishop to give administrative guidance to a district.

General officer. An individual elected by the General Conference to serve a particular field of operation in the life of the denomination.

Itinerant ministry. The process of sending out ministers from a conference by a bishop annually to serve various pastoral charges.

Bibliography

Bradley, David Henry, Sr. *A History of the A.M.E. Zion Church.* Part 1, *1796–1872;* part 2, *1872–1968.* Nashville: Parthenon Press, 1956–70.

Burke, Emory Stevens. *History of American Methodism.* Vol. 1. New York: Abingdon Press, 1964.

The Doctrines and Discipline of the African Methodist Episcopal Zion Church. Charlotte, N.C.: A.M.E. Zion Publishing House, 1984.

Hood, James Walker. *One Hundred Years of the A.M.E. Zion Church.* New York: AME Zion Book Concern, 1895.

——. *Sketch of the Early History of the A.M.E. Zion Church.* Vol. 2. N.p.: J. W. Hood, 1914.

Walls, William Jacob. *The African Methodist Episcopal Zion Church: Reality of the Black Church.* Charlotte, N.C.: A.M.E. Zion Publishing House, n.d.

Prepared by Mary A. Love, editor, Department of Church School Literature, AME Zion Church.

CHRISTIAN METHODIST EPISCOPAL CHURCH

General Description

The Christian Methodist Episcopal (CME) Church is a part of the Methodist tradition, which consists of many denominations throughout the world.

The Methodist movement was founded not for the purpose of establishing a new denomination but rather to stimulate the revival of spiritual life in England. Thus, John Wesley adhered faithfully to the fundamental theology of the Church of England. Therefore, the theological distinction of all Methodism is not found in any book of tenets of belief, but rather in the clearness and power with which it illustrated and applied the basic doctrines of the English Reformation. It confined its teachings to personal or spiritual religion, including repentance, faith, justification, regeneration, sanctification, and witness of the Spirit. These great spiritual truths have been the life-energy of Methodism wherever it has been founded. As a denomination or in a local church, Methodists stand squarely on the Bible for their doctrines and beliefs. It is a thoroughly Protestant Church, holding dear the essential truths of pure Christianity as reemphasized by Martin Luther and the Protestant Reformation.

Nevertheless, the Christian Methodist Church remains loyal to the principles of church organization, structure, and beliefs as developed and passed down by John Wesley, the founder of world Methodism. (Adapted from an article by Dr. William R. Johnson—no citation data available.)

Beliefs and Doctrines

As the youngest but very loyal daughter of Methodism, the CME Church strictly adheres to the beliefs of the mother church. Therefore, the reader is referred to the general chapter "Methodists" above, or to the chapters on the African Methodist Episcopal Church or the AME Zion Church for a general review of the CME beliefs or doctrinal positions.

Forms of Worship

The CME Church's *Membership Training Manual,* written by Mary Green Thomas, defines worship as seeking "to be in fellowship with [God] through prayer, praise and thanksgiving to him for his enduring [love] (p. 13). Elsewhere, Thomas calls worship "the realization of the presence of God" and the "effective means through which this realization is accomplished" (p. 32).

CME worship services are basically the same as other Methodist groups. They include hymns and other music, prayers of confession and other interests including pastoral concerns and intercessions, offering, an affirmation of faith, Bible reading, preaching, and a benediction. Christian Methodists make much of music as worship; with others, they believe that music helps worshipers to be joyful, to celebrate, and to feel victorious and hopeful of new life and a life to come.

CME churches generally follow the Christian year, emphasizing the events in the life of Christ from Christmas to Pentecost. They also use colors in the churches to remind worshipers of the appropriate Sundays and holidays.

Two sacraments are recognized by the CME Church: Holy Communion, or the Lord's Supper, and baptism—both instituted by Jesus Christ and celebrated with rituals inspired by the Methodist Church.

Unique elements in CME worship are related to praying. The standing position used in both prayer and praise shows respect to God, as does kneeling and bowing in prayer.

Organization

The CME Church, like other Methodist churches, calls itself a connectional church, meaning that all the units in the church are connected, from the local church and its church conference and the quarterly conference through the district conference and the annual conference to the General Conference of the whole church.

The local church also has an official board that is composed of the leaders of the church (presidents of groups, stewards and stewardesses), who are responsible for the operations of the congregation. It meets weekly, and the pastor presides. The church conference is the democratic body where all members have a voice and a vote in the business of the church. Also delegates are elected to the district and annual conferences at this conference. The quarterly conference controls (or reports) the actions of the church conferences, including stewards and stewardesses and other church officers. This conference hears reports from the official boards and other groups and meets every three months. It is chaired by the presiding elder (or the pastor if he is designated by the presiding elder).

The district conference is composed of representatives (delegates) from local churches. It functions as the local quarterly conference on the next higher level, hearing reports from local churches and electing district officers. Its presiding officer is the presiding elder. The annual conference also hears reports from local churches as well as reports from its own officers, boards, and departments and holds elections of conference officers and delegates to the General Conference. Also the presiding bishop assigns pastors to the local churches.

The General Conference is the highest authority in the CME Church. It meets every four years. It reviews, establishes, and changes the laws and rules that govern the whole connection, and it receives reports from bishops about the episcopal districts in their charge and from the general officers and departments. It also elects bishops as well as the general officers of the church.

Ministry

The CME Church, recognizing that ministerial development may occur in progressive stages, has designated several categories of ministry:

Exhorter. A layperson recognized as one who is deeply committed to Christian service. During a trial period to determine his or her future ministry, an exhorter is supervised by the pastor.

Licensed preacher. A layperson acknowledged by the congregation and tested by the pastor for at least three months who has been licensed to preach the gospel, supervised by the pastor.

Local deacon. An ordained local minister authorized to preach the gospel, read the Scriptures, give rites for marriage, and bury the dead, supervised by the pastor.

Local elder. He or she is the same as a local deacon but is authorized to consecrate and administer the Lord's Supper.

Traveling deacon. The same as a local deacon but authorized to consecrate and administer the Lord's Supper throughout the church.

Traveling elder. One possessing the full rights of a preacher of the gospel and usually a full member of an annual conference and subject to travel from church to church throughout the CME Church (connection).

Pastor. In charge of a local church, with the usual duties.

Presiding elder. One in charge of a district.

Bishop. Elected to preside over an episcopal district and the conferences therein.

Contributions and Influence

The CME Church takes great pride in its schools, to which it points as providing abundant leadership for their children and for the communities the schools service. There are five four-year liberal arts colleges, and two that began as industrial colleges and are now four-year institutions, and one theological seminary.

Also, the CME Church is proud of its good spirit of interracial harmony, beginning as it did with an act of interracial cooperation. Furthermore, the founding of Paine College was an example of racial good will, as is its long history of an integrated faculty. Indeed, historically all CME churches and schools have always been open to persons regardless of their race or color. They boast that their doors have always been open. According to Will E. Chambers, "This has been our heritage, and worthy to be kept alive as the world continues to face problems in the area of race. Our history points out that there is a way other than prejudice, and the least we can do is judge persons as individuals and prejudice none" *(CME Church Membership Manual,* Salisbury, N.C., Concepts Materialized, 1982, p. 24).

Significant Terms

A Methodist (as described by John Wesley). "One who makes obvious the love of God shed abroad in his heart by the Holy Ghost given unto him; one who loves his Lord with all his heart, with all his soul, with all his mind, with all his strength."

Epworth League. An early name of the youth program of the Methodist Church. Epworth (England) was the birthplace of John Wesley.

John Wesley. A son of Samuel and Suzanna Wesley, who, like his father, became a Church of England clergyman. He was converted by his experiences with Moravians in America and by a "heartwarming" experience at Aldersgate Chapel and later led the "Wesley Revival" in England. When Methodists in

America turned to Wesley for leadership, he sent Thomas Coke, Francis Asbury, and others to oversee Methodists and work in the colonies. Thus, the Methodist Church was established in the United States.

Methodist. A nickname first used to describe the "Holy Club" founded by John and Charles Wesley at Oxford University. It was later used to designate the Wesleyan societies and finally the church founded on Wesley's patterns.

Mother Liberty Church. The church in Jackson, Tennessee, where the organization of the General Conference of the Christian (Colored) Methodist Episcopal Church was held in December 1870.

Bibliography

The Book of Discipline. Memphis, Tenn.: CME Church Publishing House, 1986.

Chambers, Will E. *Christian Methodist Episcopal Church Membership Manual.* Salisbury, N.C.: Concepts Materialized, 1982.

The Christian Index. Memphis, Tenn.: CME Church Publishing Dept. A monthly journal.

Coleman, C. D. *Christian Methodist Episcopal Primer: Our Heritage.* Memphis, Tenn.: CME Church Publishing Dept., n.d.

Johnson, Joseph A. *Basic Christian Methodist Beliefs.* Shreveport, La.: Fourth Episcopal District Press, 1978.

Lakey, Q. H. *The History of the Christian Methodist Episcopal Church.* Memphis, Tenn.: CME Publishing House, 1958.

Prepared by the editor from materials supplied by the CME Church.

CHURCH OF THE NAZARENE

General Description

The Church of the Nazarene is an international denomination of nearly 1 million members, over half of whom live in the United States. The largest of the churches that came out of the American holiness revival of the nineteenth century, it was organized in 1908 through the merger of three regional bodies. It is Wesleyan in doctrines and related theologically to the Free Methodists, the Wesleyans, the Salvation Army, and the traditionalist sectors of the United Methodist Church.

Founders

Key leaders in the 1908 merger were Phineas F. Bresee, cofounder in 1895 of a church based on the Pacific Coast also known as the Church of the Nazarene; Hiram F. Reynolds, a missionary secretary of the northeastern-based Association of Pentecostal Churches of America (organized in 1896 from antecedents dating from 1890 and 1895); and Charles B. Jernigan and Mary Lee Cagle of the Holiness Church of Christ, a southern denomination (organized in 1904 from antecedents dating from 1894 and 1901). All four were ordained ministers and had backgrounds in Methodism. Bresee and Reynolds were elected general superintendents of the new denomination. Bresee's unique contribution was to shape the church's frame of government, while Reynolds stamped it with a strong missionary emphasis. Other key leaders include Roy T. Williams and James Blaine Chapman, second-generation leaders of the Board of General Superintendents. Benjamin F. Haynes was founding editor of the church paper *Herald of Holiness*. Aaron Meritt Hills (who wrote *Fundamental Christian Theology*, 2 vols. [1931]) and H. Orton Wiley (*Christian Theology*, 3 vols. [1940–43]) were significant in shaping early theological development.

Beliefs and Doctrines

The Church of the Nazarene is an orthodox Protestant body that adheres to the ecumenical creeds of the early Christian church. The theology of Methodist founder John Wesley (1703–91), who integrated the Protestant understanding of grace with the Catholic themes of holiness and love, is foundational for Nazarene doctrine. Nazarenes emphasize Christian conversion, sanctification of holiness, and the personal assurance of God's grace—Wesleyan distinctives that point back to a deeper rootage in continental European Pietism. Discipleship is a prominent concern. An emphasis on the doctrine of the Holy Spirit has generally prevented Nazarenes from slipping into the static biblicism that sometimes affects other evangelical Protestants. The Church of the Nazarene recognizes two sacraments: Christian baptism and Holy Communion. Believer's baptism and infant baptism are both allowed, though the former is most generally practiced.

Forms of Worship

Nazarene worship is evangelical, rather than liturgical. Services typically combine hymns with popular music. The sermon generally concludes the worship service. Most churches have worship services on Sunday evenings as well as mornings, and most conduct Wednesday night prayer meetings or provide other spiritual-oriented activity that evening. Nazarene churches are required to observe Holy Communion at least four times a year and may do so more frequently if desired.

Organization

Nazarene polity is a studied compromise between episcopal and congregational forms of government. While Nazarenes consider the congregation to be the basic unit of the church, the highest legislative body is the General Assembly, which meets every four years. The General Assembly (1) elects the general superintendents, who serve until the next assembly meeting, when they may be reelected; (2) elects the General Board, which meets annually and is composed of representatives of the General Assembly; and (3) decides denominational issues, many of which are incorporated into the church *Manual*. Congregations belong to districts, which hold annual assemblies and are led by the elected district superintendent. New ministers are elected to orders by the district assembly and ordained by the presiding general superintendent.

Contributions and Influence

As a religious body that originated on American soil, the Church of the Nazarene has reflected the democratic spirit throughout its history. This facet has been exemplary in two areas: clergy-laity relations, and the role of women in church life. Beginning in the parent bodies and continuing in the present denomination, all levels of church government from the congregation through the General Assembly have balanced lay and clergy representation. Moreover, all councils, whether clergy or lay, of church government have been open to women. The Southern parent-group ordained its first woman in 1899, and the other two groups both did so in 1902. After the 1908 merger, nearly 14 percent of the ordained clergy (and 18 percent of all ministers and evangelists) in the church were female.

Outside of the denomination line, Nazarenes have been active as well. Nazarene colleges have educated a number of leaders in the field of relief work, including the founders of World Vision and World Neighbors and past presidents and executive directors of the American Red Cross, Church World Service, and Compassion International. Nazarene leaders have been active in the National Association of Evangelicals, the Christian Holiness Association, and the Lausanne Committee on World Evangelization.

Significant Terms

Conversion. Nazarenes emphasize conversion as a definite experience that initiates the life of Christian discipleship.

Sanctification. The process of becoming holy, or Christlike, which Nazarenes equate with the infilling of divine love through the presence of the Holy Spirit. Nazarenes believe that this process begins at conversion and that a point can be reached, called entire sanctification, when love expels all disposition to sin.

Bibliography

Greathouse, William M. *What Is the Church of the Nazarene?* Kansas City, Mo.: Nazarene Publishing House, 1973. Rev. ed., 1984.

Jones, Charles Edwin. *Perfectionist Persuasion*. Kansas City, Mo.: Scarecrow Press, 1974.

Manual of the Church of the Nazarene. Kansas City, Mo.: Nazarene Publishing House, 1989.

Smith, Timothy L. *Called unto Holiness: The Story of the Nazarenes*. Kansas City, Mo.: Nazarene Publishing House, 1961.

Prepared by Stan Ingersol, Ph.D., denominational archivist, Church of the Nazarene.

FREE METHODIST CHURCH
OF NORTH AMERICA

General Description

The Free Methodist Church of North America was organized in 1860 in western New York by ministers and laymen who had been members of the Genessee Conference of the Methodist Episcopal Church. B. T. Roberts was the leader of the group and was elected general superintendent, later called bishop. He and other leaders of the Methodist Conference, both lay and clergy, had been expelled for "insubordination." After an appeal of the case had been denied by the General Conference of 1860, these excommunicated men and others met to form a new Methodist denomination.

Roberts and others had been calling the church to return to what they considered to be primitive doctrines and life-styles of Methodism. They especially emphasized the Wesleyan teaching of entire sanctification of life by means of grace through faith. In their writings and preaching they condemned with vigor their radical brothers for worldliness and their departure from Methodist doctrine and experience. Because of their strong opposition to quasi-religious secret societies, the leaders of Free Methodism incurred the ill will of members of the conference who held membership in such lodges and fraternal orders. Also, Roberts and most of his followers were radical abolitionists in the years prior to the Civil War, at a time when many within the Methodist Church were silent on the issue of slavery.

The official publication of the denomination is a monthly family magazine, *Light and Life*. Other publications include the monthly *Missionary Tidings*, published by Woman's Missionary Fellowship International. The Free Methodist Church is a member of the National Association of Evangelicals and the Christian Holiness Association. Denominational headquarters and publishing house are in Winona Lake, Indiana.

Beliefs and Doctrines

From its beginning, the Free Methodist Church has made Christian holiness a significant distinctive in its teaching. The church has interpreted the Bible and the writings of John Wesley to teach that all Christians may be inwardly cleansed from sinful rebellion against God's will. The sanctification of the affections and will may be experienced instantly, in a moment of faith, when the wholly committed Christian accepts the atonement of Jesus Christ and the fullness of the Holy Spirit for the cleansing of his motives and the perfection of his love toward God and man. The sanctification of life is a process of growth and development in holiness through the empowering of the Holy Spirit in the life of the Christian. The Free Methodist Church has endeavored to follow the teachings of Wesley regarding sanctification of life by forming both "general" and "special" rules to guide Christians in the way of holiness.

All adult members of the church covenant are not to indulge in the use of tobacco or alcoholic beverages. They promise to give a tithe of their income to benevolent and Christian causes. They vow to keep themselves free from membership in secret societies, that their loyalties may not be divided. They disavow all racism and political and social discrimination against ethnic minorities. They promise to regard marriage and the family as sacred and avoid divorce except for cases of adultery and desertion.

Organization

The government of the church is a modified form of the episcopacy. From the beginning, when lay leaders and ministers met to form the new denomination, provision was made for equal representation of clergy and laity in all councils of the church, both local and general. A general conference meets every four or five years to review and establish the polity and the programs of the denomination and to elect bishops. Annual conferences bring together the ministers and delegated representatives of the local congregations in thirty-six districts in the United States and Canada. Pastors are appointed by annual conference, with the bishop serving as the chairman of the ministerial appointments committee. All church property is held in trust for the denomination.

Contributions and Influence

Four accredited senior colleges and universities are sponsored by the Free Methodist Church: Roberts Wesleyan College (New York), Greenville College (Illinois), Seattle Pacific University (Washington), and Spring Arbor College (Michigan). A Bible college, Aldersgate (Saskatchewan), and a junior college, Central (Kansas), are also supported by the denomination. The church is affiliated with Azusa Pacific College (California) and two seminaries: Asbury Theological Seminary (Kentucky) and Western Evangelical Seminary (Oregon).

Social agencies sponsored by the denomination include the Deaconess Hospital and Deaconess Home (a facility for unwed mothers) in Oklahoma City, Oklahoma, and four retirement homes: Heritage Village, in Gerry, New York; Warm Beach Senior Community, in Stanwood, Washington; Wesley Manor, in New Westminster, British Columbia; and Woodstock Christian Care, in Woodstock, Illinois.

Significant Terms

Arminian heritage. The teachings and attitudes of Jacob Arminius and his followers, who emphasized the free will of all humans, in contrast to Calvinism and its doctrine of predestination, or religious determination of human behavior.

Free. Stands for basic human freedom, including freedom from slavery, freedom for the simple worship of God, freedom from pew rents and other charges, and freedom of conscience and counsel.

Holiness. Refers to scriptural holiness of the heart and life, often called "entire sanctification," which takes place subsequent to justification and is the work of God wrought instantaneously upon the consecrated, believing soul. It is a disciplined Christian life-style.

Methodist heritage. The influence of Methodism as seen in the organization of the Free Methodist Church, in its concern for all levels of the church—local, district, conference, and denominational—as well as in its dedication to social concerns and sensitivity.

Practical godliness. The sincere effort a Christian makes to implement in practical living the outcomes of a truly cleansed heart. The Free Methodist takes a firm stand against the use of tobacco, alcoholic beverages, and other drugs.

Wesleyan heritage. The teachings and attitudes of the Wesley brothers, John and Charles, emphasizing the direct witness of the Holy Spirit in the human heart granting salvation, peace, and power for Christian living.

Bibliography

(All items are published by the Free Methodist Publishing House, Winona Lake, Ind.)

Bastian, D. N. *Belonging! Adventures in Church Membership*. 1978.
Hogue, W. T. *History of the Free Methodist Church*. 2 vols. 1915.
Marston, L. R. *From Age to Age a Living Witness*. 1960.
———. *The Life and Faith of a Free Methodist*. 1976.
Yearbook: The Free Methodist Church of North America.

Prepared by Frances Haslam, executive secretary, Marston Memorial Historical Center.

PRIMITIVE METHODIST CHURCH

General Description

Primitive Methodism began as a result of an all-day prayer meeting held on May 31, 1807, on Mow Cop, a hill located on the border of Staffordshire and Cheshire in England. Those converted at this and a few other meetings, being refused membership in the Wesleyan Church, formed a new religious community in 1810. This group, meeting on February 13, 1812, assumed the name "Society of the Primitive Methodist," a name basically meaning, "original Methodist." Because members migrated to the United States, missionaries were sent, arriving in New York City in 1829. By 1840 the American group separated from England. The various conferences were combined in 1975 and continue to meet annually as the decision-making body for all the churches.

Founders

Hugh Bourne (1772–1852) and William Clowes (1780–1851) are recognized as the fathers of Primitive Methodism.

Beliefs and Doctrines

The Bible is the only true rule of faith and practice. We believe that the Old and New Testaments are the Word of God. We believe in the Trinity: the Father, the Son, and the Holy Spirit.

Salvation comes through belief in Jesus Christ as Savior and Redeemer. Man is in a fallen condition because of sin and yet has free will to accept or reject salvation. Sanctification is the work of the Holy Spirit in the heart, producing holiness in the life.

The Primitive Methodist Church holds to the Arminian position of nonpredestination, resistible grace, and free will.

Forms of Worship

Primitive Methodists emphasize congregational participation in worship, including singing, prayer, and Scripture reading. However, its main emphasis is placed on preaching and the exposition of the Bible. The Primitive Methodist Church accepts two sacraments: Communion and baptism. In Communion, the church commemorates Christ's suffering and death through the symbols of bread and wine (unfermented). In baptism, the outward sacred rite signifies an inward purity accomplished by Christ's atonement, administered by the use of water. Our emphasis is on infant baptism, although other modes of baptism are acceptable: sprinkling, pouring, or immersion.

Organization

The Primitive Methodist Church is presbyterian-congregational in form and government, with equal representation of clergy and laity in district and conference bodies. Its orders of ministry are elders and deacons. Deacons are appointed by the conference, and elders are elected to churches under the system of itinerancy at the call of a local church.

The laws of the church are established by the *Book of Discipline*. The Annual Conference is both administrative and legislative. The officers of conference are president, executive director, vice-president, general secretary, and treasurer. Primitive Methodist churches are divided into six districts, each with its own district superintendent.

The local church is in the charge of the minister regarding spiritual matters, but jointly governed by a quarterly conference (the highest official meeting of the church, composed of officials of the church and every organization). The trustees are in charge of administering the property and church finances.

Practices

The Primitive Methodist Church enjoys a family atmosphere. This is true in the local church and on the conference level. People know one another in a personal way. Obvious interest and concern is shown for laity and ministers alike. In times of sorrow and joy, people from all over the conference express their concern or congratulations. Conference becomes a time of renewing old friendships and gaining new ones.

The church believes that the use of alcohol is contrary to the teachings of the Lord, and because its use has created a serious health problem in our nation, members are encouraged to abstain. Members are instructed that the use of tobacco in all forms, illicit drugs, and all habit-forming narcotics are not recommended, since the church believes them to be injurious to the body.

Significant Terms

Church clerk. Officer elected by the congregation who acts as the secretary of all congregational meetings and the quarterly conference.

Conference. Composed of clergy and lay delegates. It is held annually and is the administrative and legislative body of the denomination.

Deaconess. A woman, led by the Holy Spirit, who gives herself to Christian service under the authority of the church. She ministers to the spiritual and the physical needs of those to whom she is directed.

District superintendent. Nominated by his district and elected by the conference, he holds official supervision over all churches and all ministers within the bounds of his district.

Itinerancy. All ministers must agree to the final authority of the conference and accept the church assigned. Elders, elected by local congregations, must be approved by the conference. All other ministers are appointed through the stationing committee. A minister refusing to accept a conference appointment would be left without a pastorate.

Local preacher. A person approved by the quarterly conference and completing a course of study by the School of Theology; he has authority to perform the rite of baptism, administer the Lord's Supper, and conduct funeral services and is eligible to serve as ministerial supply when appointed by the conference.

Station steward. Elected by the congregation, he has oversight of the church in the absence or disability of the minister and presides at the annual congregational meeting for the invitation and election of the minister.

Trustee (of a local church). One elected by the congregation to administer the church properties for the benefit of the church. Trustees are responsible for the maintenance of all church properties and for the administration of all funds.

Trustee (of the conference). One elected by the conference to administer and manage the business, property, and affairs of the conference entrusted to them.

Bibliography
Acornley, John. *A History of the Primitive Methodist Church.* Fall River, Mass.: B. R. Acornley, 1906.
Fudge, William. *The View from the Mountain.* Wilkes-Barre, Pa.: Wyoming Valley Religious Supply, 1987.
Kendall, H. B. *The Origin and History of the Primitive Methodist Church.* 2 vols. London: Edwin Dalton, n.d.
Tyrrell, W. *Steeples on the Prairies.* N.p.: Primitive Methodist Church of the United States of America, 1987.

Prepared by William O. Fudge, district superintendent, Primitive Methodist Church.

UNITED METHODIST CHURCH

See main entry under "Methodists."

WESLEYAN CHURCH

General Description
Linked historically and theologically to John Wesley and eighteenth-century Methodism, the Wesleyan Church is a worldwide denomination of 185,641 members in approximately 30 countries. The Wesleyan Church holds membership in the National Association of Evangelicals and the Christian Holiness Association. Its general office is located in Indianapolis, Indiana.

Founder
The Wesleyan Church was formed in 1968 as a result of a merger between the Wesleyan Methodist Church of America and the Pilgrim Holiness Church—two denominations rooted in the traditions of Methodism and the American holiness movement. The Wesleyan Methodist Church was organized in 1843 as a Methodist denomination that was free of slavery and

episcopacy. The leading founder of the Wesleyan Methodist Church was Orange Scott, a Methodist minister and abolitionist. The beginnings of the Pilgrim Holiness Church took shape in 1897 with the formation of the International Holiness Union and Prayer League. Founded by Seth Cook Rees, a Quaker evangelist, and Martin Wells Knapp, a Methodist evangelist, the union began as a nondenominational fellowship but evolved into a denomination through a series of mergers and name changes. The name Pilgrim Holiness Church was adopted in 1922. The similarities in doctrine and mission of the Wesleyan Methodist Church and the Pilgrim Holiness Church led to their 1968 merger.

Beliefs and Doctrines

The doctrinal beliefs of the Wesleyan Church are Wesleyan-Arminian and in harmony with those of the National Association of Evangelicals and the Christian Holiness Association. The doctrine of "entire sanctification" (also known as sanctification, perfect love, Christian perfection, or holiness) as a second definite religious experience following conversion is a primary doctrinal emphasis of the Wesleyan Church.

Forms of Worship

Worship is generally simple and nonliturgical. Congregational singing, prayer, Scripture reading, preaching, and evangelistic appeal are standard components of worship.

Organization

The quadrennial General Conference is the ultimate governing body of the denomination. Comprising equal numbers of elected lay and clergy delegates from around the world, the conference elects general officers, establishes policy, and provides overall direction for the church. Four general superintendents serve as the highest elected officials and are responsible for administering the affairs of the church. The elected General Board of Administration functions as the governing body between the quadrennial sessions of the General Conference. Local churches are clustered geographically into administrative districts that are supervised by elected district superintendents. Local churches exercise relative autonomy within the guiding structure of the district and general leadership.

Significant Term

Entire sanctification. We believe that sanctification is the work of the Holy Spirit by which the child of God is separated from sin unto God and is enabled to love God with all his heart and to walk blameless in all God's holy commandments. Sanctification is wrought instantaneously when the believer presents himself a living sacrifice, holy and acceptable to God, through faith in Jesus Christ, being effected by the baptism with the Holy

Spirit, who cleanses the heart from all inbred sin. The crisis of entire sanctification perfects the believer in love and empowers him for effective service. The life of holiness continues through faith in the sanctifying blood of Christ and evidences itself by loving obedience to God's revealed will.

Bibliography

(All items are published by the Wesley Press, Indianapolis, Ind.)

Haines, Lee M., and Paul William Thomas. *An Outline History of the Wesleyan Church.* 1985.

McLeister, Ira F., and Roy S. Nicholson. *Conscience and Commitment: The History of the Wesleyan Methodist Church of America.* 1976.

Thomas, Paul Westphal, and Paul William Thomas. *The Days of Our Pilgrimages: The History of the Pilgrim Holiness Church.* 1976.

Prepared by Daniel L. Burnett, director of archives, Wesleyan Church.

♦ ♦ ♦
MORAVIAN CHURCH

General Description
The Moravian Church in America is a small Protestant denomination with about 50,000 baptized members (including children) in the United States and 500,000 in the world. The Moravian Church has ties with ecumenical Christianity through the National Council of Churches and World Council of Churches and with other Christian churches as well, especially in relation to work outside the United States.

History
The Moravian church's historical roots are in the Hussite reform movement in the 1400s, in what is now Czechoslovakia, and in German Pietism of the 1700s. In 1547 followers of the martyred John Hus started a church called *Unitas Fratrum* (Unity of Brethren), stressing a simple, Christlike life. This church experienced initial success as a national church and then declined in the religious disputes of the 1600s. The leading figure of this period, which Moravians call the "ancient Unity," was Bishop John Amos Comenius, a noted educator.

In the late 1720s remnants of this Unity found refuge and renewal on the land of Count Nicholas von Zinzendorf, a wealthy German Pietist, who became the church's patron as well as spiritual leader. From Zinzendorf the church has inherited a Christ-centeredness, an ecumenical spirit, and a global concern.

From the church's center, the village of Herrnhut, burst a passion for mission work among isolated peoples. This took Moravians first to the Virgin Islands (1732), then to American Indians in Georgia (1735), Pennsylvania (1740), and North Carolina (1753). Since the colonial period, Bethlehem, Pennsylvania, and Winston-Salem, North Carolina, have been the centers of the Moravian Church in the United States, although there are now congregations in fourteen states and the District of Columbia, as well as three provinces of Canada.

Mission effort and worldwide understanding of the church, although tempered in our postcolonial period, have continued to be marks of the Moravian Church. The German roots and home mission work among German immigrants after 1850 made the American church to some extent a German ethnic group into this century.

During the 1700s Moravians were pacifists. While that practice has been dormant for most of the last two centuries, Moravians today are expressing new interest in that part of their heritage.

Even though small in number, the Moravian Church has contributed to Christendom a strong devotion to Christ, and awareness of the global nature of the Christian family.

Beliefs and Doctrines

While accepting the historic creeds of Christendom and such modern affirmations as the Barmen Declaration, Moravians have seen personal devotion and faithful living as more crucial in the Christian life than verbal assent to creeds. They have tried to avoid doctrinal controversy that pits one Christian or one Christian tradition against another. One motto used by the Moravians is "In essentials, unity; in nonessentials, liberty; in all things, love."

Forms of Worship

Moravian worship has stressed the element of joy and involves congregational singing and, in many places, instrumental music, especially brass. Moravians were the leading composers of vocal and instrumental music in colonial and early American periods. Although they display considerable diversity, Moravians generally stand between more liturgical traditions and freer worship.

Moravians observe two sacraments, baptism and Communion, and sometimes, in jest, call fellowship a third sacrament. Communion is generally celebrated about six times a year, with the service consisting primarily of congregational singing. The love feast, a simple fellowship meal of coffee and roll within the context of worship, is a custom in most congregations. Infant baptism is the normal practice, but believer's baptism is not unknown.

Organization

Congregational and denominational government is democratic and representative, with legislative meetings (synods) held every three or four years. The denomination recognizes the spiritual stature of some pastors by electing them bishops; yet the position does not have political or administrative responsibilities. Both men and women may be ordained for ministry.

The American Moravian church has two provinces, Northern and Southern. While administratively separate, they exchange pastors freely and jointly support the Moravian Theological Seminary, the Board of World Mission, and the *North American Moravians* magazine. Both are part of the worldwide Moravian Unity, in which only 20 percent live in Canada, the United States, or Europe. The largest numbers of Moravians are in Tanzania, South Africa, Surinam, Nicaragua, and the Caribbean basin. Ties among Moravians around the world are growing through educational exchanges, short-term mission work, and migration.

Significant Terms

Bishop. A pastor to pastors and spiritual leader of the denomination; not an administrative office.

Chief elder. At one time, the title of the executive head of the Moravian Church; since 1741, reserved for Jesus Christ.

God's acre. The church graveyard, site of the Easter sunrise service.

Holy Week service. A series of services during which the entire Passion narrative is read from a harmony of the Gospels and interspersed with appropriate hymns.

Love feast. A service of fellowship with hymn singing and a simple meal, most often coffee and a bun, marking an anniversary or special occasion.

Bibliography

(All items are published by the Moravian Church, Bethlehem, Pa., and Winston-Salem, N.C.)

Groenfeldt, John. *Becoming a Member of the Moravian Church.* 1976.

Hymnal and Liturgies of the Moravian Church. 1969.

Moravian Daily Texts. Published annually. Schattschneider, Allen W. *Through Fi: Hundred Years.* 1974.

Taylor, J., and Kenneth G. Hamilton. *History of the Moravian Church.* 1967.

Weinlock, John R. *Count Zinzendorf.* 1956.

Prepared by Hermann I. Weinlock, director of publications and communications, Moravia: Church, Northern Province.

◆ ◆ ◆
MORMONS
CHURCH OF JESUS CHRIST
OF LATTER-DAY SAINTS

General Description

The Church of Jesus Christ of Latter-Day Saints (CLDS) is the largest extant American-born religion—more than 7 million members strong in 1989; it is the true church of Jesus Christ restored in latter days. (Mormons believe that apostasy from the original church established by Christ resulted in the need for restoration.) With headquarters in Salt Lake City, Utah, the CLDS has members in more than 100 countries and 36,000 full-time missionaries.

The nickname "Mormons" has been used because of their belief in the *Book of Mormon,* a scripture from ancient America. Other Scriptures are the Holy Bible, *Doctrine and Covenants,* and *Pearl of Great Price.*

Leaders

The organizer and first president was Joseph Smith. He was born in Sharon, Vermont, on December 23, 1805. Smith saw God the Father and the Son, Jesus Christ, in a vision in 1820 in western New York State. Smith also received from a heavenly messenger ancient records from which the *Book of Mormon* was translated and published. The CLDS was organized as a church on April 6, 1830. Unfortunately Smith was slain in 1844 by a mob in a Carthage, Illinois, jail.

Later prophet-presidents were the famed American colonizer Brigham Young, who led the "Mormons" from Nauvoo, Illinois, to Salt Lake City in 1847, as well as John Taylor, Wilford Woodruff, Lorenzo Snow, Joseph F. Smith, Heber J. Grant, George Albert Smith, David O. McKay, Joseph Fielding Smith, Harold B. Lee, Spencer W. Kimball, and Ezra Taft Benson.

Beliefs and Doctrines

The CLDS continues revelation from God through a living prophet. Temple ceremonies include marriage for eternity and baptism of the living on behalf of the dead. Baptism is by immersion for the remission of sins at eight years or older. The church believes in premortal life.

Father, Son, and Holy Ghost are one in purpose, separate in being. There was apostasy after the death of Christ's apostles, but the church and its authority (the priesthood) were restored through Joseph Smith. Through

Christ, all will be resurrected, but to different levels of reward, depending upon their performance in mortality. There is free agency, or freedom for oneself—God will force no one to heaven.

A code of health called the Word of Wisdom counsels against use of tobacco, alcoholic beverages, tea, and coffee and emphasizes the use of wholesome grains, herbs, and fruits. Great emphasis is laid on strengthening the family with strict morality. The church believes in eternal family relationships.

The church has no paid clergy. It is supported by the voluntary tithes and offerings of faithful members.

Forms of Worship

Services are simple, with opening and closing prayers, communion, sermons, and hymns. Clergy do not wear robes. Any member of the congregation may preach a sermon in a worship service, if so assigned. CLDS worshipers use bread and water (rather than wine) for communion.

Contributions and Influence

A CLDS worldwide missionary force of 36,000 results in some 300,000 converts annually; in 1989 there were 17,000 congregations. The church has contributed to the settlement of more than three hundred communities from Canada to Mexico.

A small percentage of CLDS members practiced the biblical principle of polygamy in the nineteenth century until the Supreme Court finally ruled it unconstitutional in 1890. The practice is now grounds for loss of membership.

CLDS leaders emphasize education. "Mormon" scriptures maintain that "the glory of God is intelligence" and "no man can be saved in ignorance."

A self-help welfare system provides for needy members, but not as a dole.

Significant Terms

Apostle. A position in the Melchizedek Priesthood of the church. Apostles are general authorities of the church and, with few historical exceptions, are members of the Council of Twelve Apostles, the second highest governing body in the church.

Bishop. A lay leader who presides over a ward, or congregation, of the church.

Book of Mormon. A volume of Christian scriptures similar to the Holy Bible, the difference being that it is the translated writing of prophets in the ancient western hemisphere, as opposed to the Bible, which is a record from the eastern hemisphere.

Counselor. An adviser or aide to a bishop, branch president, district president, stake president, or president of the church.

Deacon. The first office in the Aaronic Priesthood. Young boys in the church become eligible for ordination to this office at the age of twelve and are normally eligible for advancement to a higher office by the age of fourteen. The deacon's responsibility is primarily to distribute the sacrament (bread and water) to members of the congregation during the worship services. The deacons also go to the homes of members once a month to collect "fast offerings," or cash donations for the poor.

Elder. An office in the Melchizedek or higher priesthood of the church; a title given to full-time general authorities and full-time missionaries.

Family home evening. A program of the church wherein each family is encouraged to set aside at least one evening a week where they spend time together in appropriate activities designed to strengthen family relationships.

Fast and testimony meeting. The worship service on the first Sunday of each month, culminating a day of fasting. The fasting is ended with the serving of the sacrament, or bread and water, during the service. Members are encouraged to donate at least the amount of money that would have been spent on the missed meals to a fund for needy members. During the service, members of the congregation are invited to express publicly their convictions about the gospel of Jesus Christ and about the church; the entire service is devoted to such expressions.

General conference. Twice-a-year meetings held in Salt Lake City for leaders of the church from throughout the world. The two-day conferences in the historic Mormon Tabernacle on Temple Square are televised live via satellite to nearly two thousand locations throughout the United States and in parts of Canada. Speakers at the conference are the general authorities of the church.

High priest. An office in the Melchizedek Priesthood. The office is required for, but not limited to, general, regional, and local officers of the church.

Hill Cumorah. A location in present-day western New York State where, in ancient times, a prophet buried secular and religious records kept by Christian prophets in the western hemisphere over many centuries. The records were unearthed in 1827 by the prophet Joseph Smith, who translated and published them as the *Book of Mormon.*

Latter days. The period of time immediately preceding the second coming of Jesus Christ and the thousand-year period known as the millennium.

Nauvoo. An Illinois community built in the late 1830s and early 1840s by the Latter-Day Saints. At its peak, it grew to some twelve thousand residents, rivaling the fledgling city of Chicago at the time. Nauvoo means "beautiful city."

Patriarchal blessing. A blessing given through the laying on of hands by one with priesthood authority in which the recipient's lineage is declared and a prophetic statement of the life mission of the recipient is made, complete with promised blessings, which are conditional upon faithfulness to the principles of the gospel of Jesus Christ.

Priest. The third office in the Aaronic Priesthood; generally young men, ages sixteen to eighteen. A priest has the authority to do all that deacons and teachers do, plus the authority to baptize and to offer sacramental (communion) prayers.

Relief Society. The worldwide women's organization of the church, which has some 1.8 million members.

Sacrament meeting. The weekly Sunday worship service of the church, during which the "sacrament," or communion (bread and water), is served to the congregation. The service also includes sermons by assigned members of the church as well as musical numbers and congregational singing of hymns.

Saint. A member of the Church of Jesus Christ of Latter-Day Saints. As in biblical times, a saint is a follower of Christ or a member of his church.

Stake. A geographic unit of the church comprising several congregations.

Temple. A house of worship, not to be confused with a regular church or meetinghouse. The temples serve larger areas and are open every day but Sunday, the Sabbath day. They are used for marriages, baptisms, and other sacred ordinances. They are closed on Sundays, when members meet in their local churches, or meetinghouses, for worship services.

Temple marriage. Marriage for time and all eternity performed within a temple of the church by one with the proper priesthood authority and calling.

Visiting teachers. A program of the Relief Society, the church's organization for adult women. Each member of the Relief Society is assigned a pair of visiting teachers, who regularly visit with that member and assist her in appropriate ways with her spiritual, social, and emotional needs.

Ward. A congregation.

Word of Wisdom. The health code of the church, which promotes good physical and spiritual health, including encouraging the use of fruits, vegetables, grains, and other healthful foods and warning against the use of alcohol, tobacco, and harmful drinks such as coffee and tea. The principle was revealed to the prophet Joseph Smith in 1833.

Bibliography
Allen, James B., and Glen, M. Leonard. *The Story of the Latter-Day Saints.* Salt Lake City: Deseret, 1976.

Arrington, Leonard, and Davis Blitton. *The Mormon Experience: A History of the Latter-Day Saints.* New York: Alfred A. Knopf, 1979.

Prepared by L. Don LeFevre, Media Relations, the Church of Jesus Christ of Latter-Day Saints.

REORGANIZED CHURCH OF JESUS CHRIST OF LATTER DAY SAINTS

History

In 1830 Joseph Smith, Jr., had what he later described as significant religious experiences, which led to his organizing a church in Fayette, New York, on April 6. Shortly thereafter he and a small group of members moved to Kirtland, Ohio, where a dynamic minister, Sidney Rigdon, and some of his followers joined the infant church and with Smith created a religious and social community to serve as the base for spreading the gospel message. Missionaries ventured as far as Jackson County, Missouri, and founded a colony there, which Joseph Smith called the center of God's earthly kingdom (Zion) in 1831. But tensions developed between the Saints and local residents, which resulted in church members moving northward from county to county. Subsequently Saints from Jackson County and the Kirtland experiment joined to form a new center at Far West, Missouri, with Joseph Smith as the leader.

By 1839 the church was forced to move again, evicted from the entire state of Missouri. The Saints founded the town of Nauvoo, Illinois, the "city beautiful," on the banks of the Mississippi River. Although this community grew rapidly, its success, like that of earlier attempts, was soon undermined. Unusual rites relating to the afterlife had crept into the church, causing internal dissension. Conflicts with surrounding communities also developed as Nauvoo increased in size. On June 27, 1844, an angry mob broke into the jail in Carthage, Illinois, where Joseph and his brother Hyrum had been imprisoned, and murdered them.

Following these assassinations the church was confused and disorganized for several years and divided into factions. The largest group moved westward to the Great Salt Lake valley under the direction of Brigham Young. Smaller factions scattered in all directions. By the early 1850s Jason W. Briggs and Zenus H. Gurley, Sr., began the task of reassembling the "scattered saints," who had remained primarily in Wisconsin, Illinois, and Iowa. This group believed that Joseph Smith, Jr., had designated his eldest son, Joseph III, to be his successor. Consequently, on April 8, 1860, at Amboy, Illinois, the Reorganized Church of Jesus Christ of Latter Day Saints (RLDS) was organized under the leadership of Joseph Smith, III. His fifty-four years as leader were marked by growth from a small, fragmented group to a body of over 70,000 persons, with congregations throughout the United States and other countries.

In 1915 Frederick M. Smith succeeded his father in the presidency. He emphasized the social expression of the gospel, fostering the establishment of Zionic conditions by merging spiritual and temporal affairs. Upon Frederick's death in 1946, his brother, Israel A. Smith, succeeded him. The twelve years of Israel's presidency were marked by stability and growth, undergirded by a greater missionary emphasis.

In 1958 W. Wallace Smith became the third of Joseph III's sons to follow him in the presidency. Under his leadership opportunities arose for the expansion of the church into other cultures, Western and non-Western. It was also marked by an evaluation of program and message and the adoption of a more decentralized style of church administration. In 1976 W. Wallace Smith designated his son, Wallace B. Smith, to succeed him as prophet-president.

Beliefs and Doctrines

We believe that God is self-revealing and that he acts in history. We affirm that God is just as active in the lives of individuals and nations today as in times past. Jesus Christ is the central revelation of God. In Christ, persons experience God and God-created humanity at the same time.

The Scriptures are inspired writing, the product of the Holy Spirit working within persons who have witnessed God at work. Scripture has both external and internal authority. We use and respect Scripture because the church says it is important. We also know it can change our lives for the better, so we say that it has internal authority. The Saints believe that the canon of Scripture includes the *Book of Mormon* and the *Doctrine and Covenants* in addition to the Bible.

The Saints' Bible is one of the group of three Scriptures frequently referred to as "the three standard books" of the church. It is a compilation of numerous books written at various times by people of many cultures. These books represent attempts to respond in words to the revelation of God.

Joseph Smith, Jr., under strong direction by the Spirit, worked for many years on a revised version of the Bible. His final work was not published in his lifetime, but in 1867. Although officially titled "The Holy Scriptures," this version is popularly known as the Inspired Version. The basic style and content of the King James translation are preserved, but Joseph Smith frequently modernized the language.

Like the Bible, the *Book of Mormon* is a collection of books—fifteen in all—whose central testimony is of Jesus Christ. Fourteen of these books tell the story of a colony of people called Nephites who left Jerusalem in 586 B.C. and traveled across the ocean to another land. The remaining book is about another colony, the Jesredites, who migrated from the Tigris-Euphrates valley at the time of the building of the Tower of Babel. The focal point of the book as a whole is the visit and ministry of Jesus Christ to the people. Throughout the *Book of Mormon* principles of strict morality and adherence to religious standards are taught.

The *Book of Mormon* was first published in 1830, just prior to the organization of the Church of Jesus Christ (the original name of the Saints' church). In the years immediately after its publication the book was the primary missionary tool of the infant church. More than any other single thing, it was responsible for the way both supporters and opponents viewed the church. In fact, early Latter Day Saints were called Mormons, after the title of their book.

The *Doctrine and Covenants* is a compilation of documents the church accepts as inspired statements representing "the mind and will of God" and as a standard of church law and practice. The documents date back to 1828 and cover the period from then until the present. One of the functions of the prophet-president is to present in written form what he perceives as God's will for the church. The documents are presented to the various councils of the church and to the World Conference for consideration. After a formal vote, approved sections are printed as additions to the doctrine and covenants.

Church Life

The Saints' church has always affirmed that it was brought into existence to fulfill God's purposes. Two emphases have been prevalent in its self-image. First, it is called to witness for Christ in the modern age. Second, it sees itself as called to build God's kingdom on earth—a process of community transformation and redemption.

The Saints have always stressed the worth of each member's contribution to the church's life. No role, function, or responsibility is more important than the other. Thus, congregational life is carried on by individuals who share responsibilities and are nonsalaried. This structure of shared responsibility has the advantage of involving a large number of members in the functions of ministry.

Although various responsibilities of church life are shared among a number of people, some are carried out by an ordained ministry, or a priesthood. The 1984 World Conference of the church authorized the ordination of women to priesthood, which previously had been open only to men.

Saints believe that a sacrament is a religious act or practice in which symbols are used to signify the covenant relationship between God and the human creation. We have eight sacraments.

Baptism is the celebration of God's gift of grace to humanity and the response of the individual in commitment to God. As the rite of initiation into the church, persons are eligible for baptism when they reach the age of eight—sometimes called the age of accountability. Baptism is by immersion in water, usually in a worship setting.

Confirmation represents the response of God to the one who has been baptized. It conveys the promise of the Holy Spirit as an abiding comforter and sustaining presence. It represents the completion of the initiatory rite and admission to full membership in the church. Confirmation is by the laying on of hands by elders.

Blessing of children normally occurs when a child is a few weeks or months old, but it may occur later. The parents and members of the church acknowledge the new life and accept responsibility for the child's nurture. Elders also conduct this ceremony.

The Lord's Supper is customarily celebrated at the regular worship on the first Sunday of each month. Members of the church kneel while prayers are read over the bread and wine by priests or elders, who then serve the symbols to the assembled members.

Marriage signifies a bond of mutual commitment between two persons and is solemnized by priests or elders. It acknowledges their individuality and also their oneness.

Administration to the sick is available on request to persons whether or not they are members of the Saints' church. Persons who are experiencing physical, mental, or other forms of suffering may call for elders to administer to them, usually in a private home or a hospital. The rite takes the form of anointing the person's head with consecrated olive oil and offering a prayer for the person's welfare.

Ordination of persons to the priesthood and the designation of persons for specific responsibilities are also accomplished by the laying on of hands. The procedure traditionally occurs in a public worship setting.

Patriarchal blessings are prayers offered by evangelist-patriarchs using the laying on of hands. Individuals above the age of approximately sixteen may request such a blessing, for wisdom and guidance throughout the person's life. Only one blessing is given to each individual; it is usually requested at a turning point in a person's life.

Ethics

The church emphasizes certain ethical principles that have been helpful in guiding decision making by individuals and by the church. First, each person has a special worth and uniqueness in the sight of God. This principle, the core of ethical belief, is rooted in the very heart of the gospel. It reminds us that no matter how right we think we are, we must treat all people, whether they agree with us or not, as persons who are loved by God.

Second, our personal ethics should be such that they allow us to serve God as fully as possible. A "word of wisdom" delivered to the church by Joseph Smith in 1833 counsels persons to see that their personal behavior does not detract from their physical well-being. It suggests that we should eat wisely, rest adequately, and avoid the use of anything that might impair our health. A more recent position taken by the World Conference in 1970 urges persons to use wisdom in their choice of activities and relationships and in the stewardship of their resources. Members are advised to avoid experimentation with harmful substances and to adhere to strict moral principles, but are also counseled to refrain from passing unrighteous judgment on others' behavior.

Third, in keeping with the belief in Zion, Saints' participation in the social order should be directed toward building a society of peace, justice, and personal fulfillment for all persons. Ethics is not simply a matter of personal behavior. It must inevitably touch the society in which we live.

Contributions and Influence

As members of the RLDS church, we affirm the uniqueness of our calling and of the resources we bring to it. The church exists to make God's kingdom a reality in a world of need. However, the Saints are interested in reaping all the benefits available for communication and cooperation with other denominations. All individuals and organizations of society are potential partners in God's work.

In sum, the church, with its emphasis on community development and social activism, has assisted in raising the level of religious principles in the United States. For Saints this emphasis is epitomized in the term "Zion" (the kingdom of God on earth). Whether through the utopian goals of Joseph Smith in the 1830s or the social reformation theology of Frederick M. Smith in the 1930s or the current communities working to be good citizens, the church has contributed to the building of God's kingdom on earth.

Significant Terms

Aaronic Priesthood. An order of ministers named for Aaron, the brother of Moses, having congregational functions. It includes the offices of deacon, teacher, and priest.

Melchisedec Priesthood. An order of ordained ministers; it includes the offices of elder and high priest, with the various specialized functions of the office of high priest.

First Presidency. A three-member instrumentality made up of the president and two counselors, presiding over the international church.

Council of the Twelve Apostles. A ministerial body composed of not more than twelve apostles, whose responsibilities include church expansion and other duties assigned by the First Presidency, relating to administrative supervision of field jurisdictions.

Standing High Council. An advisory body of twelve high priests functioning under the presiding leadership of the First Presidency, to whom they offer guidance in the field of ethical conduct and standards of church membership. It is also the final appellate court in the church and has original jurisdiction in cases involving general officers and high priests.

World Conference. The title adopted after 1962 for the church's international legislative assembly. It meets biennially and is composed of members in good standing who have been elected to serve as delegates by local jurisdictions.

Bibliography

(Except as noted, all items are published by Herald House, Independence, Mo.)

Flanders, Robert. *Nauvoo, Kingdom on the Mississippi.*
    Champaign: University of Illinois Press, 1956.

Ham, Wayne. *Publish Glad Tidings: Readings in Early Latter Day Saint Sources.* 1970.

Howard, Richard. *Restoration Scriptures: A Study of Their Textual Development.* 1969.

Judd, Peter. *Distinctives: Yesterday and Today.* 1983.

Judd, Peter, and Bruce Lindgren. *An Introduction to the Saints Church.* 1976.

Launius, Roger. *Joseph Smith, III, Prophet.* Champaign: University of Illinois Press, 1988.

O'Dea, Thomas. *The Mormons.* Chicago: University of Chicago Press, 1957.

RLDS. *Expanding the Faith of the Church.* 1987.

Smith, Joseph, III, F. Heman, and Henry Edwards. *The History of the Reorganized Church of Latter Day Saints.* 8 vols. 1896–1976.

Prepared by the editor from material furnished by the RLDS Church's Public Relations Committee.

♦ ♦ ♦

PENTECOSTALS
INTERNATIONAL PENTECOSTAL
HOLINESS CHURCH

General Description
The Pentecostal Holiness Church looks to the Day of Pentecost as her "spiritual" birthday and looks to the Bible, both the Old and New Testaments, as her ultimate authority. The desire of the church is to be led by the Holy Spirit and to see the works of God accomplished in earth today as in the New Testament days.

The church is identified with evangelical Protestantism. Along with others of like faith, we believe in the basic doctrines of historic Christianity, such as the Trinity, the deity of Christ, salvation by faith, the Bible as the uniquely inspired revelation from God, eternal life, heaven, and hell. Three great spiritual reform movements have shaped the history and theology of the Pentecostal Holiness Church. First, from the Reformation came the doctrines of justification by faith and the priesthood of all believers. Second, from the Wesleyan movement of the 1700s came the doctrine of sanctification as a second work of grace, which identifies the church as part of the holiness movement. Third, the Pentecostal revival of the twentieth century has shaped the denomination. This movement reemphasized the place of the Holy Spirit in the life of the church. More specifically, it developed the doctrine and experience of baptism in the Holy Spirit with the initial evidence of speaking in tongues and subsequent evidences of the gifts of the Spirit.

Beliefs and Doctrines
The Pentecostal Holiness Church sees her special theological contribution to the body of Christ as combining the Holiness and Pentecostal emphasis. The result is a three-part work of grace beginning with the new birth followed by a second experience of entire sanctification, and finally the baptism in the Holy Spirit with the initial evidence of speaking in tongues. In addition, we believe in divine healing and practice prayer for the sick accompanied by the laying on of hands and anointing with oil. In our eschatology we are premillennial. We expect the rapture of the bride of Christ at any time and encourage one another with this blessed hope.

Organization

Organizationally, the church began as two separate bodies. The first congregation to bear the name of the Pentecostal Holiness Church was organized in Goldsboro, North Carolina, in 1898 as the result of the ministry of evangelist A. M. Crumpler. From Crumpler's ministry the Pentecostal Holiness denomination was formed in 1900. The Fire-Baptized Holiness Church was formed through the ministry of B. H. Irwin of Nebraska, who organized the first Fire-Baptized Holiness Association in Olmitz, Iowa, in 1895. Other associations were formed over the next few years. And in 1898, in Anderson, South Carolina, he organized the Fire-Baptized Holiness Association as a national body.

During the world-famous Azusa Street revival in Los Angeles (1906–9), many persons experienced the baptism in the Holy Spirit with the initial evidence of speaking in tongues. G. B. Cashwell, a minister in the Holiness Church of North Carolina, traveled to Los Angeles in 1906 to attend the revival and make his evaluaticn. The result was that he received the Pentecostal experience and came back to North Carolina to share the message. In a historic meeting in Dunn, North Carolina, in 1907, Cashwell led many of the leaders of the southern holiness movements into the Pentecostal experience.

Since leaders of both the Pentecostal and the Fire-Baptized Churches, who shared the same holiness doctrine, then accepted the Pentecostal doctrine, a strong fellowship developed. On January 30, 1911, in Falcon, North Carolina, the two groups merged to form what is now the International Pentecostal Holiness Church.

The new group based its organizational structure on the Methodist system of episcopal government, electing a general superintendent over the entire body and conference superintendents over the various conferences. Only the conference has authority to license and ordain ministers and to assign pastors to the various local churches. Today, this governmental structure has been modified, but basically the structure remains generally the same. Polity for the denomination is determined by the general conference, which meets quadrennially and is made up of all pastors and one lay delegate from each local church. General officials are elected for four-year terms.

Assisting the ministers of the church are various agencies, such as the Advocate Press, Holmes College of the Bible, Emmanuel College, Southwestern College of the Christian Ministries, Falcon Children's Home, Carmen Home, and Children's Convalescent Center.

The church has always seen herself as strongly evangelistic. The Great Commission gives orders to make disciples of all nations. Both in the United States and abroad, the Pentecostal Holiness Church seeks to evangelize the lost. At the time of the consolidation in 1911, missionaries from the various local churches and associations were in the field. Since that time, the church has sent and supported missionaries and evangelists to plant the church wherever possible.

Today the church ministers in 53 countries through 176 missionaries and several thousand national workers. In the United States we have 1,461 churches with 116,673 members. Overseas there are 137,653 members in 1,699 churches. In addition, affiliates in several countries bring the International Pentecostal Holiness Church family to 1,833,964 members. We see ourselves as a vital part of the worldwide Pentecostal revival of the twentieth century that is now the fastest growing family of Protestant churches in the world.

The current general superintendent of the Pentecostal Holiness Church is Bishop B. E. Underwood. Our international offices are located in Oklahoma City, Oklahoma. We are active members of the National Association of Evangelicals, the Pentecostal Fellowship of North America, and the World Pentecostal Fellowship.

Significant Terms

Justification by faith. We believe, teach, and firmly maintain the scriptural doctrine of justification by faith alone. We do not believe that good works can produce or contribute toward our justification or salvation; this is accomplished solely by our faith in the shed blood, the resurrection, and the justifying righteousness of our Lord Jesus Christ; we do, however, believe in good works as a fruit of salvation. We are saved not by, but unto, good works. When we believe on him as our Savior, our sins are pardoned, we are justified, and we enter a state of righteousness not our own but his, both imputed and imparted.

Cleansing. We believe that Jesus Christ shed his blood not alone for our justification and the forgiveness of actual transgressions but also for the complete cleansing of the justified believer from all indwelling sin and from its pollution, and that this takes place after the new birth. This is the negative side of sanctification, the circumcision of the heart so as to make it possible for us to love the Lord our God with all our heart and soul. It is the crucifixion of "the old man," the destruction of "the carnal mind," the purging of the fruit-bearing branch so "that it may bring forth more fruit."

Entire sanctification. In its relation to the above cleansing, entire sanctification is an instantaneous second work of grace, obtainable by the fully justified believer. It includes a full and undeserved "setting apart," or "consecration," of the life to God. This is purity and dedication; it is not maturity, but the crisis experience that marks the beginning of the sanctified life, in which there is room for development, progress, and growth in grace and in the knowledge of our Lord and Savior, Jesus Christ. It is not absolute perfection, if the term is used to imply the impossibility of a sanctified person's falling into sin. We do not believe it is impossible for the sanctified person to commit sin. This is the Christian perfection—in which we love the Lord with all our heart, soul, mind, and strength and our neighbors as ourselves and in which we love Christ and keep his commandments. The sanctified life is one of separation from the world, a selfless life, a life of devotion to the will of God, and a life of holiness.

The baptism with the Holy Ghost and speaking with other tongues. We believe that the Pentecostal baptism with the Holy Ghost and fire is obtainable by faith on the part of the fully cleansed believer. We believe, because the Bible teaches and requires it, that a person in order to receive baptism with the Holy Ghost must have a clean heart and life as a prerequisite for this great blessing. Moreover, we believe that in order to live in the fullness of the Holy Spirit's power and possession, one must continue to live a clean and consecrated life, free from sin, strife, worldliness, and pride, and must avoid attitudes and actions that tend to "grieve" or "quench" the Holy Spirit of God.

We believe that the initial evidence of the reception of the baptism of the Holy Spirit is the speaking with other tongues as the Spirit gives utterance. We do not believe this is the only evidence of the Spirit's baptism, but it is the initial evidence, just as it occurred in the repeated accounts of the Spirit's outpouring in the Acts of the Apostles. But there will be other evidences spelled out in our lives such as the power to witness for Christ and power to endure the testings of faith and the opposition of the world. We believe that the initial evidence of speaking in tongues is for everyone who receives the Pentecostal baptism with the Holy Spirit, and we distinguish between this initial manifestation and the gift of tongues, which is not given to every Spirit-filled believer.

Gifts of the Spirit. The Pentecostal Holiness Church believes in the gifts of the Spirit as set forth by the apostle Paul in 1 Corinthians 12–14. We believe that they are "set in the church" by the Holy Spirit and that he retains the control of these gifts, or "enablements," distributing them "severally as he will." And we desire that our people may live so under the control of the Holy Spirit that these gifts may be manifested through consecrated individuals in the worship services—where, when, and as they are needed, but used always to the glory of God and the edifying of the body of Christ and in accordance with the decorum set forth in the Bible.

Divine healing. We believe that provision was made in the atonement for the healing of our bodies, as set forth in the Scriptures. While we do not condemn the use of medical means in the treatment of physical disease, we do believe in, practice, and commend to our people the laying on of hands by the elders or leaders of the church, the anointing with oil in the name of the Lord, and the offering of prayers for the healing of the sick.

The second coming of Jesus. We believe in the imminent, personal, pre-millennial second coming of our Lord Jesus Christ. The word "imminent" means that the second coming of Christ is near, and likely to occur at any moment. The word "personal" means that "the Lord himself" shall return, the "same Jesus" who was taken up into heaven "shall so come in like manner" as he will come before the millennium, during which the "blessed and holy" of the "first resurrection" will live and reign with Christ "a thousand years." There will be two stages of the second coming of Christ: the first to take away his saints who are prepared for the rapture before the Great Tribulation period, and the second at the end of the Great Tribulation, when he shall come back with his saints to destroy the armies of the Antichrist, to judge the nations of the world, and to inaugurate his millennial reign. The proper attitude of Christians toward the coming of Christ should be to love his appearing, to watch and pray to escape the things that will come upon the earth during the Great Tribulation, to pray for his coming, and to live faithfully until he comes.

Bibliography

(Except as noted, all items are published by Advocate Press, Franklin Springs, Ga.)
Beachman, A. D., Jr. *A Brief History of the Pentecostal Holiness Church*. 1983.
The International Pentecostal Holiness Church Manual. 1989 ed.
Synan, Vinson. *The Holiness-Pentecostal Movement in the United States*. Grand Rapids, Mich.: Eerdmans, 1971.
——. *The Old Time Power*. 1973. The official history of the denomination.
Underwood, B. E. *Spiritual Gifts: Ministries and Manifestation*. 1984.

Prepared by Harold Dalton, director of research, World Missionary Department.

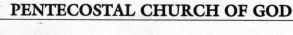

PENTECOSTAL CHURCH OF GOD

General Description

Growing out of the Pentecostal revivals at the turn of the century, the Pentecostal Church of God was organized in Chicago, Illinois, on December 30, 1919, as the Pentecostal Assemblies of the U.S.A. In 1922 the name was changed to the Pentecostal Church of God, and again in 1934 to the Pentecostal Church of God in America, Inc.; finally, in 1979, it became the Pentecostal Church of God (Incorporated).

The denomination is evangelical and Pentecostal in doctrine and practice. It is an active member of the National Association of Evangelicals and the Pentecostal Fellowship of North America.

History

On a cold wintry day in December 1919, seven dedicated men met on State Street in Chicago. These men were destined to organize what is known as the Pentecostal Church of God. Eli DePriest, one of the seven, reported that after they concluded the business, prayer was offered to God. While they were praying, the building where they assembled was actually shaken by the power of God. The objective of these men was to unite their resources for the purpose of spreading the gospel. Cooperative evangelism was the strength of their effort.

From this small group emerged one of the leading Pentecostal denominations of our day—the Pentecostal Church of God. The church is part of the great Pentecostal revival that began around the turn of the twentieth century with the work of Charles Fox Parham mainly in Topeka, Kansas, and Houston, Texas, and of evangelist William J. Seymour in Los Angeles.

In the first thirty-two years of the church's existence, its headquarters were moved three times: from Chicago to Ottumwa, Iowa, in 1927, and six years later from Ottumwa to Kansas City, Missouri. In 1951 the offices were moved to Joplin, Missouri, where they have remained to the present time.

Beliefs and Doctrines

Our doctrinal statement includes these points:

We believe:

1. In the verbal inspiration of the Scriptures, both Old and New Testaments;
2. Our God is a trinity in unity, manifested in three persons: the Father, the Son, and the Holy Ghost;
3. In the deity of our Lord Jesus Christ, in His virgin birth, in His sinless life, in His miracles, in His vicarious and atoning death on the cross, in His bodily resurrection, in His ascension to the right hand of the Father, and in His personal return in power and glory;
4. That regeneration by the Holy Ghost for the salvation of lost and sinful man, through faith in the shed blood of Christ, is absolutely essential;
5. In a life of holiness, without which no man can see the Lord, through sanctification as a definite, yet progressive, work of grace;
6. In the baptism of the Holy Ghost, received subsequent to the new birth, with the speaking in other tongues, as the Spirit gives utterance, as the initial physical sign and evidence;
7. In water baptism by immersion for believers only, which is a direct commandment of our Lord, in the name of the Father, and of the Son, and of the Holy Ghost;
8. In the Lord's Supper and washing of the saints' feet;
9. That divine healing is provided for in the atonement and is available to all who truly believe;
10. In the premillennial second coming of Jesus: first, to resurrect the righteous dead and to catch away the living saints to meet Him in the air, and, second, to reign on the earth a thousand years;
11. In the bodily resurrections of both the saved and the lost: they that are saved unto the resurrection of life, and they that are lost unto the resurrection of damnation.

Forms of Worship

One's first observation upon visiting a Pentecostal church is the distinctively different style of worship. It is nonliturgical, with congregational participation expected and encouraged. Spontaneity and freedom of expression are Pentecostal trademarks.

While Pentecostals follow no formal or precise schedule, there are certain elements found in most services. When Pentecostals assemble for worship, opportunity is provided for prayer, Scripture reading, music, offertory, praise, testimony, preaching, and closing prayers around the altar.

A Pentecostal service includes speaking in tongues (languages unknown to the speaker). This experience makes Pentecostal churches unique. Tongues are used in three ways: praying, praising, and the giving of messages from God by the Holy Spirit. By means of "praying in tongues," one is able to pray according to the will of God without the interference of one's natural desire (Rom. 8:27). "Praising in tongues" allows the worshiper the freedom to express his love for God without the inhibiting limitations of his natural language. It is the outward manifestation of the infilling of the Holy Spirit. There may also be "messages in tongues" given during the course of a service. According to the Scriptures, an interpretation should follow so that the message is edifying to the whole body of believers (1 Cor. 14:27).

Pentecost was born in a prayer meeting; therefore, much emphasis is placed on the power of prayer. Pentecostals firmly believe that they have direct access to the Father and that miracles will transpire as a result of prayer. During the worship service, the congregation often offers prayers audibly and collectively. Opportunity is also given for individual as well as silent prayer.

Since all beliefs and practices must have their bases in the Word of God, extensive use of the Holy Scripture is an essential part of Pentecostal worship.

From its earliest beginnings, Pentecostal worship has been identified with lively, vibrant, and anointed music. Congregational participation in the singing of Scripture, hymns, gospel songs, and choruses is the norm.

Worshiping God through the giving of tithes and offerings is a special and necessary part of each service. Participation in this segment of the service will often reflect a person's depth of commitment to Christ and his church.

Worship consists of many expressions. It has been said that "worship is man's foremost duty and his greatest privilege." Giving audible praises with uplifted hands (an act of surrender) is common in Pentecostal worship.

Another form of worship is the giving of audible testimony concerning God's intervening power. Believers may relate present-day answers to prayer they have personally experienced such as salvation, healing, guidance, and deliverances.

Proclaiming the gospel is the central ingredient of the worship service. Christ-oriented, anointed preaching is the powerful and passionate proclamation of the Word of God.

Pentecostal preaching is preaching for a verdict. A decision and response are called for and expected. Some of the most precious and meaningful times for Pentecostal believers are found around the altar in a special time of prayer and commitment.

Organization

The Pentecostal Church of God has a combination of representative and congregational forms of government. The local church is self-governing and elects its own pastor and local leadership. The local church is expected to work in harmony with the district and general organization. It may have bylaws, but these must not conflict with the district or general bylaws.

The General Convention is the highest legislative body in the movement. The General Executive Board is the policy-making and governing body, whose policy and actions are in accord with the General Constitution and Bylaws. The Executive Committee is a committee of the General Board empowered to act for and on behalf of the board between regular board meetings. The Executive Committee functions as an administrative, interpretive committee of General Board policy and General Convention action.

The ministries of the organization are instituted by General Convention action, coordinated nationally, promoted by the districts, and participated in by local churches. Each minister is directly accountable to his district board in all matters of faith and conduct. The district board may exercise any disciplinary action to be taken.

All members of the local church are to work in harmony within the framework of the local church structure and the district. The pastor is the spiritual head of the local church.

Contributions and Influence

The Pentecostal Young People's Association, the first department of the national level, was developed to establish and promote the varied ministries concerning youth.

Although missions had been a vital part of the movement since its inception, the World Missions Department was not organized until 1929. Today, through its World Missions Department, the Pentecostal Church of God ministers to people in thirty countries and maintains a ministry to schools in many of these regions. In addition, the Hispanic Missions ministry was organized to reach Spanish-speaking Americans.

In 1949 the Indian Mission Department was established. The new "Key to Life" curriculum published by the department is a full line of Pentecostal-oriented literature. In 1957 the Pentecostal Church of God had active-duty chaplains as well as two reserve chaplains ministering to the men and women in the military.

The King's Men Fellowship, Senior Christian Fellowship, Home Missions/Evangelism, and Department of Evangelists' ministries have been established in the last few years. In the fall of 1983 the decision was made to merge the denomination's two colleges, Southern Bible College, Houston, Texas, and Evangelical Christian College, Fresno, California. The formation of a new nationally sponsored learning center known as Messenger College and located in Joplin, Missouri, is the outgrowth of this merger.

Several economic pressures required an inordinate amount of administrative time and effort throughout the decade of the 1970s and into the 1980s. By the help of God and the conscientious efforts of the leaders, in combination with the wisdom, direction, and support of the General Board and the general constituency, the financial picture of the organization has greatly improved.

Under the capable leadership of General Superintendent James D. Gee, the Pentecostal Church of God approaches the decade of the 1990s with an enthusiastic, bold venture in evangelism—Strategy 2000.

Significant Terms

Anointing with oil. An ancient Christian practice in which the sick are anointed with oil in the name of the Lord, along with prayer for healing (James 5:14).

Foot washing. A Christian practice begun by Jesus Christ. The Pentecostal act commemorates Christ's washing of his disciples' feet in the upper room, but its observance is left to local churches for form and frequency.

Lifting up of hands. A Pentecostal practice of holding up one's hands during prayer and praise in anticipation of receiving the presence and power of the Holy Spirit.

Sanctification. A Pentecostal doctrine according to which holiness is a regard for the progressive work of God's grace beginning with regeneration and continuing until full salvation.

Bibliography

Bartleman, Frank. *Azusa Street: The Roots of Modern-Day Pentecost.* Plainfield, N.J.: Logos International, 1980.

——. *What Really Happened at Azusa Street?* Northridge, Calif.: Voice Publications, 1962.

Burgess, Stanley M., Gary B. McGee, and Patrick H. Alexander. *Dictionary of Pentecostal and Charismatic Movements.* Grand Rapids, Mich.: Zondervan, 1988.

DePriest, Eli J. *The Story of My Life.* Joplin, Mo.: Messenger Publishing House, n.d.

Frodsham, Stanley Howard. *With Signs Following.* Springfield, Mo.: Gospel Publishing House, 1946.

Moon, Elmer Louis. *The Pentecostal Church: A History and Popular Survey.* New York: Carlton Press, 1966.

Pentecostal Church of God. *General Constitution and Bylaws.* Joplin, Mo.: Messenger Publishing House, 1988.

"Pentecostal Church of God of America," *Pentecostal Messenger* 43, nos. 6–7 (July–

August 1969, pp. 1–3, 94). Published by Messenger Publishing House, Joplin, Mo.

Tadlock, Howard G. *This We Believe*. Joplin, Mo.: Messenger Publishing House, 1987.

Waggoner, Berten. "History of the Pentecostal Church of God." Unpublished paper presented in Directed Study in Church History class at Nazarene Theological Seminary, 1969.

Wilson, Aaron M. *Basic Bible Truth*. Joplin, Mo.: Messenger Publishing House, 1987.

Prepared by Ronald R. Minor, general secretary-treasurer, The Pentecostal Church of God.

UNITED PENTECOSTAL CHURCH INTERNATIONAL

General Description

The United Pentecostal Church International (UPCI) is a Christian organization with a worldwide constituency of approximately 1.4 million people, including more than 3,500 churches and 7,000 ministers in the United States and Canada. The UPCI is the largest Oneness Pentecostal body. With churches in over 120 nations, its international growth rate is approximately 10 percent per year.

Founding

Oneness Pentecostals trace their origin to the founding of the New Testament church on the Day of Pentecost (Acts 2), affirming the experience and doctrine of the apostles.

The modern Oneness movement originated with Pentecostal ministers such as Frank Ewart, Glenn Cook, and G. T. Haywood, who in 1914 began to baptize "in the name of the Lord Jesus Christ" instead of with the Trinitarian formula. By 1917 these ministers began to organize, and several Oneness groups came into being over the next decade. The UPCI was formed in 1945 by a merger of the two largest Oneness Pentecostal bodies: the Pentecostal Church, Incorporated, and the Pentecostal Assemblies of Jesus Christ.

Beliefs and Doctrines

The Bible is the inspired, infallible Word of God. It is the sole authority for faith, doctrine, and instruction in Christian living. God is absolutely one, with no distinction of persons. "Hear, O Israel: The LORD our God is one LORD" (Deut. 6:4; see also Isa. 44:8; 45:5–6, 21–23; 46:9; Rom. 3:30; Gal. 3:20; James 2:19).

In order to save sinful humanity, God provided a sinless Man as a sacrifice of atonement—Jesus Christ, the Son of God. In begetting the Son and in relating to humanity, God is the Father. In working to transform and empower human lives, God is the Holy Spirit. Thus, for our salvation, God has revealed himself as Father (in parental relationship to humanity), in his Son (in human flesh), and as the Holy Spirit (in spiritual action). (See Mal. 2:10; Luke 1:35; 2 Cor. 3:17–18; 1 Tim. 2:5.)

Jesus Christ is the one God incarnate, the manifestation of God himself in flesh. He is the union of absolute deity and sinless humanity. "For in him dwelleth all fullness of the Godhead bodily" (Col. 2:9; see also Isa. 9:6; 35:4–6; Matt. 1:23; John 1:1–14; 8:58; 10:30; 14:9–11; 20:28; 2 Cor. 5:19; 1 Tim. 3:16; Titus 2:13). Jesus is our Savior; his name is the only name given for our salvation (Matt. 1:21; Acts 4:12).

All humans have sinned and need salvation from eternal death (Rom. 3:23; 6:23). The gospel of Jesus Christ is the good news that Jesus died in our stead for our sins, was buried, and rose to provide eternal life for us (1 Cor. 15:1–4). Salvation comes by grace through faith in Jesus Christ, on the basis of his redemptive work (Rom. 3:21–25; Eph. 2:8–9).

Saving faith involves obedience to the gospel (Rom. 1:5; 6:17; 10:16; 16:26; 2 Thess. 1:7–10; Heb. 5:9; 11:6–8). The proper response to the gospel is to repent, be baptized in water, and receive the Holy Spirit; in this way a person identifies with Christ's death, burial, and resurrection (Rom. 6:1–7; 8:1–11).

The experience and message of the New Testament church is that "they were all filled with the Holy Ghost and began to speak with other tongues, as the Spirit gave them utterance. . . . Then Peter said unto them, 'Repent, and be baptized every one of you in the name of Jesus Christ for the remission of sins, and ye shall receive the gift of the Holy Ghost. For the promise is unto you, and to your children, as God shall call'" (Acts 2:4, 38–39; see also John 3:5; Acts 8:12–17; 10:44–48; 19:1–6; 1 Cor. 6:11).

Thus the UPCI has adopted the following statement regarding the experience of salvation: "The basic and fundamental doctrine of this organization shall be the Bible standard of full salvation, which is repentance, baptism in water by immersion in the name of the Lord Jesus Christ for the remission of sins, and the baptism of the Holy Spirit as he gives utterance."

The UPCI affirms the creation of all things by God; the Christian life of holiness, both inward and outward, including standards of conduct and dress; the operation of spiritual gifts, including divine healing; the priesthood of believers; tithing; the existence of angels, demons, and the devil; the catching away of the church and the second coming of Jesus to earth; the future millennial kingdom of Jesus on earth; the resurrection; the final judgment; eternal punishment for the wicked; and eternal life for the righteous.

Forms of Worship

The forms of worship are simple and include congregational singing, special singing (including choirs), testifying, praying, Scripture reading, preaching (which is emphasized), and altar calls. Worship is spontaneous, joyous, demonstrative, and free. In accordance with scriptural patterns, expressions of praise typically include raising hands, clapping of hands, vocal prayer, dancing in the Spirit, and playing of musical instruments. The UPCI observes the Lord's Supper and foot washing.

Organization

The basic form of church government is congregational. The local body controls its own affairs, and the pastor is the leader under Christ. There is a strong district and national organization for the sake of ministerial standards, fellowship, and world evangelism.

The headquarters of the international organization is known as World Evangelism Center and is located in Hazelwood, Missouri, a suburb of St. Louis. The international work is carried out by the following divisions: Church Administration, Editorial, Education, Foreign Missions (United States and Canada), Ladies Auxiliary, Sunday School, and Youth. The organization owns the Pentecostal Publishing House, which prints books and tracts under the name of Word Aflame Publications. The official organ is the *Pentecostal Herald*.

Among the endorsed institutions of the church are nine Bible colleges in North America and some eighty overseas, an orphanage, a rehabilitation center for boys, a ministry to alcohol and drug abusers, and an international relief agency.

Significant Terms

Baptism in the name of Jesus. Being immersed in water with oral invocation of the name of Jesus, thereby relying upon his saving power and authority; it is part of the salvation experience, it is valid only upon repentance and faith, and it is for the remission of sins.

Baptism of the Holy Ghost (or Holy Spirit). Being immersed in and filled with God's Spirit; it is part of the salvation experience, it comes only through repentance and faith, and it is accompanied by the initial sign of speaking in tongues.

Father. The one God in parental relationship to humanity.

Holy Spirit. The one God in spiritual existence and action.

Oneness. The doctrine that there is one God, with no distinction of persons, and that Jesus is all the fullness of the Godhead incarnate.

Repentance. A turn from sin to God, which includes recognition of sin, confession of sin, contrition (godly sorrow) for sin, and a decision to forsake sin.

Son of God. The manifestation of the one God in human flesh; the human person in whom God revealed himself.

Speaking in tongues. Speaking by the miraculous work of the Holy Spirit in a language unknown to the speaker.

Word (Logos). The one God in self-revelation, self-disclosure, or self-utterance; the mind, thought, plan, and reason of God, which is God himself.

Bibliography
(All items are published by Word Aflame Press, Hazlewood, Mo.)
Bernard, David. *Essential Doctrines of the Bible*. 1988.
———. *Series in Pentecostal Theology*. 4 vols. 1981–85.
Clanton, A. L. *United We Stand*. 1970.
Foster, Fred. *Their Story: Twentieth Century Pentecostals*. 1981.
Hall, J. L. *The United Pentecostal Church and the Evangelical Movement*. Booklet.
Hall, J. L., and David Bernard, eds. *Doctrines of the Bible*. 1990.
What We Believe and Teach: Articles of Faith of the United Pentecostal Church. Tract.

Prepared by David K. Bernard, associate editor, United Pentecostal Church International, copyrighted © 1989, David K. Bernard.

POLISH NATIONAL CATHOLIC CHURCH

General Description
The Polish National Catholic Church (PNCC) is a Christian denomination formed in 1897 in Scranton, Pennsylvania. The church was initially organized to serve the spiritual needs of Polish-Americans but today welcomes all people who wish to follow Christ. The organizers severed their ties with the Roman Catholic Church to follow beliefs they felt were closer to Christ's original spirit and teachings and to create a testimony to the unity of the Polish people in God. Apostolic succession is through the archbishop of the Old Catholic Church of Utrecht. The orders and sacraments of the PNCC are considered valid by the Roman Catholic Church, even though the church is autonomous from Rome.

The mission of the PNCC is to help members remember that their purpose in life is to know and serve God and establish his kingdom on earth; to live according to Christ's principles of truth, righteousness, and love for all people; to grow spiritually through faithful worship and participation in the sacraments and by fulfilling duties to family, nation, and humanity.

Founder
The founder of the PNCC was the Most Reverend Francis Hodur (1869–1953). Hodur was born near Cracow, Poland, and was baptized a Roman Catholic. He prepared for the priesthood at the Jagiellonian University. He was ordained a priest at St. Peter and Paul's Cathedral in Scranton shortly after immigrating to the United States in 1893. In 1897 Father Hodur became the pastor of St. Stanislaus Church.

Bishop Hodur was devoted to Christianity and believed that Christ's ideals should be lived by everyone. He sought to promote the human dignity of the Polish people. Love for the Polish people led him to encourage their unity in God and loyalty to America while maintaining a deep respect for their ethnic traditions.

Hodur composed the "Confession of Faith" and the "Eleven Great Principles" of the PNCC. He published the first church newspaper, *Straz,* in 1897 and ordained the Polish National Union, a home for the aged and a camp for the children and youth. In 1923 he began publishing the present church newspaper, *God's Field*.

Beliefs and Doctrines

Beliefs are based on Holy Scripture, Christian tradition, and church ecumenical synods.

God is one in three persons: the Father, who created all; the Son, who died for our sins and rose from the dead; the Holy Spirit, who regenerates and sanctifies souls. Christ is the Son of God, who became a human being and died on the cross for our salvation and is always with believers who try to live according to his teachings. The Holy Spirit is the third person of the Blessed Trinity, who abides in the church to teach, govern, and sanctify its members.

It is the duty of every Christian to help establish God's kingdom on earth through the grace and virtue of love, justice, and dedication to the will of God. The sin of the "first parents" (so-called original sin) does not pass to succeeding generations. The soul is immortal and ultimately destined for eternal life with God. Faith in God *and* good works will save us from our sins.

The church is made up of baptized Christians who worship together, partake of the sacraments, and hear and obey the Word of God. Worship is celebrated in the language of the people so that all can understand God's message. Church property is owned by people of the parish, who purchase, build, and maintain it. God wishes all nations to act together in brotherhood and justice.

Bishops and priests are permitted to marry even after ordination or consecration. Divorce is not recognized, but marriage may be annulled for a variety of reasons. Birth control is permitted.

Forms of Worship

The PNCC forms are given in Polish and English missals and *Ritual*. Most services are conducted in English. Both the Tridentine and a contemporary Mass form are in use. There are many paraliturgical forms of worship, particularly Benediction of the Most Blessed Sacrament, Stations of the Cross, and Marian Devotions.

The church recognizes the following sacraments:

1. Baptism/confirmation;
2. The Word of God (preached and heard);
3. Penance (both general and private);
4. Holy Eucharist (Real Presence under both species);
5. Holy unction (of the sick);
6. Holy orders (deacon, priest, bishop);
7. Matrimony.

Organization

In the church at large, a prime bishop is the chief executive. He consecrates bishops, convenes synods, presides at the Supreme Council, controls church publications, and dispenses discipline in the dioceses. The General Synod is convened every four years. It discusses church matters and interprets religious teachings, selects candidates for bishop, and establishes church policy, law, and discipline. Lay and clergy delegates are sent by parishes, dioceses, and church organizations. Special synods are convened as needed. The Supreme Council consists of the prime bishop, bishops, and lay and clerical delegates. It meets annually to review church work and to administer all business that concerns the whole church.

In each diocese, bishops appoint priests, preside at diocesan councils, visit parishes, and confer sacraments. Senior priests are appointed by the bishop to guide and oversee diocesan business as instructed by the bishop. Each diocesan synod meets within two years after the General Synod to enact laws pertinent to the diocese. The diocesan council administers the business of the diocese.

In the parish, pastors are priests appointed by the bishop to guide church members in the faith, organize their church school, and administer parish affairs. General parish meetings are held every year to elect committee members, call for actions necessary for parish welfare, review parish reports, and so forth. Special meetings may also be called as needed. The Parish Committee is elected by the parish. At least nine members serve to assist the pastor, fulfill parish and synodal resolutions, keep records, and so on.

Contributions and Influence

The church restored the pride of Polish and other ethnic groups in their religious and cultural heritage. Although small in size (165 parishes), the PNCC has influenced Catholic thought by demonstrating that Catholicism can exist independent of the papacy. The PNCC anticipated Vatican II by thirty years in areas of lay participation in worship, church government, and liturgical renewal.

Significant Terms

Apostolic succession. The doctrine that there has been an uninterrupted transmission of the episcopate (bishops) from the apostles who were commissioned by Christ, down to the present day. Roman Catholic Church, the Orthodox churches, the PNCC, and the Anglican (Episcopal) churches all claim apostolic succession.

Benediction of the Blessed Sacrament. This devotion to the Eucharistic Christ consists of the exhibition of the Blessed Sacrament in the monstrance, or a pix; adoration by the faithful, with hymns; and the blessing, during which the priest makes the sign of the cross with the Blessed Sacrament over the people. It also includes the recitation of divine praises.

Tridentine Mass. A development of the Council of Trent (1545–63) and the Counter-Reformation, the Tridentine Mass was a response to the Lutheran and Reformed claims that the Roman Catholic Mass was a reenactment of the sacrifice of Christ. The Tridentine Confession pointed out that there was only one sacrifice of Christ on the cross but that the celebrating priest simply represented Christ's once-and-for-all offering at the altar.

Bibliography

(All items are published by the PNCC, Scranton, Pa.)

Fox, Paul. *The Polish National Catholic Church.* 1957.

Hodur, Francis. *Apocalypse of the Twentieth Century.* 1930.

——. *Works and Writings.* 1984.

Wlodarski, Stephen. *The Origins and Growth of the Polish National Catholic Church.* 1974.

Prepared by Rev. Kenneth S. Kraska, parish administrator, St. Valentine's PNCC Church, Philadelphia.

PRESBYTERIANS

General Desription

Presbyterians (from the Greek *presbyteros*, "elder") are a part of a worldwide Christian fellowship known as the Reformed tradition. With other Reformation churches, Presbyterians look back to the apostolic faith and separated from the Church of Rome in the sixteenth century, when the latter refused to deal with abuses that had crept in during the Middle Ages. The Reformed churches throughout the world include over 90 branches embracing over 55 million people in 60 nations.

In 1989 the oldest and largest denomination representing the Presbyterian/Reformed tradition in America was the Presbyterian Church (USA). Like many of the mainline denominations in the United States, this church has suffered significant losses in the last thirty years, while some of the smaller Presbyterian bodies have been growing rapidly. Mergers in 1958 and 1983 added members and churches to the major body but did not stem the overall decline. In 1963 this body had 3,292,000 members and 11,573 churches.

Founders

Before the pope or the emperor or even Luther had fully realized the significance of the events in Wittenburg, an almost completely independent series of Reformation events was taking place in Switzerland, where there was much discontent with Rome. By 1523 the magistrates of Zurich, led by the preacher Huldreich Zwingli (1484–1531), had begun a full-fledged purge of the church, going even further than Luther in many areas. The Reformed tradition was an established reality by the time John Calvin (1509–64) took over as its chief theologian and author.

Calvin, a Frenchman, became converted to evangelical views in 1534 and fled from French persecution to make Geneva his permanent home in 1541. There he not only infused renewed zeal into the movement but also developed particular viewpoints and emphases that influenced most of the Protestant Reformation in time. Chief among these are Reformed theology's stress on the sovereignty of God, the sinfulness of humans, the work ethic, and the judgments of God on society, the world, and history. In addition, it had a distinctive view of connectional church government (by elders), a more dynamic method of church planting than Lutheranism possesses, which explains some of its later successes.

Calvin very directly influenced John Knox (1513–72), who took the Reformed viewpoint to Scotland and formed the national church upon it. This system of theology and church government also made significant advances in the Netherlands, England, France, Bohemia, Austria, Poland, and the German Rhineland. The most influential figure of the English Reformation, Thomas Cranmer (1489–1556), the archbishop of Canterbury, was generally Reformed in his theological views. When the Puritan movement began in England in the late 1580s, it held to Calvinistic theology, although those who eventually became Congregationalists rejected its polity.

Presbyterians first came to America before 1640. Several Presbyterian congregations on Long Island trace their origins to the years 1640–62. Under the leadership of Rev. Francis Makemie, the first presbytery was organized in Philadelphia in 1706. The General Synod, with four presbyteries, was organized in 1717. The Westminster Standards (Confession of Faith, Larger and Shorter catechisms) were adopted in 1729. The Presbyterian Church in the USA was organized in 1789, with the meeting of the first General Assembly in Philadelphia. In 1837 the denomination divided into Old School and New School factions but reunited in 1870. In 1861 the southern presbyteries (Old School) withdrew to organize the Presbyterian Church in the Confederate States of America. This split was not healed until 1983, when the Presbyterian Church (USA) ended the major division of American Presbyterians. In 1958 another group, the United Presbyterian Church of North America, came into union with the major body. Other groups, such as the Cumberland Presbyterian Church, which split from the major body in 1810, the Presbyterian Church in America, and others maintain separate existences.

Beliefs and Doctrines

Theologically, Presbyterians hold generally to the views of John Calvin as given in his *Institutes of the Christian Religion*. While there is some latitude of belief, Presbyterians hold to the following doctrines: the deity of Jesus Christ, a regenerate church membership, symbolic significance of the sacraments, the priesthood of all believers, and the church as a gathered company of believers professing personal confession of faith in Jesus Christ as Lord and Savior. They form "confessional" churches, holding such statements as the Gallican Confession (1550), the Belgic Confession (1561), the Heidelberg Catechism (1562), the Canons of the Synod of Dort (1619), and the Westminster Confession of Faith (1646) as articulations of the Christian faith set forth in the Holy Scriptures. Some of the emphases that have been enunciated over the past 450 years are set forth above, especially the sovereignty of God, the sinfulness of humanity, and the lordship of Christ in history.

Forms of Worship

The *Book of Common Worship* was for decades the chief directory for worship. Usually no detailed liturgy is prescribed, but a basic outline is ordered. Historically, the Reformed tradition has always been noted for its stress on the teaching of the Word and the centrality of the sermon in worship. In many Presbyterian churches, the sermon will thus traditionally take up about one-half of the total worship period. In the Presbyterian Church (USA), the *Directory of Worship* establishes the guidelines for formal worship, and the *Book of Common Worship* and other guides contain the various liturgies recommended but not required.

Organization

All Presbyterian churches of whatever denomination are governed by a pyramidal system of judicatories: the "session" (over the local congregations); the "presbytery," "classis," or "colloquy" (including all pastors and representative lay elders from each congregation in local areas); and the "Synod," or "General Synod" (at the national level). The parity of all clergy and elected elders at each level is basic to Presbyterian polity.

Significant Terms and Names

Calvinism. The system of theology and of church organization that grew out of the work of John Calvin. It is marked by the acceptance of the supreme role of Scripture, the total sovereignty of God, and the predestined election of history and individuals.

John Knox. The leading churchman in the Reformation of Scotland. Knox was influenced by John Calvin and imported both the theology and the church organizational system of Calvinism to Scotland.

Presbytery. Literally, "a body of presbyters," a term from 1 Timothy 4:14, which has its principal use in Presbyterian polity. Usually it consists of ministers and elders (laymen) representing local churches. It also possesses authority over churches in its region.

Puritans. A group of churchmen in England and the American colonies who wanted a greater reformation, a "purification" of the Church of England—more particularly, of traces of Roman Catholic forms and ceremonies. New England was largely settled by Puritans through the Massachusetts Bay Colony.

Reformed tradition. A Protestant tradition, established by reformers Huldreich Zwingli and John Huss of Czechoslovakia, that fired John Calvin in Geneva and influenced the development of Protestantism in both theology and a certain theocratic view of politics.

Session. The local governing body of Presbyterian congregations, with oversight over the spiritual welfare of the congregation. It is made up of the pastors and the active ruling elders.

Westminster Confession of Faith. The confession of faith presented by the

Puritan divines at the suggestion of the British House of Commons. It received partial parliamentary approval, and its life as a creed of the Church of England was brief. However, it is now authoritative in most of the Presbyterian churches.

Huldreich Zwingli. The Swiss theologian and reformer who, as a student of the Greek New Testament, began to base his preaching on the gospel and to emphasize the Bible as a sufficient revelation of God, in opposition to the people of Zurich. Zwingli became a powerful leader in the Reformation.

Bibliography
Armstrong, Maurice W., et al., eds. *The Presbyterian Enterprise: Sources of American History.* Philadelphia: Westminster Press, 1956. Reprinted in 1963.
Jamison, Wallace. *The United Presbyterian Story: A Centennial Study, 1858–1958.* Pittsburgh: Geneva Press, 1958.
Loetscher, Lefferts A. *The Broadening Church: A Study of Theological Issues since 1869.* Philadelphia: University of Pennsylvania Press, 1954.
Presbyterian Historical Society. *Journal of Presbyterian History,* vol. 1 beginning in 1901. Philadelphia.
Trinterud, Leonard J. *The Forming of An American Tradition: A Re-Examination of Colonial Presbyterianism.* Philadelphia: Westminster Press, 1949.

Prepared by Keith J. Hardman, Ph.D., professor of philosophy and religion, Ursinus College; terms by the editor.

CUMBERLAND PRESBYTERIAN CHURCH

General Description

The Cumberland Presbyterian Church (CPC) began in 1810 in dissent from predestination as framed in the Westminster Confession of Faith and as an outgrowth of the Second Great Awakening revivals of the first decade of the 1800s in Kentucky and Tennessee. It spread across the South, Midwest, and West as population increased in those regions. A large portion, especially in the Midwest and the West, united with Northeastern Presbyterians in 1906 after a statement interpreting predestination was adopted by that church.

The CPC enjoys ecumenical cooperation especially with other Reformed Churches through membership in the World Alliance of Reformed Churches and other consortiums for educational and mission projects. It has union congregations with the Presbyterian Church (USA) in several locations.

The CPC numbers about 100,000 members in the states of Alabama, Arizona, California, Florida, Georgia, Illinois, Indiana, Iowa, Louisiana, Michigan, Mississippi, Missouri, New Mexico, Oklahoma, Tennessee, and Texas and in Columbia, Hong Kong, Japan, Liberia, and Portuguese Macau.

Leaders

Founders were Finis Ewing, Samuel King, and Samuel McAdow, ministers of the Presbyterian Church who constituted the Cumberland Presbytery on February 4, 1810, in McAdow's log house near Dickson, Tennessee. Later leaders were Richard Beard, Robert Donnell, Reuben Burrow, Stanford G. Burney, Milton Bird, T. C. Blake, D. W. Fooks, William T. Ingram, Morris Pepper, Hubert Morrow, and Shaw Scates.

Beliefs and Doctrines

The CPC has seen itself as taking a middle position between the traditional theological categories of Calvinism and Arminianism, confessing the mystery of God's sovereign grace but holding that people have free choice concerning God's offer of salvation in Christ.

Forms of Worship

The Cumberland Presbyterian Church has never adopted a liturgy. It has adopted so-called directories for worship, which have stressed the need for balance between the sermon and other aspects of worship such as hymns and prayers. Many Cumberland Presbyterian services include confession of sin, affirmation of faith, and other corporate liturgical expressions. Other congregations have a freer or revivalist style of worship. Communion is observed quarterly in many churches, monthly in many others. Baptism is administered to infants and adults, generally by the mode of sprinkling.

Organization

The Cumberland Presbyterian Church follows a presbyterian form of government. Local churches are governed by a session, composed of the pastor as moderator and the elders elected by the congregation. All the ministers in a certain geographic district along with elder representatives from the churches form a presbytery. Three or more presbyteries compose a synod. The annual General Assembly comprises an equal number of ministers and elders representing their presbyteries. The General Assembly supports boards of mission, finance, and Christian education, a General Assembly office, a historical foundation and Memphis Theological Seminary, all headquartered in Memphis; Bethel College in McKenzie, Tennessee; and a children's home in Denton, Texas.

Contributions and Influence

As an outgrowth of the Second Awakening, the CPC was an important component in the expanding westward movement of free church influence. The church was able to remain united during the Civil War. The church has sponsored several colleges that remain today, including Bethel College, McKenzie, Tennessee (the only college still related directly to the CPC);

Trinity University, San Antonio, Texas; and Millikin University, Decatur, Illinois.

Significant Term

Medium theology. The Cumberland Presbyterian view of predestination, which takes a middle ground between Calvinism and Arminianism. It holds that God's grace moves on the human heart in a mysterious way, so that repentance is not possible without grace, but that human choice is still genuinely free.

Bibliography

Campbell, Thomas H., et al. *A People Called Cumberland Presbyterians.* Memphis, Tenn.: Frontier Press, 1972.

Confession of Faith for Cumberland Presbyterians. Memphis, Tenn.: Frontier Press, 1984.

Prepared by the Office of the General Assembly.

PRESBYTERIAN CHURCH IN AMERICA

General Description

The Presbyterian Church in America has a strong commitment to evangelism, to missionary work at home and abroad, and to Christian education.

Organized at a constitutional assembly in December 1973, this church was first known as the National Presbyterian Church but changed its name in 1974 to Presbyterian Church in America (PCA). It separated from the Presbyterian Church in the United States (southern) (PCUS) in opposition to its long-developing theological liberalism, which denied the deity of Jesus Christ and the inerrancy and authority of the Scripture. The PCA held to the traditional position on the role of women to serve in offices. The PCUS had not only permitted women officers, but began to force all churches to comply. There was also opposition to the PCUS affiliation with the National Council of Churches, which supported the radical left political and social activism. As conservatives in the southern church, there was opposition to the movement toward merger with the more liberal United Presbyterian Church in the U.S.A. (northern).

Beliefs and Doctrines

The PCA made a firm commitment on the doctrinal standards that had been significant in Presbyterianism since 1645, namely, the Westminster Confession of Faith and Catechism. These doctrinal standards express the distinctives of the Calvinistic, or Reformed, tradition.

Among the distinctive doctrines of the Westminster Standards and of Reformed tradition is the unique authority of the Bible. The reformers based all of their claims on the Scriptures alone *(sola Scriptura)*. This included the doctrine of their inspiration, which is a special act of the Holy Spirit by which he guided the writers of the books of Scriptures (in their original autographs) so that their words should convey the thoughts he wished conveyed, being free from errors of fact, of doctrine, or of judgment, all of which were to be an infallible rule of faith and life.

Other distinctives are what are known as the doctrines of grace, which depict what God has done for mankind's salvation. These doctrines have five parts:

1. Total depravity of man. Man is completely incapable within himself to reach out toward God. Man is totally at enmity with God (see Rom. 3:10–23).
2. Unconditional election in any person whom God would grant salvation. As a matter of fact, long before man was created, God chose or predestined some to everlasting life. He did this out of His mere good pleasure (see Eph. 1:4–5).
3. Particular atonement. God in His infinite mercy, in order to accomplish the planned redemption, sent His own Son, Jesus Christ, to die as a substitute for the sins of a large but specific number of people (see Rom. 8:29–30).
4. The irresistible grace of God operates when the Holy Spirit moves upon a particular person whom He has called to apply the work of redemption, and does so effectually (see John 3:5–6).
5. The perseverance of the saints is that gracious work of God's sanctification whereby He enables a saved person to persevere to the end (even though it is as good as accomplished; see Rom. 8:30, 39; Phil. 1:6).

Organization

The PCA maintains the historic polity of presbyterian governance— namely, rule of presbyters (or elders) and the graded courts, which are the session governing the local church, the presbytery for regional matters, and the General Assembly at the national level. It has taken seriously the position of the parity of elders, making a distinction between the two classes of elders, teaching and ruling. It has self-consciously taken a more democratic position (rule from the grass roots up) on presbyterian governance, in contrast to one that is more prelatic (rule from the top assemblies down).

Contributions and Influence

In 1982 the Reformed Presbyterian Church, Evangelical Synod, joined the PCA. It brought with it a tradition that had antecedents in colonial America. It also included Covenant College in Lookout Mountain, Georgia, and Covenant Theological Seminary in St. Louis, Missouri, both of which are the national denominational institutions of the PCA.

PCA headquarters is in Atlanta, where most of the work of the denomination is coordinated. That work is carried on by three program committees—Mission to the World, Mission to North America, and Christian Education and Publication. In addition, besides the Office of the Stated Clerk, which is responsible for the administration of the General Assembly, there are other agencies: PCA Foundation; the Insurance, Annuities and Relief Boards; and the Investors Fund. Ridge Haven is the PCA conference center, located near Rosman, North Carolina.

The PCA is one of the fastest growing denominations in the United States, with 1,130 churches and missions throughout the United States and Canada. There are more than 172,000 communicant members augmented by almost 40,000 noncommunicant members as of December 1988.

The influence of the PCA extends far beyond the walls of the local church. Because of the unique relationship between Mission to the World and over thirty mission agencies, with whom some of our missionaries are working, some consider that the influence is far greater than our size might indicate. Furthermore, the gospel is proclaimed to a rather large audience around the world not reached through usual ecclesiastical channels. Because of the emphasis on an educated ministry, there are many members of the PCA who are teachers and professors at all levels of education, including large universities and quite a few theological seminaries.

Bibliography

Boice, James Montgomery. *Foundations of the Christian Faith*. Downers Grove, Ill.: Inter Varsity Press, 1986.

Richards, John Edwards. *The Historical Birth of the Presbyterian Church in America*. Liberty Hill, S.C.: Liberty Press, 1986.

Smith, Frank Joseph. *The History of the Presbyterian Church in America*. Manassas, Va.: Reformation Education Foundation, 1985.

Smith, Morton H. *How Is the Gold Become Dim*. Jackson, Miss.: Steering Committee for a Continuing Presbyterian Church, 1973.

Prepared by Paul R. Gilchrist, Ph.D., stated clerk, assisted by Laurel De Bert, administrative assistant.

PRESBYTERIAN CHURCH (USA)

See main entry under "Presbyterians."

REFORMED CHURCH

CHRISTIAN REFORMED CHURCH
IN NORTH AMERICA

General Description

The background of the Christian Reformed Church is in the Netherlands. In the 1830s some members of the Reformed Church of the Netherlands sought to resist an attempt to bring this church under the control of the Dutch monarchy. This unsuccessful attempt was the occasion for harassment by the government, leading in turn in 1834 to a secession of several congregations under the leadership of such ministers as Hendrik Decock, Hendrik Scholte, and Albertus C. Van Raalte. These believers saw themselves as defenders of the historic faith that was being lost through the indifference of the national church. Following persecution and economic hardship, many members of the seceding church made plans to emigrate to the United States.

A group of settlers under the leadership of Dr. Van Raalte arrived in western Michigan in 1847 and by 1848 had formed themselves into an ecclesiastical body that they called Classis Holland. Having been aided by members of the Reformed Church in America, with whom they shared the same faith, they united with that denomination in 1850, becoming a classis within the Reformed Church in America. They were assured that they could leave the newly joined denomination if the ecclesiastical connection should prove a threat to their interests. For most, it never did. In 1857, however, four congregations left the Reformed Church in America, forming a new denomination that eventually came to be known as the Christian Reformed Church in North America (CRCNA). The separation was sparked by accusations of doctrinal laxity, open communion, the use of unsound hymns, and neglect of catechism preaching. Furthermore, the dissidents felt that their fellow believers in the Netherlands believed that the secession in the Netherlands had been unjustified.

The new denomination went through a series of name changes that reflected a gradual process of decreasing isolation and increasing adjustment to their American environment. Growth in membership was initially slow but increased rapidly within a few years because of large-scale immigration from the Netherlands. Immigration continued to be the principal source of growth until the end of the nineteenth century. About one-fourth of the denomination's membership is now found in Canada, largely as a result of emigration from the Netherlands following World War II.

The CRCNA is a member of the North American Presbyterian and Reformed Council, the Reformed Ecumenical Council, and the National Association of Evangelicals. It participates in a variety of ecumenical studies.

Emphasis and Influences

The CRCNA lays a great deal of emphasis on education. Catechismal instruction of the youth of the church is stressed. Moral and financial support is given to a system of Christian day schools, which, however, are independent of church control. Since 1857 the church has owned and operated Calvin College and Calvin Theological Seminary. In addition, Dordt College, Trinity Christian College, The King's College, Redeemer Christian College, and the Reformed Bible College are closely affiliated with the church.

Home missions carries on a wide-ranging program, and local evangelism is encouraged. The world mission outreach includes church planting and social development work in twenty-five nations in Africa, South America, Latin America, the Pacific, and Asia. The denominational broadcast ministry is known as the "Back to God Hour" and includes worldwide radio broadcasts in several languages as well as a television ministry.

Beliefs and Doctrines

The CRCNA subscribes to the following ecumenical creeds: the Apostles' Creed, the Nicene Creed, and the Athanasian Creed. Our doctrinal standards are the Heidelberg Catechism (1563), the Belgic Confession (1618–19), and the Canons of Dort (1618–19). The church places emphasis upon a church school program in which the youth are guided through a unified curriculum. This curriculum includes instruction in the Heidelberg Catechism as a part of preparation for professing membership in the church.

All office bearers in the church are required to subscribe to the three doctrinal standards mentioned above. The church practices infant baptism, administered only to the children of confessing members. From its earliest days, the denomination has opposed those lodges that have a religious ritual.

Forms of Worship

The churches are relatively formal in worship, giving emphasis to the proclamation of the Word. Choirs assist in worship, and the *Psalter Hymnal,* published in 1987 by CRC Publications, is the songbook used for worship. Worship services are held twice each Lord's Day. The *Church Order* of the CRCNA specifies that sermons regularly follow the order of the Heidelberg Catechism.

The forms of government, worship practices, and hymnody were originally based on models from the Netherlands but have been subject to considerable adaptation. An original insistence on the exclusive use of psalms in public worship has given way to use of both psalms and hymns.

Organization

The CRCNA is presbyterian in polity and has a Reformed Church government in which there are three ecclesiastical assemblies: the local church council, made up of a consistory (elders) and a diaconate (deacons); the classis, a group of neighboring churches; and the synod. The classis and synod are major assemblies to which the council and classis delegate responsibility. The decisions of the major assemblies are binding upon the minor assemblies unless it is proven that the decisions are in conflict with the Word of God and the *Church Order*. The authority of the local church is original, whereas that of major assemblies is delegated.

The broadest assembly is the General Synod, which meets annually and is constituted of two ministers and two elders from each of the forty-four classes. The classes meet two or three times a year.

Significant Terms

Minister. A person ordained to the ministry of the Word.

Elder. An office bearer charged with the responsibility of supervision and discipline.

Consistory. A body of elders.

Deacon. An office bearer charged with a ministry of mercy.

Diaconate. The body of deacons.

Council. The office bearers of the church; the Board of Trustees.

Classis. A group of neighboring churches, made up of a minister and an elder of each member congregation.

Synod. The general assembly, made up of two ministers and two elders from each classis.

Baptized member. A person who is a member of the local church by virtue of infant baptism.

Professing member. A person who is a member of a local church by virtue of both baptism and profession of faith.

Bibliography

(All items are published by Christian Reformed Church Publications, Grand Rapids, Mich.)

Van Dyk, W.M. *Belonging.* 1982.

Brink, W.P., and R.R. De Ridder. *Manual of Christian Reformed Church Government.*

Ecumenical Creeds and Reformed Confessions. 1988.

Psalter Hymnal. 1987.

Prepared by Leonard J. Hofman, stated clerk, CRCNA.

REFORMED CHURCH IN AMERICA

General Description

The Reformed Church in America is a Protestant denomination in the Calvinistic tradition with a baptized membership of more than 340,000 individuals. The denomination includes about 950 congregations throughout North America. Its mission efforts are evidenced in India, the Middle East, Japan, Africa, Taiwan, the Philippines, and in North, Central, and South America.

The Reformed Church in America is an ecumenical church and participates in both the National and the World Council of Churches, the World Alliance of Reformed Churches, and other ecumenical agencies and groups. Its purpose, together with all other churches of Christ, is to minister to the total life of all people by preaching, teaching, and proclaiming the gospel of Jesus Christ, the Son of God, and by all Christian good works.

The church was known as the Reformed Dutch Churches in North America and the Reformed Protestant Dutch Church prior to 1867. Established during the initial Dutch colonization of New Amsterdam in the seventeenth century, it has had continuous ministry since 1628.

Founder and Major Leaders

The Reformed Church traces its heritage to the church of the New Testament. The American church is the ecclesiastical child of the Netherlands Reformed Church. As a Reformation church, it follows in the tradition of John Calvin as it was interpreted in the Netherlands.

While communicant members reached the New World earlier, the first ordained minister, Johannes Michaelius, arrived in 1628. The colonial church was under the ecclesiastical supervision of the Dutch Church in Amsterdam. An independent American denomination was established following the American Revolution under the leadership of Rev. John Henry Livingston (popularly known as the Father of the Reformed Church in America).

Beliefs and Doctrines

The Reformed Church is reformed and reforming itself according to the Word of God as evidenced in the Old and New Testaments. Yet the Bible is not the only infallible rule of faith and practice: other denominational major standards of faith and unity include the Apostles', the Athanasian, and the Nicene creeds, along with the Belgic Confession, the Heidelberg Catechism, and the Canons of the Synod of Dort.

The Reformed Church has upheld a tradition of a well-educated clergy. From the earliest years of the seventeenth century, both collegiate and graduate theological education were deemed essential for the faithful and careful proclamation of the Word. In addition, the church has worked extensively as a leader in world missions and the wider church. The motivation to spread the gospel has served as a rallying point and a common theme that tied together a denomination rich in its diversity.

Forms of Worship

The church's liturgy is set forth in the *Liturgy of the Reformed Church in America*. Forms for the order of worship and for prayers are clearly set out. However, no attempt is made to restrain individuals into strict patterns of practice or worship. It is left to the faithfulness and gifts of the ministers to structure worship in a manner that is acceptable to God and edifying to his people.

The *Liturgy* has been revised a number of times in order to enable it to be meaningful to the contemporary church and to reflect properly our understanding of worship. Though not bound to any hymnal, the Reformed Church has recently produced its own *Rejoice in the Lord,* which has proved to be useful beyond the bounds of the denomination. Ongoing matters of revisions of forms and practices of worship are the responsibility of the denomination's Commission on Worship.

Organization

The Reformed Church in America is a church with a presbyterial system of government. Its governmental organization exists to assist the church as it engages in its ministry. Four basic structures in the Reformed Church are the consistory (minister, elders, deacons) of the local congregation, the classis, the particular synod, and the General Synod. The four bodies are both judicial and legislative.

Local congregations are led by an installed minister, who serves as the president of the consistory. The consistory is the elected governing body of the congregation and consists of elders, who are responsible for temporal affairs. The classis is a regional body composed of ministers and elders from the several congregations within its boundaries. The General Synod is the highest body of the church and consists of ministers and elders delegated from each of the classes. Among other responsibilities, the classes have the responsibility to examine, license, and ordain candidates for the ministry, to supervise congregations within their boundaries, to install ministers in congregations, and to form, dissolve, and disband churches.

The program of the Reformed Church in America is carried out by the General Program Council. The General Synod functions through several committees, commissions, and agencies as well as with a national staff serving the council and the synod.

Contributions and Influence

The Reformed Church in America has made a significant contribution in the forward movement of world missions. John Henry Livingston was instrumental in the early development of mission societies in the eighteenth century. David Abeel was a pioneer in China and widely publicized the plight of women in nineteenth-century China. Guido Verbeck played a major part in the development of modern educational systems in Japan. The Reformed Church has contributed a great number of world church leaders. The church is ecumenically minded and has always developed indigenous, independent national churches rather than merely extending its own boundaries.

Its heritage of education has led to the establishment of three colleges, a state university, and two seminaries. The church was active in the establishment of elementary schools, providing for a teacher in congregations during the colonial period and supporting public education in a democratic society and in post-Revolutionary America.

Significant Terms

Classis. A regional assembly of the church consisting of all enrolled ministers of that body and elders from each congregation. The classis has responsibility for the supervision of churches and ministers as well as judicial responsibilities in matters of discipline.

Consistory. The governing body of a local congregation. Membership includes the installed ministers, elders, and deacons.

Deacon. An ordained office in the consistory. Deacons are responsible for financial and temporal oversight of the congregation. They receive the contributions and oversee their distribution as well as the care of the poor and the whole benevolence program.

Elder. An ordained office in the consistory. Elders are responsible for all matters relating to the welfare and good order of the congregation. They have oversight over preaching, teaching, and conduct.

General Program Council. The program agency of the Reformed Church in America. This body is responsible for program organization, implementation, and development in Christian discipleship, church planning and development, and world mission.

General Synod. The highest assembly in the denomination, consisting of minister and elder delegates from each of the classes, as well as delegates from the seminaries, particular synods, and mission and chaplaincies. The General Synod supervises the whole church and serves as a judicial body for appeals from particular synods.

Particular synod. A regional assembly of ministers and elders delegated by each of the classes within its boundaries. Synods have superintendence over the classes within the boundaries and exercise responsibility on cases appealed to it from a classis.

Bibliography

Brouwer, Arie. *Reformed Church Roots.* New York: Reformed Church Press, 1978.
Cook, James I. *The Church Speaks.* Grand Rapids, Mich.: Eerdmans, 1985.

De John, Gerald. *The Dutch Reformed Church in the American Colonies*. Grand Rapids, Mich.: Eerdmans, 1978.

Esther, James R., and Donald J. Bruggick. *Worship the Lord*. New York: Reformed Church in America, 1987.

Hesselink, I. John. *On Being Reformed: Distinctive Characteristics and Common Misunderstandings*. Ann Arbor, Mich.: Servant Books, 1983.

Historical Series of the Reformed Church in America. Grand Rapids, Mich.: Eerdmans. 17 vols. as of 1989.

Osterhaven, Maurice Eugene. *The Spirit of the Reformed Tradition*. Grand Rapids, Mich.: Eerdmans, 1971.

Vandenberge, Peter N. *Historical Directory of the Reformed Church in America*. Grand Rapids, Mich.: Eerdmans, 1978.

Prepared by Russell L. Gasero, Reformed Church in America, archivist.

RELIGIOUS SOCIETY OF FRIENDS (QUAKERS)

History

The Religious Society of Friends (Quakers) began in England in the late 1650s, during the last stages of the Reformation and from the dream of a government that would be the kingdom of God on earth. The Quaker faith spread rapidly, but its adherents were persecuted for offenses to the norms and procedures of civil duty (required by law): refusal to enter the army or navy, to swear oaths, to attend liturgical worship services, to pay tithes to the state church, to take off hats to honor an official, and to use titles. Quakers insisted upon holding their own study groups and "meetings for worship"—practices seen as further threats to established Christianity. Persecutions occurred throughout England and Wales and in the Massachusetts Bay Colony. In Delaware, New Jersey, North Carolina, Rhode Island, and Pennsylvania, Quakers were instrumental in establishing freedom of worship and strong community life.

George Fox (1624–91) and his wife, Margaret Fell (1614–1702), are considered the founders. They nurtured many new leaders in England, who traveled widely and founded local "meeting," or faith, communities that often met in barns, fields, or farmhouses. Quaker ministers did not need university training or receive salaries; worship occurred in quiet, expectant waiting before God; men and women were equally equipped to be ministers of all kinds. During the nineteenth century in the western United States, several changes occurred; some meetings began to hire pastors and to follow what was called programmed worship with music, prepared messages, and other parts of familiar Protestant worship services. Despite these differences in practice, Quaker organizations have sprung up to work on shared concerns.

Beliefs and Doctrines

Friends do not have creeds or doctrinal statements. Religious principles are expressed through testimonies, advices, and queries; these are intended as ideals. Attenders who express a desire for membership in a meeting are asked to wait for a period of time, to be sure that they can unite with both the style of worship and the Quaker form of decision making.

A basic concept affirmed by Friends is that every human being, regardless of gender, age, race, or condition, has access to the Divine Light. This Inward Light enables persons to grow in recognition of moral truth, to communicate with each other about this truth (frequently referred to as knowing God's will), and to want to change wrongdoing, evil, or injustice. While this inner spark is referred to differently by various Friends (as the Spirit of the Living God, the Seed of Christ, the God in everyone, the Source, the Eternal Presence), Friends agree that it is available to everyone and is known inwardly and experimentally.

Friends believe that the Judeo-Christian scriptures were written under the guidance of this Spirit, and most Friends still turn to them for guidance. However, Friends also believe that revelation from God is continuous and did not end when the biblical canon closed. Many Friends take the Bible seriously, but not literally, continuing to study the Scriptures for what can be learned about God's will and work among human beings. To discern whether one is truly led by the Spirit of God, one must check at least three authorities: guidance received in individual prayer, wisdom recorded in the Bible and other inspired texts, and the Quaker community's discernment of God's will.

Believing that humans are not born guilty, many Quakers reject the concept of original sin. The Inward Light will direct the developing conscience of a child raised in a loving, gentle home where the testimonies of community, equality, harmony (peace), honesty, moderation, and simplicity are evident. Children in this environment are as capable of ministry as their elders.

Friends are best known for their "Peace Testimony" and refusal to take part in any war. They have also been advocates for prison reform, abolition of the death penalty, abolition of slavery, and, most recently, the sanctuary movement for victims of the war in Central America. These acts are based on belief in the universal human potential for experience of the Divine Light.

Practices

Everyone shares responsibility for the meeting of worship. Friends wait upon the Spirit of God in worship and in learning what their form of ministry will be. Vocal ministry occurs when someone feels led to stand and share aloud what the Spirit is directing. When these messages "weave together," or the silence is deep and connecting, worship is referred to as gathered or covered. Worship is held on first-day (Sunday) morning; in some cases, any Friend can call for silence as a way of reminding the group to seek divine guidance.

In meetings for business, Friends do not vote. They seek to know the will of God and to reach unity in making communal decisions. This is one hallmark of a Friends meeting, regardless of the form of worship. Spiritual unity (as distinct from a secular consensus) takes much more time than parliamentary procedure and gives Quakers a reputation for being slow in deliberation. Since all bring a measure of God's Light to the meeting, they dare not rush to meet a worldly schedule.

Organization

Monthly meetings are the congregational units that meet once a month for the business of the faith community, and more frequently for worship. A monthly meeting forms a quarterly or regional meeting, and a group of quarterly meetings forms a yearly meeting. Young Friends have formed an organization called Young Friends of North America to reach across yearly meetings and differences in local practices and to encourage the development of new leadership. There are also several organizations that hire staff to provide educational resources, programs, and services that a yearly meeting cannot as easily provide on its own: Friends General Conference, Friends United Meeting, American Friends Service Committee, Friends World Committee for Consultation, and the Evangelical Friends Alliance. Their staff people frequently work together on joint projects and conferences.

Contributions and Influence

Friends' testimony to the dignity and worth of every person and the faith that every group has the ability to work together with other groups for good are Quaker contributions to society. With other peace churches, Friends have helped legalize in many countries the right to conscientious objection to war. William Penn's Constitution for Pennsylvania had a profound influence upon the authors of the Constitution of the United States. Quaker women have been strong, steady workers for suffrage and in women's rights movements around the world. Latin American and African Friends, who now outnumber their cousins in the northern hemisphere, are now broadening the meaning of evangelism by working toward a radical change in the colonial structures that have kept their countries underdeveloped. William Penn's words remain a standard: "True godliness does not turn us out of the world but enables us to better live in it and excites our endeavors to mend it."

Significant Terms

Affirm. An acceptable word to Friends, substituted for "swear" in judicial oaths. The privilege of "affirming" rather than "swearing" is now available in both British and American systems of law.

After the manner of Friends. A phrase that characterizes the friendly processes of conducting both meetings and ceremonies. Business meetings find "a sense of the meeting," and ceremonies forgo the pomp of many churches for the quiet way that is the way of the Friends.

American Friends Service Committee. A service organization established by the Society of Friends but independent from it, founded in 1917 to aid in human service and to provide an outlet for the energies of those opposed to war. It was awarded the Nobel Peace Prize in 1947.

Birthright Friend. A term for those born into the society by the circumstance of both parents' being Friends. A convinced Friend is a member who chose the society as his or her spiritual family. A paper Friend is one whose name is on the membership list but who is inactive.

Cherish. A lovely word rarely heard in today's language, but Friends have kept it as a part of their standard vocabulary. We all need cherishing, and its use in meetings and services reminds all of those who especially need to be cherished.

Clearness. A term usually applied to applications for membership and marriage as a Committee on Clearness determines obstacles and tries to help resolve difficulties. The committee may also be asked to help in personal dilemmas.

Conscientious objection (pacificism). An official position a person of draft age may take to avoid military service or to be placed in a noncombat role. The Friends are a positive force for peace and harmony, even though they are often objectors to the social and political patterns of the larger world.

First-day. Early Friends refused to apply the old heathen terms to the days of the week or the months of the year. The usage survives, such as, "The meeting will be held on the first-day evening, seventh month, twenty-four o'clock."

Inner Light. In its full form, "the light that lights every man," the society's distinctive belief that the Inward Light is divine truth that informs, nourishes, and guides the human conscience. Indeed, one of the names the early Friends took for themselves was "Children of Light."

Sense of the meeting ("Quaker process"). In decision making, Friends seek to discern the will of God on many issues by a different understanding of consensus than that used by other groups. They seek neither agreement nor unanimity but an articulation of what action or witness they can now unite on. The result is often less than many activists want, but Friends see an ongoing process as more viable and tender than voting can produce. (Adapted from Warren Sylvester Smith, *One Explorer's Glossary of the Quaker Terms*, Philadelphia, Friends General Conference, n.d.)

Bibliography

Bacon, Margaret H. *The Quiet Rebels: The Story of Quakers in America.* New York: Basic Books, 1969.

Brinton, Howard H. *Friend for Three Hundred Years.* Wallingford, Pa.: Pendle Hill, 1956. Reprinted in 1987.

——. *Guide to Quaker Practice.* Wallingford, Pa.: Pendle Hill, 1972.

Christian Faith and Practice. London Yearly Meeting, 1960.

Hall, Francis B., ed. *Friends in Americas.* Friends World Committee for Consultation, 1976.

Kenworthy, Leonard. *Quakerism: A Study Guide on the Religious Society of Friends.* Kennett Square, Pa.: Quaker Publications, n.d.

Newby, James R. *Reflections from the Light of Christ: Five Quaker Classics.* Richmond, Ind.: Friends United Meetings, 1980.

Newman, Daisy. *A Procession of Friends.* New York: Doubleday, 1972.

Whalen, William J. *The Quakers.* Philadelphia, Pa.: Friends General Conference, 1984. Pamphlet.

Williams, Walter R. *The Rich Heritage of Quakerism.* Newburg, Oreg.: Barclay Press, Evangelical Friends Alliance, 1986.

Prepared by Cynthia B. Taylor, religious education coordinator, Friends General Conference; terms by the editor from a glossary by Warren Sylvester Smith.

ROMAN CATHOLIC CHURCH

General Description and History

Roman Catholics constitute a worldwide communion of Christians who view themselves as belonging to a church whose history leads back to the very earliest moment in the unfolding of the Christian religion. If we think in terms of the role and significance of religion in culture, three phases in the development of Roman Catholics may be distinguished.

The first phase consisted in an initial period of growth in the Mediterranean basin, where Christianity mingled with Greco-Roman civilization. Then and there the church took on its characteristically hierarchical form, with the Roman see emerging as the linchpin, especially in the West.

With the disintegration of the Roman Empire, the stage was set for the second phase: the great experiment of Christendom. During this period of approximately a thousand years, the Roman Catholic Church played a decisive role in the common task of constructing a culture that would be Christian through and through. Popes, bishops, and monks cooperated in the effort to achieve freedom for the church; with the development of the Western nations, a sort of dynamic unity of the civil and ecclesiastical elements of society was momentarily wrought. The thirteenth century might be identified as the high-water mark of this medieval synthesis. In the meantime, however, Rome's hegemony had been challenged by Constantinople; and at a later date, Christian unity in the West unraveled in the Reformation.

That shattering series of events called forth a world with its own agenda and cleared the way for the third and latest phase in the history of Roman Catholicism. At first, modern empirical science, modern philosophy (dominated by rationist elements), and modern historical scholarship were viewed from within the church, without differentiation, as inimical forces; and this perception resulted in a reaction to modernity that separated Roman Catholics from the mainstream of culture. Only toward the end of the nineteenth century did the idea take hold that dialogue with modernity might be possible. Our own century has seen a remarkable struggle in that direction, accelerated particularly by Pope John XXIII and the council that he convoked. The council's Pastoral Constitution on the Church in the Modern World (1965) is the charter for Roman Catholic involvement in the building of the global village.

Founder

When Roman Catholics describe the church as apostolic, they mean to trace her existence historically to the era of Jesus himself. Critical scholarship combines with this basic conviction to yield the notion of a developing tradition, with Jesus as the originator. He is the focal point of a circle of disciples who believed in his resurrection, and this circle eventually became the movement, the growth of which is described in the Acts of the Apostles. From this point of view, the transition to the so-called early Catholicism of the second century (as exemplified by figures such as Ignatius of Antioch) does not seem to be such a big leap.

Beliefs and Doctrines

Roman Catholic belief is grounded in the creeds of the ancient church and the dogmas of the early councils (Christological and Trinitarian). Today, scholars generally recognize that these formulas emerged in response to a twofold demand: (1) that the Christian message be expressed in a compendious form, especially for use in sacramental catechesis (hence the creeds); (2) that the good news be formulated in terms that represent its accurate meaning in the culture of that place and time (the dogmas). This latter move involved the use of language that did not occur in Christianity's original cultural context, a transition that itself fueled intense theological controversy. The commitment was made, however, and became the foundation of an ongoing doctrinal tradition, which includes the burden of authentic interpretation and development.

Forms of Worship

"Sacramental liturgy" is the generic term for the Roman Catholic worship. It is a set of rituals, at the heart of which is the Eucharist (the Mass), wherein the church is thought of as fully actualized, that is, as a hierarchical community, intentionally united with other elements in a worldwide communion, celebrating the death and resurrection of Christ, with a view toward implementing the love symbolized in the sharing of the body and blood of the Lord. The general pattern of such worship has the following elements: (1) liturgy of the Word (reading of the Scriptures, with prayers and homiletic interpretation); (2) symbolic action, wherein bread, wine, water, oil, and so forth are employed in religious ritual (the seen sacraments). In modern times, especially by way of reaction to the Protestant Reformation, the second of these elements has been the object of close scrutiny. Liturgical renewal functions to bring back into prominence the Word. Again modern scholarship has done much to make real to Roman Catholics the developing nature of sacramental liturgy, after a period of relative stability, even fixedness, that characterized the post-Reformation period.

Organization

To describe the Roman Catholic Church as papal, that is, as organized under the leadership of the pope, in contrast with all other Christian churches, is quite to the point, but possibly misleading. In fact, the papacy itself, as a historical institution, has in the course of the centuries undergone much change. First, it emerged under the pressure of the circumstances of the early history of the church. The popes finally settled on the tradition of Peter's presence in Rome as the foundation of their claim to hierarchical hegemony. Today, after centuries of development, the papacy is recognized by Roman Catholics to be the center of a collegial hierarchy. An ecumenical council, for example, is thus constituted of the collegium of bishops who are in communion with Rome, working together with the pope. The most recent example of this type of cooperation is the Second Vatican Council (1961–65). The dialectic of the Roman primacy and the relative autonomy of the local churches is a feature of historical Roman Catholicism.

Contributions and Influence

The history of Western civilization is interlaced with the development of the Roman Catholic tradition. When there occurred a power vacuum in the West, on account of the demise of the ancient Roman Empire, authority structures that had developed in the church served to keep a semblance of order. Monasticism then became responsible for the preservation of the cultural tradition. As indicated above, the church figured as a principal agent in the building of the cultural edifice historians call Christendom. Moreover, this grand movement provided the womb for the conception and birth of the medieval universities, which attempted to develop the riches of the Greek philosophical tradition into a kind of intellectual synthesis in which the Christian religion would be the transforming agent. All the while, the fundamental thrust remained the promotion of authentic spirituality. Noteworthy in such efforts were Augustine and Benedict, Francis and Dominic, Catherine and Teresa, Eckart and Tauler, Ignatius and John of the Cross, Therese de Lisieux and Teilhard de Chardin.

In our own nation, despite the presence of Roman Catholics from the outset, particularly in Maryland, the image of the church right into the twentieth century was that of an immigrant community, quite suspect on account of its allegiance to Roman authority. At the present time, however, integration is in progress, and Catholics take part in American culture on all levels. As the largest church body in the United States, with membership exceeding fifty-five million, the Catholic presence is strongly felt throughout the social strata. They are present among the wealthy, as well as in the middle and working levels of the economy. The church has given impetus and support to the labor movement. Catholic schools and universities provide diversity in the arena of education. In politics, Catholics are distributed across the spectrum. In the most recent past, however, the leadership has devoted a good amount of its energy to a critical participation in the movements of renewal, in elements of geopolitics (e.g., the peace movement) and justice in the social order at home (e.g., the preferential option for the poor and involvement in all aspects of the endeavor to respect life).

Significant Terms

Apostolic succession. The historical tradition of ecclesiastical authority, vested in the bishops of the church.

Bishop (episcopate). Chief pastor of a local church, whose functions are to preach the Christian message, to guide members of the church in their conduct of the Christian life, and to preside at the church's worship.

Deacon (diaconate). Ordained assistants in the order of the clergy, especially commissioned to minister to the poor and to care for the material goods of the church.

Ecumenism. The effort to reestablish the unity of the church and generally to promote it among the religions of the world and within the human community.

Eucharist (the Mass). Principal worship of the church, the sacramental celebration of the death and resurrection of the Lord.

Hierarchy. The order of ordained members of the church, to whose leadership the community is committed.

Laity. The people who constitute the church, in discipleship and the representation of Christian values in the marketplace.

Liturgy. Symbolic worship, centered in the sacraments and including all public services in which the church gathers to pray in common.

Monasticism (religious life). Those forms of Christian life characterized by the vows of obedience, chastity, and poverty.

Priesthood (presbyterate). Ordained assistants to the bishop in the general conduct of the ministry (responsible for preaching and teaching, pastoral guidance, and leadership in worship).

Pope (papacy). Bishop of Rome and chief pastor of the entire church; head of the college of bishops.

Tradition. In an active sense, the handing on of the Christian message and way of life; in a more objective sense, the content of that message and way of life, as it is transmitted from one culture to another.

Bibliography

Congar, Y. *The Mystery of the Church.* London: G. Chapman, 1960.

deLubac, H. *The Church: Paradox and Mystery.* Shannon, Ireland: Ecclesia Press, 1969.

Dulles, A. *Models of the Church.* Garden City, N.Y.: Doubleday, 1976.

Flannery, A., ed. *Vatican II: Conciliar and Post-Conciliar Documents.* Collegeville, Minn.: Liturgical Press, 1975.

McBrien, R. *Catholicism*. 2 vols. Minneapolis: Winston Press, 1980.
McKenzie, J. L. *The Roman Catholic Church*. New York: Holt, Rinehart & Winston, 1969.

Prepared by Maurice Schepers, O.P., professor of religion, LaSalle University.

UKRAINIAN CATHOLIC CHURCH

General Description

The Ukrainian Catholic Church is one of the Eastern churches that is in full communion with the see of St. Peter, the pope of Rome. Hence, the term "Catholic" in the sense used here indicates that this church is hierarchically related to the supreme pontiff and that the church recognizes him as the vicar of Christ on earth and is in accord with the teachings of the Holy Father. The Ukrainian Catholic Church, while Catholic, is not a Latin rite church. It belongs to the generic family of Byzantine rite churches, since much of the liturgical tradition was introduced to the Slavs in the ninth century by the missionaries Cyril and Methodius by way of Constantinople (Byzantium). Hence, the term "Byzantine rite."

Because of the unique relationship to Rome, while retaining the Byzantine liturgical and spiritual tradition, which in many respects is identical to those of Eastern Orthodox churches (which are not in union with Rome), the Ukrainian Catholic Church has experienced significant persecution over the centuries since 1595, the date of the historic Union of Brest-Litovsk, which formalized the relationship with the Vatican.

First the czars were responsible for much of this persecution. Then after the Bolshevik revolution in 1917, the Communists continued this campaign aimed at destroying the Ukrainian Catholic Church. In 1946 Joseph Stalin, in cooperation with the Russian Orthodox Church, attempted to sound its death knell by claiming that the church "voluntarily liquidated itself" and joined the Russian Orthodox Church.

Since that time, the Ukrainian Catholic Church has been officially outlawed in the Soviet Union. In spite of imprisonment of its bishops, clergy, and faithful and the confiscation and destruction of its churches, schools, and seminaries, the church has continued to thrive as an "underground church of the catacombs," with an estimated 5 million followers, primarily in western Ukraine. To this day, the church is illegal in the Soviet Union. However, there is some optimism that the present leadership in Moscow may legalize it. The Ukrainian Catholic Church is found not only in the Soviet Union but in what is considered the diaspora throughout the world.

In the United States, the first Ukrainian Catholic Church was founded in 1884 in the anthracite coal-mining borough of Shenandoah, Schuylkill County, Pennsylvania. With increased immigration, more and more parishes were established, and finally, on August 27, 1907, the Holy See appointed Soter Ortynsky the first Ukrainian Catholic bishop for the United States. However, at this time, he had to receive all jurisdiction from Latin rite ordinances. He was finally accorded full ordinary jurisdiction on May 28, 1913. The first priest in the United States was Father John Volansky.

Presently, there is one archdiocese and three dioceses of the Ukrainian Catholic Church in the United States. They are the Metropolitan Archdiocese of Philadelphia; the Diocese of Stanford, Connecticut; the Diocese of St. Nicholas in Chicago; and the Diocese of St. Josephat in Parma, Ohio. There are approximately 300,000 Ukrainian Catholics in the United States.

Founder

Since the Ukrainian Catholic Church is in full communion with Rome, its founder is Jesus Christ. Legend has it that the apostle Andrew brought Christianity into many lands that are now Ukrainian. In the ninth century, Cyril and Methodius introduced Christianity to the Slavs. However, 988 A.D. is the significant date in Ukrainian Church history. In that year Prince Wolodymyr (Vladimir) proclaimed Christianity the official religion of Kiev. This marked the baptism of Ukraine, the millennium of which was celebrated worldwide in 1988.

Parenthetically, it must be noted that many asserted incorrectly that 1988 marked the millennium of Russian Christianity. Ukraine and Russia are two distinct republics, two distinct peoples, with two distinct languages, cultures, and identities. In fact, Ukraine has a separate vote in the United Nations. Ukraine evolved from the principality of Kiev, while Moscovy, which was founded in the thirteenth century, evolved into Russia.

Beliefs and Doctrines

The Ukrainian Catholic Church adheres to all the teachings, revealed truths, dogmas, and doctrines of the Catholic Church. Vatican II, in the decree *Orientalium Ecclesarium,* declared, "The Holy Catholic Church, which is the Mystical Body of Christ, is made up of the faithful who are organically united in the Holy Spirit by the same faith, the same sacraments, and the same government. They combine into different groups, which are held together by their hierarchy and so form particular churches or rites. Between those churches, there is such a wonderful bond of union that this variety in the Universal Church, so far from diminishing its unity, rather serves to emphasize it."

Forms of Worship

The most important service is the divine liturgy. During this service, the gospel is proclaimed and the Eucharist is offered and received. In the liturgy, the Eucharist is offered with leavened bread and wine, which becomes the body and blood of Christ during the anaphora, or eucharistic prayer, which includes the epiclesis, the invocation of the Holy Spirit upon the gifts offered.

The churches are designed according to standards that contribute to the rich liturgical tradition. The Ukrainian Catholic Church does not use any statues, but rather uses icons, sacred images of Christ, Mary, and the saints or of events in their lives. The church represents heaven on earth, and therefore the icons are ornately painted and decorated to lift one away from the earthly life and to give a foretaste of heaven. The liturgies are sung a cappella in Ukrainian, English, or the official church language; no instruments of any kind are ever used. Incense also figures prominently in the service.

Organization

The Ukrainian Catholic Church is headed by a major archbishop, who is similar in function to a patriarch. He has most of his rights and privileges, except the title "patriarch." The major archbishop with the Synod of Hierarchs of the Ukrainian Catholic Church can implement liturgical and disciplinary law for the Ukrainian Catholic Church worldwide, subject to review by the Holy See. The most important governing takes place on a diocesan level, which is headed by a bishop. He, with his curia, governs the diocese. The parishes are staffed by priests, who provide the pastoral and administrative care of the faithful of the parish. The bishops are appointed by the pope, usually after being recommended by the Synod of Hierarchs. In keeping with the spirit of the Vatican II and the principle of subsidiarity in the hierarchically structured church, decisions should be made at the lowest level where the decision can be responsibly made—whether on a parish, diocesan, or synodal level.

Contributions and Influence

The church has always been a center for prayer and activity for Ukrainian Catholics. It helped to preserve the cultural identity of the immigrants in the United States and provided a sense of support and security for those in a strange land. In the Ukraine, the faithful have always had a deep attachment to the church. In the United States, Ukrainian Catholics have made contributions in their liturgical music, their church architecture with the onion-shaped domes, their iconography, and their folk arts, such as *pysanky* (egg decorating), embroidery, folk dancing, and ethnic foods.

In the future, it is anticipated that the Ukrainian Catholic Church, in keeping with the mandates of Vatican II, will serve as a bridge in helping the Vatican achieve unity with the Orthodox Churches of the East.

Significant Terms

Archeparchy. An archdiocese.

Autonomous churches. Groups of Christian faithful bound together by a hierarchy according to the norm of the law and that are expressly or tacitly acknowledged as autonomous by the supreme authority of the church.

Divine liturgy. the service of prayer, readings, and offerings of the Eucharist, usually called Mass in the Latin tradition.

Eparchy. A diocese.

Iconostasis. The icon screen that separates the sanctuary from the nave of the church.

Metropolitan. An archbishop who presides over several dioceses that collectively form a province.

Rite. The liturgical, theological, spiritual, and disciplinary patrimony, culture, and historical circumstances of a distinct people, by which each autonomous church expresses its own manner of living the faith.

Bibliography

Canadian Catholic Conference. *The Byzantine-Ukrainian Rite.* Toronto: Canadian Catholic Conference, 1975.

Meyendroff, John. *Byzantine Theology: Historical Trends and Doctrinal Themes.* New York: Fordham Press, 1974.

Petras, David M. *Eastern Catholic Churches in America.* Parma, Ohio: Office of Religious Education, 1987.

Shewchuk, Marie, and Patricia Lacey. *Journey of Faith: Ukrainian Millennium.* Toronto: Sister Servants of Mary Immaculate, 1987.

Prepared by Rev. Fr. John Shields, pastor, Presentation Ukrainian Catholic Church, Lansdale, Pennsylvania.

SALVATION ARMY

General Description

The Salvation Army, founded in 1865, is an international religious and charitable movement organized and operated on a quasi-military pattern and is a branch of the Christian church. Its membership includes officers (clergy), soldiers/adherents (laity), members of varied activity groups, and volunteers who serve as advisers, associates, and committed participants in its service functions.

The motivation of the organization is love of God and a practical concern for the needs of humanity. This is expressed by a spiritual ministry, the purposes of which are to preach the gospel, disseminate Christian truths, supply basic human necessities, provide personal regeneration and physical rehabilitation of all persons in need who come within its sphere of influence, regardless of race, color, creed, sex, or age.

The Salvation Army's basic aim is to bring people into a right relationship with God, and it tries to return people to their faith. Its evangelical efforts are reflected in renewed interest in religion through all denominations and faiths.

Founder and Leaders

The Salvation Army was founded by William Booth, an ordained minister, who left the Methodist New Connexion to become a full-time evangelistic preacher. In 1865 this step led him to the worst slum areas in London's East End and to a dedication of his life to the poverty-stricken, unchurched masses in that area. His first plan was to make his work supplementary to that of the churches, but this proved impractical because many converts did not want to go where they were sent; often they were not accepted when they did go, and Booth soon found that he needed his converts to help handle the great crowds that came to his meetings. Booth commenced his work in Mile End Waste under the name of the Christian Mission, but in 1878 the name was changed to the Salvation Army.

When Booth died on August 20, 1912, he was succeeded by his eldest son, William Bramwell Booth. Bramwell's failing health forced him to retire in 1929. His successor was Edward J. Higgins, the first elected general.

Evangeline Booth, daughter of the founder, took command of the Salvation Army on November 11, 1934. At the age of seventeen she had entered full-time service in the Salvation Army. She was a striking, auburn-haired girl with a flair for the dramatic and a voice that was compared to Sarah Bernhardt's. Along with other Salvationists, she endured violence and persecution in the 1880s. In 1896 she arrived in the United States and succeeded in restoring the unity threatened by a splinter movement. In 1904 she became national commander of the Salvation Army in the United States. She was famous as a leader for women's suffrage and prohibition.

The next general was George L. Carpenter, who took command on November 1, 1939. On June 21, 1946, he was succeeded by Albert Osborn, who was followed by Wilfred Kitching on July 1, 1954. Frederick Coutts took office in the fall of 1963, followed by Erik Wickberg in 1969, Clarence Wiseman in 1974, Arnold Brown in 1977, Jarl Wahlstrom in 1981, and Eva Burrows in 1986.

Beliefs and Doctrines

The following eleven points summarize Salvation Army doctrines.

1. We believe that the Scriptures of the Old and New Testaments were given by inspiration of God and that they only constitute the divine rule of Christian faith and practice.
2. We believe that there is only one God, who is infinitely perfect, the Creator, Preserver, and Governor of all things, and who is the only proper object of religious worship.
3. We believe that there are three persons in the Godhead—the Father, Son, and the Holy Ghost, undivided in essence and coequal in power and glory.
4. We believe that in the person of Jesus Christ the divine and human natures are united, so that He is truly and properly God and properly man.
5. We believe that our first parents were created in a state of innocency, but by their disobedience they lost their purity and happiness, and that in consequence of their fall all men have become sinners, totally depraved, and as such are justly exposed to the wrath of God.
6. We believe that the Lord Jesus Christ by His suffering and death made an atonement for the whole world, so that whosoever will may be saved.
7. We believe that repentance toward God, faith in our Lord Jesus Christ, and regeneration by the Holy Spirit are necessary to salvation.
8. We believe that we are justified by grace through faith in our Lord Jesus Christ and that He that believes has the witness in himself.

9. We believe that continuance in a state of salvation depends upon continued, obedient faith in Christ.
10. We believe that is the privilege of all believers to be wholly sanctified and that their whole spirit and soul and body may be preserved blameless until the coming of our Lord Jesus Christ.
11. We believe in the immortality of the soul, in the resurrection of the body, in the general judgment at the end of the world, in the eternal happiness of the righteous, and in the endless punishment of the wicked.

Forms of Worship

The Salvation Army brass band is a unique feature of worship services. Music provides both a joyful expression of faith and a form of recreation. Most officers play some musical instrument. The bands have been commended for musical excellence by many famous conductors and composers.

Open-air meetings are an army tradition, taking the gospel to those who need it where they are. The "open-air" is followed by a march to the citadel, or corps building. The street-corner congregation is invited to follow.

Organization

The Salvation Army, as the name implies, is organized along military lines. Instead of congregation members attending church, there are soldiers marching to the citadel. Its ordained ministers are known as officers.

Candidates for officership undergo an intensive two-year course in residence as cadets at officers' training schools. A cadet is commissioned a lieutenant and assigned to active duty. Lieutenants are required to devote four years to postgraduate studies. Promotion is based on length of service, character, efficiency, devotion to duty, and capacity for greater responsibility. Degrees of rank are lieutenant, captain, major, lieutenant colonel, colonel, and commissioner. The general, or international leader, is elected by a high council composed of all active commissioners and territorial commanders who have held the rank of colonel for at least two years.

Women are admitted to officers' training schools and promoted up through the ranks just as men are. They have always participated in the army on an equal basis. There have been two women generals. The Salvation Army officer must devote his or her full time to army work. If an officer wishes to marry, he or she must marry only another Salvation Army officer. Both spouses hold equal rank and share their duties. Officers receive a modest salary, out of which they must purchase their own uniforms and food. The army provides living quarters and furnishings.

Contributions and Influence

From the beginning, the Salvation Army has been active in what is now termed social welfare and has played an important role in developing effective methods of aiding the poor and those afflicted in mind or body. Its founder was among the first to recognize that alcoholism is a disease and must be treated as such. The army's shelters, its use of group and work therapy, its work with alcoholics, prisoners, and unwed mothers, as well as its youth programs and summer camps all play an important role in American life and have often served as models for others to follow.

Significant Terms

Articles of War. Declaration of faith.

Cadet. A trainee for officership.

Corps/Community Center. The basic unit of the Salvation Army. It serves as a neighborhood center for varied religious and welfare programs.

Division. An administrative unit containing several corps in a given area, usually bounded by state lines.

Eventide home. A boarding house operated by the Salvation Army, which provides comfortable accommodations at reasonable rates for senior citizens.

Girl Guards. A nondenominational organization established by the Salvation Army for girls ages 10–13, who subscribe to a program that promotes God's character and good citizenship. Sunbeams is a junior division for girls ages 6–10. The Senior Guards enroll girls ages 14–18.

Harbor Light Center. A chain of centers operated by the Salvation Army with a program designed especially for the treatment of alcoholics and socially disinherited in skid row areas of the larger cities.

Harvest Festival. An autumn commemoration during which the Salvation Army soldiers and interested friends give a thank-offering.

Home League. An organization within a Salvation Army Corps or institution for all women sixteen years of age or over. It follows a program of dedication, worship, fellowship, and service.

League of Mercy. A volunteer group of Salvationists and friends who regularly visit institutions to provide spiritual and social therapy.

Officer. A Salvationist engaged in full-time service as an ordained minister of religion in the Salvation Army.

Red Shield Clubs. These Salvation Army clubs are divided into three groups, serving boys, boys and girls, and servicemen and women.

Salvationist. A lay member or officer of the Salvation Army.

Self-denial/World service. An annual observance during Holy Week characterized by prayer and a fund-raising project for the army's missionary work.

Soldier. A lay member of the Salvation Army.

Citadel. A regular place of worship of the Salvation Army.

Promoted to Glory. The Salvation Army way of saying that a member has died.

Open-air. A worship meeting held outdoors.

"The War Cry." Official weekly publication of the Salvation Army.

Bibliography

The History of the Salvation Army. Vols. 1–3, *1865–86,* by Robert Sandall; vols. 4–
    5, *1886–1904,* by Arch Wiggins; vol. 6, *1914–46,* by Frederick Coutts. New
    York: Thomas Nelson & Sons, 1979.
McKinley, Edward H. *Marching to Glory.* San Francisco: Harper & Row, 1980.

Prepared by Leon Ferraez, director, Communications Department, Salvation Army.

◆ ◆ ◆
SCHWENKFELDER CHURCH

General Description

The Schwenkfelders are spiritual heirs of Caspar Schwenckfeld von Ossig (1499–1561). Schwenckfeld was a German nobleman from Silesia who was spiritually awakened by Martin Luther and became involved with other reformers during the Protestant Reformation. The church that bears his name today is composed of 2,800 members in five congregations located in Lansdale, Norristown, Palm, Philadelphia, and Worcester, all in Pennsylvania.

The purpose of the Schwenkfelder Church is to make Christ known and to enable its members to express that knowledge in the way they live and serve the needs of people everywhere. Seeking to carry on their work in the tradition of Schwenckfeld, the five Schwenkfelder churches remain Christ-centered in theology, congregational in church polity, and ecumenical in ecclesiology. New members are received by baptism after catechetical instruction, by profession of faith, and by letters from other churches.

Founder

Technically, Caspar Schwenckfeld is not the founder of the Schwenkfelder Church as it exists today. He labored for a reformation of life, for liberty of religious belief and conscience, and for a fellowship of all believers in one united Christian Church. He never attempted to form an ecclesiastical organization.

Schwenckfeld was educated in the best schools and universities of his day and was influenced by the cultural styles of German nobility. By profession, he was a courtier—that is, adviser to several dukes and diplomats in the German courts. Influenced by the writings of Martin Luther, he undertook a detailed study of the Scriptures in Greek and Hebrew as well as the writings of the church fathers and the medieval mystics. He became a lay preacher and author of the Reformation in Silesia.

Believing that all persons who accept Jesus Christ as Savior and Lord of life are part of the Christian church, he sought fellowship with all such persons regardless of denominational names. He did not start a church called by his name. Those who agreed with his teachings met in small groups for prayer, study, and worship to assist one another in spiritual growth toward the "fullness of the stature of Christ." He called these groups simply Confessors of the Glory of Christ.

His teachings emphasize the centrality of Jesus Christ as a living person, the right of the individual to do his own thinking and deciding, the use of all externals (the visible church, the Bible, the sacraments, preaching, teaching, etc.) as pointers to Jesus Christ as the only Savior and Lord of persons, and the importance of living one's faith in all relationships rather than merely subscribing to a creed or dogma.

Schwenckfeld wrote numerous letters and discourses on theological and religious subjects throughout his years of voluntary exile from 1529 to the end of his life in 1561. Because of the severity of persecution throughout the intolerant sixteenth century, he became a fugitive and was constantly on the move during the later years of his life. He was in personal contact with the major and minor reformers of the day. From 1884 to 1962 his writings were collected and published in a nineteen-volume collection called the Corpus Schwenkfeldianorium. The collection is maintained at the Schwenkfelder Library in Pennsburg, Pennsylvania.

Beliefs and Doctrines

Caspar Schwenckfeld was an original thinker, one who was not bound by traditional creeds and articles of faith. At the center of his mature theology was a concern with the glory of the risen Christ. Until late in the eighteenth century, his followers called themselves Confessors of the Glory of Christ. Schwenckfeld insisted on the unity of the divine and human natures in Christ's person, but Jesus' humanity, he insisted, was not as ours. His body was not that of a creature but that of a being of heavenly origin, a celestial flesh. Christ was the firstborn of a new creation. From the moment of his birth, a progressive deification took place in which the God in him more and more divinized the celestial, but human flesh. The progress of the divination can be marked by the transfiguration witnessed by the three disciples. After the crucifixion and resurrection, this process was completed by his glorification, as true God and true man, at the right hand of the Father.

Schwenckfeld's Christology had anthropological implications as well. Man, he taught, is totally corrupted by the Fall, but by the grace of God he may participate in the new creation through faith. Faith not only declares that a man is justified (as Luther taught), but as knowledge, it unites the believer with that in which he believes. In baptism, one is united with the glorified body of Christ; one feeds on it spiritually. Faith is a seed of the divine in man, God's very being in the old creature. It works a real change in the sinner. It is not simply an initial act at the beginning of the new life, but it fills the whole life of the believer, from spiritual rebirth to physical death, and continues in action through the believer's resurrection and final glorification in the Son. In the believer, faith develops parallel to the way the divine progressed in Christ's celestial flesh. Because it is a part of the flesh, it leads the believer through suffering into glory, if man allows.

The focus of Schwenckfeld's life and teaching was on the personal experience of the living, glorified Christ in the school of Christ. For him, God alone is the teacher. He touches the inner life of the seeker by granting experiential knowledge of Christ. He called this learning and growing process "Erkenntnis Christi." In general, this term defines the dawning awareness on the part of the believer that he or she is empowered daily by Christ to live for God and for others. Maturity is never a static goal that can be achieved at some point in this life but is a goal achieved only after death and resurrection, when the believer is glorified in heaven.

The following beliefs of the Schwenkfelders today are in keeping with Schwenckfeld's teaching.

1. The centrality of Jesus Christ, the living Word of God, as our Savior and Lord of life.
2. The Bible as the written record of the Word of God in history and as the directive authority for our faith and life.
3. The need for one to think for oneself and for individual, unforced commitment to the living Christ.
4. Respect for the rights of Christian laity in the church and toleration of individual differences.
5. Spiritual rebirth through faith in Jesus Christ, which is essential to salvation.
6. The inner experience of Christ within us, which is more important than the outward forms, practices, and structures of religion.
7. The need for faith to be seen in the way we conduct our lives.
8. The unity of all Christians in Jesus Christ as one in the family of God.
9. As honest seekers after truth, openness to the Holy Spirit so that He may lead us into all truth.
10. Growth toward spiritual maturity, which is a lifelong process.

Forms of Worship

Schwenckfeld himself worshiped in the formal state churches of his day. Before his reformatory activity, he grew up in the Roman Catholic tradition of his family estate in Ossig, Silesia. Later he worshiped in a variety of ways in Roman Catholic monasteries, in cathedrals, and in small Protestant groups called conventicles. His followers worshiped mainly in private homes until their flight to America in the 1730s. In the small groups the practice was to sing, pray, and study the Scriptures. In the early colonial days, they worshiped in private homes and constructed meetinghouses primarily for the purpose of education. Music and Bible study were central to their worship from earliest times. Today, each local church of the five is free to use whatever style of worship it desires. Typically, the worship service is centered on a biblically based sermon and congregational participation through responsive readings, singing, and prayers with a sharing of prayer concerns.

Organization and History

Schwenckfeld never organized a church. His followers, after his death in 1561, became known as Schwenkfelders but continued the conventicle method of worship centered in private homes. Because of severe persecution from the state churches, about two hundred of them came to Philadelphia in the 1730s. On September 22, 1734, the largest group arrived in the sailing vessel the *St. Andrew*, with George Weiss as their spiritual leader. The next day they affirmed their allegiance to King George II of England, and on September 24, 1734, they held a service of thanksgiving to God for deliverance from persecution and safe arrival in Pennsylvania. Commemorating that event, a memorial thanksgiving service has been held each September 24 (or the Sunday nearest that date). The traditional meal eaten at this service is bread and apple butter because that is all they had to eat at the first service.

In spite of their avoidance of institutional structures, the Schwenkfelders were not without compelling leaders during the first fifty years in Pennsylvania. The colonial Schwenkfelders settled in Philadelphia, Montgomery, Bucks, Berks, and Lehigh counties, many of them becoming farmers. Education of families was very important to them. On November 8, 1735, nine heads of families met and selected George Weiss (1687–1740) as their first minister, and Balthasar Hoffman and David Seipot as deacons. On Weiss's death, he was succeeded by Hoffman (1687–1775), who, like his predecessors, was much troubled by the geographic dispersion of his people and the difficulties of country travel. Several times during his life he resigned from a leadership position, but each time he was persuaded to take up the task once again. In 1753, in spite of much resistance, formal religious meetings were established. Hoffman was the most consummate scholar of all eighteenth-century Schwenkfelders, completing in his life three major biblical studies as well as hymns, letters, sermons, and a series of theological and religious tracts, all of which are extant in manuscript form at the Schwenkfelder Library.

In 1762 Christopher Schultz (1718–89), who did much to organize the Schwenkfelders and maintain them as a distinctive group, edited the first Schwenkfelder hymnbook, printed by the Sauer Press in Germantown. Schultz wrote a catechism in 1763 and *Vindication of Casper Schwenckfeld* (1771), printed in German in Silesia. In 1782 Schultz also wrote the constitution of the "Society of Schwenkfelders," which was patterned after the Society of Friends.

The Schwenkfelders continued as "the Society of Schwenkfelders" until the incorporation of "the Schwenkfelder Church" in 1909. Just prior to the turn of the century, ordained clergy became the formal spiritual leaders of the congregations. However, each congregation maintains congregational polity with elected laity as well as delegates to the General Conference, which meets twice each year.

The General Conference deals with such matters as publications, education, missionary endeavors, charitable requests, and financial concerns that involve all five congregations. Each congregation is autonomous and conducts its own internal affairs. The General Conference also appoints representatives to serve on the Pennsylvania Council of Churches, the State, International, and World Christian Endeavor, and other ecumenical organizations.

Contributions and Influence

Schwenkfelders were concerned with education as early as 1759, when they conducted nonsectarian, public, and free classes in private homes. In 1765 they built a school at Towamencin. Other schools were established in meetinghouses, as these were erected in the late eighteenth and early nineteenth centuries. In 1891 the Schwenkfelders moved into secondary education with the purchase of the Perkiomen Seminary. Under the leadership of Oscar S. Kriebel (1863–1932), Perkiomen School was started, and it continues to flourish today as a coeducational independent college-preparatory school.

Schwenckfeld and his followers can be characterized as a bookish people. During the eighteenth century they circulated their writings in manuscript form. In the early nineteenth century, they began to print the works of Schwenckfeld in German and English. At the 115th Day of Remembrance in 1884, a Schwenkfelder descendent and president of the Hartford Theological Seminary in Connecticut, Chester David Hartranft (d. 1914), urged the collection of all Schwenckfeld's writings. The project was undertaken, and Hartranft became the first editor. But before the final folio volume of *The Corpus Schwenkfeldianorum* in 1961, valuable contributions were made by Elmer E. S. Johnson (1872–1959). The Board of Publication of the Schwenkfelder Church was formed to publish Schwenckfeld's works and sponsored the compilation and printing of *The Genealogical Record of the Schwenkfelder Families* (1923), Selina Schultz's biography of Schwenckfeld and the Schwenkfelders.

The Schwenkfelders have also contributed magnificently to housing for the elderly. In 1974 they opened Schwenkfeld Manor Apartments in Lansdale. Today, some two hundred apartments provide low-cost housing for many people. The Board of Advanced Living joined Wyncote Homes (UCC) to create a similar housing unit in Red Hill. Schwenkfelders have also been instrumental in developing Meadowood, a continuing care retirement community for over five hundred elderly citizens in Worcester.

Significant Terms

Christian liberty. Schwenckfeld was a champion of religious freedom and toleration. He said, "Let no one permit himself to be deprived of his Christian liberty or allow his mind to be bound by human creeds. . . . Let every Christian both teacher and hearer, use with gratitude whatever talents God has given him for the good of others and the glory of God."

Conventicle. A term used to describe the small group meetings conducted by Caspar Schwenckfeld and his early followers for prayer, Bible study, and nurture of one another in the Christian life and faith.

The living Christ. A term used for the risen and glorified Christ, who is present within the life of every believer. It sometimes is used interchangeably with terms such as the Holy Spirit, the Spirit of God, and the Spirit of Christ.

The Word of God. Schwenckfeld preferred to use this term when speaking directly of Jesus Christ, based on the prologue of John's Gospel. The Bible, he said, is really the written record of the voice of God, which points the believer to the Living Word, Christ himself.

Bibliography

(Except as noted, all items are published by the Board of Publication of the Schwenk-felder Church, Pennsburg, Pa.)

Brecht, Samuel K., ed. *The Genealogical Record of the Schwenkfelder Families.* 1923.

Erb, Peter C. *Schwenkfelders in America.* 1987.

———, ed. *Schwenckfeld and Early Schwenckfeldianism.* 1986.

———, ed. *Schwenckfeld in His Reformation Setting.* 1978.

Kriebel, Howard W. *The Schwenckfelders in Colonial Pennsylvania.* Lancaster, Pa., 1904.

Kriebel, Martha B. *Schwenkfelders and the Sacraments.* 1968.

McLaughlin, R. Emmet. *Caspar Schwenckfeld, Reluctant Radical: His Life to 1540.* New Haven, Conn.: Yale University Press, 1986.

Mescheter, W. Kryel. *Twentieth Century Schwenkfelders.* 1984.

Rothenberger, Jack R. *Caspar Schwenckfeld von Ossig and the Ecumenical Ideal.* 1967.

Schultz, Selina Gerhard. *A Course of Study in the Life and Teachings of Caspar Schwenck-felder (1489–1561).* 1964.

———. *The History of the Schwenkfelder and Religious Movement (1518–1964).* 1964.

Schwenkfeldiana. 1940–52. Eleven short monographs on the Schwenkfelders in America.

Weigelt, Horst. *The Schwenkfelders in Silesia.* 1985.

Prepared by Rev. Jack R. Rothenberger, senior minister, Central Schwenkfelder Church, Worcester, Pennsylvania.

◆ ◆ ◆

SCIENTOLOGY

General Description

Scientology is an applied religious philosophy designed to make the able more able. It deals with the study of knowledge, which, through its application, can improve life in a troubled world. It comes from the Latin *scio*, meaning "know" or "knowing" and the Greek word "logos" meaning "the word," or "the way," or "study of."

Scientology is a path, discipline, and study of how to know. A Scientologist is one who is studying and learning to apply the knowledge and wisdom of life to better his survival, the survival of others and his environment, while gaining an understanding of the Supreme Being and his relationship to it.

Scientology is based on the fact that man is a spiritual being and that man has a mind and a body through which he, as a spiritual being, operates. A person is not his body or mind—a person has a body and a mind; he is both a spiritual being himself who is aware of the universe around him and one who directs his activities.

Founder

The founder of the applied religious philosophy Scientology is L. Ron Hubbard (1911–86). Mr. Hubbard has been widely recognized for his contributions in many fields, but he is best known as one of the most acclaimed and widely read authors of all time.

From his earliest days, he was a man whose inquisitive nature led him to explore every nook and cranny of existence and to experience every possible part of life. By the time he was nineteen, Hubbard had traveled more than quarter of a million sea miles and thousands more on land. In a real sense, the world itself was his classroom.

In 1948 Hubbard's first writings on the nature of life and human mind began to circulate privately, and the word got out that he had made a breakthrough. In 1950 Hubbard released his discoveries in the book *Dianetics: The Modern Science of Mental Health*. It became a nationwide best-seller almost overnight.

Soon after the release of *Dianetics* Hubbard made his next major discovery. It had become clear to him that there was something much more basic and important to life than the brain, the mind, and the body. After discovering that the basic common denominator of all life was "the urge to survive," Hubbard established conclusively that man was basically a spiritual being, inhabiting a body and using a mind. His first findings on the spirit of man were published in 1951 in his next book, *Science of Survival*.

This was the beginning of Hubbard's researches into man and his nature. Between 1951 and 1954 alone, he wrote twenty books and gave over a thousand lectures on Scientology. As Hubbard's research time and time again broke new ground, he wrote millions of words over the next thirty-five years.

Hubbard wrote in 1965, "I have lived no cloistered life and hold in contempt the wise man who has not lived and the scholar who will not share. There have been many wiser men than I, but few have traveled as much road. I have seen life from the top down and the bottom up. I know how it looks both ways. And I know there is wisdom and that there is hope."

Beliefs and Doctrines

The basis of Scientology is in the writings of L. Ron Hubbard. Scientology believes that man is a spiritual being, that he is what is commonly known as "the soul." In Scientology, the term "thetan" is used, which is derived from the Greek *theta*, meaning "life." Scientology has found that man is basically good and that he is here to find his own salvation.

Since Scientology is an applied religious philosophy, the stress is on application and workability. It addresses the individual and brings about self-improvement by increasing a person's awareness and ability to handle life. In this way, the individual takes more responsibility for himself, others, organizations to which he belongs, his community, and mankind generally.

Scientology does not have a dogma about God. Scientology is a non-denominational religion, which means that membership does not require that one leave any other religion. Scientology does not conflict with other religions or religious practices, as it clarifies and brings understanding of the spiritual nature of man. Scientology has among its members people of all the major faiths, including many priests, bishops, and other ordained communicants of the major faiths.

Forms of Worship

Church services include a Sunday service, marriage ceremonies, naming ceremonies, funeral services, and some formal prayers and a creed, which can be found in the book *Background and Ceremonies* (see Bibliography).

Scientology is a very practical religion, intended to be applied in one's life and to improve conditions. The two most major practices in the Church of Scientology are study and auditing.

Pastoral counseling in scientology is called auditing, which comes from the latin *audire*, meaning "to listen." Auditing is the practice in which individuals, with the aid of a minister or auditor (one who listens), come to confront experiences in life that are troublesome to themselves and rid themselves of these negative influences so that they can go on to live life anew. There is a very important point in auditing that must not be confused with counseling. The auditor does not counsel the person, evaluate the person's experiences or life, or tell him he should think this or that. It is the person himself who must confront his own past and present life and thereby come to gain new self-determinism and choice, and therein total freedom.

Study comprises both the techniques of auditing, which contain much in understanding man, and the self-improvement courses. The self-improvement courses assist a person by addressing specific life problems, such as handling drug addiction, improving human relations, or raising a family.

Organization

In 1954 the first Church of Scientology was founded by Scientologists in Los Angeles, California. This was at the time a grass-roots movement that had exploded in size overnight; organizing as a formal religious body was its natural course.

The church has grown considerably from its founding in 1954. In just thirty-five years, the church has grown from one church in Los Angeles to more than 600 churches, missions, and groups in more than 30 countries around the world. In just the past five years, 60 churches and 130 new missions have opened. The estimated membership from enrollment and registration is 6 million worldwide and 3 million within the United States. Over 11 million people have bought Hubbard's book *Dianetics*.

The churches are organized in a hierarchical manner internationally with the mother church, the Church of Scientology International in Los Angeles. The smallest organization in Scientology is a group, which is simply a number of Scientologists who meet regularly for purposes of union and study; it might vary in size between five and thirty members. A mission is a group that has been recognized by the mother church and has facilities to perform regular church services with at least one ordained minister and a small staff. A mission is responsible only for its own parishioners. A church is larger in size; for instance, the Boston Church has approximately five thousand members, has been recognized by the mother church, and geographically is responsible for its own parishioners and any missions or groups it forms. Each church is autonomous, but tithes are sent to the mother church, and each church in turn receives assistance and direction. In order to facilitate managing an international organization, each continent has a central church for advanced religious studies, training staff persons, and relaying communications.

Contributions and Influence

Hubbard was an outspoken advocate of man's humanity to man—and took an active role in human rights, social reform, and religious freedom. As a Scientologist improves his own life, there is a noticeable change that takes place. His awareness of the condition of the world around him, his friends, relations, and the community in which he resides come up to a level where he will act to improve life around him. Because of this factor, Scientologists are well known for taking interest in many problems of life and community activities.

One noteworthy area of interest followed Hubbard's research into the degrading effects of drugs and drug abuse. Over thirty years ago, the church became an advocate for a drug-free society. First using techniques to help Scientologists deal with the effects of both medicinal and street drugs, these techniques are now in use by many drug rehabilitation organizations in over eleven countries around the world.

Thus, Scientologists are helping to solve the problems of drug abuse and addiction. Many celebrity Scientologists have become directly involved. The results are the programs such as "Right Track" and "Hollywood Says No to Drugs." The Narconon drug rehabilitation group, which uses Hubbard's research, has successfully delivered drug education and rehabilitation programs to over 150,000 persons.

Hubbard also spent years researching the subject of study—seeking to discover the various barriers to study. Education Alive and Applied Scholastics are two organizations that use Hubbard's discoveries to rehabilitate students and revitalize entire educational systems. In China, for example, L. Ron Hubbard's study of technology has been introduced in two universities, and the program has been so successful that educational authorities are expanding it to the entire country.

Significant Terms

Scientology. The word "Scientology" literally means "knowing how to know." It comes from the Latin *scio,* meaning "know" or "knowing," and the Greek *logos,* meaning "word" or "way" or "study of."

Dianetics. This word comes from the Greek *dia,* meaning "through," and *nous,* which means "soul."

Thetan. The person himself—not his body or his name, the physical universe, his mind, or anything else; that which is aware of being aware; the identity that is the individual. The thetan is most familiar to one and all as "you."

Bibliography

(All items are published by Bridge Publications, Los Angeles, the printing house of the Church of Scientology.)

The Background and Ceremonies of the Church of Scientology of California, World Wide. 1970.

Hubbard, L. Ron. *Dianetics: The Modern Science of Mental Health*. 1950.
———. *Fundamentals of Thought*. 1956.
What Is Scientology? 1978.

Prepared by Rev. Stephen B. Ford, an ordained minister of the Church of Scientology. Parts of this chapter copyright © 1964, 1965, 1967, 1971, 1975, 1981, 1986 by Ron L. Hubbard. All rights reserved. Reprinted with the permission of the Religious Technology Center.

◆ ◆ ◆

SPIRITUALISM

NATIONAL SPIRITUALIST
ASSOCIATION OF CHURCHES

General Description
It is thought that modern Spiritualism's philosophical father was Immanuel
Swedenborg (1668–1772), said by some to be the most pivotal and influential figure from the eighteenth century. Swedenborg was a man of intellectual gifts, manifest in science, engineering, politics, and psychology. Later
in his life, however, at about the age of fifty-five, spiritual visions of the
departed and God appeared to him with perfect clarity and reality. Moreover,
he told of lengthy journeys "in the spirit" to places on earth, in heaven and
hell, which he described with great detail. He even gave accounts of personal
interviews with dead notables, including Plato and Luther. Swedenborg was
most effective in popularizing the ideas later developed by Spiritualism as
well as by many other occult and metaphysical movements.

Spiritualism was born as an institution in 1848 in upstate New York—
specifically in the home of John Fox. The Fox family had experienced puzzling
noises, mostly "rappings," which they proceeded to decode as messages. News
of these experiences caused much interest, which exposed the phenomena.
Critical clergy and scholars investigated and denounced it, but circles began
meeting all over to reproduce the special experiences. Spiritualism grew with
remarkable speed, encouraged by the support of prominent Americans such
as Horace Greeley, James Fenimore Cooper, William Cullen Bryant, Gov.
Nathaniel P. Tallmadge, and, by 1857, Abraham Lincoln. At one point, six
or seven Spiritualist newspapers and magazines were published in 1857. It
was reported that the majority of the people of Cleveland, Ohio, were spiritualists. However, the Civil War and other circumstances, including incidents
of medium fraud and excesses, combined to cause fluctuations in public
support.

The faithful remnant was nourished by the writings of Andrew Jackson
Davis (1826–1910), the most important American Spiritualist teacher-
writer. Davis was fundamentally a Swedenborgian with an evolutionary view
of nature and the upward progress of the soul. The idealism of Davis carried
into occult dimensions, providing the foundation for the Spiritualist claim
that "vibrational frequency of consciousness" is the only difference between
the earth plane and the higher spaces. Others, such as the Spanish writer

Unamuno, have claimed that consciousness is fundamental to existence. However, Spiritualists speak of an "unobstructed universe" in which mind and body as the "uncircumscribed" mind constructs one's self, life history, and world, all of which emerges from psychic phenomena and the images and persons within the experience of spiritual consciousness.

Beliefs and Doctrines

Spiritualism does not subscribe to creed or dogma but has, as the foundation of its beliefs, a Declaration of Principles as follows:

We believe in Infinite Intelligence.

We believe that the phenomena of nature, both physical and spiritual, are the expression of Infinite Intelligence.

We affirm that a correct understanding of such expression and living in accordance therewith constitutes true religion.

We affirm that existence and personal identity of the individual continue after the challenge called death.

"Life here and hereafter is all one life whose continuity of consciousness is unbroken by that of mere change in form, whose process we call death." (Lilian Whiting)

We affirm that communication with the so-called dead is a fact, scientifically proven by the phenomena of Spiritualism.

We believe that the highest morality is contained in the Golden Rule, "Whatsoever ye would that others should do unto you, do ye also to them."

We affirm the moral responsibility of the individual and that he makes his own happiness as he obeys or disobeys nature's physical and spiritual laws.

We affirm that the doorway to reformation is never closed against any soul, here or hereafter.

We affirm that the precepts of prophecy and healing contained in the Bible are divine attributes proven through mediumship.

Spiritualism accepts and teaches the philosophy attributed to Jesus and endeavors to emulate this demonstration of mediumship. Spiritualism does not accept Jesus as a savior or his virgin birth. Nor does it accept the Bible as "the Word of God," but as a historical record written by men, which has been interpreted and revised many times by men.

Spiritualism is not built around the life or works of any one individual in any one era of time, nor does it accept but one Bible. It is eclectic in nature, accepting truth wherever it is found.

Spiritualism believes the Infinite has ever and always been interested in the advancement of the human race, not just that section of humanity that has lived in the past two thousand years. Hence, their objection to vicarious atonement, which they consider contrary to and inconsistent with the operations of universal, immutable, eternal natural law.

Organization

The National Spiritualist Association is directed by a board of nine trustees elected by the delegates at annual conventions. State organizations are subject to the national body, and individual churches report to the state association. "Direct churches" report to the national body.

Before a member can be certified or commissioned as a lay worker or ordained as a minister, the association requires completion of studies outlined by the Morris Pratt Institute, plus further examination and demonstration of ability and understanding prior to the issuing of any certificate of ministry by the association.

To some observers, Spiritualist churches seem to be less structured and more dependent on the charisma of the medium than on his or her loyalty to the national association.

Prominent Adherents

Some of the well-known people active in U.S. Spiritualism were the Fox sisters, Dr. J. M. Peebles, Prof. J. B. Loveland, Emma Hardinge Britten, Hudson Tuttle, the Bangs sisters, Cora L. V. Richmond, Mary Piper Vanderbilt, Mattie and Moses Hull, Morris Pratt, Dr. J. V. Mansfield, Will J. Coville, Luther R. Marsh, Mr. and Mrs. E. W. Sprague, J. C. Grumbine, Harrison D. Barrett, Thomas Grinshaw, the Hon. Mark A. Barwise, Daniel Dunglas Home, Mrs. M.E. Cadwallader, Lenora Piper, and Maggie Waite. We could list many more, including Arthur Conan Doyle, Sir William Crookes, and Prof. Robert Hare.

Significant Terms

Spiritualism. The science, philosophy, and religion of a continuous life, based upon the demonstrated fact of communication, by means of mediumship, with those who live in the spirit world.

Spiritualist. One who believes, as the basis of his or her religion, in the communication between this world and the spirit world by means of mediumship, and who endeavors to mold his or her character and conduct in accordance with the highest teaching derived from such communion.

Medium. One whose organism is sensitive to vibrations from the spirit world and through whose instrumentality intelligences in that world are able to convey messages and produce the phenomena of spiritualism.

Spiritualist healer. One who, either through his own inherent powers or through his mediumship, is able to impart vital, curative force to pathological conditions.

Infinite Intelligence. The way Spiritualists express their belief in a supreme impersonal power everywhere present, manifesting itself as life, through all forms of organized matter; it is called by some, God; by others, Spirit; and by Spiritualists, Infinite Intelligence.

Clairvoyance. Properly speaking, a clairvoyant can see, hear, and sense the spirit people and their messages. So that the term may be more clearly understood, Spiritualists subdivide it into three phases: clairvoyance, clairaudience, and clairsentience. *Clairvoyance* is the ability to see with the spiritual eye those who have made the change called death and to see their names, symbols, and messages, often written in the air. It is sometimes called soulseeing or lucidity. *Clairaudience* is the ability to hear with the spiritual ear the whisperings of those who have made the change called death; it is sometimes called soul hearing. *Clairsentience* is the most common of all these phases of a clairvoyant, more generally known as impressional mediumship. Many mediums get their messages entirely in this way, neither hearing nor seeing the Spirit people, only sensing them and receiving impressionally their messages.

Trance. A sleeplike state that takes form in two phases: partial trance and deep trance. *Partial trance* is when the spirit entity so overshadows the medium that the medium has no recollection of what is said or done yet retains the mobility of the body. *Deep trance* is when the consciousness of the medium is in a comatose state, actually unconsciousness. The spirit entity takes control of the person's larynx, and the voice becomes the voice of the spirit entity, as nearly as is possible. In this state, the medium has no control of the body. It is possible to bring about a self-induced trance, but this is dangerous without a thorough knowledge and understanding of the laws of mediumship because spirit entities of the wrong character can step in and control an individual. Such a condition can bring on a mental breakdown.

Apports. In physical phenomena, it is possible to transport an object from one location to another. This is known as apportism. To accomplish this, it is necessary to dematerialize an object by increasing and decreasing the rate of vibration of the object.

Bibliography

Austin, B. F. *ABC of Spiritualism*. Indianapolis, Ind.: Summit Publications, n.d.

Barwise, Mark A. *Preface to Spiritualism*. Cassadaga, Fla.: National Spiritualist Association of Churches, 1987.

Crookes, William. *Phenomena of Spiritualism*. London: J. Burnes, 1874.

Doyle, Arthur Conan. *History of Spiritualism*. New York: Arno Press, 1975.

Greber, Johannes. *Communication with the Spirit World of God*. Teaneck, N.J.: Greber Memorial Foundation, 1987.

Peebles, J. M. *General Principles and Standard Teachings of Spiritualism*. Mokeamme Hill, Calif.: Health Research, 1972.

Spiritualists Manual. Washington, D.C.: National Spiritualist Association of Churches, 1987.

Prepared by Rev. Elizabeth R. Edgar, revised by the editor.

THEOSOPHICAL SOCIETY

General Description

The Theosophical Society is an international organization with three declared objectives: (1) to form a nucleus of the universal brotherhood of humanity, without distinction of race, creed, sex, caste, or color; (2) to encourage the study of comparative religion, philosophy, and science; and (3) to investigate unexplained laws of nature and the latent powers of man.

The Theosophical Society was founded in New York City in 1875. The international headquarters of the society is located at Adyar, India. The Theosophical Society in America has its headquarters in Wheaton, Illinois.

Founders

Helena P. Blavatsky, H. S. Olcott, and W. Q. Judge were the major figures in the group that founded the society in 1875. Madame Blavatsky remained the spiritual head of the movement until her death in 1891. Colonel Olcott was the society's first international president and remained so until his death in 1907. Mr. Judge was the first head of the American Section.

Annie Besant became president upon Olcott's death and served in that capacity until her death in 1933. Besant established small temples of the world's religions on the property of the headquarters at Adyar to reflect the society's commitments to the brotherhood of humanity and to the "divine wisdom" and the "wisdom about the divine" expressed in the many different religious traditions throughout history. That wisdom is Theosophy.

Beliefs and Doctrines

No philosophical or theological doctrine is mandated by the society. The motto of the Theosophical Society, adopted from the family of the Maharajah of Benares, is "There is no religion higher than truth."

The Theosophical worldview is based on three fundamental propositions. First, the universe and all that exists within it form one interrelated and interdependent whole. Second, every existent being—from atom to galaxy—is rooted in the same universal, life-creating reality. This reality is all-pervasive, but it can never be summed up in parts, since it transcends all its expressions. It reveals itself in the purposeful, ordered, and meaningful processes of nature as well as in the deepest recesses of the mind and spirit. Third, recognition of the unique value of every living being expresses itself in reverence for life, compassion for all, sympathy with the need of all individuals to find truth for themselves, and respect for all religious traditions. The ways in which these ideals become realities in individual life are both the privileged choice and the responsible act of every human being.

Other concepts found in a study of Theosophical literature include the following: cycles from the tiny lives of cells to the birth and death of galaxies and universes; the cycle of reincarnation for human beings; the principle of karma, which holds that we eventually receive the consequences of all our actions, in either this life or another one; the reality of a spiritual self or soul within each person; and the growth of the soul through life's experiences and through spiritual practices. The Theosophical Society imposes no dogmas but instead points toward the source of unity beyond all differences. All people, whatever their race, religion, sex, or color, are invited to participate in the life and work of the society.

Forms of Worship

Members of the society have many different religious affiliations and worship according to their own tradition. No specific form of worship is stipulated by the society, which shows respect for them all. For many Theosophists, consciousness is where the unity of all being is directly experienced and is the highest expression of truth.

Organization

The basic unit of organization consists of lodges, or branches, which are composed of at least seven members, though most are much larger. These are grouped into regional federations, and federations into national sections. There are sections of the society in all the free countries of the world, with the Indian section being the largest.

Contributions and Influence

The society is the parent of a number of other organizations, and there are still others that have taken up different aspects of Theosophical teachings. Since its inception, the society has been steadfast in its commitment to the brotherhood of humanity and to the appreciation of differing religious traditions, truly a novel idea when the society was founded. It has actively expressed compassion and idealism through a century of struggle for civil rights and religious tolerance.

Significant Term

The most important term, unique to Theosophy, is the word "Theosophy" itself. Literally, it is taken from the Greek words *theos* and *sophia,* or "God" and "wisdom," and is taken to mean "divine wisdom" by the Theosophical Society. It is a combination of philosophy, religion, and science that, according to Theosophists, has been in process of discovery and accumulation for thousands of years.

Bibliography

(Except as noted, all items are published by the Theosophical Publishing House, Wheaton, Ill.)

Blavatsky, H. P. *Key to Theosophy: An Abridgement*. Edited by Joy Mills. 1972.

Cooper, Irving S. *Theosophy Simplified*. 1989.

Jinarajadasa, C. *Golden Book of the Theosophical Society*. Adyar, Madras, India: Theosophical Publishing House, 1975.

Layton, Eunice, and Felix Layton. *Life: Your Great Adventure*. 1988.

Nicholson, Shirley. *Ancient Wisdom—Modern Insight*. 1985.

Ryan, Charles J. *H. P. Blavatsky and the Theosophical Movement*. Point Loma, Calif.: Point Loma Publications, 1975.

Prepared by Shirley Nicholson, senior editor.

UNIFICATION CHURCH

General Description

The Holy Spirit Association for the Unification of World Christianity, also known as the Unification Church, was founded in Korea in 1954 to embody and propagate the teachings of Rev. Sun Myung Moon. Now in over 120 nations, the first missionaries arrived in the United States in 1959.

The church is the spiritual center of a larger movement of unification whose purpose is to bring unity and harmony to all areas of human life through God's love and thus to realize the kingdom of God on earth. It has spawned organizations in many fields: science, peace studies, religion, the media, politics, and the arts. There are newspapers, a hospital, an international relief organization, and diverse business enterprises worldwide. The church sponsors and facilitates these movement activities for the benefit of the world, and they draw supporters who hold every sort of belief, religious and secular.

Founder

At age sixteen, when Rev. Sun Myung Moon was deep in prayer, Jesus appeared to Moon in a vision and told the young man that he had died on the cross before he could complete his mission. Jesus commissioned Moon to complete the unfinished task, which is to establish the kingdom of God substantially on the earth. Unsuccessful in his attempts to work with other Christian ministers, in 1948 he was imprisoned by the Communists in North Korea and suffered in a labor camp until he was liberated in 1950. His church began from a cardboard shack in Pusan. Despite these humble beginnings, Moon has never deviated from his original revelation and its world-embracing vision.

Rev. Sun Myung Moon is regarded as Lord of the Second Advent, but not in the apocalyptic sense of the second coming of Christ as believed by some Christians. Rather Moon, together with his wife, Hak Ja Han, has fulfilled the conditions within their family to restore the original sinlessness of Adam and Eve before the Fall. As the church grows and more and more people join this seed-family, the kingdom of God will grow and become manifest in the world. As people learn to live the Principle, hatred and wars will cease, and God will dwell with humanity as one family.

Beliefs and Doctrines

The Principle, as Unification doctrine is called, is based upon the Bible as interpreted through the revelations to Moon. Its doctrine of creation emphasizes God's work. Humans were created to be objects of God's love who should bring joy to God. But because of the Fall, God grieves, lacking a true object. Since God created us for the purpose of love, he gave us responsibility for our spiritual growth and will not dominate us by force. The love of God should be brought to reality in the family. But the doctrine of the Fall teaches that while Adam and Eve were immature, their love was corrupted through an adulterous relationship with the angel Lucifer, who became Satan. This corruption of human love into something selfish, domineering, and false is the source of all humanity's evils. To heal the broken family and restore true love, God sends the Messiah. But the Messiah can succeed only on a foundation to receive him—Jesus could not find that foundation and was killed. The Principle teaches how our biblical forefathers built their strong foundations; we are able to do likewise. We are required to serve: "Let us go forth, with the heart of a father, in the shoes of a servant, shedding tears for man, sweat for earth, and blood for heaven."

The central rite in the Unification Church is the holy wedding, called the Blessing. Through partaking of holy wine and being sprinkled by holy water, each couple is engrafted onto the new, pure lineage of God as restored by Adam and Eve. Moon ordinarily matches the couples and encourages interracial and international marriage to overcome racism and nationalistic hostility. Mass weddings symbolize the greater family of God.

Persecution

The church has endured much hostility: from Christians for its heresy, from leftists for its anti-Communism, from conservatives for its vision of one world and interracial unity, and from secularists who liken its intense religiosity to brainwashing. Moon has been jailed in Japan, in Korea, and, most recently, in the United States, which raised concerns in many quarters over violations of religious liberty.

Significant Terms

True parents. Adam and Eve, had they not fallen, would have become the natural channels of God's love to all their descendants. Because of the Fall, however, love in the family has been tainted by selfish, Satanic elements. God has been seeking to restore the true parents and reestablish true love at the center of the family. Mr. and Mrs. Moon have fulfilled the qualifications to be the true parents.

True love. Love that is unreservedly giving and unselfish. It flows vertically from God and should be manifest horizontally in acts of love, service, and self-sacrifice.

Divine Principle. The teachings based upon the Bible, which were revealed to Moon.

God's heart. The deepest part of God is the spontaneous impulse to love others. In perfection humans come to feel God's heart within themselves.

Restoration. To establish God's kingdom we must first correct and overcome the failures of the past.

The Blessing. The holy wedding, conducted by Mr. and Mrs. Moon, which sacramentally removes original sin.

Cain-Abel relationship. Any conflict between people at different spiritual levels should be resolved through love and service to restore brotherhood and prevent violence.

CAUSA. An anti-Communist education movement founded by Moon.

Bibliography

Moon, S. M. *God's Warning to the World.* New York: HSA-UWC, 1985.

Outline of the Principle, Level 4. New York: HSA-UWC, 1980.

Sontag, F. *Sun Myung Moon and the Unification Church.* New York: Abingdon, 1977.

Wilson, A., ed. *The Future of the World.* New York: International Cultural Foundation, 1987.

Prepared by Andrew Wilson, International Religious Foundation, Inc.

UNITARIAN UNIVERSALISTS

General Description

The Unitarian Universalist Association (UUA) was formed in 1960 when the American Unitarian Association and the Universalist Church of America merged. The association accounts for over 200,000 adults and children, generally centered in metropolitan and university areas. Unitarianism is found in countries around the world from Great Britain and Romania to India, Japan, and Australia.

Unitarian Universalism is a faith whose focus is this-worldly. It offers the strength and solace of community for those who find the answers to the mysteries and responsibilities of life beyond the answers of dogma and revelation.

Founding

The Unitarian branch had its theological origins in the Arian controversy in the third century of the Christian era. The issue erupted as the Reformation began and the Scriptures became more widely available. Some found that the Trinity was not scripturally based, and they were branded Unitarians to distinguish them from Trinitarians.

The Universalist branch had its theological origins in the contradiction, noted by Origin in the second century, implied by a good, just, and all-powerful God and the eternal damnation of any of his creatures. In the eighteenth century, the heresy of universal salvation again arose in this country and became institutionalized. It claimed 500,000 followers by the mid-nineteenth century.

Leaders

The founding of the United States and the establishment of our democracy were deeply influenced by the liberal beliefs of the Unitarian Thomas Jefferson, who expected to see everyone a Unitarian by the time he died. The two Adamses were also Unitarian. Their desire for religious freedom, not just from the tyranny of the state, but also between religions, was rooted in the religious tolerance first practiced by Unitarians in 1568 in Transylvania. Unitarians and Universalists took leading roles in areas from literature (Emer-

320 ·

son, Hawthorne, Thoreau, Longfellow, Lowell, Holmes, Alcott, Whittier, Fuller, Browning, Markham, Potter, Melville) to the woman's movement (Anthony, Barton, Nightingale, Livermore, Dix, Addams).

Beliefs and Doctrines

Unitarian Universalists believe in the never-ending search for truth, using all the means of verification at hand. They do not believe that it can be captured in a single statement (creed), book, or personage. They believe in the worth and dignity of every human being, no matter what his or her ideology is. Indeed, the quality of each person's theology is to be practiced, and the UUA provides the freedom to develop and establish one's own expression of faith. Justice is another cornerstone of Unitarian-Universalist religion. Living and acting justly is more important than any symbolic act.

Forms of Worship

The Unitarian Universalist approach to worship is clearly cerebral as well as emotional, where the arts of critical thinking and the real experiences of life are the fires through which the principle and celebration are tempered. Music, readings (from all the world's literature), singing, and silence are also regular parts of the service.

Organization

The twin concerns of independence and community are blended in the democratic structure of the UUA, as are the beliefs of the Unitarian-Universalist. An individual church is responsible to run its affairs, including calling and ordaining ministers, owning property, and determining policies. As members of the continental association (United States, Canada, Mexico), churches and lay-led congregations participate in the wider movement and share in supporting critical services and creating programs and materials. The UUA Service Committee, which provides aid and education around the world, is an independent but closely related organization.

Significant Terms

Freedom (religious liberty). Literally, "the state or quality of being free to choose one's religious faith, practice, and affiliation."

Justice. Literally, "the quality of being right and correct, fair or impartial"; also, the use of sound reason or validity in judgment.

Reason. To think logically or analytically about religious issues and to form sound judgments and conclusions (with support and justifications) on those issues.

Tolerance. Literally, "to recognize, respect, and allow the beliefs and practices of others without prejudice or bigotry."

Unitarianism. Literally, "belief in the personal unity of God, as opposed to the doctrine of the Trinity (three persons in one God)." However, modern

Unitarians stress more vigorously the three principles of freedom, religion, and tolerance in religious matters.

Universalism. The belief that, in the goodness and love of God, all humanity will find salvation in the grace of God (universally). That is, we will all be brought into harmonious relations with God in the end, thus negating hell and eternal damnation.

Bibliography

Cassara, Ernest. *Universalism in America: A Documentary History of a Liberal Faith.* Boston: Skinner House Press, 1984.

The Epic of Unitarianism: Original Writings from the History of Liberal Religion. Edited by David Parke. Boston: Skinner House Books, 1985. Reprint.

Marshall, George. *Challenge of a Liberal Faith.* Boston: Unitarian Association, 1987. Reprint.

Mendelsohn, Jack. *Being Liberal in an Illiberal Age: Why I Am a Unitarian Universalist.* Boston: Beacon Press, 1984.

Miller, Russell. *The Larger Hope.* 2 vols. Boston: Unitarian Universalist Association, 1979. The basic history of Universalism.

Robinson, David. *The Unitarians and the Universalists.* Westport, Conn.: Greenwood Press, 1985.

Wilbur, Earl M. *A History of Unitarians.* 2 vols. Boston: Beacon Press, 1977. The basic Unitarian history text.

Prepared by W. Bradford Greeley, parish minister, Main Line Unitarian Church, Devon, Pennsylvania.

UNITY

General Description
Unity is a nondenominational Christian movement dedicated to emphasizing the teachings of Jesus Christ as a practical, contemporary life-style. It is headquartered at Unity Village, Missouri, an incorporated municipality, located southeast of Kansas City, Missouri. It is represented by two organizations.

Unity School of Christianity is the parent organization, dating from 1889. It features three basic areas of ministry. The prayer ministry, conducted by Silent Unity, is a continuous ministry, twenty-four hours a day, every day of the year. Prayer requests are handled by telephone and by letter. The education ministry conducts a ministerial education program through which Unity ministers are prepared, a continuing education program for laypeople, and a retreat program. Unity Village Chapel is the on-campus congregational ministry. The publishing ministry produces two periodicals, including *Daily Word Unity* and *Wee Wisdom,* the oldest continually published children's magazine in the United States. Unity School also publishes books, pamphlets, and other materials with its message of practical Christianity.

Association of Unity Churches is the field services organization for field ministries. It was established in 1966 to replace the Field Department of Unity School. The association is responsible for licensing teachers and ordaining ministers. It is a corporate body made up of churches and centers that are individually incorporated and autonomously governed. The association also assists local congregations with ministerial placement and produces resource material for congregation use.

Unity's published statement of purpose reads: "Unity School of Christianity is dedicated to teaching and demonstrating the spiritual Truth as taught by Jesus Christ. Unity believes that God is absolute to everyone. All of the activities of Unity School are designed to help people understand their own spiritual nature and to express spirituality in their lives in practical ways. The outreaches and services of Unity School are evaluated on the basis of how well they meet the spiritual needs of people. Unity is committed to doing its part to bring forth God's divine plan for good and to spreading Truth throughout the world."

Founders

The cofounders of Unity are Charles and Myrtle Fillmore. Charles Fillmore was a real estate developer in Kansas City, and Myrtle was a former schoolteacher. Myrtle had a tuberculosis condition that she had been told was hereditary. She had been given a short time to live. After attending a lecture, she came away with the prayer statement, "I am a child of God and therefore do not inherit sickness." With this as her healing credo, she was healed. She then established a prayer group in her home with the view of sharing this positive approach to Christianity with others in need. This prayer group was the foundation for the present Silent Unity ministry. Charles became interested in the endeavor, and together they founded the Unity Tract Society, which grew into the Unity School of Christianity. Unity School was located in Kansas City for many years and moved to its present location in 1949.

Beliefs and Doctrines

Unity does not have doctrines per se. It does offer a teaching that is best described as a positive approach to the teachings of Jesus. It is Bible-based. Unity does not encourage beseeching prayers, but rather recommends affirmative prayers, or affirmations. It also has a prayer technique called denials. Denials deny permission of adverse conditions to enter into one's life. Unity's teachings have a general compatibility with those of most other Christian organizations. Unity believes that all people are created in the image and likeness of God and therefore have the potential of expressing their innate divinity. Unity followers are called truth students, and their spiritual mission is to touch their innate divinity and bring it forth into expression. We do not dwell on the person of God or his qualities. Unity followers are encouraged to accept those parts of Unity teachings that they can apply to their lives. No one is required to subscribe to set doctrines. Truth students are asked to seek the truth of life and live it to the best of their ability.

Forms of Worship

There is no set formula for worship in Unity. Differing orders of service may be found in congregations throughout the world. Most Sunday worship services include a sermon, meditation, and music. Unity does not use adapted forms of other Christian traditions. Communion is conducted, but without the use of sacramentals. Baptism is practiced, but without the use of water. The spiritual ideals behind the sacraments are emphasized. Wine, representing the blood of Christ, is the ideal of life. Bread, the body of Christ, is spiritual substance. Baptism is spiritual, involving inward cleansing through the use of prayer. Unity does not have a common book of rites and ceremonies.

Organization

The Unity School of Christianity is governed by a board of trustees that includes a chairman of the board, president, secretary/treasurer, and vice-presidents. Each vice-president oversees and is responsible for a major area of service.

The Association of Unity Churches is governed by a board of trustees made up of a president, first vice-president, second vice-president, and twenty-one trustees. An executive director, located at the headquarters of the Association at Unity Village, is the chief executive officer. All members of the board, with the exception of the executive director, are field ministers and are elected to specific terms by their fellow ministers.

Contributions and Influence

The major influence of the Unity movement is its ability to touch the lives of persons who are affiliated with other religious organizations, mainly within the Christian community. Because of the nondenominational aspect of its organization and teachings, many persons feel that they can embrace Unity without being disloyal to their religious affiliation.

Unity publications have been translated and printed in ten languages and are distributed in 153 countries. The message through the printed word has been far-reaching and has served as Unity's missionary church. Unity's Overseas Department offers assistance and service to congregations in twenty-five countries around the world.

Significant Terms

Consciousness. The awareness one has of the presence of God within; a high state of consciousness being desired.

Divine Mind. A description of the presence and activity of God indwelling all persons.

Indwelling Christ. A reference to the part of us that is created in the image and likeness of God.

Manifestation. The degree to which the innate divinity of the individual is expressed.

Metaphysics. A system of study referring to the spiritual meaning underlying the teachings of Jesus Christ and other biblical writers.

Omnipotence. The almighty power of God evidenced everywhere in creation.

Omnipresence. The inescapable presence of God.

Bibliography

(All items are published by Unity, Unity Village, Mo.)
Bach, Marcus. *The Unity Way.* 1982.
Cady, H. Emillie. *Lessons in Truth.* 1903.
Fillmore, Charles. *Christian Healer.* 1909.
Fillmore, Myrtle. *Myrtle Fillmore's Healing Letters.* 1936.
Freeman, James D. *The Story of Unity.* 1954.

Prepared by William L. Fischer, director of retreats, Unity School of Christianity.

◆ ◆ ◆
APPENDIX A.
OTHER GROUPS

The editor prepared the following articles about religious groups that did not submit self-descriptions. Information was obtained largely from *World Religions: Major Religious Systems in Comparative Outline Form*, by Charles L. Manske, Ph.D. (Irvine, Calif.: Institute for the World Religions, 1988), and also from *Religious Requirements and Practices: A Handbook for Chaplains* (Washington, D.C.: U.S. Government Printing Office, 1978), and *Religious and Spiritual Groups in Modern America*, by R. S. Ellwood and H. B. Partin (Englewood Cliffs, N.J.: Prentice Hall, 1988).

• • •
BUDDHIST HERITAGE

NICHIREN SHOSHU OF AMERICA

General Description

Nichiren Shoshu is a school of Buddhism based mostly on Gautama Buddha's teaching in the Lotus Sutras. It was formally established in Japan by Nichiren Daishonin (1222–82). Nichiren was not a conventional Buddhist. He was trained in the famed Mount Fuji monastery of the Tendai tradition, but he was far from traditional, asking more personal questions than the esoteric teachings of the monastery allowed. Actually, he turned to the sure answers of the Lotus Sutra with the final answer that simple devotion is a certain key to personal liberation as philosophy or meditation. While knowledge of the Lotus Sutra is important, Nichiren discovered that to chant the *Daimuku* in the presence of the *Gohonzon* (a religious scroll that contains the names of the principal Buddhas and bodhisatvas) is to harmonize oneself mystically with its contents.

The Buddhism of Nichiren became very popular, and his followers began to teach that Nichiren is the Buddha for his age and that the Lotus Sutra is the authoritative book. Also, Nichiren taught a monism of body and mind, individual and environment, Buddhism and the state, as well as a simple and united concept of almost everything. His head temple was established on the slopes of Mount Fuji, a most auspicious spot.

The contemporary form of Nichiren Shoshu is the work of T. Makiguchi, who founded a lay movement in 1930 called Soka Gakkau, or "value-creation study society." Makiguchi and his new organization soon merged with Nichiren Shoshu. In the years before World War II, Makiguchi fell out of favor with Japan's militaristic government, and he died in prison in 1944. His successor, J. Toda, proved to be a great leader, and in postwar Japan, Nichiren Shoshu Soka Gakki grew until it embraced 10 million members and created its own political party, the Komeito, now one of the strongest parties. Indeed, the movement is one of the most important social forces in Japan.

The movement finally made its way to the United States, first in the persons of Japanese "war brides," and formally in the person of Masayasu Sadanaga, who was sent to America in 1960 by Daisaku Ikeda, Toda's successor. Sadanaga (who later changed his name to George M. Williams) discovered about five hundred followers in the United States, most of them Japanese wives of American servicemen. These he organized and recruited as enthusiastic missionaries. Eighteen years later, a Chicago convention of the group revealed they had approximately 300,000 members and 150 chapters. By that time, many non-Japanese had been recruited. As an international movement, Nichiren Shoshu now claims to have 20 million members in 90 countries.

Beliefs and Doctrines

The basic belief is that each person can attain "enlightenment" as part of the universality of life within oneself. Happiness and peace are one's birthright but can be achieved only by harmonious relations with the universal law, made possible only by chanting *Nam-myoho-renge-kyo* and by reciting the Lotus Sutra *(Gongyo)*. In this, the individual is united with his or her environment as a mirror image of the eternal. Nichiren Shoshu insists that each person has the immediate potential for enlightenment in his or her lifetime by right beliefs and practices, more specifically, by the utilization of Gohonzon, since it represents "the entity of life itself."

Religious Requirements and Practices, which gives information on religious groups, quotes the article on Nichiren Shoshu in *NSA Handbook No. 2*, which notes that their "Buddhism is simply humanism—not the academic humanism of early Western scholars . . . but humanism which embodies a philosophy that leads to happiness, both individually and in the social context" *(The Buddhist Tradition* [Santa Monica, Calif.: World Tribune Press, 1972], p. 3). Furthermore, "While attaining his/her own enlightenment, or 'human revolution,' each member is achieving harmony with his/her surroundings and contributing to a better world" *(Religious Requirements and Practices,* p. IV.20).

Forms of Worship

The basic worship requirements of Nichiren Shoshu are very simple: morning and evening recitations of portions of the Lotus Sutra, along with repeated invocations of *Nam-myoho-renge-kyo,* done before an altar or worship center containing the Gohonzon. According to tradition the Gohonzon is enshrined in an altar that should contain offerings—candies, fruits, evergreens, water, and incense. Also, the worshiper uses prayer beads and a bell for the service. Group worship in Nichiren Shoshu centers, along with teaching and group discussion, is available both to encourage individual worship and to attract new members.

Nichiren Shoshu emphasizes a postworship phenomenon called *shakubuku,* which is the belief and practice of unity being put to work dynamically in the world. A slogan of Nichiren Shoshu says, "Other religions promise good things after you die, but only Nichiren Shoshu can deliver them now." Another urges, "Try chanting for something you want to see if it works." Under the later development of the religion by Soka Gakkai, *shakubuku* was sometimes disruptive, involving business boycotts and interruptions of the meetings of other religious and civil groups, a tactic that won Nichiren Shoshu both many critics and many converts.

The Gohonzon, which represents the enlightened life of the universe, is inscribed under the authority of the high priest and given to each member of the group as he or she is initiated.

Nichiren Shoshu requires a written application for membership, followed by an initiation ceremony (called *Gojukai,* or "conversion"), during which converts receive their own Gohonzon. Weddings, funerals, meetings, and other religious functions are officiated by senior members of the group.

Organization

The world leader of the international movement is Daisaku Ikeda, the president of Nichiren Shoshu. A well-developed organizational structure and modern communication link have been designed to keep President Ikeda in touch with all of the group's members and seekers. In the United States, Nichiren Shoshu of America (NSA) is headed and directed by George M. Williams, general director of NSA, with the help of the NSA Executive Planning Board.

NSA's basic unit is either a group meeting in a member's home or a center that usually is near a concentration of members in an area. The name for such a concentration is the district. A district usually meets several times a week under the supervision of experienced individuals mostly for communication and mutual support. Above the district are regional chapters, and above these, general chapters. In addition there are special divisions: men's, women's, youth/student, and one that promotes and oversees pilgrimages to Japan. Furthermore, there is a music division and one that oversees an active publication program that includes the newspaper *World Tribune.*

Organizational activism is a key characteristic of Nichiren Shoshu, as both its critics and its converts point out. There are also two temples in the United States; one in Honolulu and another in Etiwanda, California, which are used mostly for formal weddings and the consecrations of Gohonzons by the high priest or another NSA priest.

Contributions and Influence

The ethical teachings of Nichiren Shoshu are especially advanced and liberal. No ethical code, recommended laws, or prohibitions are prescribed for the members of NSA. The teachings prescribe simply the use of the member's common sense in the light of the social mores and codes of moral conduct that stem from the culture of one's country. Thus, NSA asks only that individual members develop their ethical codes as a result of their practices on the basis of both their personal character and the experiences growing out of their religious beliefs and worship.

NSA also teaches and practices an underlying philosophy that is compatible with many non-Buddhist religions. They believe that NSA is simply an extension of the more familiar Judeo-Christian heritage of the United States. It takes an altogether different attitude toward other Buddhist sects, which they believe are not helpful to modern seekers. Yet the fundamental principle remains: the granting of freedom of religion to all.

Significant Terms

Daimoku (Nam-myoho-renge-kyo). The main slogan, which is repeated as part of meditation.

Gohonzon. A sacred scroll that represents the enlightened life of the universe and that, when enshrined in the altar, becomes the center of worship.

Goshu. The collected writings of Nichiren Daishonin.

Lotus Sutra. A teaching of Gautama Buddha chosen by Nichiren to be the main sacred writing of NSA.

Bibliography

Anesaki, Masaharu. *Nichiren: The Buddhist Prophet*. Cambridge, Mass.: Harvard University Press, 1916.

Daishonin, Nichiren. *Gosho: Collected Writings of Nichiren*.

Ellwood, Robert S. *The Eagle and the Rising Sun: Americans and the New Religions of Japan*. Philadelphia: Westminster Press, 1974.

Gautama (Buddha). *Lotus Sutra*. Many editions are available.

Prebish, Charles. *American Buddhism*. North Scituate, Mass.: Duxbury Press, 1979.

Seikyo Times. A periodical.

Soka Gakkai News. A monthly.

World Tribune. An NSA newspaper.

HINDU HERITAGE

DIVINE LIGHT MISSION

General Description

The Divine Light Mission was founded in India by Shri Hans Ji Maharaj. The founder designated the youngest of his four sons, Sant Ji, his successor. Therefore, at the founder's death, Guru Maharaj became the next perfect master and head of the Divine Light Mission. The result was that this religious group born in India became a worldwide movement under the inspired leadership of Guru Maharaj Ji and is active in fifty-nine countries.

In 1970 Maharaj Ji announced that he would take his mission to the West, and in 1971 he came to the United States for a lecture tour in hopes of establishing the Divine Light Mission in America. Indeed, in 1971 the Divine Light Mission was formally established as a religious organization (incorporated in Colorado) and ultimately recognized as a church by the U.S. Internal Revenue Service in 1974. Shortly afterward, in 1977, some 50,000 members were reported with 23 churches or centers in the United States.

Beliefs and Doctrines

Specific information on the content of the mission's beliefs are not available, but the literature insists that the reason for the existence of this religious group is simply to present and encourage the appropriation of the teachings of Guru Maharaj Ji. Disciples believe that Guru Maharaj Ji revealed knowledge that they suggest cannot be adequately described in words but that can be experienced through satsang (a discourse of believers), meditation, and service, the fundamental practices of the mission's worship.

The authoritative teachings of Guru Maharaj Ji are given in satsang programs in the form of readings. Such materials are circulated and read throughout the organization in its many branches or centers. Films and tapes are also available. Disciples believe that such active participation in satsang meditation and service is a living program that will dispel inner conflict and give the individual inner peace and light.

The Divine Light Mission teaches some dietary laws and restrictions. Members are encouraged to be vegetarians, although they are given individual choice on this restriction. However, ministers or members in the Monastic Order of the church must adhere to vegetarian dietary laws, refraining from the eating of meat, fish, or eggs.

Forms of Worship

The spiritual teachings of Guru Maharaj Ji translate readily into the worship activities of the Divine Light Mission. Indeed, the spiritual discourse of services (satsang, meditation, and service) are the basic activities of the church. Ministers are the only members authorized to teach meditation, although "Community Coordinators" (formally appointed by the mission) may conduct satsang programs nightly. In case there is no church or formal community, two or more members may hold nightly courses, since this worship activity is required of every member, as is daily meditation.

Each of the branches maintains a center or a private, quiet room for this purpose, although services may be held in a member's home. One unique feature of Divine Light Mission's worship is the wearing by some meditators of a blanket to cover them and conceal their special meditation techniques. Each member is also asked to do "service"—performing deeds for others and the special service of giving 10 percent to one's church.

Three religious holidays are observed by the Divine Light Mission, and each one lasts for one full week. Attendance is required for active members, as these holidays are said to be of great assistance to an individual's spiritual growth. The holidays fall in March (Holi Festival), in July (Guru's Paja), and in November (Hans Jayanti). Other festivals and holidays may be declared by Guru Maharaj Ji, which members are also expected to attend. Members may also participate in the religious holidays and programs of their families' faith.

Organization

The spiritual master and head of the Divine Light Mission is Guru Maharaj Ji—both in the international movement and in the U.S. Mission, which is managed by a board of directors with headquarters in Colorado. The board is responsible for the supervision of the more than twenty-three branches in the United States.

The ministers of Divine Light Mission (also called Maharmes, or initiators) are deputy spiritual heads of the mission's branches or communities throughout the world. Interestingly enough, many ministers are missionaries who travel from branch to branch mainly to check on the faithfulness of churches to the spiritual teachings of Guru Maharaj Ji. They also conduct the initiation of new disciples into the branches and more specifically into the experience of meditation as the means of self-realization and peace.

Contributions and Influence

One positive influence of the Divine Light Mission is its benign relation with other religions. Because the mission insists that the teachings of Guru Maharaj Ji involve members in an experience and do not require a creed or specific belief, there is therefore no conflict between the Divine Light Mission and other faiths.

Another positive contribution is the mild recruitment program of the mission. While the Divine Light Mission does hold and advertise introductory lectures and programs, most members are brought to the mission by friends or family members who invite them to investigate the mission's programs. No doubt this is a good reason why this religious group has survived the decline seen in the influence of other groups.

Significant Terms

Baragon. A T-shaped device used by a meditator to aid in meditation.

Mahatman. An Indian term meaning "greater soul," which may be applied to outstanding spiritual leaders.

Satsang. A basic (and required) Divine Light Mission service, or meeting, in which spiritual discourses are presented.

Bibliography

(No formal bibliography seems to be available. However, two periodicals are published: *Divine Times* and *Edam Vital,* which are available from the International Headquarters [in Colorado] or from the North American Headquarters [in Miami Beach, Fla.]. Films, tapes, and pamphlets are also available.)

SELF-REALIZATION FELLOWSHIP

General Description

The Self-Realization Fellowship (SRF) was founded by Paramahansa Yogananda, who, following a visit and an address to the International Congress of Religious Liberals sponsored by the Unitarian Church, decided to remain in the United States to continue to teach and complete his spiritual mission. A charismatic Yogi, not at all withdrawn and conservative, and content to remain in this country, Yogananda had an immediate impact on his American audiences. His warm personality and his understanding of American publicity methods, plus his use of American idioms and attitudes, convinced listeners that he had principles and techniques for enabling people to do something about his teachings.

Yogananda wrote an autobiography that lucidly tells his most interesting story. It is fascinating and well worth reading. From his name, we know his title: Paramahansa means "master Yogi," and Yogananda lived up to the title. He lectured widely, wrote most extensively (seven books), and founded the Self-Realization Fellowship. The fellowship was a great success because of Yogananda's major emphases in his teaching of Yoga: first, a syncretism of Hinduism and Christianity, based on their common features; second, a teaching and a practice that accommodated Hinduism with American culture.

One reason for his success is said to be his easy use of the vocabulary of Western science interspersed with metaphors. It is said that he made the age-old Yoga philosophy appear to be reinforced by the empirical data of science without reference to Scripture or religious authority. It appears that Yogananda was especially successful in stimulating trust in his hearers. Indeed, he also noted a similar relation of empirical data to all religions and their teachings, presumably because all religions point to the truth and goals of Yoga. He also identified Jesus and other spiritual leaders as Yoga masters.

Beliefs and Doctrines

The basic concept of the SRF is that self-realization and God-realization yield spiritual bliss and human happiness. Furthermore, the Hindu notion of *samadhi* is the state of perfect union of the human soul with the Infinite Spirit.

Yogananda taught the basic philosophy of the Yoga Sutras and the specific teachings of *kriya yoga*. The best description of the combination of belief and practice is that the practice of withdrawal enables the movement of a person's life-energy from external material concerns to the inner spiritual centers of the soul. Thus, meditating on the cosmic syllable "aum," along with the Yoga exercises, will open the spiritual centers, which will enable one to attain bliss.

Furthermore, the Self-Realization Fellowship teaches the famous "Eight Steps" of Raja Yoga, which are at the same time both beliefs and ethical prescriptions. They are:

1. *yama,* or negative rules for moral conduct;
2. *niyama,* or positive rules for living;
3. *asanas,* or postures for life;
4. *pranayama,* or control of life-energy;
5. *pratyahara,* or sense-withdrawal;
6. *dharana,* or concentration;
7. *dyhana,* or meditation;
8. *samadhi,* or union;
9. cosmic consciousness.

Some scholars have pointed out that the Ten Commandments are in a sense similar to these Eight Steps in that they articulate moral laws (*yama*) necessary for spiritual growth.

Forms of Worship

The Sunday (and other) worship or lecture of the Self-Realization Fellowship is held, as in other religious groups, in a chapel or meeting room where worshipers may meditate at other times during the week. Generally, there are evidences in the room or chapel of the fact that what goes on is experienced in all religions; for instance, a worship center symbol of the Christian cross and the Eastern lotus as well as pictures of the Yogananda and Jesus (and others). SRF meetings begin with chants such as, "Filling the mind with God," given by a knowledgeable minister, usually an American wearing an orchid robe.

SRF worshipers greet each other and visitors with the Indian *namste* (a bow with both palms pressed together), rather than with a handshake. The invocation addresses God as Father, Mother, and Friend and often mentions the saints of all religions as well as "our guru," Yogananda (often referred to as Master). The address also is a blend of religious scriptures—Old Testament, New Testament, the Bhagavad Gita, and the writings of Yogananda. As indicated above, the syncretism is deliberate and compatible with the basic premises of SRF. Furthermore, there is a populist atmosphere that fits the spirit of Yogananda, who, like Jesus, was concerned with bringing his "good news" to the common people.

Personal worship is mostly meditation that often includes a recitation and the dedication of the individual to the eightfold path of Samadhi.

Organization

The SRF consists of laity and renunciants—those who have completed the introductory series of lessons and have begun the practice of Kriya Yoga (which requires meditation for two or more hours a day and the living of a monastic life). The head of the fellowship at present is a nun, Daya Mata, a Sanskrit name meaning "Mother of Compassion." She and her name were chosen by Paramahansa himself. There is also a governing board, presided over by the head of the fellowship. It consists of eight senior members.

The fellowship has branches all over the world. The Indian Yogoda Satsang is large in both size and influence. There are forty-four centers in the United States, nine of them in California. In West Los Angeles, the SRF maintains a Lake Shrine and the impressive Mahatma Ghandi Memorial. Yogananda is said to have initiated Ghandi into Kriya Yoga and was one who knew Ghandi well and admired him greatly. The SRF also has a retreat center in Encinitas, California.

Contributions and Influence

As the second oldest Hindu group in the United States, the SRF's well-established and widely accepted doctrine and practice of accommodating Hinduism with both American culture and Christianity demonstrates the feasibility of syncretism in religious groups, especially those with "a core of common features." Furthermore, the masterful teaching and leadership of Yogananda demonstrates that even the most ancient truths (in this case, Yoga philosophy) can be interpreted and presented in the form and language of contemporary reality and idioms. This skillful Yoga master shows that Yoga philosophy and methods can be reconciled with the empirical and experimental modes of Western science and the experimental method.

Significant Terms

Amruta. The blissful reward of self-realization, "the nectar of immortality."

Aum. A "cosmic" syllable used in meditation and to achieve self-realization.

Church of All Religions. One of the names used to describe the SRF.

Kriya Yoga. The Yoga techniques for moving one's life-energy from other concerns to one's spiritual centers.

Pranayama. One of the eight steps of Raja Yoga, dealing with the control of life-energy.

Samadhi. The state of perfect unity of the individual with the Infinite Spirit (God).

Bibliography

(Except as noted, all items are published by Self-Realization Fellowship, Los Angeles.)
Self-Realization Fellowship. Golden Anniversary Books. 1970.
Wendall, Thomas. *Hinduism Invades America*. Boston: Beacon Press, 1950.
Yogananda, Paramahansa. *Autobiography of a Yogi*. 1968.
——. *The Science of Religion*. N.d.

TRANSCENDENTAL MEDITATION

World Plan Executive Council

General Description

The Maharishi Mahesh Yogi's Transcendental Meditation (TM) movement was born with the arrival in the United States of this now-famous Yogi. In India, he had studied physics at the Allahabad University and then, after returning to religion, studied Yoga, under the master Swami Brahmananda Saraswati. It is reported that the swami had counseled his precocious student-disciple to go to the United States.

On his arrival, Maharishi Mahesh Yogi sought and won publicity, on which he capitalized by secular personal appearances. Crowds filled every place he appeared. And he pleased them, with his long, flowing gray hair and beard, sitting on a tiger-skin pallet, twirling roses in his hands and looking like an other-worldly ambassador inspiring thoughts of temple incense and ashrams. He also appeared on numerous TV talk shows and was subject of numerous articles, all arranged by public relations specialists he hired. All of this exposure encouraged the acquaintance and discipleship of TV, movie, and sports personalities (e.g., Mia Farrow, the Beatles, and Joe Namath). TM became the "in" thing.

A major step was taken when the Transcendental Meditation movement obtained the campus of the former Parsons College in Fairfield, Iowa, and established Maharishi International University on the site. It was an immediate success, even offering a Ph.D. program in "Neuro-Science of Human Consciousness." The daily program included an assembly devoted to the two "Golden Domes of Pure Knowledge" aimed at inspiring the practice of TM.

The movement however, has experienced several levels of popularity. Following its early heyday, there was a decline after the Beatles were disenchanted and pictures appeared showing the master's luxurious life-style. Also, he had arranged a tour with the famous rock band, which turned out to be ill-advised and contributed to a decline of popular enthusiasm.

The 1970s, however, witnessed a resurgence of TM's popularity, due in part to a change in the movement's presentation. It was presented less as "pop" spirituality and more as a scientific method of achieving creativity and peace of mind—not to the youth but to the "yuppies" and professionals. Unfortunately, Maharishi precipitated a brief decline when he announced that TM would teach its meditators levitation. Presently, the movement has two branches, the Student International Meditation Society and the adult Spiritual Regeneration Movement. It appears that the former is the more vigorous.

Beliefs and Doctrines

Transcendental Meditation offers teachings on two levels: the theoretical, based on its basic concept of the science of creative intelligence (its international title); and the practical, based on the practice of TM for contacting the limitless source of energy within. The U.S. Army *Handbook for Chaplains* notes that TM is "not a religion, philosophy, or belief system" per se, but an "automatic procedure for allowing the mind gradually to settle down until the least excited state of mind is reached . . . a state of inner wakefulness, or pure consciousness aware of its unbounded nature. It is wholeness, beyond the division of subject and object—transcendental consciousness. It is a state of perfect order, the matrix from which all the laws of nature emerge, the source of creative intelligence" (*Religious Requirements and Practices: A Handbook for Chaplains* [Washington, D.C.: Department of the Army, 1978], p. II-20-4).

In an interview with *Time* magazine in February 1968, the Maharishi is quoted as saying, "The purpose of human life is to realize the godliness in oneself. . . . God is to be found in every creature and every object." Also he asserted that "the Wisdom of Vedanta is a philosophy rather than a creed" (ibid., p. 53).

The basic teaching of TM is that it is possible to enjoy life by getting to the ground of joy through meditation, which is a natural method, rather than Yoga, or an unnatural meditation like the orthodox Zen method, which reverses the normal human function. TM uses the natural human desire for joy and bliss similar to Brahman in Vedanta belief. (Some say that Maharishi's method is simply a popularized version of Vedanta.) For TM, meditation is not about anything or through any unnatural mood; it is the natural seeking of one's own center and thus one's latent joy. The movement claims both psychological and physiological evidence for the efficiency of their meditation, citing the fact that deep rest and reduced metabolism and oxygen consumption occur while the mind is completely active. Indeed, they claim one is not only more refreshed and vital but also creative and content (happy).

There is a standard seven-step program both for learning TM beliefs and for achieving the age of enlightenment. The seven goals are:

1. to develop the full potential of the individual;
2. to improve personal and social achievements;
3. to realize the highest ideal of education;
4. to eliminate the age-old problem of crime and behavior that brings unhappiness to the family of man;
5. to maximize the intelligent use of the environment;
6. to bring fulfillment to the economic aspirations of individuals and society; and
7. to achieve the spiritual goals of mankind in this generation.

Since the TM program requires no specific creed, faith commitment, or belief and no changes in affiliation or personal preferences, it is compatible with all religions and faiths. Furthermore, the World Plan Executive Council does not make any formal effort to recruit meditators. People join mostly through the recommendations of meditating family and friends. However, most centers do advertise their introductory lectures through the media.

There is some controversy within the movement over the decision of the World Plan Executive Council's pronouncement that TM is not a religion and the acceptance by the council of grants to teach TM in schools and the armed forces. Some members have challenged that decision, pointing to the religious nature of the movement's emphasis on Japa Yoga and on theology in the title "Science of Creative Intelligence" and Hindu prayers in the initiation ceremony. They also claim that the council is a religious body. But its refusal to provide a self-description of TM for this volume is one proof that the council remains unmoved by the dissenters.

Forms of Worship

Worship, per se, for Transcendental Meditation is contained in meditation as well as in instruction as qualified teachers conduct courses in both the beliefs and techniques of TM. However, since meditation is done alone, no group sessions are needed or provided. Individual worship, or meditation, lasts from fifteen to twenty minutes, twice a day. Special days of religious significance are not celebrated in TM, although awards are presented at quarterly celebrations. And the initiation of disciples contains some elements of what the Western religions call worship; for instance, the initiator gives the initiated his mantra and instructs him in how to use it. The initiate practices meditation and meets daily with a small group to discuss his progress. Indeed, the initiation is called the "seven steps to bliss," perfect happiness, and the ultimate in "attractiveness."

Organization

The Transcendental Meditation movement in the United States is governed by the World Plan Executive Council, which oversees 7,000 instructors and about 400 TM centers. The International Association for the Advancement of the Science of Creative Intelligence oversees the TM's movements and activities worldwide. The association acts through a board of directors, but it is often guided by the founder, the Maharishi. In the United States, TM offers instruction in its beliefs and techniques. In the United States alone, almost a million people have taken the basic TM course. Another interesting feature of TM is that the movement is staffed primarily by volunteers who receive neither expense money nor any stipend.

Contributions and Influence

One important contribution of TM lies in its acceptance of all other religions and faiths, mainly because it is a technique of probing the depths of an individual and moving one to find one's full potential of happiness.

Another contribution is the success of the TM program in the field of motivating people in the worlds of business, education, and the armed forces to function and achieve up to their full potential. Furthermore, the technique has been used to increase physiological, psychological, and even sociological benefits to individuals and their society. There is even talk of an "ideal society" as TM enlightens and empowers both the individual and the community to live a more harmonious life.

Significant Terms

Mantra. A sound that the meditator says "internally" to help him or her begin and complete a good meditation.

Meditation. A vehicle that enables the meditator to transcend external mental stimuli and focus on his or her center, the true and natural bliss, or joy.

Transcendental. From the Latin, meaning "climb over," and used to describe going beyond sense experience to find reality and knowledge in human thought and mind.

Bibliography

Bainbridge, William S., and Daniel H. Jackson. "The Rise and Decline of Transcendental Meditation." In *The Social Impact of New Religious Movements*, ed. Bryan Wilson. New York: Rose of Sharon Press, 1981.

Bloomfield, Harold, et al. *TM: Discovering Inner Energy and Overcoming Stress.* New York: Delacorte Press, 1975.

Campbell, Anthony. *Seven States of Consciousness: Vision of Possibilities Suggested by the Teaching of Maharishi Mahesh Yogi.* New York: Harper & Row, Torch Books, 1973.

Denniston, Denise, and Peter McWilliams. *The TM Book.* Allen Park, Mich.: Three Rivers Press, 1975.

Forem, Jack. *Transcendental Meditation.* New York: E. P. Dutton, 1973.

Invitation to Create an Ideal Society. Los Angeles: World Plan Executive Council, n.d.

Jackson, M. B. *Transcendental Meditation.* Los Angeles: Spiritual Regeneration Movement Foundation, 1967.

The Social Impact of New Religious Movements. New York: Rose of Sharon Press, 1981.

♦ ♦ ♦

ISLAMIC HERITAGE

AMERICAN MUSLIM MOVEMENT
World Community of Al-Islam in the West

General Description

The World Community of Al-Islam in the West had its beginning in the nationalist movements in the early 1930s—specifically the Moorish Science Temple and the Marcus Garvey movement, both of which laid the foundation for the Black Muslim movement. However, the movement gained great impetus through the efforts of W. D. Farad Mohammed, who began teaching the Qur'an in the black ghetto of Detroit. He also taught the "true" history and religion of the blacks along with practical references to nutrition, health, and politics. His teaching also contained negative references to the white race.

Farad Mohammed disappeared in 1934 and was succeeded by a trusted student and disciple, Elijah Poole, who later took the name of the founder, Elijah Muhammed. At that time, another follower of the founder, Abdul Muhammed, separated himself from the movement and established another temple in Detroit. The result was fierce competition that led Elijah Muhammed to establish a temple in Chicago, where he became immensely popular and emerged as the undisputed leader of the movement and the Nation of Islam (in America). He defined black nationalism as Islamic and urged separation from white people, whom he described as blue-eyed devils.

The conversion of Malcolm X gave the movement a real boost, and Malcolm emerged quickly as a dynamic and appealing spokesperson for Elijah Muhammed. The early 1960s proved to be productive for the movement, and the membership grew dramatically, prompted by the recruitment of sports and entertainment personalities such as Cassius Clay, who took the Muslim name Muhammed Ali. Indeed, in 1965, at Malcolm X's death, the movement listed seventy temples in the United States. At the death of the Honorable Elijah Muhammed, his son Wallace Muhammed succeeded him. Wallace Muhammed made drastic changes in the movement, with the goal of bringing it closer to orthodox Islam than his father had positioned it. Whites were no longer to be condemned but encouraged to join the movement, and Christianity was no longer to be attacked in a radical way. Yet the membership continued to grow, as did the number of temples.

Beliefs and Doctrines

Elijah Muhammed's Islam was significantly different from orthodox Islam, for his version of Islam was to be relevant to the needs of American blacks as he understood them. Allah was claimed to be the Supreme Black Man. However, he did hold fast to many important elements of Islam, namely, self-identification as Muslims, the reading of the Qur'an, Muslim prayers, and dietary restrictions.

American Muslims are taught to accept without reservation the creed of Islam, including the fervent belief in Allah as the true and supreme God, and in Muhammed as Allah's holy prophet and servant. Furthermore, the movement teaches the Muslim principle of complete submission and obedience to Allah and absolute respect for Muhammed. Also, it teaches that the divine message of Allah is disclosed in the Qur'an and that all the great prophets of history are authentic and God's messengers, including Moses, Abraham, Jesus, Buddha, Muhammed, and so forth. Finally, the basic duties of Muslim worship are to be performed: (1) saying the five daily prayers, (2) fasting during the month of Ramadan, (3) giving alms to the poor, and (4) making a pilgrimage to Mecca.

The movement stresses the brotherhood of all men. American Muslims are also taught specific ethical practices, namely, cleanliness, good conduct, chastity, clarity, honesty, courtesy, proper appearance, sobriety, brotherhood, equality, justice, and love.

Forms of Worship

Muslims worship as a group or individually (if prevented from being with a group) by five daily prayers (particularly at noon on Fridays). Any Muslim may lead such services, but they are usually conducted by ministers of the various temples, or mosques. The chief imam (chief ministers, or spiritual leaders) may also conduct services. There is no priesthood or ordination in Islam. Muslim ministers are teachers (imams) who exemplify great knowledge and can handle religious responsibilities, such as preach from the Qur'an, lead in prayers, render counsel, and officiate at weddings and conversions. They are approved by the body of the movement.

Prerequisites for worship in Islam are the cleansing of the body (face, mouth, nostrils, arms, feet, and so on) and the person's clothing as well as the place of worship. Members are to have a prayer mat or rug for prayers on Friday and Sunday. Also, Muslims are required to abstain from food between dawn and dusk in preparation for worship. Prohibited are pork and its derivatives as well as alcoholic beverages and drugs.

Muslim holidays are the birthday of Muhammed (born in Mecca in 570), every Friday (noon prayers), and the thirty days of Ramadan, when serious fasting is continuous from dawn to dusk, at the end of which a prayer celebration takes place with the giving of money to the poor. No less important is the *hajj,* or the pilgrimage of each Muslim to Mecca, at least once in his or her lifetime.

Muslim funeral practices are unique. After death, the body is washed and wrapped in a cotton sheet for burial. Members pray for the soul of the deceased member. Cremation is not permitted, since Muslims believe that the body should return to earth in its natural state.

Organization

Wallace D. Muhammed (he later changed his given name to Warith, its Arabic equivalent) is the chief imam and leader of the Community of the American Muslim Mission (a name he chose to match his more orthodox Islamic emphasis). Warith Muhammed is assisted by a group of Muslim ministers who are regarded as authorities on theological and practical issues and who assist the chief minister as spokesperson. Generally, these assistants are leaders of the sixty-five or seventy temples in the United States. The international branch of the community has an Imam Consultation Board that functions as a similar authority for the World Community, which is under the directorship of Sheikh James Abdul Aziz Shabazz.

A dissident group was organized by Minister Louis Farrakhan, which has attained much publicity and popularity because of the charisma of Minister Farrakhan and his open admiration for the Honorable Elijah Muhammed and his continuity with the Islamic ideology of the great imam. It is his group that is referred to as the Black Muslims.

Contributions and Influence

The American Muslim Mission teaches that there is authenticity in all religious groups and urges that all religious leaders unite to promote pro-human goals and survival. For this reason and also because all religious prophets are respected, tolerance of other religious groups is encouraged.

However, the World Community's relationship with other Muslim groups has not been as congenial. In spite of Warith Muhammed's conciliatory trip to the Middle East and his general achievement of good will and acceptance, the movement still is at odds with Hanafi Muslims in the United States. The World Community (and all Black Muslims) maintains strict security at all levels.

Significant Terms.

Imam. The Islamic name of a spiritual leader or chief minister of Muslim groups.

Hadith. The traditions, or Islamic elaborations on the Qur'an.

Hajj. A holy pilgrimage to Mecca, required of all Muslims at least once.

Masjid. Arabic for "mosque," or Islamic "temple."

Shirah. The Islamic law based on the Qur'an.

Tribe of Shabazz. The lost—and later found—black tribe of Islam (not the "slave religion" of white Christians).

Bibliography

Abilla, Walter D. *The Black Muslims in America.* Kampala: East African Literature Bureau, 1977.

Baldwin, James. *The Fire Next Time.* New York: Dial Press, 1963.

Bilalian News. The World Community's newspaper.

Lincoln, C. Eric. *The Black Muslims in America.* Boston: Beacon Press, 1973.

Malcolm X, with the assistance of Alex Haley. *The Autobiography of Malcolm X.* New York: Grove Press, 1964.

Pinkney, Alphonzo. *Red, Black, and Green: Black Nationalism in the U.S.* New York: Cambridge University Press, 1976.

Poole, Elijah. *Our Saviour Has Arrived.* Chicago: Muhammed's Temple of Islam, 1972.

♦ ♦ ♦

JAPANESE HERITAGE

CHURCH OF PERFECT LIBERTY

General Description

The Church of Perfect Liberty was born in Japan in 1912 as Tokumitsu Kyo, the brainchild of Tokumitsu Kanada, a Shinto priest and ascetic. As it happened, Miki Tokuhara, a former Zen Buddhist priest, was a disciple of Kanada, who at the master's death, "worshiped" a shrub planted at Kanada's death as Miki had been instructed by his master. In 1924 Miki received the revelation promised by Kanada and founded Hitono Michi, "the Way of Man." This new religious group emphasizing the reality and meaning of both art and nature was quite successful in Japan. Unfortunately, the government of Japan prohibited Hitono Michi, and Miki was put in prison, where he died in 1938.

Miki's son, Tokuchika, took up the leadership of the Way of Man and led its restoration until the Supreme Court of Japan upheld the prohibition in 1943 and Hitono Michi was disbanded. In 1946, however, Tokuchika and others from Hitono Michi established the Church of Perfect Liberty. Finally, in 1957 missionaries from the church in Japan began working in the United States, and lay missionaries were soon imported after the arrival of the first minister of the church in 1960. Today, the church reports 50,000 families as adherents in the United States.

Beliefs and Doctrines

We list here the twenty-one basic teachings of the Church of Perfect Liberty (PL).

1. Life is art.
2. Man's life is a succession of self-expressions.
3. Man is a manifestation of God.
4. Man suffers if he fails to express himself.
5. Man loses his true self when swayed by feelings and emotions.
6. Man's true self is revealed when his ego is effaced.
7. All things exist in mutual relationship to one another.
8. Live radiantly as the sun.
9. All men are equal.

10. Strive for creating mutual happiness.
11. Have true faith in God.
12. There is a way (function) peculiar to every "name" (existence).
13. There is a way for men, and there is another way for women.
14. All is for world peace.
15. All life is a mirror [a concept from Shinto].
16. All things progress and develop.
17. Comprehend what is most essential.
18. At every moment man stands at the crossroads of good and evil.
19. Act when your intuition dictates.
20. Live in perfection of mind and matter.
21. Live in perfect liberty.

The Perfect Liberty Declaration is a statement of PL faith.

> Life is Art. Man realizes life's true beauty, charm, and meaning only when he lives an artistic life. Then, what is an artistic life? It is to freely express one's true individuality in his particular field of work. However, one's true individuality cannot be expressed to the best degree unless one is free of egotistic interest and selfish gains. One must live in a state of objectivity expressing one's individuality in the interest and welfare of all mankind. We, members of PL, hereby declare to live an artistic life, detaching ourselves from egocentricity and expressing our individuality in complete freedom and spontaneousness. We, members of PL, also declare that it is our duty to propagate and implant the teachings of PL to the world, and we shall contribute to the world community of men.

The PL creed affirms: "I live for the joy of an artistic life. I pray for happiness of others. I live with true effort and sincerity. I maintain the highest dignity and honor. I strive for the great peace of the world."

The world leader of PL, currently Tokuchika Miki, is the *Oshigoya* (father of the teachings, or patriarch) and as such is the sole authority for rules and teachings. PL holds that God in fact invests the *Oshigoya* with such authority. His writings are considered by the faithful as divine.

Forms of Worship

Private and group worship are both encouraged. Indeed, morning and evening services in members' home are required, and an individual may conduct an abbreviated version of the service alone (with family or other members also) if he has a portable or family shrine. Also important to PL worship are a prayer book *(Kyoten)*, a book of divine instruction *(Mioshie)*, and an envelope for offerings *(Hosho)*.

Allied to worship are other requirements, such as visitation to churches, attendance at meetings, classes, and seminars, devotional service (to mankind), officiating at divine services, conducting special prayers, and making special pilgrimages and special offerings for the welfare of man.

Special religious holidays are celebrated. For instance, the twenty-first day of each month is a thanksgiving day, celebrated with ceremonies in each PL church. Four annual festivals are also celebrated: Founder's Day, August 1; New Year's Day, January 1; Oshigoya's Birthday, April 8; and PL Establishment Day, September 29.

Organization

As noted above, *Oshigoya*, the patriarch, is the sole and supreme head of PL. Ministers of the church may be selected and designated as *Yuso*, or disciples, and after achieving enlightenment and the PL state of mind are granted the title of *Oya*. The succession of the patriarch is assured by tradition. The successor is elected from among the *Yuso*s and elevated and trained for that high office.

Church of Perfect Liberty ministers function in the usual manner. They administrate churches, educate the church's members and nonmembers, young and old, convey the teachings of PL, and perform divine rites, services, and ceremonies with the authority of the patriarch, who invests them in the office and to whom they are responsible.

Contributions and Influence

Members of the Church of Perfect Liberty have been exemplary citizens. Indeed, PL teachings explicitly require members to abide by and uphold the laws of the land and to live in strict accordance with their teaching. Furthermore, the church encourages its members to be of service wherever and whenever they are needed. PL is vigorously pacifistic, following the highly regarded teaching that they should work and strive to bring about world peace.

While members are encouraged by PL teachings to share their beliefs and experience with others and also to invite neighbors and friends to attend church with them, PL supports any endeavor that will bring about religious unity and social harmony as well as a ministry to the suffering and needy of the community. In fact, many PL members belong to other churches and practice the teachings of other religions.

Significant Terms

Hitono Michi. Japanese for "the Way of Man," the predecessor to the Church of Perfect Liberty.

Hosho. The envelope used for offerings in PL worship services.

Kyodan. Japanese name for the church.

Kyoten. The prayer book used in PL worship.

Mioshie. Japanese for "the Book of Divine Instructions."

Oshigoya. The title of the patriarch of the Church of Perfect Liberty.

Oya. The title of a minister who has been enlightened and has achieved the PL state of mind.

Yuso. The title of an ordained disciple of the Church of Perfect Liberty who is invested as minister of a church.

Bibliography

(Readers wishing bibliographic material should write to Rev. Tashio Kazama, Church of Perfect Liberty, 700 S. Adams St., Glendale, Calif. 91205.)

⬧ ⬧ ⬧
OCCULT HERITAGE
ROSICRUCIANISM

General Description

The first mention of Rosicrucianism came in 1614 with the appearance in Cassel, Germany, of a pamphlet known as *Fama*, or *The Fame of the Fraternity of the Meritorious Order of the Rosy Cross Addressed to the Learned in General and the Governors of Europe*. The pamphlet called for men of learning to unite to bring about a reformation of science like that of religion, and for them to turn to a hidden brotherhood—the Rosicrucians. The *Fama* tells the story of a German knight, Christian Rosencrentz, who, on his travels to the Near East and North Africa, had been instructed by many wise men in the occult sciences, including the invocation of spirits and the making of the elixir of life.

On his return to Europe, Rosencrentz organized a secret society that continued to exist in secret after the founder's death in 1484. The *Fama* also tells the story of the discovery of Rosencrentz's burial place and the more amazing discovery that his body was uncorrupted and all in the tomb was bathed with a strange light. This discovery prompted the release of the *Fama*, which was followed a year later by another pamphlet, *Confession of the Rosicrucian Fraternity*, which presented a call to persons publishing tracts and other material to identify themselves to the order. The results were not clearly reported. Indeed, the credibility of the two documents has been questioned.

Contemporary Rosicrucians seem not to be too concerned by the historical discrepancies and claim their group is part of a universal secret order that includes Ikhnaton, Solomon, Jesus, Plato, Philo, Plotinus, the Essenes, the early Christians, the Kabbalists, and even Benjamin Franklin. The evidence for such a claim is not given. Interestingly enough, the symbols of the rose and the cross appear on the coat of arms of Martin Luther. The very existence of Christian Rosencrentz has been questioned by scholars, yet the existence of an alchemic society is highly possible, since many alchemists practiced at that time.

The appeal of Rosicrucianism was probably its archetypal accommodation of naturalism and Christianity. The next appearance of Rosicrucianism was in England, where Robert Fudd (1626–37), John Heydon (1629–?), and Thomas Vaughan (1626–66) embraced it and where Rosicrucianism seemed to find a place on the occult fringe of Platonism that encouraged writings on astrology, numerology, and mystic arts.

Rosicrucianism came to the United States in 1907 in the person of Max Heindel, who first was a member-leader in Theosophy. However, he claimed that in 1907, when he was in Europe, he had a vision of an "elder brother"— of the occult Rosicrucian Order, which offered Heindel help in his quest. Heindel was taken to a temple of the "Rosy Cross" where he was fully instructed by the elder brothers. It is this experience that Rosicrucians claim as the group's founding. Heindel told his story in a book, *Rosicrucian Cosmo—Conception*. By the time of his book's publication, Heindel had established several fellowship centers and a temple at Mount Ecclesia, California. Another Rosicrucian group was also organized by H. Spencer Lewis, the Ancient and Mystical Order Rosae Crucis (AMORC). The latter group is in reality the best known and the largest, mainly because of a nationwide advertising campaign, carried on for many years.

Beliefs and Doctrines

The belief of Rosicrucianism is a blend of occultism and Theosophy and based broadly on Neoplatonism. Its basic teachings are interlaced with astrology, alchemy, and Kabbalism. The Divinity of Rosicrucianism is a great being who is power, motion, and word that proceeds from the very root of existence. This notion of God is referred to as either the impersonal spirit, who is a collective or pantheistic God, or "the seven spirits." They refer to Jesus Christ, but in terms of a human Jesus into whose body the cosmic Christ's spirit entered.

The Rosicrucian teaching about man is that humanity is evolving into divine being, a righteousness accomplished by choosing rightly. The concept of reincarnation is declared to be "the one great answer" of evolution and salvation. Furthermore, in keeping Rosicrucian tradition, the contemporary groups believe in secret initation, invisible helpers, and elder brothers, and the initiated must give up meat, liquor, and tobacco.

Forms of Worship

In spite of the secrecy of the Rosicrucian order, the Rosicrucian Fellowship groups are now much like Protestant churches in their worship. There are altars with curtains or drapes, a rose-bedecked cross, and hymns with a musical instrument. There are spiritual and other readings and prayers that are often in the "new thought" style, providing "good vibrations" rather than intercession. There are no ministers in the professional sense, and members lead the services. The atmosphere is quite Western, but there is special emphasis on astrology and healing.

The AMORC is another matter. This Rosicrucian group claims to be not a religion but a worldwide fraternal organization like the Masons generally, but one that teaches doctrines and practices to help the individual improve both self-understanding and live up to his or her abilities. The group has a temple, and ceremonies of a lodge type are based on the mystery religions of the Near East (e.g., from Egypt) and augmented by Greek and later influences throughout history. The AMORC is very active in its advertising and also in educational programs. Home study lessons are available from the headquarters of the group, which help the initiate to learn the great "secret" (that each one know his or her "greater inner self") and the psychic powers this knowledge brings.

Organization

The Rosicrucian Fellowship has headquarters in Oceanside, California, and Tucson, Arizona, from which information on the organization of the group can be obtained.

The Ancient and Mystical Order of the Rosae Crucis has headquarters in San Jose, California, from which information on the organization of the group may be obtained.

Contributions and Influence

The character of AMORC and the similarity of the organization, ceremonies, and terminology of the group to Freemasonry have aided both that very popular American lodge as well as itself. And AMORC's claim not to be a religion has found a sympathetic public in the United States, since many Americans are loathe to give up their traditional religious groups for one reason or another.

Another reason is the Rosicrucian teaching concerning the concept of "the greater inner self," which underlies Goethe's observation that as far as man is concerned, "the whole is greater than the sum of its parts" (the physical body). This truth is an essential concept in much "new thought" in religion.

Significant Terms

Alchemy. From Latin *alchemia,* "to change" (chemically). Its basic use was in the medieval hope to change base metals to gold.

Kabbalism. From Hebrew *kabel,* "to receive" (tradition); a mystic lore of Judaism based on an occult interpretation of the Bible as well as Talmudic and Midrashic literature.

Neoplatonism. Originally, the work of Plotinus, a disciple of Plato, who taught that God was at the center of all reality—the one from which all emanates and to which all returns.

Occultism. From Latin *occultis,* "concealed"; a name given to those who practice astrology, alchemy, and so forth.

Pantheism. Derived from Greek *pan,* "all," and *theos,* "God"; the view that all of reality is God.

Bibliography

Allen, Paul M., ed. *A Christian Rosencrentz Anthology*. New York: R. Steiner Pubs., 1968.

Clymer, R. S. *The Rosy Cross, Its Teachings*. Quakertown, Pa.: Beverly Hall Corp., 1965.

Fama Fraternitatis. 1614. Some republishings are available.

Heindel, Max. *The Rosicrucian Cosmo-Conception*. Oceanside, Calif.: Rosicrucian Fellowship, 1909.

Plummer, George W. *Principles and Practice for Rosicrucians*. New York: Society of Rosicrucians, 1947.

Waite, A. E. *The Brotherhood of the Rosy Cross*. London: Rider, 1924.

Yates, Frances A. *The Rosicrucian Enlightenment*. London: Routledge & Kegan Paul, 1972.

APPENDIX B.
Statistics

TABLE 1.
Membership of Religious Groups in the United States, 1989

Religious Group	Membership	Churches
Roman Catholic Church	52,893,217	23,561
Southern Baptist Convention	14,477,364	37,072
United Methodist Church	9,192,172	37,876
Moslems	6,000,000+	Unknown
National Baptist Convention of the U.S.A.	5,500,000 *	26,000
Evangelical Lutheran Church in America	5,341,452	10,791
Church of Jesus Christ of Latter-Day Saints (Mormons)	3,860,000	8,396
Church of God in Christ	3,709,661 *	9,982
Church of Scientology	3,500,000	200
Presbyterian Church (USA)	3,007,322	11,531
National Baptist Church Convention in America	2,688,799 *	11,398
Lutheran Church—Missouri Synod	2,630,588	5,897
Episcopal Church in the U.S.A.	2,504,507	7,054
African Methodist Episcopal Church	2,210,000 *	6,200
Assemblies of God (General Council)	2,135,104	10,886
Greek Orthodox, Archdiocese of North and South America	1,950,000	535
United Church of Christ	1,676,105	6,406
Church of Christ	1,623,754	13,364
American Baptist Churches in U.S.A.	1,576,483	5,864
Baptist Bible Fellowship	1,500,000	3,500
Union of American Hebrew Congregations (Reform Judaism)	1,300,000	804
United Synagogue of America (Conservative Judaism)	1,250,000 *	800
African Methodist Episcopal Zion Church	1,195,173	6,057
Christian Church (Disciples of Christ)	1,106,692	4,221
Christian Churches and Churches of Christ	1,063,469	5,566

Religious Group	Membership	Churches
Progressive National Baptist Convention	1,000,000+	1,000
Orthodox Church in America (Russian)	1,000,000 *	440
Union of Orthodox Jewish Congregations in America	1,000,000	1,700
Jehovah's Witnesses	752,404	8,336
Christian Methodist Episcopal Church	718,922	2,340
Seventh-Day Adventist Church	666,199	4,055
Church of the Nazarene	530,912	5,018
Church of God (Cleveland, Tenn.)	505,775	5,346
United Pentecostal Church International	500,000	3,410
Armenian Orthodox Church	450,000 *	66
Salvation Army	432,893	1,092
Wisconsin Evangelical Lutheran Synod	416,493	1,180
Reformed Church in America	340,359	928
Polish National Catholic Church	282,411 *	162
National Primitive Baptist Convention	250,000 *	606
American Baptist Association	250,000	1,705
Christian and Missionary Alliance	238,734	1,691
Baptist Missionary Association of America	228,125	1,359
Conservative Baptist Association	225,000	1,140
Christian Reformed Church in North America	219,968	650
Free Will Baptist Church	205,546	2,483
Reorganized Church of Jesus Christ of Latter Day Saints	192,077	1,094
Church of God (Anderson, Ind.)	188,662	2,296
Presbyterian Church in America	188,063	913
International Church of the Foursquare Gospel	186,213	1,250
Unitarian Universalist Association	173,167	952
Church of the Brethren	155,000	1,050
Ukrainian Catholic Church (Uniate)	148,371	199
Baptist General Conference	131,480	762
Independent Fundamental Churches of America	120,446	1,019
International Pentecostal Holiness Church	118,095	Unknown
Coptic Orthodox Church	115,000	28
Religious Society of Friends	112,191	1,255
Wesleyan Church	109,196	1,704
Baha'i Faith	100,000	1,650
Buddhist Churches of America	100,000	100
Cumberland Presbyterian Church	96,103	811
Evangelical Free Church	95,722	880
Unity School of Christianity	95,000	512
Worldwide Church of God	95,000	800

Religious Group	Membership	Churches
Mennonite Church	91,167	989
Pentecostal Church of God	90,900	1,444
Congregational Christian Churches	90,000	400
Free Methodist Church of North America	71,682	1,048
Reconstructionist Judaism	60,000	70
Moravian Church	53,902	157
Evangelical Congregational Church	41,237	160
Church of Perfect Liberty	30,000	10
Advent Christian Church	19,946	352
Brethren in Christ Church	16,693	183
Unification Church	10,000	300
Primitive Methodist Church	8,625	86
National Spiritualist Association of Churches	5,658	142
Theosophical Society	5,500	150
Sufi Order	5,000	105
Church of the New Jerusalem (Swedenborgian)†	4,879	56
American Ethical Union	3,500	21
Schwenkfelder Church	2,647	5
Vedanta Society	2,500	13
International Sivananda Yoga Vedanta Center	2,000	8
Fellowship of Religious Humanists	700	1

Source: *World Almanac and Book of Facts* (New York: Pharos Books, 1989).

Note: Statistics were not available for the following groups: (Al-Hanif) Hanafi-Madh-hab, Christian Science Churches (1,869 churches), Church of God in Christ, Eckankar, Freedom from Religion Foundation, Krishna Consciousness, Liberty Baptist Fellowship, Society for Humanistic Judaism, Society of Natural Science, United Church of Religious Science, and Zen Buddhism.

*Statistics are from 1988 or earlier.

†Statistics are from the Church of the New Jerusalem Convention.

TABLE 2.
Adherents to Religions Worldwide, Mid-1989

Religious Group	Adherents	Percentage of Total Population
Christians	1,711,897,000	32.9
Roman Catholics	971,702,000	18.7
Protestants	351,220,000	6.7
Orthodox	163,622,000	3.1
Anglicans	71,209,000	1.4
Other Christians	154,143,000	3.0
Muslims*	924,611,000	17.8
Hindus†	869,205,100	13.2
Buddhists‡	311,438,000	6.0
Chinese Folk Religionists	170,236,200	3.3
New-Religionists	126,819,500	2.4
Tribal Religionists	90,810,200	1.7
Sikhs	17,735,100	0.3
Jews	17,357,000	0.3
Confucians	5,821,400	0.1
Baha'is	5,072,000	0.1
Ja'ins	3,581,500	0.1
Shintoists	3,205,300	0.1
Others	11,205,300	0.2

Source: *1990 Britannica Book of the Year* (Chicago: Encyclopedia Britannica, 1990), chart by David Barrett.

Note: Not included here are those professing no religion (nonbelievers, agnostics, atheists, freethinkers, etc.).

*Among Muslims, 83 percent are Sunnites, 16 percent are Shiites, and 1 percent belong to other schools.

†Vashnavites represent 79 percent of the Hindus; Shaivites, 25 percent; and Neo and Reform Hindus, 2 percent.

‡Mahayana Buddhists compose 50 percent of the total number of Buddhists; Theravada Buddhists, 38 percent; Tantrayana Buddhists, 6 percent.

APPENDIX C
A Time-Line Chronology of Religious Groups in the United States

I • Colonial Religious Groups
  (Seventeenth Century)
1619
Church of England (Va.)
1620
Pilgrims-Congregationalists (Mass.)
1628
Dutch Reformed Church (N.Y.)
1630
Puritans-Congregationalists (Mass.)
1634
Roman Catholic Church (Md.)
1639
Baptist Church (R.I.)
1640
Lutheran Church (N.Y. and Pa.)
1654
Judaism (N.Y.)
1656
Society of Friends (Quakers) (Pa.)
1683
Mennonite Church (Pa.)

II • Eighteenth-Century Religious
  Groups
1706
Presbyterian Church (Pa.)
1723
Dunkards (German Baptists) (Pa.)
1723
Church of the Brethren (Pa.)
1727
Free Will Baptist Church
1735
Moravian Church
1769
Methodist Church
1773

Black Baptist Church
1775–1783
Revolutionary War
1780
Brethren in Christ
1782
Schwenkfelder Church
1785
Universalist Church
1788
Church of the New Jerusalem
1789
Protestant Episcopal Church in the
  U.S.A.
1792
Russian Orthodox Church
1796
African Methodist Episcopal Zion
  Church

III • Nineteenth-Century Religious
  Groups
1803
Christian Church (Disciples of Christ)
1810
Cumberland Presbyterian Church
1816
African Methodist Episcopal Church
1819
Unitarian Church
1830
Church of Jesus Christ of Latter-Day
  Saints
1831
Church of Christ
1840
Primitive Methodist Church
1843

Millerism/Adventism
1845
Southern Baptist Convention
1847
Lutheran Church—Missouri Synod
1848
Spiritualism
1848
Christian Reformed Church in America
1850
Lutheran Church—Wisconsin Synod
1851
Young Men's Christian Association
1852
Baptist General Conference
1860
Free Methodist Church of North
    America
1860
Reorganized Church of Jesus Christ of
    Latter Day Saints
1860
Seventh-Day Adventist Church
1866
Young Women's Christian Association
1870
Christian Methodist Episcopal Church
1873
Reform Judaism
1875
Theosophical Society
1876
Society for Ethical Culture
1879
Christian Science Church
1881
Church of God (Anderson, Ind.)
1884
Ukrainian Catholic Church
1886
Church of God (Cleveland, Tenn.)
1887
Christian and Missionary Alliance
1889
Unity (School of Christianity)
1889
Armenian Orthodox Church
1889
Buddhist Churches of America
1893

Baha'i Faith
1893
Vedanta Society
1894
Evangelical Congregational Church
1895
Black Baptist Convention in America
1896
Salvation Army
1897
Polish National Catholic Church

IV • Twentieth-Century Religious
    Groups
1901
United Pentecostal Church
    International
1906
Christian Church and the Churches of
    Christ
1907
Church of God in Christ
1907
Rosicrucianism
1908
Church of the Nazarene
1911
International Pentecostal Holiness
    Church
1914
Assemblies of God
1915
National Baptist Convention in the U.S.A.
1917
Sufi Order
1919
Pentecostal Church of God
1922
Reconstructionist Judaism
1923
International Church of the Foursquare
    Gospel
1924
American Baptist Association
1927
United Church of Religious Science
1930
Independent Fundamental Churches of
    America
Early 1930s

American Muslim movement
1950
Baptist Missionary Association of
America
1954
Church of Scientology
1955
Congregational Christian Churches
1957
United Church of Christ
1957
International Sivananda Yoga Vedanta
Center
1957
Church of Perfect Liberty
1959
Unification Church
1959
Transcendental Meditation Movement
1959
Zen Buddhism
1960
Nichiren Shoshu of America
1961
Unitarian-Universalist Merger
1961
Progressive National Baptist
Convention
1963
Fellowship of Religious Humanists
1963

Society for Humanistic Judaism
1965
Coptic Orthodox Church
1965
Eckankar
1965
Krishna Consciousness
1968
Wesleyan Church
1971
Divine Light Mission
1973
Presbyterian Church in America
1978
Freedom from Religion Foundation
1981
Liberty Baptist Fellowship
1985
Society of Natural Science
1988
Evangelical Lutheran Church in America

V • Not included for lack of dates of
establishment
Baptist Bible Fellowship Mission
Conservative Baptist Association
Orthodox Judaism
Greek Orthodox Church
Advent Christian General Conference
(Al-Hanif) Hanafi Madh-hab
Self-Realization Fellowship